CRITICAL SURVEY OF POETRY
Nature Poets

Editor

Rosemary M. Canfield Reisman
Charleston Southern University

SALEM PRESS
A Division of EBSCO Publishing, Ipswich, Massachusetts

Cover photo:
Robert Frost (© Bettmann/Corbis)

Copyright © 2012, by Salem Press, A Division of EBSCO Publishing, Inc.
All rights in this book are reserved. No part of this work may be used or reproduced in any manner whatsoever or transmitted in any form or by any means, electronic or mechanical, including photocopy, recording, or any information storage and retrieval system, without written permission from the copyright owner except in the case of brief quotations embodied in critical articles and reviews or in the copying of images deemed to be freely licensed or in the public domain. For information address the publisher, Salem Press, at csr@salempress.com.

ISBN: 978-1-42983-656-2

CONTENTS

Contributors iv

Ecopoetry and Nature Poets 1

A. R. Ammons 5
William Cullen Bryant 15
Raymond Carver 23
Rosalía de Castro 34
William Cowper 44
Du Fu 54
Ralph Waldo Emerson 61
Robert Frost 75
Thomas Hardy 87
Gerard Manley Hopkins 101
Matsuo Bashō 117
W. S. Merwin 125
May Swenson 138
Rabindranath Tagore 147
Edward Thomas 159
Henry David Thoreau 166
Jones Very 177
David Wagoner 183
Alice Walker 196
Wang Wei 205
Phillis Wheatley 215
Walt Whitman 228
John Greenleaf Whittier 244

Checklist for Explicating a Poem 255
Bibliography 258
Guide to Online Resources 261
Geographical Index 265
Category Index 266
Subject Index 269

CONTRIBUTORS

Karley K. Adney
University of Wisconsin, Marathon County

Andrew J. Angyal
Elon University

Walton Beacham
Beacham Publishing Corp.

Todd K. Bender
University of Wisconsin-Madison

Harold Branam
Savannah State University

David W. Cole
University of Wisconsin Colleges

Delmer Davis
Andrews University

Bill Delaney
San Diego, California

Lloyd N. Dendinger
University of South Alabama

Cliff Edwards
Fort Hays State University

Richard A. Eichwald
St. Louis, Missouri

William J. Heim
University of South Florida

Sarah Hilbert
Pasadena, California

Kenneth A. Howe
Michigan State University

Philip K. Jason
United States Naval Academy

Jeffry Jensen
Pasadena, California

Perry D. Luckett
United States Air Force Academy

Sara McAulay
California State University, Hayward

Julia M. Meyers
Duquesne University

Allene Phy-Olsen
Austin Peay State University

Francis Poole
University of Delaware

Richard J. Schneider
Wilson, North Carolina

John C. Shields
Illinois State University

Jack Shreve
Allegany Community College

Vivien Stableford
Reading, United Kingdom

Shelby Stephenson
Pembroke State University

Pauline Yu
University of Minnesota

ECOPOETRY AND NATURE POETS

Nature has long been a favorite subject of poets. Many cultures revere wilderness and have created whole mythologies surrounding life outside of civilization. Some believe that life in its original, purest form can only exist away from what man has created. There is a spiritual quality to the natural world that has drawn the earliest poets and modern man, a tug of the wild or a drive to return to what may be described as the source of all life. Facing the prospect of the earth's destruction, many contemporary poets have embraced the cause of speaking up for the very survival of the natural environment. Whether it is a lost cause, a noble cause, or a little of both, poets are determined not to remain silent as the earth continues to be polluted, ravaged, and torn apart.

One of the ancient masters of the nature poem was the eighth century Chinese poet Du Fu. As a Confucian scholar, Du Fu had absolute control of the poetry he composed. He is considered to be one of the greatest Chinese poets, having written more than one thousand poems on a vast number of topics. His work demonstrates his mastery of form and his preeminent ability to render serenity without effort. In countless poems, Du Fu employs the natural elements to symbolize human dilemmas, using water in all of its various forms as a symbol to create the appropriate mood. The seventeenth century Japanese poet Matsuo Bash{o} also reveled in writing about nature. He wandered throughout Japan, his travels inspiring him to compose some of the most miraculous haiku now known.

Nature Becomes the Ideal

As one of the leading English Romantic poets, William Wordsworth helped to usher in a revolutionary approach to poetry. The Romantic poets believed first and foremost in the value of the individual person and the inherent beauty of the natural world, necessitating a healthy respect for the goodness within both man and nature. In Wordsworth's famous preface to the second edition of *Lyrical Ballads* (1800), he states that man must strip off the influence of civilization in order to find his natural, more primitive state of being. This philosophy shaped Wordsworth's approach to his own poetry. He made it his life's work to write about the common man, somebody who lived in the rural areas away from the corrupting influence of cities. This concept has been considered naive or idealized, but at the time it was a powerful ideology that became extremely influential. One of his most brilliant poems is "Lines Composed a Few Miles Above Tintern Abbey," included in the 1798 edition of *Lyrical Ballads*. The poem was inspired by a walking tour that he took with his sister Dorothy. In it, he speaks of being a free man, connected to nature:

> Of aspect more sublime; that blessed mood,
> In which the burthen of the mystery,
> In which the heavy and the weary weight
> Of all this unintelligible world,
> Is lightened—that serene and blessed mood,
> In which the affections gently lead us on—
> Until, the breath of this corporeal frame
> And even the motion of our human blood
> Almost suspended, we are laid asleep
> In body, and become a living soul;
> While with an eye made quiet by the power
> Of harmony, and deep power of joy,
> We see into the life of things.

Several other Romantic poets were also nourished by what nature offered, including Samuel Taylor Coleridge, John Keats, and Percy Bysshe Shelley. Nature continued to inspire English poets from the mid-nineteenth into the twentieth century. Such poets as Gerard Manley Hopkins, Thomas Hardy, and William Butler Yeats also embraced the power of the natural world. During the mid-to-late nineteenth century in America, three towering writers directed their focus toward nature: Ralph Waldo Emerson, Henry David Thoreau, and Walt Whitman, who are remembered not only for their verse but also for their spirit and the tone of their work. As a poet, Emerson strived to bring purpose to the everyday in American life. For Whitman, poetry needed to be full of life and the spirit of America. He was not wedded to any particular poetic form; his poetry needed to be free to breathe. His *Leaves of Grass* is an American classic of epic proportions. The first edition was published in 1855, and for the rest of his life, he continued to expand it; as he saw America growing, so, too, did his poem. *Leaves of Grass* is a living testament to American life and landscape.

Speaking for the Environment

Ecopoetry is a term that entered the lexicon in the final decades of the twentieth century. The increasingly popular wave of ecopoetry encompasses those poets who have made a point of deliberately emphasizing the ecological thread in their work. In his article "The Language of Habitat: An Ecopoetry Manifesto," published in the online *Octopus Magazine*, James Engelhardt claims that ecopoetry creates a "connection" with "non-human nature." It is not intended to merely "praise" nature or the ways that man can manipulate nature; these traditions must be discarded. The ecopoet should look to science for help in understanding nonhuman nature. With a greater understanding of how to recognize the forces of both culture and nature, it then becomes possible for the ecopoet to write an ecopoem that will at least attempt to connect the contradictions that exist in the world.

Some of the most noteworthy contemporary American nature poets are William Carlos Williams, Robinson Jeffers, W. S. Merwin, David Wagoner, Robert Bly, Wendell Berry, Gary Snyder, Donald Hall, and Mary Oliver. Each of these poets has written about the natural world in striking and profound ways. Never sentimental, their poems wrestle with the conflicts that exist between preserving nature and the encroachments of civilization. Berry represents the strong voice of the farmer, the father, the person who fights against the bloodthirsty corporation. A man of Kentucky, Berry has gained prominence not only as a poet, but also as an essayist and novelist. He has a strong connection with the land and is a fierce advocate for the survival of the small farmer. Bly, on the other hand, is a poet who believes in study, and his poetry is an outgrowth of his interests in mythology, psychology, and meditation. Since the 1960's, Snyder has focused on writing about how any relevant approach to living must also consider the role of the environment. For him, it has been, in a very direct sense, a lifelong pursuit. In both his poetry and his essays, Snyder is committed to the survival of the earth.

There are many more poets who have felt that the natural environment must be supported, promoted, and saved. Other American poets such as A. R. Ammons, Joy Harjo, Alice Walker, Raymond Carver, and Baron Wormser have written about the environment with profound eloquence. Whether they view nature as a symbol of beauty and freedom or as a neutral force that must be allowed to have its place in a coherent whole, poets from all continents have written forcefully and passionately about how humans must come to terms with their connection and responsibility to the earth.

Jeffry Jensen

BIBLIOGRAPHY

Bryson, J. Scott, ed. *Ecopoetry: A Critical Introduction.* Salt Lake City: University of Utah Press, 2002. A collection of essays concerning both literary and environmental issues in ecopoetry.

Elder, John. *Imagining the Earth: Poetry and the Vision of Nature.* Urbana: University of Illinois Press, 1985. A look at how poets see the natural world.

Englehardt, James. "The Language Habitat: An Ecopoetry Manifesto." *Octopus Magazine*, no. 9 (2007). A discussion of ecopoetry and its connection to science and nonhuman nature.

Felstiner, John. *Can Poetry Save the Earth? A Field Guide to Nature Poems.* New Haven, Conn.: Yale University Press, 2009. Discusses how poets of the past and present have attempted to speak with conviction in support of the earth.

Keith, W. J. *The Poetry of Nature: Rural Perspectives in Poetry from Wordsworth to the Present.* Toronto: University of Toronto Press, 1980. An overview of how poets have responded to the natural world around them.

Quetchenbach, Bernard W. *Back from the Far Field: American Nature Poetry in the*

Late Twentieth Century. Charlottesville: University Press of Virginia, 2000. A discussion of Robinson Jeffers, Theodore Roethke, Robert Bly, Gary Snyder, and Wendell Berry, and how each of them portrays nature in their poetry.

Spiegelman, Willard. *How Poets See the World: The Art of Description in Contemporary Poetry.* New York: Oxford University Press, 2005. A presentation of the various ways an observant poet can see the world.

A. R. AMMONS

Born: Near Whiteville, North Carolina; February 18, 1926
Died: Ithaca, New York; February 25, 2001

PRINCIPAL POETRY
Ommateum, with Doxology, 1955
Expressions of Sea Level, 1963
Corsons Inlet: A Book of Poems, 1965
Tape for the Turn of the Year, 1965
Northfield Poems, 1966
Selected Poems, 1968
Uplands, 1970
Briefings: Poems Small and Easy, 1971
Collected Poems, 1951-1971, 1972
Sphere: The Form of a Motion, 1974
Diversifications, 1975
The Selected Poems, 1951-1977, 1977
The Snow Poems, 1977
Highgate Road, 1978
Six-Piece Suite, 1979
Selected Longer Poems, 1980
A Coast of Trees, 1981
Worldly Hopes, 1982
Lake Effect Country, 1983
The Selected Poems: Expanded Edition, 1986
Sumerian Vistas, 1987
The Really Short Poems of A. R. Ammons, 1990
Garbage, 1993
The North Carolina Poems, 1994
Brink Road, 1996
Glare, 1997
Bosh and Flapdoodle, 2005
A. R. Ammons: Selected Poems, 2006 (David Lehman, editor)

OTHER LITERARY FORMS

Although A. R. Ammons (AM-uhns) is known primarily for his poetry, he also published reviews and essays. Central to an understanding of his work are "A Poem Is a Walk" and his short autobiographical reflection "I Couldn't Wait to Say the Word."

Ammons's several published interviews, especially one by Cynthia Haythe, give additional insight into his poetics. *Set in Motion: Essays, Interviews, and Dialogues* (1996) collects his most important writings about poetry.

Achievements

Throughout a distinguished and prolific career, A. R. Ammons observed and presented the particulars of the world while projecting his longing for a sense of unity. He immersed himself in the flow of things, celebrating the world and the self that sees and probes it.

Ammons's work lies within the Emersonian tradition: He wrote from life without being a slave to any set poetic form. However, more than any other poet since Ralph Waldo Emerson, he developed a transcendentalism rooted in science and in a poetic that includes the self in the work. His epigrams, his short to moderate-length nature lyrics, and his long verse-essays are popular reading among poets.

His many awards include the Bread Loaf Writers' Conference Scholarship (1961), a Guggenheim Fellowship (1966), an American Academy of Arts and Letters Traveling Fellowship (1967), a National Endowment for the Arts grant (1969-1970), the Levinson Prize (1970), a National Book Award (1973) for *Collected Poems, 1951-1971*, an honorary Litt.D. from Wake Forest University (1973), the Bollingen Prize for Poetry for *Sphere* (1975), an Academy Award in Literature from the American Academy and Institute of Arts and Letters (1977), a National Book Critics Circle Award (1981) for *A Coast of Trees*, a John D. and Catherine T. MacArthur Foundation Award (1981), and the North Carolina Award for Literature (1986). In 1990, he was inducted into the American Academy and Institute of Arts and Letters. Ammons won the Lannan Literary Award for Poetry (1992), a second National Book Award (1993) for *Garbage*, the Poetry Society of America's Frost Medal (1994), the Bobbitt National Prize for Poetry (1994), the Ruth Lilly Poetry Prize (1995), and the Wallace Stevens Award (1998). Ammons is recognized as one of the most significant and original voices in twentieth century poetry.

Biography

A. R. Ammons was born Archie Randolph Ammons near Whiteville, North Carolina, in a house bought by his grandfather and situated on the family farm. The main book in the house was the Bible. Ammons's early experiences on the farm, working the land, helped shape his imagination. The self in his poems appears most frequently in relation to the natural world he knew as a child.

He was his parents' fourth child. Three sisters were born before him and two brothers after; one sister lived for only two weeks, and both brothers died, one in infancy and the other at birth. Ammons remembered the deaths of his brothers, saying that they accounted in part for the undercurrent of loss and loneliness in his work.

Upon graduation from high school in 1943, Ammons took a job in the shipyard in Wilmington, North Carolina. In 1944, he joined the U.S. Navy, spending nineteen months in service, including time in the South Pacific, where he began writing poems. Returning home after the war, Ammons attended Wake Forest College (his tuition paid for by the G.I. Bill) and graduated with a B.S. in 1949. That year he married Phyllis Plumbo and took a job as principal of an elementary school in the remote coastal community of Hatteras, North Carolina. From 1950 to 1952, he studied English at the University of California, Berkeley. In 1952, he took a position with his father-in-law's New Jersey medical glassware firm, a job he held for twelve years. He soon began to send poems to literary magazines, and in 1953, *Hudson Review* accepted two of them. His first book of poetry, *Ommateum, with Doxology*, appeared in 1955. Eight years later, *Expressions of Sea Level* appeared. In 1964, he began teaching at Cornell University. Other books of poems followed, and in 1972, most of his poems were published as *Collected Poems, 1951-1971*. *Sphere*, his poem of more than two thousand lines, published in 1974, gained for him the Bollingen Prize in Poetry for 1974-1975. Whitmanesque in its tendency toward democratic feeling, *Sphere* presents Ammons's aesthetic of continual motion and a musical affirmation of interdependence in the energy of all life. Ammons continued to be highly productive in his later years. *The North Carolina Poems* appeared in 1994; *Brink Road* was published in 1996; and his final book during his lifetime, *Glare*, appeared in 1997.

Ammons served for many years as the Goldwin Smith Professor of Poetry at Cornell University. In 1998, the university honored him with a celebration of his monumental achievement. He died from cancer in February of 2001, leaving behind his wife, his son John, and two grandchildren. Throughout his career, Ammons made frequent trips to eastern North Carolina, a place that figures prominently in his poems.

ANALYSIS

In one of A. R. Ammons's early poems, "So I Said I Am Ezra," from *Ommateum, with Doxology*, the speaker is whipped over the landscape, driven, moved by the natural elements. He is at once ordered and disordered, close and far, balanced and unbalanced, and he exclaims, "So I Ezra went out into the night/ like a drift of sand." The line is representative of Ammons's entire body of work, for it announces a search through language in an attempt to mean and to be clear, and failing to succeed completely in such clarity, the line ends by affirming a presence of radiance.

EXPRESSIONS OF SEA LEVEL

Ammons's poems have a tendency, like most contemporary poems, to take their own process, their own making, as a theme. Wanting to express something changeless and eternal, Ammons is constrained by his own intricate mortality. So in the title poem of *Expressions of Sea Level*, he presents the ocean as permanent and impermanent, as form and formlessness. He is interested in what humanity can and cannot know, giving full sway and expression to the ocean's activity: "See the dry casting of the beach worm/ dissolve at the delicate rising touch." The range and flow in Ammons's poetry, his search for balance, moved him to create his philosophical music, using a vocabulary drawn largely from everyday speech. He celebrates the need in every human being to discover a common experience in the least particular thing.

POEMS OF NORTH CAROLINA

Ammons attempts always to render visual details accurately. Some of the most moving poems in this regard are the poems inspired by his background in Columbus County, North Carolina. "Nelly Meyers" praises and celebrates a woman who lived on the farm where Ammons grew up; "Silver" records Ammons's love for and rapport with a mule he used for work. "Hardweed Path Going" tells of his life as a boy, doing chores on the farm, his playtime with a pet bird (a jo-reet) and a hog named Sparkle. These poems re-create Ammons's past, particularly his boyhood, which he renders in astonishingly realistic details.

CORSONS INLET

Ammons infuses the natural world with his own attuned sensibilities, acknowledging in the title poem of *Corsons Inlet* that "Overall is beyond me." The form of the poem is a walk over the dunes. What lives beyond his perception reassures, although he knows "that there is no finality of vision." Bafflement is a primary feeling in the poem, which may be studied for what it says about the relationship between logic and reason, imposed order and discovered order, art and life, reality and illusion, and being and becoming. "Corsons Inlet" concludes the walk/quest on the note that "tomorrow a new walk is a new walk." Ammons's desire to say something clearly, therefore, is not so much a search for the word as it is an attempt to find original ways to make and shape poetry.

TAPE FOR THE TURN OF THE YEAR

With *Tape for the Turn of the Year*, Ammons writes a long, narrow poem on adding-machine paper. The poet improvises and spontaneously records his thoughts and moods in what resembles a poetic diary. In one place, he praises how writing gets done, suggesting that doing it is almost its own practical reward, as the speaker acknowledges in another poem, "Identity," "it is wonderful how things work."

MAJOR THEMES

By the mid-1960's, Ammons's major themes had emerged, his sensibility oscillating between extremes: formlessness-form, center-periphery, high-low, motion-stasis, order-disorder, and one-many. One of his most constant themes has been the self in the work and in the world. He is concerned not only with the form of natural fact but also with form in the abstract sense, that is, with physical laws that govern the way individual entities act and behave. Ammons reaffirms the resonance of his subject, as in "The Eternal City," in which destruction must "accept into itself piece by piece all the old/ perfect human visions, all the old perfect loves."

Motion within diversity is perhaps Ammons's major theme. In "Saliences," from *Northfield Poems*, he discovers continuity in change. In "Snow Log," from *Uplands*, recognizing that nature's intentions cannot be known, he responds simply as an individual to what he sees in the winter scene: "I take it on myself:/ especially the fallen tree/ the snow picks/ out in the woods to show." In "The City Limits," from *Briefings*, a poem whose urban subject removes the speaker from nature, Ammons celebrates the "goldskeined wings of flies swarming the dumped/ guts of a natural slaughter or the coil of shit."

COLLECTED POEMS, 1951-1971

Receiving the National Book Award in Poetry in 1973, *Collected Poems, 1951-1971* comprises most of Ammons's first six volumes, except for *Tape for the Turn of the Year* and three long verse-essays—"Extremes and Moderations," "Hibernaculum," and "Essay on Poetics." In "Extremes and Moderations" and "Hibernaculum," Ammons is a seer, lamenting humankind's abuse of Earth and appreciating the immediacy of a world that takes care of itself. "Essay on Poetics" considers the structural advantages and disadvantages of poetry. One reads this essay to appreciate more fully Ammons's views on writing.

SPHERE

In perhaps his major work, the book-length poem *Sphere*, Ammons explores motion and shape in a set form: sentences with no full stops, 155 sections of four tercets each. He relies on colons, perhaps suggesting a democratization and a flow. Shifting freely, sometimes abruptly, within a given stanza, phrase, or word, Ammons says, "I do not smooth into groups." Thus the book explores the nature of its own poetics, the poet searching everywhere for a language of clarity. In one place, he says that he is "sick of good poems." Wanting the smooth and raw together, Ammons reminds the reader that his prejudice against neat, traditional structures in poetry relates to the natural world where "the shapes nearest shapelessness awe us most, suggest the god." He regards a log, "rigid with shape," as "trivial." Ammons, therefore, makes his case for the poem of the open form as opposed to strong, traditional verses.

Ammons demythologizes poetics and language, while testifying to an Emersonian faith in the universe as flowing freely and spontaneously. At the same time, there is a counter feeling always working. He refers often to clarity and wants his poems to arrive and move forward "by a controlling motion, design, symmetry."

While he is writing the poem, commenting on it, writing himself into it, he shows his instinct for playfulness, for spoofing. This aspect of his work—the clowning humor—adds an inherent drama to his work, as critic Jerald Bullis has written:

> The tone of the poem or, I should say, of the voices of its "parts," ranges and range from that of the high and hard lyric, the crystalline and *as if* final saying, through a talky and often latinate professorial stance, to permutations of low tone: "bad" puns, catalogues that seem to have been lifted from a catalogue, and, in the example below, the high-pressure pitch-man tone of How-To scams: "Now, first of all, the way to write poems is just to start: it's like learning to walk or swim or ride the bicycle, you just go after it."

The poem goes on, praising the ability of humanity to write and to appreciate being alive.

Reverence for creation runs throughout *Sphere*, investing the work with a vision beyond and through the details of the poet's aesthetic. This religious strain has its source in Ammons's absolute reverence for the natural world. A religious vocabulary, then, is no surprise in his work and connects with his childhood, when church services and hymn-sings were dominant parts of his life. As in *Sphere*, he questions what is "true service," saying "it must be a service that is celebration, for we would celebrate even if we do not know what or how, and for He is bountiful if/ slow to protect and recalcitrant to keep." Ammons goes on to say, "What we can celebrate is the condition we are in, or we can renounce the condition/ we are in and celebrate a condition we might be in or ought/ to be in." Ammons fuses and plays on the relationship between creation and imagination, hoping and trying to discover "joy's surviving radiance." In the presence of this radiance—the hues and bends of Ammons's music—exist the crux of his aesthetic, his art and his being: the solitary man never surrendering as he is being imposed on and whipped about, as he writes in one of his earliest poems, "So I Said I am Ezra/ and the wind whipped my throat/ gaming for the sounds of my voice." However, the self is not dwarfed by the world. Ammons understands his moral and aesthetic convictions and will not cease to assert them. Such desire allows the visionary in Ammons constantly to discover new ways to see and understand his life. In this regard, key words crop up often: "salience," "recalcitrant," "suasion," "periphery," "possibility," tentative words that tend to illuminate or seek the proper blend in experience. So *Sphere* ends as it began, clear and free of all encumbrances except the spoken voice: "we're ourselves: we're sailing." The ending is right for the "form of a motion," the sense of wonder and uncertainty going on beyond the finality of the poem. Past, present, and future are one, and the poem and its end recall Walt Whitman's absorption into the dirt in "Song of Myself."

THE SNOW POEMS

In *The Snow Poems*, Ammons continues his experimental attempt to arrange a poetic journal, recounting in lyrical splendor the concerns of daily life, including details about weather, sex, and the poet's attempt to write and to experience a dialogue between the specific and the general. Ammons's work since the mid-1970's marks a return to the more visionary tendencies contained in his earlier terse, fierce lyrics of short or moderate length. "Progress Report" is an epigram from *Worldly Hopes*: "Now I'm/ into things// so small/ when I// say boo/ I disappear." The words flow in natural motion.

LAKE EFFECT COUNTRY

Lake Effect Country continues Ammons's love of form and motion. The whole book represents one body, a place of water, a bed of lively recreation. In "Meeting Place," for example, "The water nearing the ledge leans down with/ grooved speed at the spill then,/ quickly groundless in air." His vision comes from the coming together of the natural elements in the poem, rising and falling, moving and forming the disembodied voices that are the real characters in his poems: "When I call out to them/ as to the flowing bones in my naked self, is my/ address attribution's burden and abuse." "Meeting Place" goes out "to summon/ the deep-lying fathers from myself,/ the spirits, feelings howling, appearing there."

A COAST OF TREES

A major contemporary poem is "Easter Morning," from *A Coast of Trees*. Based on the death in infancy of the poet's younger brother, the poem is filled with reverence for the natural world, Ammons's memory ever enlarging with religious and natural resonances. "I have a life that did not become,/ that turned aside and stopped,/ astonished." The poem carries the contradictory mysteries of the human condition—death, hope, and memory—working together in a concrete and specific aesthetic. Presented in the form of a walk, "Easter Morning" reveals the speaker caught in the motion, as two birds "from the South" fly around, circle, change their ways, and go on. The poem affirms, with the speaker in another poem ("Working with Tools"), "I understand/ and won't give assertion up." Like Ezra going out "into the night/ like a drift of sand," the poet celebrates "a dance sacred as the sap in/ the trees . . . fresh as this particular/ flood of burn breaking across us now/ from the sun." Though the dance is completed in a moment, it can never be destroyed, because it has been re-created as the imagination's grand dance.

SUMERIAN VISTAS

Another major contemporary poem is "The Ridge Farm" from *Sumerian Vistas*. In fifty-one parts, the poem renders the farm itself on a ridge, on the edge of everything and nothing. Ammons's speaker joyfully resigns himself to the "highways" and the dammed-up brooks. The implication is that poetry—like nature—breaks through and flows, exploring the motion and shape of the farm's form. The farm itself is a concrete place wherein Ammons explores the nature of poetics and other realities.

The Really Short Poems of A. R. Ammons

In *The Really Short Poems of A. R. Ammons*, the poet continues his necessity to really see the natural world. That seeing becomes the poem; its motion, the story moving through the images. The form and subject move in a terse, fierce way as the poem discovers itself. In "Winter Scene," for example, the natural world changes radiantly when the jay takes over the leafless cherry tree. The landscape transformed, the poet notes what he sees: "then every branch/ quivers and/ breaks out in blue leaves." Motion formerly void of color brightens with vision and sway.

Garbage

Many consider *Garbage* to be a capstone of Ammons's maturity. Inspired by a massive landfill along Florida's portion of Interstate 95, this book-length poem continues Ammons's contemplation of and reverence for nature, this time positing the theme of regeneration following decay. It is a theme he applies to the human condition as well as to the sorry condition humanity has brought to nature. According to David Lehman, in his profile of Ammons published in the Summer, 1998, issue of *American Poet*, Ammons was attracted to the garbage mound for several reasons, including its geometry. Writes Lehman,

> The mound struck him as a hierarchical image, like a pyramid or the triangulation of a piece of pie. The pointed top corresponded to unity, the base to diversity. This paradigm of unity and diversity—and the related philosophical question of "the one and the many"—has been a constant feature of Ammons's work from the start.

Glare

Ammon's penchant for stretching out his thoughts and words is nowhere as evident as in his 1997 volume, *Glare*. Comprising two sections, "Strip" and "Scat Scan," and written in his familiar couplet style, it is a work that is self-deprecating and spontaneous. Ammons speaks of "finding the form of the process," and critics have noted that his apparent ambition in *Glare* was "to make the finished form of the poem indistinguishable from the process of composition." In doing so, it reveals an immediacy of experience and thought, a kind of poetry in real time. In "Strip," he writes, "I have plenty and/ give plenty away, why because here/ at nearly 70 stuff has bunched up/ with who knows how much space to/ spread out into." The themes of "Scat" are harder to discern. Overall, he uses twisted proverbs and recalls Robert Frost's poetry to sum up his life.

Other major work

NONFICTION: *Set in Motion: Essays, Interviews, and Dialogues*, 1996.

Bibliography

Bloom, Harold, ed. *A. R. Ammons.* New York: Chelsea House, 1986. This volume contains eighteen essays on Ammons's work, plus an introductory essay by Bloom. Among the contributors are contemporary poets John Ashbery, Richard Howard, and John Hollander. Perhaps the central theme of all the essays is that Ammons, like Walt Whitman, is a solitary self in the world.

Burak, David, and Rogert Gilbert, eds. *Considering the Radiance: Essays on the Poetry of A. R. Ammons.* New York: W. W. Norton, 2005. A collection of essays on Ammons's poetry, some of which were written by fellow poets.

Elder, John. *Imagining the Earth: Poetry and the Vision of Nature.* Urbana: University of Illinois Press, 1985. Elder writes about poets who remember and re-create Earth. His chapter on Ammons is called "Poetry and the Mind's Terrain." Elder's prose is clear and uncluttered; he presents Ammons from the fresh perspective of contemporary poets. Includes chapter notes and an index.

Hans, James S. *The Value(s) of Literature.* Albany: State University of New York Press, 1990. This book addresses the ethical aspects of literature by discussing three major American poets: Walt Whitman, Wallace Stevens, and A. R. Ammons. The chapter on Ammons is called "Ammons and the One: Many Mechanisms." In a concluding chapter, "The Aesthetic of Worldly Hopes," Hans speculates that one of the reasons poetry is not read widely in the United States is that it is "perceived to have nothing of ethical value inherent in it." What Hans calls "patterns of choice" exist in poems such as "Corsons Inlet" and "Essay on Poetics."

Holder, Alan. *A. R. Ammons.* Boston: Twayne, 1978. This introductory book-length study presents Ammons's life and works through *Sphere.* The text is supplemented by a chronology, notes, a select bibliography (with annotated secondary sources), and an index.

Kirschten, Robert. *Approaching Prayer: Ritual and the Shape of Myth in A. R. Ammons and James Dickey.* Baton Rouge: Louisiana State University Press, 1998. A mythopoetic study of each author that focuses on ceremonial strategies, this analysis examines the nature of Ammons's interest in ancient Sumerian as well as other traditions.

Schneider, Steven P., ed. *Complexities of Motion: New Essays on A. R. Ammons's Long Poems.* Madison, N.J.: Fairleigh Dickinson University Press, 1999. Essays by Helen Vendler, Marjorie Perloff, and other major critics examine the genre of the long poem as individualized by Ammons. Rationale, shape, structure, and strategy are explored, along with recurrent themes.

Sciagaj, Leonard M. *Sustainable Poetry: Four American Ecopoets.* Lexington: University Press of Kentucky, 1999. Along with Ammons, discusses and compares Wendell Berry, Gary Snyder, and W. S. Merwin and their treatment of nature and environmental concerns in their works. Bibliographical references, index.

Spiegelman, Willard. *The Didactic Muse.* Princeton, N.J.: Princeton University Press,

1989. Spiegelman's chapter on Ammons is called "Myths of Concretion, Myths of Abstraction: The Case of A. R. Ammons." Spiegelman ranges over Ammons's work, particularly the longer poems through *Sumerian Vistas*. Spiegelman's concern is the relation between poetry and philosophy. He contends that Ammons's dominant conceit is motion: his attempt to find that place where the conscious and unconscious move, yet stay. The book is important to any student who wishes to see Ammons's work within the larger context of contemporary poetry.

Vendler, Helen, ed. *Voices and Visions: The Poet in America*. New York: Random House, 1987. A companion to *Voices and Visions*, a Public Broadcasting Service television series. Calvin Bedient's essay on Walt Whitman discusses Ammons's *Sphere* within Whitman's energetic thrust out—toward a desire to create a motion within the American attraction for space, for going on, for expanding one's self in a larger world. The book contains pictures of poets, illustrations, notes on chapters, suggestions for further reading, notes on contributors, a list of illustrations, and an index.

Shelby Stephenson; Philip K. Jason
Updated by Sarah Hilbert

WILLIAM CULLEN BRYANT

Born: Cummington, Massachusetts; November 3, 1794
Died: New York, New York; June 12, 1878

PRINCIPAL POETRY
The Embargo: Or, Sketches of the Times, a Satire, 1808
Poems, 1821, 1832, 1834, 1836, 1839, 1854, 1871, 1875
The Fountain, and Other Poems, 1842
The White-Footed Deer, and Other Poems, 1844
Thirty Poems, 1864
Hymns, 1864, 1869
The Poetical Works of William Cullen Bryant, 1876
The Flood of Years, 1878

OTHER LITERARY FORMS

William Cullen Bryant wrote a substantial body of prose: tales, editorials, reviews, letters, appreciations, sketches or impressions, and critical essays. In 1850, he published *Letters of a Traveller: Or, Notes of Things Seen in Europe and America*; in 1859, *Letters of a Traveller, Second Series*; and in 1869, *Letters from the East*. He reviewed the careers of a number of his contemporaries in such pieces as *A Discourse on the Life and Genius of James Fenimore Cooper* (1852) and *A Discourse on the Life and Genius of Washington Irving* (1860). In 1851, he published his *Reminiscences of the "Evening Post,"* and in 1873, a collection of *Orations and Addresses*. His *Lectures on Poetry*, delivered to the Athenaeum Society in 1826, was published in 1884.

ACHIEVEMENTS

William Cullen Bryant's central achievement as a man of letters was his contribution to the developing sense of a national identity. Although Bryant's verse is often indistinguishable from the eighteenth and nineteenth century English verse of his models, he begins to draw lines of contrast, first, by his choice of subject matter—prairies, violets, gentians, Indian legends—and, second, by developing a characteristic poetic voice that can be seen in retrospect to be the early stage of the development of a nationally distinctive poetry.

Bryant's participation in the formative stages of American poetry was a natural corollary to the second of his two major achievements, his career as a journalist. As the editor and part-owner of the New York *Evening Post* for almost fifty years, he championed liberal social and political causes that were as much a part of the newly emerging national identity as was his poetry. His vigorous support of freedom of the press, of aboli-

William Cullen Bryant
(National Archives)

tion, of the Republican Party, and of John Frémont and Abraham Lincoln, are among his most notable achievements as a journalist.

Although minor in comparison with his two major achievements, Bryant's lectures on poetic theory to the Athenaeum Society in 1826 shed light on his own poetry and on some of the cultural assumptions of his period. Bryant's emphasis on "moral uplift and spiritual refinement" as the aim of poetry is balanced by his interest in native speech and natural imagery as resources to be tapped by the poet.

Biography

William Cullen Bryant was born on November 3, 1794, in Cummington, Massachusetts, to Peter Bryant and Sarah Snell Bryant. The poet enjoyed a close family life and, from an early age, benefited from the positive influences of both parents, as well as from those of his maternal grandfather, Ebenezer Snell. The latter's Calvinist influence, though muted, is evident in the language of the poetry and in the recurrent image of an angry God threatening retribution for humankind's sins. His mother's gentler religious influence bore directly on his precocity as a reader in general, and of the Bible in particular, at the age of four. Bryant was later to remember those conducting the religious services of his very early childhood experiences as "often poets in their extemporaneous prayers."

A counter, and as time passed more prevailing, influence was that of his liberal physician father, Peter Bryant, who encouraged the poet in his early experiments with satires, lampoons, and pastorals. Under that encouraging tutelage, Bryant published his first poem of substance, "The Embargo," in 1808, at the age of thirteen; three years later, he set about translating the third book of the *Aeneid*. In 1817, Peter Bryant took copies of several of his son's poems to his friend Willard Phillips, one of the editors of the *North American Review*. "Thanatopsis" and one other poem were published immediately in the journal's September issue. "Inscription for the Entrance to a Wood" and "To a Waterfowl" appeared subsequently.

Meanwhile, Bryant had been preparing himself for a legal career and was admitted to the bar in 1815. He began practicing law in 1816 in Great Barrington, Massachusetts. In 1825, he assumed editorship of the *New York Review*, and in 1829, he began his fifty-year career as a major journalist when he became part-owner and editor-in-chief of the New York *Evening Post*. From that position he was to champion freedom of speech, abolition, the right of workmen to strike, Frémont, the Republican Party, and Lincoln and the Union cause. When he died in 1878, the *Evening Post* continued his policies under the leadership of his son-in-law, Parke Godwin.

Although Bryant was to continue writing poetry throughout his life, most of it, and particularly those poems on which his reputation rests, was written by the early 1830's. By the middle of the century, though he was still an active and vigorous journalist, he had become something of an institution to writers such as Nathaniel Hawthorne, Herman Melville, and Oliver Wendell Holmes. Ralph Waldo Emerson included Bryant among the imagined faculty of his ideal college, because, as he noted in his journal, "Bryant has learned where to hang his titles, namely by tying his mind to autumn woods, winter mornings, rain, brooks, mountains, evening winds, and wood-birds. . . . [He is] American."

Bryant married Frances Fairchild in 1821. They had two daughters, Fanny and Julia, who inherited the sizable estate left at his death on June 12, 1878. His death resulted from a fall and head injury on May 29.

Analysis

William Cullen Bryant wrote his poetry over a fifty-year span, but the apex of his career came in the early 1830's, very close to an exact midpoint between William Wordsworth's 1800 preface to the second edition of *Lyrical Ballads* and Walt Whitman's *Leaves of Grass* (1855). In retrospect, Bryant's poetry, especially his blank verse, can be seen in terms of a development moving from Wordsworth's theories and examples to the American model of Whitman's free verse, celebrating the self and the newly emerging national identity. At its best, Bryant's verse reflects the evolutionary dynamics of a national poetry in the making; at its worst, it is stale repetition of eighteenth century nature poetry, cast in static imitation of Wordsworthian models.

Bryant's affirmative resolution of his brooding preoccupation with the mutability of all things is another characteristic that places him in the early mainstream of the emerging national literature. He will continue to be read for his place in literary history, for the fuller understanding of the development of that national literature of which he contributes, even if his verse is wholly uncongenial to the contemporary reader. His celebration of the American landscape and his affirmation of a progressive spirit became overtly central themes for Ralph Waldo Emerson, Henry David Thoreau, and Whitman. Bryant's best poetry prefigures the American Renaissance in both content and form, theme and style, and thus he continues to be read, and to be readable, as one of America's literary pioneers.

"THANATOPSIS"

"Thanatopsis," one of Bryant's earliest successes and his most enduring one, survives as a poem rather than as an artifact because its rhythmic and syntactic fluidity has kept it readable. Blank verse has always offered the poet writing in English the best medium, short of free verse, for such fluidity, and that fact, along with the survival of the Romantic ideal of a natural or colloquial language, goes a long way toward explaining the poem's survival. Because, however, it is obvious that not all of Bryant's blank verse has been so successful, "Thanatopsis" invites a more detailed examination. The basis of its rhythmic character lies primarily in the relationship between the blank verse structure and the sentence structure. Because few of the lines are end-stopped, the syntactic rhythm is stronger than the theoretical rhythm of blank verse—that is, of five-stress, iambic lines. An examination of the great variety of sentence length relative to line length and of the accentual stress pattern of both will provide some illustrative detail for this aspect of the poem's character.

There are three thematic sections in the poem, the second beginning at line 31, with "Yet not to thine . . . ," the third at line 73, with "So live. . . ." The opening independent clause of section 1, ending with a semicolon in line 3, has all the rhetorical quality of a sentence. It and the opening sentence of section 2 are two-and-a-half lines long. The third section has only one sentence, running through the final nine lines of the poem. Two other very long sentences are those beginning at line 8, running over eight lines, and at line 66, running over six. The two shortest sentences are at lines 29 and 60, respectively. The first of these, beginning with "The oak/ Shall send his roots abroad," has twelve syllables, two more than the blank verse line. The latter has only nine syllables, one short of the prescribed ten. Even this shortest sentence, however, occupies parts of two lines, thus contributing to rather than diminishing the dominance of the syntactic over the verse structure. That dominance prevails in large part simply because of the variety of sentence lengths, which constitute a variety of rhetorical subunits within the thematic and blank verse structures of the poem. The relationship between these syntactical subunits and the blank verse can be best illustrated by simple scansion of representative passages.

The poem begins with a two-and-a-half line independent clause: "To him who in the love of Nature holds/ Communion with her visible forms, she speaks/ A various language...." If, for the sake of illustration, one ignores the sentence-sense of this phrase, the first two lines scan perfectly as iambic pentameter. The artificiality of the resulting illustration is so apparent, however, as to prompt a quick second scansion of the clause as a whole, which shifts the emphasis from line units to grammatical units—to, in this case, an introductory prepositional phrase, a relative clause, and a main clause. In that second scansion, "who," as the first word of the relative clause, is stressed, immediately throwing off the iambic regularity of the first reading. "In" loses its stress, becoming the first syllable of an anapest, "in the love." A second anapest occurs in line 2 in "visible forms." The most dramatic alteration of the blank verse line comes at the end of the grammatical unit in line 3, where the rhythm shifts momentarily from rising to falling, to the dactyl of "various," and the trochee of "language."

The opening lines of section 2, lines 31 through 33, maintain a greater iambic regularity than does the first clause, although at the end of the sentence, "couch," the first word of line 33, is stressed and is followed by the anapest "more magnificent."

In the closing nine-line sentence of the poem, the syntactic counterpoint to the blank verse rhythm is of a more subtle kind. The opening anapests of line 74, "The innumerable," *if* one sounds the schwa in the middle of the word, is followed immediately by the initial stress of "caravan." The rhythm of the prepositional phrase "in the silent halls," of line 76, prevails over the artificiality of a strict iambic reading, which calls for a stress on "in." Anapests occur in each of the final four lines. Line 78 has an initial stress on "Scourged," and the final line has the interesting juxtaposition of stresses in "About him," that is probably best described as a spondee.

The language of "Thanatopsis," particularly the dominance of syntactical over blank verse rhythm, is very close to what might be called the vernacular mode. Except for its diction, the "still voice" of the poem approximates, almost as closely as does Whitman's free verse, the voice of American colloquial speech. A dramatic illustration of that characteristic can be made by reading "Thanatopsis" side by side with almost any poem of Henry Wadsworth Longfellow's. Adjustments must be made from the late twentieth century perspective to accommodate Bryant's diction and imagery to that sense of his achievement, but in "Thanatopsis" those adjustments can be made rather easily. Except for the second-person pronouns, "thee," "thou," and "thine," there is very little diction that dates the poem.

Imagery

If Bryant's rhythm and diction point forward in time to the emerging American voice, his imagery and overt moral didacticism provide the ballast that holds him most securely to his own time. The general and abstract plane of much of his imagery clearly reflects eighteenth century influence. In some instances, it clogs the otherwise fluid syntax, effectively cutting off any prospects of vitality for the modern sensibility. One of his better poems, "A Forest Hymn," suffers in this way because of the density of images such as "stilly twilight," "mossy boughs," "venerable columns," "verdant roof," and "winding aisles."

Although the imagery of "Thanatopsis" is typical in this respect—that is, its imagery is more general and abstract than particular and concrete—it does not impede the syntactic flow of the poem. This is due, in part, to the fact that the subject of the poem, the meditation on death, calls for and sustains general imagery as much as any subject can. The "innumerable caravan" of the dead and the "silent halls of death" have no concrete, experiential counterparts. The "gay" and "the solemn brood of care," on the other hand, do, and they contribute to that eighteenth century ballast that counteracts Bryant's forward motion. Those countermelodies of the static and the dynamic, of the past and of the present progressive, are nowhere more evident than in the closing lines of the first section of the poem, which juxtapose the stock images of the "insensible rock" and the "sluggish clod" with the concrete imagery of one of the most memorable lines in American poetry: "The oak/ Shall send his roots abroad and pierce thy mould."

The blank verse and the theme of "Thanatopsis" together make the general imagery less obtrusive than it is in many of Bryant's poems. The same can be said of his overt moral didacticism, which is better sustained in this blank verse meditation on death than it is in poems such as "The Yellow Violet," "To the Fringed Gentian," and "To a Waterfowl," where the fragile lyricism is overburdened for twentieth century sensibility by the didactic uses to which he puts the flowers and the birds.

"A Forest Hymn" and "The Prairies"

Other blank verse poems that hold up well in much the same way as does "Thanatopsis" are "A Forest Hymn" and "The Prairies," although the eighteenth century stock imagery somewhat impedes the syntactic and rhythmic flow of the former. "The Prairies," on the other hand, is remarkable for the fluid sweep of its opening thirty-four lines of impressionistic description, motivated by Bryant's first visit to Illinois in 1832. The marvelously vibrant sense of life in these lines provides an excellent example of the major counterpoint in Bryant's poetry to the stoic resignation evinced in the earlier meditation on death. The terms of that early poem are broader than those of what might be called a mortality theme; the counterpoint in Bryant is really between the two larger themes of mutability and plenitude. His prevailing preoccupation is not so much with mortality as with change, and that somber theme is countered by his affirmative sense of a natural plenitude that guarantees a continuing replenishment of all that passes.

OTHER MAJOR WORKS

NONFICTION: *Letters of a Traveller: Or, Notes of Things Seen in Europe and America*, 1850; *Reminiscences of the "Evening Post,"* 1851; *A Discourse on the Life and Genius of James Fenimore Cooper*, 1852; *Letters of a Traveller, Second Series*, 1859; *A Discourse on the Life and Genius of Washington Irving*, 1860; *Letters from the East*, 1869; *Orations and Addresses*, 1873; *Lectures on Poetry*, 1884; *The Letters of William Cullen Bryant*, 1975-1992 (6 volumes; William Cullen Bryant II and Thomas G. Voss, editors); *Power for Sanity: Selected Editorials of William Cullen Bryant, 1829-1861*, 1994.

TRANSLATIONS: *The Iliad of Homer*, 1870; *The Odyssey of Homer*, 1871, 1872.

EDITED TEXT: *A Library of Poetry and Song*, 1871.

BIBLIOGRAPHY

Brown, Charles H. *William Cullen Bryant*. New York: Charles Scribner's Sons, 1971. A well-written, comprehensive, and reliable account of Bryant's life. The study of Bryant's long career at the *New York Evening Post* is excellent. Little literary analysis.

Donovan, Alan B. "William Cullen Bryant: Father of American Song." *New England Quarterly* 41 (December, 1968): 505-520. Identifies the importance of Calvinism and neoclassicism in shaping Bryant's Romantic verses. Finds in Bryant's work "the first native articulation of the art of poetry."

Foshay, Ella M., and Barbara Novak. *Intimate Friends: Thomas Cole, Asher B. Durand, and William Cullen Bryant*. New York: New York Historical Society, 2000. An examination of the friendship among Bryant and the two painters.

Justice, James H. "The Fireside Poets: Hearthside Values and the Language of Care." In *Nineteenth-Century American Poetry*, edited by A. Robert Lee. New York: Barnes & Noble, 1985. Asserting that the Fireside poets established poetry as an American treasure, Justice presents Bryant as one of the firmest to show how personal values could be merged with public service. His conversion from older verse styles to newer, Romantic ones is the focus of the discussion of his work. Includes notes and an index.

Krapf, Norbert. *Under Open Sky: Poets on William Cullen Bryant*. New York: Fordham University Press, 1986. This resource, which includes both prose and poetry by twenty contemporary poets, pays tribute to Bryant, the United States' first nature poet. The writings give both a broad and deep appraisal of Bryant's poetic legacy.

McLean, Albert F. *William Cullen Bryant*. Rev. ed. Boston: Twayne, 1989. The first four chapters survey Bryant's life, examine his poems of nature, analyze "Thanatopsis" in detail, and classify several poems of "progress." The last three chapters evaluate Bryant's prose and translations, explicate his poetic theory and style, and review his reputation. Includes chronology, notes, a select bibliography, and an index.

Muller, Gilbert H. *William Cullen Bryant: Author of America*. Albany: State University of New York Press, 2008. A biography of Bryant that looks at him as an important American literary voice.

Nevins, Allan. *The "Evening Post": A Century of Journalism*. New York: Russell and Russell, 1922. Includes a long account of Bryant's accomplishments as an editor, praising his business judgment, his cultural influence, and his liberal stance on social issues.

Peckham, Harry Houston. *Gotham Yankee: A Biography of William Cullen Bryant*. 1950. Reprint. Folcroft, Pa.: Folcroft Library Editions, 1970. Correcting misrepresentations of Bryant, Peckham describes him as a poet with an interesting personality and an interesting career as a journalist and poet. In eleven chapters, Bryant's life is narrated from its beginnings, when he was a delicate child, through his legal work of drudgery, to his last years of eloquence. Contains illustrations, notes, a bibliography, a chronology, and an index.

Phair, Judith Turner. *A Bibliography of William Cullen Bryant and His Critics: 1808-1972*. Troy, N.Y.: Whitston, 1975. An extremely useful annotated bibliography of critical commentary on Bryant.

Ringe, Donald A. *The Pictorial Mode: Space and Time in the Art of Bryant, Irving, and Cooper*. Lexington: University Press of Kentucky, 1971. Bryant is given priority among writers who shared a pictorial aesthetic. Representation of space in Bryant's poetry is analyzed as a view of expansive nature, with precision of detail in the play of light and shadow. Time is examined as a force of contrast and continuity. Includes notes and an index.

Lloyd N. Dendinger

RAYMOND CARVER

Born: Clatskanie, Oregon; May 25, 1938
Died: Port Angeles, Washington; August 2, 1988

PRINCIPAL POETRY
Near Klamath, 1968
Winter Insomnia, 1970
At Night the Salmon Move, 1976
Two Poems, 1982
If It Please You, 1984
This Water, 1985
Where Water Comes Together with Other Water, 1985
Ultramarine, 1986
A New Path to the Waterfall, 1989
All of Us: The Collected Poems, 1996

OTHER LITERARY FORMS

Raymond Carver is perhaps best known as a writer of short fiction. In addition, he wrote a screenplay and edited a collection of short stories.

ACHIEVEMENTS

Raymond Carver has been credited with rescuing both poetry and the short story from the elitists and obscurantists and giving them back to the people. His honors include the National Endowment for the Arts Discovery Award for Poetry in 1970, the Joseph Henry Jackson Award for fiction in 1971, a Wallace Stegner Creative Writing Fellowship from Stanford University in 1972-1973, a National Book Award nomination in fiction in 1977, a Guggenheim Fellowship in 1977-1978, a National Endowment for the Arts Award in fiction in 1979, the Carlos Fuentes Fiction Award in 1983, the Mildred and Harold Strauss Living Award in 1983, a National Book Critics Circle Award nomination in fiction in 1984, a finalist for the Pulitzer Prize in fiction in 1984 and 1989, *Poetry* magazine's Levinson Prize in 1985, and a Washington State Book Award in 1987. Carver was elected to the American Academy of Arts and Letters in 1988 and in that same year was awarded a doctorate of letters from the University of Hartford.

BIOGRAPHY

Raymond Clevie Carver, Jr., was born in Clatskanie, Oregon, and grew up in Yakima, Washington, where his father worked as a saw filer in a lumber mill. Like most young men growing up in that heavily forested, sparsely populated region, Carver enjoyed hunting and fishing; however, he seems to have inherited unusual intelligence, sensitivity, and ambition. His life is a story of his struggle to achieve self-actualization in spite of an impoverished background. His parents were poor and uneducated, and he himself was extremely ignorant about literature. In his teens, he enrolled in a correspondence course in creative writing, but he never finished it. His early reading was typically the westerns of Zane Grey, the fantasies of Edgar Rice Burroughs, and magazines celebrating rugged outdoor adventure.

At the age of nineteen, Carver married his teenage sweetheart, who gave birth to their first child less than six months later. Another child was born the following year, and from then on, Carver was torn between the desire to become a writer and the need to support his family. "Nothing—and, brother, I mean nothing—that ever happened to me on this earth," he said, "could come anywhere close, could possibly be as important to me, could make as much difference, as the fact that I had two children."

In 1958, Carver and his family moved to Paradise, California, where he enrolled at Chico State College (now Chico State University). One of the major turning points in his life was a course in creative writing taught by the inspiring writer and teacher John Gardner. Carver began publishing poems and short stories in college literary magazines. He continued to do so when he transferred to Humboldt State College (now University) in Arcata, California, and finally his work began to be accepted by respected literary quarterlies.

Carver was tortured by the fact that he had to support himself and his family by working at a series of mindless and often physically exhausting dead-end jobs. Among other things, he worked as a mill hand, a farm laborer, a delivery boy, a service station attendant, a stock clerk, and a janitor. His poems and stories are haunted by guilt. He felt guilty because he was not providing his family with a decent standard of living and because he did not want to be burdened with a family at all. He drank because he felt guilty, and then he felt guilty for drinking. Many American writers have been heavy drinkers, including Ernest Hemingway, William Faulkner, and Sinclair Lewis, but few have admitted it so frankly or used it so freely as subject matter for his or her work.

In 1967, Carver obtained his first white-collar job, as an editor of textbooks for Science Research Associates in Palo Alto, California. By this time he had become a heavy drinker, and only a few years later, he was fired. Still, he had continued to write stories and poetry, and in 1970, he received a National Endowment for the Arts Discovery Award for Poetry. Other monetary awards helped him to devote more time to writing. In 1971, his poems and stories began to appear in magazines such as *Esquire*, *Harper's Bazaar*, and *Playgirl*.

Part-time teaching assignments helped Carver survive to produce more stories and poetry. In 1971, he began teaching creative writing at the University of California, Santa Cruz; in 1972, he began teaching at Stanford University. In 1975, he had to drop out of an assignment at the University of California, Santa Barbara, because of his alcoholism;

in the late 1970's, however, Carver was teaching writing again, even though he said he felt uncomfortable doing it.

Carver taught at Goddard College in the late 1970's and then at the University of Texas, El Paso, and at the University of Vermont. He was appointed professor of English at Syracuse University in 1980. In 1983, he was at last able to give up teaching and devote his full time and attention to writing, after receiving a Strauss Living Award, which guaranteed him an annual stipend for five years.

Carver was separated from his wife in the late 1970's and began living with Tess Gallagher, a poet and college teacher like himself who had also been born in the Pacific Northwest. Gallagher helped him to cope with his drinking problem and provided him with understanding and emotional support. She was with Carver until the time of his death from lung cancer in 1988; they were married in Reno, Nevada, less than two months before he died. Years of worry, chronic insecurity, and hard living had cut short the career of one of America's most promising writers at the age of fifty.

Analysis

Raymond Carver certainly had his faults, but he also had many strengths that were responsible for making him better loved than most other writers of his generation and ultimately more famous. He was humble, modest, honest, sincere, and dedicated. He was not ashamed to acknowledge his lower-class background or the fact that he had done a considerable amount of work that required him to get his hands dirty. He did not pretend to know all—or even any—of the answers. The reader senses that Carver was someone like himself or herself, struggling to make sense out of a life that actually did not make much sense at all.

Carver's writing was always personal and autobiographical. He did not seem to know how to write any other way. This quality made him seem primitive and a mere literary curiosity to certain sophisticated critics but also endeared him to ordinary readers, many of whom felt betrayed by the trickery and emotional emptiness of much modern literature. Carver said, "My poems are of course not literally true" but acknowledged that, as in most of his short stories, "there is an autobiographical element."

Carver never got on a pulpit or a soapbox. He never blamed anyone but himself for his troubles. His writings are remarkably devoid of allusions to religion and politics, the Scylla and Charybdis of most modern writers. This was probably another thing that annoyed his critics: They wanted him to take a position—preferably one aligned with their own. A writer can toil in obscurity forever without a glance from such people, but if he begins receiving recognition, then they immediately want to bring him into their camp. Thus critics have complained that in Carver's poems there are no resolutions, no epiphanies—as if resolutions and epiphanies were something that came in boxes of twelve at the supermarket. One of Carver's writing mottos was "No cheap tricks." He steered by this motto all his life, and it always guided him in the direction of unadorned self-revelation. The photographs that appear on the backs of many of his published volumes show a big, awkward, shy-looking man with questioning eyes that are hard to look at and hard to look away from. He was the sort of plain-spoken American that Americans have always admired, not unlike Abraham Lincoln, Mark Twain, Will Rogers, and Jimmy Stewart. In an age when every television personality seems to have all the answers to life's biggest questions, it is refreshing to come upon a writer such as Carver who has no easy answers to offer. Carver will be remembered not for his depth of thought but for his depth of feeling. He saw life as a mystery, but a wonderful and fascinating mystery.

FIRES

When Carver published *Fires: Essays, Poems, Stories* in 1983, he said that he had collected in the book everything he had previously written that he considered worth keeping. In addition to two very illuminating essays about his life and his writing values, the book contains fifty of his poems dating back to 1968. Most of the themes that would appear in his later poems are evident in these early works. "Near Klamath," for example, is one of many expressions of his love for nature and particularly for fishing. Many of Carver's poems about nature remind the reader of Hemingway's passionate love for physical action in the outdoors. Hemingway was one of Carver's early literary models; they have a similar simple, straightforward style of writing and have a similar reticence to express sentimental feelings.

With Carver, one senses that his love of nature was connected with a yearning for escape from the responsibilities that plagued him—the menial jobs, the coin-operated laundries, the crying children, the endless bills, the junk cars, the squatter's life in cheap apartments and borrowed dwellings—and kept him from his writing, the only thing that gave his life meaning. In one of his better-known poems, "Winter Insomnia," he writes:

> The mind would like to get out of here
> onto the snow. It would like to run
> with a pack of shaggy animals, all teeth.

"Drinking While Driving" is one of the many pieces Carver wrote about drinking during his lifetime. "Bankruptcy" tells with wry humor how he became bankrupt for the first time at the age of twenty-eight. A similar story is told in a later poem titled "Miracle," published in *A New Path to the Waterfall*; the wry humor is still there (as it remained for the rest of his life), but his wife's reaction to this second bankruptcy was far more violent. "Deschutes River" is an interesting poem because it brings together his love for the outdoors and his personal guilt and anxiety: The poem ends with the lines "Far away—/ another man is raising my children,/ bedding my wife bedding my wife."

Some of the poems collected in *Fires* show the bad habits a naïve beginner can pick up from other writers who substitute stylistic legerdemain, erudition, wit, and exoticism for genuine feeling. "Rhodes," "The Mosque in Jaffa," and "Spring, 480 B.C." are among the poems in which Carver deals with foreign sights and sounds, evidently trying to evoke refined sentiments. Poems with this foreign flavor continue to appear in his subsequent volumes and are among the least appealing of his works. Many of them have a certain artificial or chapbook quality, as if written by a professor on sabbatical. It was inevitable that Carver's growing fame as well as his exposure to academia would tempt him to seem more cultivated than he actually was; he was most likable and most effective, however, as a simple lad from the Pacific Northwest who had barely managed to obtain a bachelor's degree.

ULTRAMARINE

The poems collected in *Ultramarine*, published in 1986, represent Carver at his best. These poems are longer, more confident. The words march across the pages almost with the brave assurance of John Milton's iambic pentameter in *Paradise Lost* (1667, 1674). Carver, however, always shunned rhyme and meter. Stylistically, he belongs to that vast modern school of poets who have abandoned all poetic conventions and try to write like someone talking to a close friend. Though his poems have rhythm, rhyme and meter would seem as grossly out of place in a poem by Carver as he himself would look in an Elizabethan costume with lace ruffles.

The question arises, why then did he continue to arrange his words in lines to look like poems? Why did he not abandon this last vestige of conventional poetry and write his thoughts as plain prose? There are several possible answers. Probably the most important one is that the appearance of a poem gives the author more freedom. Prose poems such as those written by Charles Baudelaire have never gained wide popularity. A reader faced with a prose paragraph expects a reasoned utterance, a logical progression of ideas from the first to the last sentence. The poetic format allows Carver the freedom to use exclamations, interjections, incomplete sentences, neologisms, allusions, abrupt changes of subject, or whatever else he wishes. Here are the first four lines of "In the Lobby of the Hotel del Mayo":

> The girl in the lobby reading a leather-bound book.
> The man in the lobby using a broom.
> The boy in the lobby watering plants.
> The desk clerk looking at his nails.

These fragments would seem surrealistic in a straight prose paragraph; such prose might remind one of the experimental writing of Gertrude Stein. An arrangement in lines like those of a traditional poem, however, prepares the reader to approach the words in a different way.

One of the most interesting poems in *Ultramarine* consists entirely of short fragments describing an oldcar that Carver once owned—or that once owned Carver.

> The car with a cracked windshield.
> The car that threw a rod.
> The car without brakes.
> The car with a faulty U-joint.
> The car with a hole in its radiator.
> The car I picked peaches for.

The poem continues in this vein for forty-four more lines and ends with the words "My car." By the time the reader finishes the poem, he or she has formed a remarkably complete picture not only of the car, but also of Carver's life and state of mind over the long period during which he was chained to this horrible automobile. It is characteristic of Carver to take his imagery from the external world rather than search for it in his own memory. There seems to be a Japanese influence here, perhaps by way of his favorite poet, William Carlos Williams. Like many of the poems in *Ultramarine*, "The Car" deals with themes of alcoholism, debt, meaningless work, domestic unhappiness, and the longing for escape. As always, there is also a note of unconquerable humor even in this Job-like litany of despair.

There is, however, a slightly different note, a slightly different perspective. In most of these poems, Carver is now talking about the past. Life has improved for him. He has achieved recognition. He is earning some money and not having to do it with a mop or a broom. He has quit drinking. Perhaps most significantly, *Ultramarine* is dedicated to Gallagher, a fellow writer and evidently a real soul mate, someone who would be with him for the rest of his life.

"NyQuil" is one of the poems in which Carver remembers his nightmare with alcohol. NyQuil is a well-known cold medicine, but Carver was doggedly drinking it as a substitute for liquor. An acquaintance, he says, was similarly trying to break his addiction to Scotch whiskey by drinking mouthwash by the case. This externalization or projection of feelings is a common characteristic of Carver's writing—both in his poems and in his short stories. The image of a man drinking NyQuil by the tumblerful gives the reader a vivid conception of the depth of Carver's addiction to alcohol.

"Jean's TV" is another poem in which an external object serves as an extended metaphor. A former girlfriend and drinking companion named Jean calls to ask when he plans to return the black-and-white television set she had left with him when she moved out. He hems and haws until the reader finally understands: He must have sold it a long time ago to buy liquor. Carver has confessed in interviews that he was capable of doing almost anything in his drinking days; he was also apparently unusually susceptible to feelings of remorse.

In "The Possible," he talks about another former drinking companion, this one a fellow college teacher, and makes the following interesting statement about his many years of teaching: "I was a stranger,/ and an impostor, even to myself." "Where They'd

Lived" is among the poems that deal with his unhappy marriage. Like most of the poems collected in this volume, these two pieces seem to be looking back at a receding past.

One new theme appears quite prominently among the poems collected in *Ultramarine*, the book that established Carver's reputation as a poet. It is the theme of unexpected death. "Egress" tells of a man who "fell dead/ one night after dinner, after talking over some business deal." "Powder-Monkey" is the story of a coworker who is killed in a head-on collision with a logging truck. In "An Account," a friend dies of a heart attack while watching the television serial *Hill Street Blues* (1981-1987). In each of these poems, Carver seems stunned. "What does this mean?" he seems to be asking the reader. "How can this happen?"

Somehow the black shadow of death makes Carver's message to the world suddenly stand out bright and clear. Life itself is beautiful in any aspect. The human tragedy and the human comedy are two sides of the same coin. Drinking, toiling, fighting, and lying to the landlords and the bill collectors are all a part of life, and consequently they all contain their own weird beauty. Clearly, Carver was experiencing strong premonitions of his own approaching death.

A NEW PATH TO THE WATERFALL

Carver finished *A New Path to the Waterfall* shortly before he died of lung cancer. The title of the book is taken from one of the poems in the volume, "Looking for Work." The speaker dreams that he is out fishing: "Suddenly, I find a new path/ to the waterfall." His wife wakes him up, however, and tells him that he must go out and find a job. The themes of unhappy marriage, responsibilities, shortage of cash, and a desire to escape to nature are still here, even though Carver's troubles were at this point only ghosts of the past. One of the most harrowing poems in the book is "Miracle," in which he matter-of-factly and in excruciating detail describes the aftermath of his second bankruptcy proceeding. On the way home on the airplane, his wife turns in her seat and begins hitting him in the face with clenched fists.

> All the while his head is pummeled,
> buffeted back and forth, her fists falling
> against his ear, his lips, his jaw, he protects
> his whiskey.

The shadow of death is the subject that dominates this last collection of Carver's poetry. What he sensed intuitively in *Ultramarine* has become an unblinking reality. Early in his career, he had chosen to write short stories and short poems because his struggle to support a family left him no time to contemplate larger projects; ironically, now that he had leisure and a certain amount of financial security, death was pressing him even harder than the bosses and bill collectors of old. In September, 1987, Carver, a heavy cigarette smoker for many years, was diagnosed with lung cancer. Two-thirds of his left lung was removed, but the cancer recurred as a brain tumor in March of the following year. He underwent seven weeks of full-brain radiation; however, by early June, the doctors found tumors in his lungs again. He knew he had only a short time left to live.

Some of Carver's last poems are not only his most moving but also his most successful in terms of realizing his artistic aims. "Poems" reveals how he understood his creative process. His poems "came to him," and he wrote them down as if he had heard them whispered in his ear. Frequently they came to him in the form of dreams, as was the case with "Looking for Work." He was never satisfied with the original versions of his poems, however, and he polished them painstakingly for a long time before letting them out of his hands. At their best, these poems seem to have no need for rhyme or meter or any of the other paraphernalia of conventional poetry. His method might be described as functionalism: The thought finds its own form, so that thought and form seem molded to each other. "Through the Boughs" comes close to perfection in this style of poetic composition.

> Down below the window, on the deck, some ragged-   looking
> birds gather at the feeder. . . .
> The sky stays dark all day, the wind is from the west and
> won't stop blowing. . . . Give me your hand for a time.
>   Hold on
> to mine. That's right, yes. Squeeze hard. Time was we
> thought we had time on our side. *Time was, time was,*
>   those ragged birds cry.

These last poems by Carver are almost the royal road to understanding what many modern poets have been trying to do. They have abandoned rhyme and meter. They have abandoned what used to be called poetic diction. They write in a conversational style. They attempt to allow the poetic message to dictate the poem's own unique form. No one has expressed the essential notion behind modern poetry better than the great American thinker Ralph Waldo Emerson, who said in his essay "The Poet" that "For it is not metres, but a metre-making argument that makes a poem—a thought so passionate and alive that like the spirit of a plant or an animal it has an architecture of its own, and adorns nature with a new thing."

Ironically, the circumstances that originally kept Carver from writing became the principal material of much of his poetry and fiction. His recognition of this fact may partially explain the wry humor found in many of his most doleful poems. Drinking bouts, hangovers, guilt, divorce, and debt were recurring themes of his stories and poems. He recognized that even his own terminal illness was a powerful subject for his poetry. With characteristic naïveté and improvidence, Carver had chosen precisely the two literary forms that are hardest to sell and pay the least money when they do sell—poetry and short stories. These choices automatically condemned him to long years of poverty, with all the problems that accompanied it. (Gardner had not warned Carver and his classmates of this reality when he advised them to forget about the "slicks" and concentrate on the "little" magazines, "where the best fiction in the country was being published, and all of the poetry.") Even had he lived longer, Carver would have had a hard time making a living as a writer: He was dependent on the various disguised forms of charity that are the creative writer's lot in the age of television.

"Proposal," "Cherish," "Gravy," "No Need," and "After-Glow" all confront the imminence of death. "What the Doctor Said," in which Carver relates how a doctor informed him that he had at least thirty-two malignant nodules on one lung and was doomed, still is tinged with that ineradicable Carver humor, his most endearing quality. Though he has no resolutions or epiphanies to offer the reader, his invincible spirit, his truthfulness and dedication, and his admirable humanity are resolution and epiphany in themselves.

Carver had started as a country yokel in a rocky region whose literary roots did not run deep; he had made the painful climb from ignorance to enlightenment, from inarticulate frustration to masterful eloquence, from anonymity to fame. Many of his poems and stories are confessions of his sins, but readers have forgiven him because they recognize in him their own faults as well as some of their virtues. He had more than mere talent with words: He had the extra quality of soul that only great writers possess. He saw literature not as a stylish game but as the most important job a person can do. When he died on the morning of August 2, 1988, his works were being read in twenty different languages, and he has a better chance of being remembered for the next few centuries than do most of his contemporaries. His career was a striking illustration of what Emerson meant when he said in "The Poet," "Thou must pass for a fool and a churl for a long season. This is the screen and sheath in which Pan has protected his well-beloved flower. . . . and though thou shouldst walk the world over, thou shalt not be able to find a condition inopportune or ignoble."

OTHER MAJOR WORKS

SHORT FICTION: *Put Yourself in My Shoes*, 1974; *Will You Please Be Quiet, Please?*, 1976; *Furious Seasons, and Other Stories*, 1977; *What We Talk About When We Talk About Love*, 1981; *Cathedral*, 1983; *Elephant, and Other Stories*, 1988; *Where I'm Calling From*, 1988; *Short Cuts: Selected Stories*, 1993.

SCREENPLAY: *Dostoevsky*, 1985.

EDITED TEXT: *American Short Story Masterpieces*, 1987 (with Tom Jenks).

MISCELLANEOUS: *Fires: Essays, Poems, Stories*, 1983; *No Heroics, Please: Uncollected Writings*, 1991 (revised and expanded as *Call If You Need Me: The Uncollected Fiction and Prose*, 2000).

BIBLIOGRAPHY

Adelman, Bob, and Tess Gallagher. *Carver Country: The World of Raymond Carver.* Introduction by Gallagher. New York: Charles Scribner's Sons, 1990. Produced in the spirit of a photographic essay, this book contains excellent photographs of Carver, his relatives, people who served as inspirations for characters in his stories, and places that were important in his life and work. The photographs are accompanied by excerpts from Carver's stories and poems.

Carver, Maryann Burk. *What It Used to Be Like: A Portrait of My Marriage to Raymond Carver.* New York: St. Martin's Press, 2006. Maryann Burk Carver recounts her tumultuous twenty-five-year marriage to Raymond Carver.

Carver, Raymond. Interviews. *Conversations with Raymond Carver.* Edited by Marshall Bruce Gentry and William L. Stull. Jackson: University Press of Mississippi, 1990. A wide-ranging collection of interviews covering Carver's career from the early 1980's until just before his death.

Gallagher, Tess. Introduction to *A New Path to the Waterfall*, by Raymond Carver. New York: Atlantic Monthly Press, 1989. The collection in which this essay appears, a collection of Carver's last poems, includes some moving reflections on his life and values as he faced the fact that he was dying of cancer. The writer of the informative and moving introduction is the person who knew him best, the poet Gallagher, who lived with him for many years and was with him at the time of his death.

Halpert, Sam, ed. *Raymond Carver: An Oral Biography.* Iowa City: University of Iowa Press, 1995. An expanded edition of a collection of conversations originally published in 1991 as *When We Talk About Raymond Carver.* Includes contributions from Carver's first wife, his daughter, an early writing instructor, and some of his lifetime friends.

Kleppe, Sandra Lee, and Robert Miltner, eds. *New Paths to Raymond Carver: Critical Essays on His Life, Fiction, and Poetry.* Columbia: University of South Carolina Press, 2008. This collection has a number of essays on his poetry as well as Tess Gallagher's introduction to the Japanese edition of *Ultramarine.*

Kuzma, Greg. "*Ultramarine*: Poems That Almost Stop the Heart." *Michigan Quarterly Review* 27 (Spring, 1988): 355-363. In her introduction to *A New Path to the Waterfall*, Tess Gallagher calls Kuzma's review of *Ultramarine* "the most astute essay on [Carver's] poetry."

Saltzman, Arthur M. *Understanding Raymond Carver.* Columbia: University of South Carolina Press, 1988. A short overview of Carver's life and work with the emphasis on Carver's short stories and one chapter devoted to his poetry. Contains a valuable bibliography of works by and about Carver.

Sklenicka, Carol. *Raymond Carver: A Writer's Life.* New York: Scribner, 2009. Biography of Carver that looks at his life and works. Contains analyses of *Ultramarine* and *A New Path to the Waterfall.*

Stull, William L., and Maureen P. Carroll, eds. *Remembering Ray: A Composite Biography of Raymond Carver*. Santa Barbara, Calif.: Capra Press, 1993. Though not a formal biography, this collection of essays covers Carver's working-class origins, his troubled first marriage, his battle with alcoholism, his teaching style, and his ultimate happiness until his death from cancer.

Bill Delaney

ROSALÍA DE CASTRO

Born: Santiago de Compostela, Spain; February 24, 1837
Died: Padrón, Spain; July 15, 1885

PRINCIPAL POETRY
La flor, 1857
A mi madre, 1863
Cantares gallegos, 1863
Follas novas, 1880
En las orillas del Sar, 1884 (*Beside the River Sar*, 1937)
Obras completas, 1909-1911 (4 volumes)
Poems, 1964
Poems, 1991

OTHER LITERARY FORMS

Rosalía de Castro (KOS-troh) was a novelist as well as a poet. Her five novels—*La hija del mar* (1859; *Daughter of the Sea*, 1995), *Flavio* (1861), *Ruinas* (1866; ruins), *El caballero de las botas azules* (1867; the knight with the blue boots), and *El primer loco* (1881; the first madman)—span the transition from Romanticism to realism. Although Castro herself put considerable stock in her novels, she is remembered only for her poetry.

ACHIEVEMENTS

Rosalía de Castro has been called Spain's foremost woman poet; Gerald Brenan has gone further, asserting that if she had written more in Spanish than in her native Galician dialect, she would be recognized as the greatest woman poet of modern times. Her unabashedly heart-throbbing lyrics are saved from mawkishness by her disciplined style. Castro's poetry, along with that of Gustavo Adolfo Bécquer, is the most representative of Spanish poetry at the time of its transition from Romanticism to the modern lyric. Some critics believe that she interacted with Bécquer—that in fact she lent him in 1857 a copy of Gérard de Nerval's translation of Heinrich Heine's *Tragödien, nebst einem lyrischen Intermezzo* (1823; *Tragedies, Together with Lyric Intermezzo*, 1905), a book said to have influenced Bécquer. It was not until the second decade of the twentieth century, when Azorín (José Martínez Ruiz) and Miguel de Unamuno y Jugo recommended her to the public, that her reputation as a poet became assured. Later, even poet Luis Cernuda, who found her work uneven and sentimental, recognized the rare timelessness of her observations. Antonio Machado borrowed images from her poetry, Juan Ramón Jiménez referred to her as "our Rosalía," and Gerardo Diego used her name as a metaphor in his own poetry. Her Galician poetry inspired Federico García Lorca to write his own "poemas gallegos," including a "Canzón de cuna pra Rosalía Castro, morta" ("Lullaby for the Late Rosalía de Castro").

With her contemporaries Manuel Curros Enríquez (who wrote an elegy for her) and Eduardo Pondal, Castro made up a triad of Galician poets who effected a renaissance of their provincial literature. Using the folk songs of Galicia as her models, she bonded modern Spanish poetry to oral forms that would have otherwise been lost. She led the way for subsequent poets to utilize folk tradition, and her work tolled the death knell for urban Romanticism. Modernist poets availed themselves of the revolutionary meters used by Castro (her ennea-syllabic verse in *La flor*—the flower—predates the so-called innovations of Rubén Darío), and her use of free verse heralded the boldness of contemporary poetry.

To a remarkable extent, Castro's Galician and Spanish poetry has been accepted into English-language anthologies of world verse, especially in those of women's poetry (such as *A Book of Women Poets: From Antiquity to Now*, rev. ed., 1992).

Biography

Rosalía de Castro was born in Santiago de Compostela in 1837, the child of María Teresa de la Cruz de Castro y Abadía. Her mother, who came from a once-wealthy family, was thirty-three when Rosalía was born; her father, Jose Martínez Viojo, was thirty-nine and a priest. Although her father could not acknowledge Rosalía as his daughter, he may have taken some interest in her welfare. Rosalía was brought up by Francisca Martínez, who, despite her surname, does not appear to have been the priest's sister. By 1853, Rosalía was living with her real mother, and there developed between them a deep bond. In Rosalía's eyes, her mother sanctified whatever sin she may have committed by reaffirming her obligation to her daughter in defiance of a hypocritical society.

A precocious child, Castro was writing verses by the age of eleven, and by the age of sixteen she could play the guitar and the piano, had developed a fine contralto voice, and could draw well and read French. She read the foreign classics in translation and was fond of Lord Byron, Heinrich Heine, Edgar Allan Poe, and E. T. A. Hoffmann. Judging from the spelling errors in hand-written manuscripts of her poetry, however, her formal education may not have been extensive.

As a teenager, Castro was taken from Padrón to Santiago, where she attended school and where she participated in the city's cultural life. At a young people's cultural society, she met Aurelio Aguirre, one of the most representative figures of the Romantic movement in Galicia, a man who was later to be the model of Flavio in her novel of the same name, and who dedicated to her a work called "Improvisation"—apparently an attempt to console her for the discrepancy between her enchanting poetry and her less than enchanting physical appearance. Perhaps it is too facile to attribute the characteristic wistfulness of her poetry to a failed love affair, but it has been suggested that the lost love recalled in her poems and her fiction was Aurelio Aguirre. Among the poems not included in her own collections but included in *Obras completas* is an elegy for Aguirre.

In 1856, Castro went to Madrid, where she stayed at the home of a relative. It is generally said that she went "on family business," but it is possible she left home with the idea of becoming an actress in Madrid. Exposed to the cultural life of the Spanish capital, she devoted herself to writing and was able to meet other contemporary writers. In 1857, her first book of poetry *La flor* appeared and was favorably reviewed by Manuel Murguía in *La Iberia*. According to Murguía, he was not acquainted with the young author, but this is rather unlikely, not only because some of his comments presuppose a direct knowledge of Castro's personality, but also because he, too, had recently come from Galicia and, in fact, was Aguirre's best friend. Castro and Murguía were married in Madrid on October 10, 1858. Murguía, like Aguirre a Galician of Basque descent, was a journalist and historian destined to be honored in Galicia for his role in promoting regionalist literature. The couple had seven children. Their first child, a daughter, was born in 1859; their second child, also a daughter, was not born until ten years later. One of the twins Castro bore in 1871, Ovidio, was an accomplished painter of Galician landscapes but died young. Her youngest son died in his second year as the result of a fall, and her youngest daughter was stillborn in 1877.

In 1862, Castro's beloved mother died, and Castro honored her with a privately printed collection of poems, *A mi madre* (to my mother) of limited literary value but elegiac and emotional.

It remains unclear what kind of a marriage Castro had with Murguía. Gerald Brenan believes that Murguía, envious of his wife's talents, mistreated her; it is certain that Murguía destroyed his wife's correspondence after her death. Castro scholar Marina Mayoral, on the other hand, prefers to see in Murguía—who survived his wife by thirty-eight years and wrote lovingly and abundantly about her—one of the few mainstays of Castro's sad life. Despite the fulfillment of children and the security of family life, she was frequently bored, and in both her poetry and her fiction, she mourned lost happiness.

It is important, however, not to exaggerate the pathetic nature of Castro's life. She loved the arts and took great pleasure from her endeavors in the fields of music, drawing, and acting. She was a great success when she acted in Antonio Gil y Zárate's play *Rosamunda* (1839), and for the greater part of her life she enjoyed exchanging ideas with her friends. Her daughter Gala, who lived until 1964, was especially concerned that her mother not be remembered as morose. As Victoriano García Martí points out, people who are authentically sorrowful often develop a profound love of humankind and achieve a different kind of contentment. This was especially true of Castro, and after her death a legend grew concerning her generosity to others, endowing her with a kind of saintliness.

Between 1859 and 1870, the couple lived in Madrid and Simancas, where Murguía had a position as a government historian, and they traveled extensively throughout

Spain. To Castro, any terrain that was not green, damp, and lush like her native Galicia was disappointing; thus, she disliked most of the rest of Spain. She became so consumed with nostalgia for her native land that she began her *Cantares gallegos* (Galician songs), written in Galician but given a Spanish title. In the 1870's, Murguía held positions in Galicia, and Castro spent much of her time at Padron, which she considered home. Having suffered from vague ill health all her life, she withdrew completely from society in her last decade; she died of uterine cancer in 1885. In the moments before her death, she received the Sacraments, recited her favorite prayers, and begged her children to destroy her unpublished manuscripts. With her last breath, she asked that the window be opened, for she wished to see the ocean—which in fact was not visible from her home.

Castro was buried near her mother in the peaceful cemetery of Adina in Padron, a place whose enchantment she had evoked in *Follas novas* (new leaves). On the very day of her death, accolades began to arrive, and as a result of the homage paid her in death, her remains were moved in 1891 to a marble tomb in the Convent of Santo Domingo de Bonaval in Santiago. In 1917, her compatriots, together with an organization of Galician emigrants in America, organized a campaign to raise a statue to their poet in the Paseo de la Herradura in Santiago, looking toward Padron. According to biographer Kathleen Kulp-Hill, this statue is faithful to portraits and descriptions of Castro. The figure is seated in a calm, pensive attitude, projecting an aura of strength and warmth.

ANALYSIS

As Frédéric Mistral is to Provence and Joan Maragall to Catalonia, Rosalía de Castro is to Galicia, the northwest corner of the Iberian peninsula, linked politically with Spain but tied ethnically, linguistically, and temperamentally with Portugal. When Castro was nine years old, there was an unsuccessful insurrection in Galicia against the Spanish government. The unpleasant memory of the savage reprisals undertaken by the government may help explain her strong hostility toward Castile and Castilians, as in the lines, "May God grant, Castilians,/ Castilians whom I abhor,/ that rather the Galicians should die,/ than to go to you for bread."

Santiago de Compostela, Castro's birthplace, possesses the bones of Saint James the Apostle, for which reason Galicia became in the Middle Ages the third most holy shrine in Christendom (after Jerusalem and Rome). The steady stream of pilgrims traveling to Galicia from all parts of Europe made Santiago a medieval cultural center, and in the thirteenth century, Galician became the language of lyrical poetry throughout the Iberian peninsula. The Galician *jograles* (minstrels) sang characteristically of melancholy (designated in Spanish by its Galician and Portuguese name, *saudades*), as in, for example, their *cantigas de amigo*, the songs of women whose lovers were absent, either away at sea or fighting the Moors in Portugal. After the thirteenth century, however, there was an eclipse of Galician poetry, and it was not until the nineteenth century that an interest in the poetic potential of the Galician language was reawakened.

The poetry of Castro flows from line to line in a musical sequence and does not, as Gerald Brenan observes, condense well into a single epithet or phrase. She was not fond of metaphors but rather relied heavily on repetition—in such lines as ("Breezes breezes, little breezes/ breezes of the land I come from")—and contrast—as in "To them those frosts/ are the promise of early flowers;/ To me they are silent workers/ weaving my winding sheet." In her earlier poems, she sometimes used the *leixa-pren*, a special feature of the medieval *cantigas de amigo*, whereby each new stanza begins with an echo from the last line of the previous stanza. Her diction is almost colloquial, her syntax uninverted (except in her earliest poetry and in some of her later poetry), and her adjectives are always the least ornamental possible. There abound words for the lushness of Galicia, names of animals and birds, and especially of trees (such as the oaks sacred to the ancient Celts of Galicia; giant chestnuts; and the cedars of "our own" Lebanon). In her somber moods, she draws repeatedly on Spanish adjectives such as *torvo* (grim), *amargo* (bitter), and *triste* (sad), and uses verbs such as *anonadar* (to destroy), *agostar* (to wither up as in August), *hostigar* (to scourge), while she uses words such as *guarida* (lair), *nido* (nest), and *egida* (aegis) to express the security and coziness of home in Galicia. Galician, more than Spanish, is a nasal language (for example, Galician *min*, "my," as opposed to Spanish *mí*), and Castro uses its humming nasals as a tool to craft more sharply the gloom she suffers on Earth, as in the line "Pra min i-en min mesma moras" (for me and in myself you live), rom "Cando penso que to fuche" (when I think that you have gone), in *Follas novas*.

"I Used to Have a Nail"

One remarkable poem that reveals Castro's attitude toward sorrow is "Una-ha vez tiven un cravo" ("I Used to Have a Nail") in *Follas novas*. This painful nail, whether made of gold, iron, or love, leads the poet, weeping like Mary Magdalen, to entreat God to effect a miracle for its removal. When at last she gathers the courage to pluck it out, the void it leaves is something like a longing for the old pain. Some critics have speculated that without an abundant supply of sorrow for her to sublimate into poetry, Castro felt lost. This contradictory hunger for suffering cannot be reduced to the level of a personal neurosis, for it reflects the ideals of traditional Christianity. Castro believed that thistles, though harsh to the flesh, mark the road to heaven, and in "Yo en mi lecho de abrojos" ("I on My Bed of Thistles," from *Beside the River Sar*), avowedly preferred her destiny to a "bed of roses and feathers," which have been known to "envenom and corrupt."

Religion and superstition

Castro was conventionally religious; she needed God and sought him everywhere, and she fought herself for her faith, as Unamuno did. There are biblical references in her poetry, as well as her marginally Christian *sombras* ("shades"), the souls of persons no longer living whom Castro "invokes" from time to time and who respond by intervening in the lives of the living. She also draws on Galician lore concerning the supernatural world. Witches (*meigas, lurpias*), warlocks (*meigos*), and elves (*trasgos*) inhabit her forests, and the safety of the unwary nocturnal traveler may be jeopardized by the Host of Souls in Torment. In "Dios bendiga todo, nena" ("God Blesses Everything, Child," from *Cantares gallegos*), an old woman warns a young girl of the dangers of the world, whereupon the girl declares her intention never to leave her village without scapularies, holy medals, and amulets to protect her from witches. The fine line between religion and superstition is typified in "Soberba" ("Foolish Pride") in *Follas novas*, where a family frightened by a storm tries to placate God with candles, olive leaves, and prayers, and by scouring from their personal slates offenses that might have incurred his wrath. Nor is the imagery of the supernatural always to be taken literally. In an aubade, Castro has the heroine address her lover affectionately as "warlock" while he prepares to leave her bed, and elsewhere employs the same word to create a metaphor for sorrow: "N' hay peor meiga que un-ha gran pena" (there is no worse demon than a great sorrow).

CANTARES GALLEGOS

Castro's first important book of poems was *Cantares gallegos*. In the prologue to this volume, she acknowledges the inspiration of *El libro de los cantares* by Antonio de Trueba, published the previous year, and apologizes for her shortcomings as a poet, claiming that her only schooling was that of "our poor country folk." The poems are dedicated to Fernan Caballero (Cecilia Böhl de Faber), the pioneer of the realistic novel in Spain, who won Castro's appreciation with her unprejudiced portrayal of Galicians. Working without a grammar, Castro apologizes for her Galician; indeed, it is not a pure dialect unaffected by Castilian influence, and lexical and orthographic inconsistencies abound. She attempted to imitate modern Portuguese in her use of diacritical marks, contractions, and elisions, and included a short glossary of Galician words for the sake of her Castilian readers.

Castro's usual procedure was to begin her poems with a popular couplet and then to elaborate it into a ballad. Her masterpiece is perhaps "Airiños, airiños, aires" ("Breezes, Breezes, Little Breezes") in which she portrays the nostalgia of a Galician emigrant, playing upon the dual meaning of *airiños* as "little breezes" and "little songs." Everywhere this unfortunate emigrant turns in the strange country of her destination, people peer curiously at her, and she longs for the sweet breezes of home, those "quitadoiriños de penas" ("takers-away of sorrow") that enchant the woods and caress the land. Similarly as Galician poetry inspired the Castilian lyric of the fifteenth and sixteenth centuries, this poem influenced the revival of Spanish poetry that began thirty years after Castro's death. The *Romancero gitano, 1924-1927* (1928; *The Gypsy Ballads of García Lorca*, 1951, 1953) of Federico García Lorca, for example, with its themes and repetitions derived from folk tradition, owes much to this poem.

In "Pasa rio, pasa rio" ("Pass by, River, Pass By"), a disconsolate lover weeps tears into the ocean in hope that they may reach her beloved in Brazil, where he has had to emigrate. The plight of the Galician emigrant forced to leave his homeland because of economic necessity troubled Castro deeply. There are many poems of praise for Galicia, such as "Cómo chove mihudiño" ("How the Rain Is Falling Lightly"), in which she describes Padrón, lulled by the river where the trees are shady, and reminisces about the great house owned by her humanitarian grandfather. She dares to ask the Sun of Italy if it has seen "more green, more roses,/ bluer sky or softer colors/ where foam stripes your gulfs with whiteness"; and is reminded by a wandering cloud of the sad shade of her mother wandering lonely in the spheres before she goes to glory.

FOLLAS NOVAS

The poems of *Follas novas* are meant to be read and reflected upon, as opposed to the folk poems of *Cantares gallegos* with their marked oral quality. The 139 poems of *Follas novas* are more subjective and personal and bleaker than those of the earlier book, which radiate innocence and hope; they are also more innovative in form: Castro employed varying line lengths with metrical combinations then regarded as inappropriate for Spanish verse, such as combinations of eight with ten or eleven syllables or eight with fourteen. Dedicated to the Society for the Welfare of Galicians in Havana, the book was published simultaneously in Havana and Madrid in 1880. In her prologue, Castro expresses her concern for the suffering of Galicians in distant lands, and she also asserts her artistic independence as a woman. Certainly the successive deaths of her two youngest children within three months of each other in 1876-1877 did much to intensify her tragic sense of life, but many of the poems in this collection were written as long as ten years before the publication date.

Here, Castro's poetry is no longer concerned with aubades but rather with the departures of lovers and their separation. Love is no longer hopeful but rather furtive and anxious. In "¿Que lle digo?" ("What Should I Tell Her?") the emigrant may be plagued by *saudades* for his homeland but may wax cynical about love as well: "Antona is there, but I have Rosa here." The landscape of Galicia is always in the background, but is no longer decorative and is now interwoven with more complex emotions. Death is seen as a cure for the disease of life, and the poet asks God why suicide must be deemed a crime.

Although she occasionally dedicated her poems to worthy persons (such as her husband and Ventura Ruíz de Aguilera), Castro did not often exalt either historical figures or living persons in her poetry. One notable exception, written in classical form, is her elegy on the tomb of Sir John Moore, the affable British general who led a retreat to Corunna that ended in the British victory over the Napoleonic forces there in 1809, but which cost Moore his life. *Follas novas* also includes a translation into Galician of the poem "Armonias d'a tarde" (harmonies of the afternoon), by Ventura Ruíz de Aguilera, a contemporary poet who drew on the folk motifs of the Salamanca area.

BESIDE THE RIVER SAR

As a result of complaints made by her Galician readers that some of her material was scandalous, Castro vowed never again to write in Galician, and it is to this decision and the Spanish poems of her last collection, *Beside the River Sar*, that she owes her prominence in Spanish literature. Not all the critics, however, proclaim the superiority of these poems. Gerald Brenan, who prefers the softer, more tender tone of her Galician verse, finds the aloofness of her Castilian poems chilling. Many of the poems collected in *Beside the River Sar* were written between 1878 and 1884 and were published in periodicals, some as distant as *La nación española* of Buenos Aires. These late poems reflect a greater concern with ideas; they are characterized by unusual combinations of lines and broken rhythms, with lines of as many as sixteen or eighteen syllables, and by a syntactical complexity not previously seen in Castro's work.

In *Beside the River Sar*, Galicia is no longer a focal point, assuming instead the role of a backdrop, and the folk element is even less in evidence. Castro continues to excel in nature poetry, displaying in "Los robles" ("The Oaks") a distinctly modern concern for ecology when she protests the wasteful destruction of trees in Galicia with an almost druidic reverence for arboreal vitality. The River Sar of the title, the beloved river of her homeland, is a symbol for the flowing of life toward its unknown and unknowable destination.

In what is possibly her most frequently anthologized poem, "Dicen que no hablan las plantas" ("They Say That Plants Do Not Speak"), Castro asserts the importance that natural phenomena such as plants, brooks, and birds have for her. Although it seems that these natural phenomena view her as a "madwoman" because of her outlandish dreams, she exhorts them not to poke fun at her, because without those dreams, she would lack the wherewithal to admire the beauty that they themselves so generously display.

In her valorization of dreams (*sueños* or *ensueños*) and her refusal to accept the pathetic constraints by which humankind is necessarily bound, Castro prefigures the concerns of the Generation of '98, of poets such as Unamuno, Machado, and Azorín. Nevertheless, she must acknowledge that dreams can lead to folly, as they do in the poignant "La canción que oyó en sueños el viejo" ("The Song Which the Old Man Heard in His Dreams"), in which an old man, designated crazy in the poem, feels his blood pump and surge as his youthful passions return when in truth he should be reckoning with "infallible death" and "implacable old age."

In *Beside the River Sar*, the winter, symbolic of despair and the end of life in Castro's earlier work, is friendly, a herald, in fact, of spring, and is "a thousand times welcome." Even the desert of Castile, anathema in her earlier poetry and so drastically opposed to the lushness of Galicia, assumes a positive guise, coming to represent the realm beyond carnal suffering, lit by "another light more vivid than that of the golden sun."

One of the most interesting poems in the collection is the questioning and subsequently epiphanic "Santa Escolástica" ("Saint Scholastica"). In Santiago on a drizzly

April day, the poet allows herself to absorb the dismal atmosphere. "Cemetery of the living," she exclaims, as she contrasts the gloom she sees around her with the city's medieval glory. This leads to her own rephrasing of that tortured question, "Why, since there is God, does Hell prevail?" She enters the Convent of San Martín Pinario in search of comfort. Her female soul begins to feel the sacred majesty of the temple as vividly as it has felt the satisfactions of motherhood. Suddenly, the sun strikes the statue of Saint Scholastica and brings into sharper focus the saint's ecstasy, which in turn produces an ecstasy in Castro, who exclaims exultantly, "There is art! There is poetry! . . . There must be a heaven,/ for there is God."

Kulp-Hill contrasts this joyous poem from *Beside the River Sar* with a poem from *Follas novas* having the same setting, "N'a catedral" ("In the Cathedral"). In the latter, although the sun shines briefly into the dimly illuminated room, the shadows return, and the poet withdraws without consolation. As the contrast between the two poems suggests, Castro's last volume was a testament to hope.

In an age when poets declaimed, Castro had the courage to write honestly and realistically about issues that troubled her. She was unashamed to examine and interpret the feelings of the Galician peasantry, creating from their own forms and phrases a new poetry of rare beauty. As she explored her own hope and hopelessness and pondered the human condition in general, she translated her findings into poetry that speaks to all people.

Other major works
LONG FICTION: *La hija del mar*, 1859 (*Daughter of the Sea*, 1995); *Flavio*, 1861; *Ruinas*, 1866; *El caballero de las botas azules*, 1867; *El primer loco*, 1881.

Bibliography
Courteau, Joanna. *The Poetics of Rosalía de Castro's "Negra sombra."* New York: Edwin Mellen Press, 1995. A close critical examination of one of Castro's poems. Includes bibliographical references and index.
Dever, Aileen. *The Radical Insufficiency of Human Life: The Poetry of R. de Castro and J. A. Silva.* Jefferson, N.C.: McFarland, 2000. A comparison of Castro's and Silva's poetry. Their works have mean ingful differences but share remarkable likenesses in theme, tone, and style, though it is unlikely that they knew of each other's work. Of interest to feminist critics is an interpretation of Castro's literary vocation within a patriarchal society.
Geoffrion-Vinci, Michelle C. *Between the Maternal Aegis and the Abyss: Woman as Symbol in the Poetry of Rosalía de Castro.* Madison, N.J.: Fairleigh Dickinson University Press, 2002. Examines the symbolism of Castro's poetry at length. Discusses her relationship with Manuel Murguía.
Kulp-Hill, Kathleen. *Manner and Mood in Rosalía de Castro: A Study of Themes and*

Style. Madrid: Ediciones José Porrua Turanzas, 1968. A thorough critical study of Castro's writing and a bibliography of her works.

———. *Rosalía de Castro*. Boston: Twayne, 1977. Introductory biography and critical analysis of selected works. Includes an index and bibliography of Castro's writing.

Wilcox, John C. *Women Poets of Spain, 1860-1990: Toward a Gynocentric Vision*. Urbana: University of Illinois Press, 1997. This work on female poets in Spain in the second half of the nineteenth century contains a section on Castro.

Jack Shreve

WILLIAM COWPER

Born: Great Berkhampstead, Hertfordshire, England; November 26, 1731
Died: East Dereham, England; April 25, 1800

PRINCIPAL POETRY
Olney Hymns, 1779 (with John Newton)
Poems, 1782
The Task, 1785
Completed Poetical Works, 1907 (standard edition)

OTHER LITERARY FORMS

The *Olney Hymns* are now commonly studied as poems. Of the sixty-four hymns contributed to the volume by William Cowper (KEW-pur), only a very few still appear in church hymnals. The hymn, however, while certainly kin to the poem, presents unique demands on the author and cannot be judged fairly by the same critical standards. The hymn must try to reflect universal Christian feelings on a level immediately recognizable to all the human souls and intellects that make up a congregation. It must be orthodox and express only the expected. It must be simple, and above all it must not reveal what is individual about the author. To the extent that Cowper's unique genius could not always be restrained by convention, he is not consistently as good a hymnist as Isaac Watts or Charles Wesley.

In the eighteenth century, the familiar letter became so artistically refined that modern literary scholars now regard it as a minor literary form. Cowper's collected correspondence fills four volumes (Wright edition, 1904) and treats an incredible range of subjects and themes with great insight, humor, and style. Literary historians regard him as one of the finest letter writers in English.

ACHIEVEMENTS

Modern literary historians commonly assign William Cowper to the ranks of the so-called pre-Romantics, and to be sure, his subjective voice, preference for the rural to the urban, and social concern are qualities more easily discernible in the poetry of the early nineteenth century than of the late eighteenth century. Cowper, however, was not attempting to create a literary movement. The poetry characteristic of his later years is clearly a perfection of themes and forms that occupied his attention from the first, and those early efforts are not radical departures from what is considered mainstream neoclassicism. Satire, mock-heroic, general nature description, all are present, but Cowper grew in his art and was not concerned that his growth made him into something a bit different.

Cowper's satires, for example, are notable for a measure of charity toward their subjects, charity that he saw was lacking in the satires of Alexander Pope and his contemporaries. Moreover, Cowper was greatly interested in poetic structure but also felt that the poetry of his age put too much emphasis on structure at the expense of real human personality. The canon of Cowper's work is of a very uneven quality, but his finest efforts, such as *The Task*, display an unobtrusive structure and identifiable human presence uncommon in the neoclassical age, and they are fine by the standards of any age. Perhaps his outstanding structural achievement is the conversational blank verse used in *The Task*. There is no more interesting development in that form between John Milton and William Wordsworth. However, while Cowper's critical reputation is quite good, he is not regarded as one of the major figures in English letters. The conventions of neoclassical poetry had been manipulated with greater skill by Pope, and the new directions suggested by Cowper would be shortly perfected by Wordsworth. Thus, the achievement of Cowper, by no means insignificant, is somewhat obscured by the giants who surround him.

Biography

William Cowper was born on November 26, 1731, in Great Berkhampstead, Hertfordshire, England. He was the fourth child of the Reverend Dr. John Cowper, rector of Great Berkhampstead, and Ann Donne. Both parents represented distinguished families. The Cowpers had distinguished themselves by loyalty to the Crown, and John Cowper's uncle, Sir William, had been created baron in 1706 and earl in 1718. The Donnes were of even nobler lineage and traced descent from Henry III. The famous seventeenth century poet, John Donne, was of the same illustrious family. John and Ann had seven children, but only William and their last child, also named John, survived infancy. Very shortly after the birth of John, Ann died; William was only six at the time.

Cowper's father appears to have been neither a cruel nor especially loving parent. Shortly after Ann's death, young William was sent away to school. This early separation from his parent—not unusual in upper-class households—seems to have affected the poet greatly, because several years later, Cowper attacked the practice and the school system in general in a poem, *Tirocinium* (1785). While a student at Westminster, Cowper met his first love, his cousin Theodora. The affair was terminated in 1756, but it is commemorated in nineteen sentimental love poems addressed to Delia. Cowper suffered his first severe attack of depression in 1752. He was studying law at the time and was called to the bar in 1754. Although he had no great fondness for the profession, his family had thought it best that he have some livelihood.

In 1759, Cowper was appointed commissioner of bankrupts, a minor governmental post that paid very little. Out of the need for financial security, he applied for an appointment to the post of clerk of the journals of the House of Lords. When the incumbent clerk died, Cowper's appointment was put forward only to be challenged by supporters of another candidate. In 1763, Cowper learned that he would have to face an examination to determine the best applicant. This prospect greatly aggravated his already depressed state, and he experienced a severe mental breakdown during which he unsuccessfully attempted suicide. Clearly, he could not occupy a government post. The sense of rejection as a consequence of this realization joined with the recollection of his mother's death, and the broken affair with Theodora led Cowper to imagine that his exile from normal human relationships was God's sign to him that he was also excluded from the company of the blessed for all eternity.

Following an eighteen-month residence in an asylum, Cowper moved to the country, where he soon made the acquaintance of the Unwin family. He resided with that cheerful and cordial family in Huntingdon and then accompanied Mrs. Unwin in her move to the town of Olney following the sudden death of her husband. Here, Cowper met the revivalist minister John Newton, and for a time, he enjoyed a useful and productive existence. He became interested in the problems of the poor and various charitable activities and joined with Newton in writing a collection of hymns that was later published as the *Olney Hymns*. In January, 1773, however, shortly before his planned marriage to the widowed Mrs. Unwin, Cowper again suffered a period of instability. Convinced by a terrifying dream that it was God's will, he once again attempted suicide. His failure only added to his distress, for now, sure that he had failed to obey God's command, he became utterly convinced of his damnation. Although he recovered from the 1773 breakdown, despair never left him.

Largely as a distraction, Cowper turned his attention to writing poetry, and in February, 1782, he published his first significant collection. The early 1780's were made happier for Cowper by his friendship with Lady Austin, who had taken up residence near Olney. It was at the suggestion of this good-humored lady that in July, 1783, he began his masterpiece, *The Task*. That poem provided the title for his next collection that appeared in 1785. However, whatever joy Cowper may have derived from the favorable public response to his new volume was soon erased by the death of Mrs. Unwin's son, William. This shock, plus the anxiety caused by moving from his beloved Olney to Weston, was more than Cowper could endure, and in 1787, he again lost his grip on reality.

Following his recovery, Cowper again turned to writing. He began a translation of Homer and addressed himself to social issues, especially the fight against slavery. For a few years at least, he was able to reproduce the routine and uneventful living he had enjoyed at Olney. In December, 1791, however, Mrs. Unwin suffered a stroke; in May, 1792, she suffered another that rendered her immobile and speechless. She recovered somewhat, but the guilt Cowper felt at recalling how her life had been spent in his care, plunged him again into deep melancholy. His feelings are well expressed in "To Mary," written in the fall of 1793. Not even the satisfaction of his great poetic fame and an annual pension of three hundred pounds from George III could lift him from despair or silence the voices of eternal doom that came to him at night. On December 17, 1796, Mrs. Unwin died. "The Castaway," composed in 1799, is one of the bleakest poems in English and itself sufficient comment on the last three years of Cowper's life. On April 25, 1800, after a one-month struggle with edema, he died. A witness described his last facial expression as one of "holy surprise."

Analysis

William Cowper's poetic achievement is marked by a tension between subjectivity and objectivity, a tension that, at its best, produces a unique poetry defying easy classification as either neoclassical or Romantic. Cowper wrote poetry to preserve his sanity. It was a way to distract himself from the terrible brooding on the inevitability of his damnation, and even when his gloom made it impossible to focus on subjects other than his own condition, at least the very act of writing, the mechanical business of finding rhymes or maintaining meter, defused the self-destructive potential of the messages of despair that crowded his dreams and came to him in the whisperings of mysterious voices. Because the poetry was not only by Cowper but also for Cowper, it displays a subjectivity uncommon in the neoclassical tradition. Although Cowper had his own opinions about poetry and disliked the formal, elegant couplet structure that dominated the verse of his day, he was not completely a rebel. Objectivity, Horatian humor, sentimentality, respect for the classics, the very qualities that define neoclassicism are all present in Cowper's verse. Unlike William Wordsworth, he never issued a manifesto to revolutionize poetry. Indeed, the levelheaded detachment of the Horatian persona, so popular with Cowper's contemporaries, was a stance that he often tried to capture for the sake of his own mental stability. When Cowper manages a balance between the subjectivity that injects his own gentle humanity into a poem and the objectivity that allows universal significance, he is at his best.

"On the Receipt of My Mother's Picture Out of Norfolk"

One of Cowper's most famous poems illustrates the poet at less than his best when he manages almost fully to withhold his own personality and allows convention to structure his message. "On the Receipt of My Mother's Picture Out of Norfolk" was written in 1790, fifty-three years after his mother's death and only ten years before his own. The poem avoids the theme of death and rather focuses on the mother with the only tool available to it: convention. The poem begins with a reference to the power of art to immortalize, a theme that might have supported some interesting content. The poet then introduces yet another worthy theme: "And while that face renews my filial grief,/ Fancy shall weave a charm for my relief"; while the art of the picture kindles an old grief, the art of the poem will provide the balm. Neither theme, however, survives beyond the first few lines of the poem. Instead, Cowper turns to the popular conventions of eighteenth century verse to produce a proper comment on a dead mother.

The verse form is the heroic couplet, the dominant form of the age. The diction is formal because the neoclassical notion of decorum—words appropriately matched to the subject matter—demanded formality in the respectful approach of a child to a parent. Ann Cowper, the poet's mother, is unrecognizable in the poem; she has no individuality, no visual reality for the reader. Consistent with the neoclassical emphasis on the general and ideal rather than the particular and commonplace, Cowper creates a cloud of expected motherly virtues through which the face of Ann can be seen but dimly. Here it should be remembered, however, that the poet is reacting to a picture, an eighteenth century portrait, not to a tangible human being, and that portrait itself would have been an idealized representation reflective of the aesthetic principle voiced by Sir Joshua Reynolds: "The general idea constitutes real excellence. . . . Even in portraits, the grace, and, we may add, the likeness, consists more in taking the general air than in observing the exact similitude of feature."

The poem, then, does accurately treat its subject if that subject is indeed the portrait. Still, the treatment is for the most part a catalog of hackneyed images—"sweet smiles" and "dear eyes"—mixed with a few images that need more than originality to save them, such as the extended simile that likens the mother to "a gallant bark from Albion's coast" that "shoots into port at some well-havered isle," a rather unflattering analogy if the reader attempts to use it to help visualize the mother. The overall sentimentality of the poem is also no departure from neoclassical convention. Sentimentalism in all literary genres had emerged as a popular reaction to the great emphasis placed on reason by so many eighteenth century thinkers. The universe, it was held, is logical and ordered, and all nature, including human nature, is ultimately understandable by the human ability to reason. Sentimentalism answered this by calling attention to emotions and feelings. Humanity is not merely rational; there are finer qualities beyond the power of logic to comprehend. At its best, sentiment could add an element of emotion to reason and make a work more reflective of the real human psyche. At its worst, sentiment drowned reality in maudlin fictions and saccharine absurdities. Cowper's poem does not completely sink in the quagmire of sentimental syrup. It hangs on by the thread of an idea about the immortalizing power of art, a thread that is visible at the beginning and then again at the end but which for the greater part of the poem is lost in the swamp.

All this is not to say that "On the Receipt of My Mother's Picture Out of Norfolk" is a bad poem. Indeed, it remains one of Cowper's most frequently anthologized works. If it is conventional, it is still worth studying as a good example of several aspects of the neoclassical tradition unknown to readers who name the age after Alexander Pope or Samuel Johnson. Cowper, however, was capable of doing better. The problem with the mother poem was that rather than writing about his mother, he pretended to write about his own feelings and memories. The memories after so many years were probably dim, and he seems to have chosen to avoid an expression of his dark fears and utter isolation in favor of a conventional grieving son persona.

"THE CASTAWAY"

Cowper succeeds more fully when his reaction to a situation or event includes, but also goes beyond, the feelings most readers would experience when he injects enough of his purely subjective response to allow the reader to see a somewhat different but still believable dimension to what it is to be human. The loss of a mother is certainly an appropriate correlative to the emotions expressed in the poem. Moreover, the emotional response is certainly believable; it is not, however, unique. The loss of a seaman overboard during a storm is also an appropriate correlative to the emotions of the speaker in "The Castaway," but here Cowper does more than simply respond to a situation.

The episode of the seaman swept overboard in a storm, an account of which Cowper had read in George Anson's *Voyage* (1748) some years before writing the poem, is actually an extended metaphor for the poet's own condition. Interestingly, the analogy between poet and sailor is only briefly pointed out at the very beginning and again at the end of the poem. The metaphor, the story of the sailor, is for the most part presented with curious objectivity. The facts of the tragedy are all there: the storm, the struggles of the seaman, the futile attempts at rescue. There is also a respectable measure of grief in the subdued tone of the speaker; the reader, however, could not be misled by this seeming objectivity. It is at once apparent that the poem is really about the tragic fate of the poet, but it is precisely in this tension between the objective and subjective that the poem says so much. The effect of the long metaphor in keeping the poet's ego in the background is to illustrate that indeed the poet is an insignificant thing—a tiny, isolated being beyond the help of his fellows and the concern of his God. That curious objectivity is in fact the attitude of the universe toward Cowper. It does not seem to care, and it is not hostile. It has simply excluded Cowper from the scheme of things, a scheme that allows for the possibility of salvation for all humans.

The God in "The Castaway" seems strangely Deistic. He is unwilling to interfere with the predetermined operation of his universe, but unlike many of his contemporaries who viewed the universe with optimism, believing that if God was remote, at least the system that he set in motion was good, Cowper sees no goodness in his own portion. In "The Castaway," Cowper can neither bless nor curse his fate, for any action would detract from the utter futility he wishes to convey. "The Castaway," then, is highly subjective. The poet is in no way suggesting that the fate of the metaphorical sailor describes the universal human condition. Indeed, humanity is on board the ship, which survives the storm. Cowper is talking about himself, but the air of objectivity in the presentation stresses the futility and isolation he wishes to convey. In other words, the structure of the poem contributes greatly to its message. What is Cowper in the eyes of God? He is no more than the minimal first-person intrusion in the sixty-six lines that constitute "The Castaway."

"The Poplar Field"

Cowper was a fine craftsperson in the structuring of poems. His collected works clearly show a fondness for experimentation, and as is to be expected, some of those experiments were more successful than others. An interesting example is "The Poplar Field," a frequently anthologized lyric that deals with the fleeting glories of this world. Here, Cowper deliberately violates decorum and adopts a sprightly, heavily accented meter. The mere four feet to a line gallops the reader through musings on various reminders of mortality. The meter seems to mock the expected seriousness of the theme to produce a parody of melancholy landscape verse. The content of the poem consists, for the most part, of uninspired platitudes and clichés, but this is the necessary fodder for parody. A less generous reading might assert that parody is not an issue. The poem is rather a straightforward presentation of the joys of melancholy, the pleasures of the contemplative life. The meter is the vehicle for communicating the pleasure idea to the audience, and Cowper's "The Poplar Field" is really a direct descendant of John Milton's "L'Allegro." If this is the case, the trite content cannot be justified as fuel for a satiric fire and must be held to be just that: trite content. Perhaps, then, "The Poplar Field" is of the same family as "On the Receipt of My Mother's Picture Out of Norfolk": Both poems suffer from the substitution of conventions for the presence of the real Cowper.

"The Diverting History of John Gilpin"

An experiment of unchallenged success is "The Diverting History of John Gilpin." Structure is everything in this delightful ballad about the misadventures of a linen draper on his twenty-year delayed honeymoon. The lively meter and rhyming quatrains are ideally suited to the rollicking humor of the piece. Gilpin, a rather bombastic but totally good-natured hero, has his adventure told by a narrator who is himself satirized by the deceptively careless method of his composition. It soon becomes clear that the poem is everything and that the narrator will not be stopped or the rhythm broken by such concerns as taking time to find an appropriate figure rather than a silly one or even by running out of content to fill the quatrain: "So like an arrow swift he flew,/ Shot by an archer strong;/ So did he fly—which brings me to/ The middle of my song." For Cowper, the poem lived up to its title; it seems to have diverted him indeed, for the reader familiar with Cowper's voice will look in vain for a trace of the brooding author of "The Castaway." However, beneath the funny story, the brilliant metrics, and the silly narrator, there is still the gentle poet who prefers to laugh with his characters rather than reduce them to the grotesque fools that populate so much of eighteenth century satire.

Despite the success of "The Diverting History of John Gilpin," Cowper has never been considered a leading satirist of the age. Satire, especially in the popular Horatian mode, must have had its attractions for him. The detached, witty observer who by choice leaves the herd to remark on the foibles of humanity presented an ideal persona, but it was a stance that Cowper could seldom sustain. The satirist must appear objective; the folly must appear to be a genuine part of the target and not merely in the satirist's perception of the target. Cowper could maintain that kind of objectivity only when there was really nothing at stake. Poking fun at the world of John Gilpin is harmless, for there is no suggestion that the world is real beyond the confines of the poem. When the subject is real, however, Cowper cannot stand aside. He lacks wit, in the neoclassical sense of the word. Wit consisted of the genius needed to conceive the raw material of art and the acquired good taste to know how to arrange bits of that material into a unified whole. Wit did not allow for the subjective intrusion of the author's personal problems. Cowper's genius was so intertwined with his special mental condition that he could not remain detached, and when he tried, his acquired skill could only arrange conventions, substitutes for his unique raw material. Moreover, Cowper lacked the satirist's willingness to ridicule. He had nothing against humanity. The shipmates are guiltless in the tragedy of the castaway. Humanity, to be sure, has its delusions and vanities, but Cowper preferred the deflected blow to the sharp thrust.

THE TASK

The Task is Cowper's major achievement, and it is the satiric Cowper who introduces the work. His friend, Lady Austin, had suggested a sofa as an appropriate topic for a poem in blank verse. Of course, such a subject could only be addressed satirically, and Cowper elected the conventional form of mock-heroic. Specifically, he alluded to *The Aeneid* with "I sing the sofa" and thereby suggested that a modern Vergil would be hard pressed to find in eighteenth century society a topic deserving heroic treatment. However, the sofa is more than simply a mean subject, it is a quite appropriate symbol for sloth and luxury, the very qualities responsible for society's falling away from the truly heroic. Having called attention to the problem, there is little more for the sofa to do, except that it led Cowper to something worth saying, and he needed a structure less restrictive of his own involvement than the mock-heroic. So with a comment on how he prefers walks in the country to life on the sofa, Cowper shifts to an appreciation of nature theme and the *I* who had been the Vergilian persona of the satire suddenly becomes Cowper himself.

The Task is far too long a work for detailed analysis here. Its five thousand lines are divided into six parts: "The Sofa," "The Time-Piece," "The Garden," "The Winter Evening," "The Winter Morning Walk," and "The Winter Walk at Noon." The question of the overall unity of the work has probably attracted the greatest amount of critical attention. Cowper's own comments about the poem indicate that he was not aiming at tight thematic development; rather, the ideas were naturally suggested by immediately preceding ideas with the whole moving along with the ease of an intelligent but unplanned conversation.

Cowper's style, once the mock-heroic has been dropped, certainly suggests conversation. The diction is elegant but natural, quite different from the language of the other popular eighteenth century nature poet James Thomson, whose baroque language in *The Seasons* (1730, 1744) imitated the grand style of John Milton. Moreover, Cowper's blank verse avoids the end-stopped lines used by Thomson, which detracted from the conversational effect by their epigrammatic regularity. The deceptively artless ease of the poem with its several scenes, frequent digressions, and inclusion of highly personal material might easily lead the reader to conclude that the poet is recording a stream of consciousness with no central purpose or theme in mind. In fact, *The Task* is concerned with the need and search for balance in nature and human life. The sofa itself suggests the theme, for if it represents the scale tipping toward excessive luxury, there must somewhere in the range of experience be an ideal condition against which such excesses can be recognized and measured.

The ultimate excess to which the sofa points is the city, London, which on a physical plane reveals squalor, corruption, and insanity; its spiritual reality is sin. The opposite side of the scale also has a spiritual and physical existence. Spiritually, this extreme is the untempered wrath of God, pure divine power; on the physical level, such power is reflected in disturbances in nature and the brutalism that is the alternative to civilization. The early books explore the extremes and present the rural countryside as perhaps the best balance. This balance is insecure, however, for intrusions of both natural and human turmoil bring constant disturbance. The latter parts of the poem demonstrate the futility of finding a secure position in the physical environment. For those who enjoy God's grace, conversion can clarify the balance and bring freedom and order. The final book reveals God as the ultimate source of harmony. In his infinite kindness and infinite sternness, the Father judges all, and that judgment is perfection.

Among the landscape descriptions, character sketches, social criticism, and personal confessions, a unifying theme is perceptible if not obvious in *The Task*, and interestingly, it is the theme that best describes Cowper's life and art, the quest for a place of stability, a point of balance. In his art, he experimented to find his own voice, and he found it between the extremes of objectivity, toward which most art of his age tended, and the subjectivity that would characterize the art of the next generation. In the task of his life, he sought the balance of sanity, a quiet place of his own between the stress of urban society and the horror of being utterly alone, a castaway in a sea of despair. Tragically, he could not occupy that stable middle ground for very long; but in his best poetry, he created a remarkable sanity and said still-important things in a way that cannot easily be pigeonholed as neoclassical or Romantic but is uniquely Cowper.

OTHER MAJOR WORKS

NONFICTION: *Correspondence, Arranged in Chronological Order*, 1904 (4 volumes); *The Centenary Letters*, 2000 (Simon Malpas, editor).

Bibliography

Brunström, Conrad. *William Cowper: Religion, Satire, Society*. Lewisburg, Pa.: Bucknell University Press, 2004. A critical study of the poet's significance. Aimed at serious scholars.

Cowper, William. *The Centenary Letters*. Edited by Simon Malpas. Manchester, England: Fyfield Books, 2000. A collection of Cowper's correspondence with a biographical introduction by Malpas.

Ella, George Melvyn. *William Cowper: Poet of Paradise*. Durham, England: Evangelical Press, 1993. Criticism and interpretation of Cowper's work with an extensive bibliography.

Free, William Norris. *William Cowper*. New York: Twayne, 1970. This 215-page work takes a biographical approach to interpretations of *The Task, Olney Hymns*, and Cowper's short poems. Norris suggests that Cowper's experiences had influence on poetic elements such as theme, structure, tone, and metaphor. Includes a lengthy bibliography, notes, and an index.

Hopps, Gavin, and Jane Stabler, eds. *Romanticism and Religion from William Cowper to Wallace Stevens*. Burlington, Vt.: Ashgate, 2006. Contains an essay on Cowper's poetry that presents his religious views and places him among the Romanticists.

King, James. *William Cowper: A Biography*. Durham, N.C.: Duke University Press, 1986. The standard biography that corrected many of the oversights and inaccuracies of early biographies. The poetical works are discussed as markers in the chronology of Cowper's life. The 340-page work includes an extensive index and notes.

Newey, Vincent. *Cowper's Poetry: A Critical Study and Reassessment*. Totowa, N.J.: Barnes & Noble, 1982. Newey's intelligent approach closely examines Cowper's work psychodramatically and sees the poet as a genius craftsperson of complex, contemporary, relevant poetry. The 358-page volume looks at *The Task*, moral satires, hymns, and comic verse. Includes a chronology and index of persons and works.

Nicholson, Norman. *William Cowper*. 1951. Reprint. London: Longman, 1970. A comprehensive work that discusses the influence of the evangelical revival on Cowper. Nicholson sees Evangelicalism as a vigorous and emotional movement that paralleled Romanticism. Although Cowper's poetic sensibility first developed under Evangelicalism, his early poetry reflects contemporary religious and social thought and later becomes partially independent of the movement to share aspects with Romanticism.

Ryskamp, Charles. *William Cowper of the Inner Temple, Esq*. New York: Cambridge University Press, 1959. This 270-page book studies Cowper's life and works before 1786, focusing on his life and literary activities as a Templar and gentleman. Appendixes include previously uncollected letters, essays, poems, and contributions to magazines. Supplemented by illustrations, notes on Cowper's friends and relatives, and an index.

William J. Heim

DU FU

Born: Gongxian, China; 712
Died: Tanzhou (now Changsha), Hunan Province, China; 770
Also known as: Tu Fu

PRINCIPAL POETRY
Quan Tang shi, 1706
Tang shi san bai shou, 1763 (*The Jade Mountain: A Chinese Anthology*, 1929)
Tu Fu: Selected Poems, 1962 (Zhi Feng, editor; Rewi Alley, translator)
The Selected Poems of Du Fu, 2002 (Burton Watson, translator)
Du Fu: A Life in Poetry, 2008
Spring in the Ruined City: Selected Poems, 2008

OTHER LITERARY FORMS

Du Fu (dew few) is known primarily for his poetry. The 1,450 poems he wrote have been collected through the years in frequently revised and reprinted anthologies and collections such as *Quan Tang shi* and *The Jade Mountain*.

ACHIEVEMENTS

Born during the Tang Dynasty (618-907), the classical period in Chinese literary history, Du Fu was one of four poets whose greatness marked the era. Some fifty thousand poems from that period have survived, the large number resulting primarily from the talents of Du Fu; Wang Wei, basically a nature poet; Bo Juyi, a government official whose poetry often reflected official concerns; and Li Bo, probably the best known of all Chinese poets, a poet of the otherworldly or the sublime.

Du Fu sums up the work of all these poets with the wide range of topics and concerns that appear in his poems. Known variously as "poet-historian," "poet-sage," and "the Master," Du Fu may be China's greatest poet. His "Yue ye" ("Moonlit Night") is perhaps the most famous poem in Chinese literature. His more than fourteen hundred extant poems testify to his productivity; the range of topics in his poetry and the variety of verse that he employed constitute Du Fu's main contribution to Chinese literature.

One of Du Fu's major contributions to Chinese literature was his extensive occasional verse—poems inspired by a journey or by a mundane experience such as building a house. Many of Du Fu's occasional poems were addressed to friends or relatives at some special time in their lives. Distant relatives who held official positions and achieved distinction would receive a laudatory poem. These poems could also be addressed to special friends. Du Fu traveled much in his life, both by choice and involuntarily, relying on friends to shelter and support him, because, for the majority of his life, he was without an official governmental position and salary. His poems would therefore be addressed to these persons as expressions of gratitude and friendship on the occasion of his visit.

Poems about nature abounded during the Tang period, and Du Fu contributed extensively to this genre as well. In contrast to Li Bo, who followed the Daoist philosophy of withdrawal from the world, Du Fu was very much a poet of everyday life, both in his response to nature and the physical world and in his active engagement in the social and political life of his times. Indeed, it has been said that Du Fu's poetry provides a running history of the Chinese state during his era.

Finally, Du Fu was a master of poetic form; his verse forms were as varied as his content. During the Tang period, the *gutishi* (old forms) in Chinese poetry coexisted with the *lushi* (new forms). The old, or "unregulated," forms placed no restrictions on the word tones used in the verse, did not limit the number of lines in a poem, and did not require verbal parallelism. The new forms, or "regulated verse," however, were much more demanding. They mandated certain tonal patterns, especially in rhyme words, a requirement which markedly affected word choice. They also usually restricted the total number of lines in a poem and utilized verbal parallelism. Each of these two major categories of Chinese poetry was also divided into subcategories depending on the meter, which in Chinese poetry depends on the number of words in each line rather than on stressed and unstressed syllables, as in Western poetry. Du Fu adeptly used both old and new forms in his verse, justifying in this respect as in every other his reputation as "the Master."

Biography

Du Fu's life could best be described as one of frustration. Although his mother's family was related to the imperial clan, and both his father and grandfather held official positions in the government, much of Du Fu's life was spent in poverty. Unable to pass the examination for entrance into official service, Du Fu remained, more often than not, a "plain-robed" man, a man without official position and salary. His poems from the mid-730's allude to "the hovel" in which he lived on the outskirts of the capital while the court members resided in the splendor of the palace. One of Du Fu's sons died from starvation in 755 because of the family's poverty, and the poet's sadness and anguish caused by his son's death is reflected in several of Du Fu's poems.

Du Fu was born in Gongxian, Henan Province, in 712. His natural mother died at an early age, and Du Fu's father remarried, eventually adding three brothers and a sister to the family. Du Fu was apparently a very precocious child. In his autobiography, he states unabashedly that at the age of seven he pondered "only high matters" and wrote verses about beautiful birds, while other children his age were dealing with puerile subjects such as dogs and cats. At an early age, Du Fu also mastered a great number of the characters which make up written Chinese. He was writing so extensively by the age of nine, he claims, that his output could easily have filled several large bags. Not much else is known about Du Fu's early years. As would be expected, he was schooled in literary matters in preparation for entrance into official service. A firsthand knowledge of the many facets of Chinese life and the geography of the country also became a part of Du Fu's education: He traveled for about three years before taking the official examination for public service. His poetry of this period reflects the experiences and sights he encountered while traversing the countryside.

In 735, at the age of twenty-three, Du Fu finally took the test to enter government service and failed. Apparently there was something in Du Fu's writing style, in the way he handled the Chinese characters, which did not suit the examiners. This setback in Du Fu's plans ushered in the first of several important phases in his life. Since the poet had failed the examination and was without a position, he resumed his travels. During these travel years, several significant changes occurred in his life. His father died in 740, which prompted a series of poems on the theme of life's impermanence. This event was followed by Du Fu's marriage to a woman from the Cui clan, a marriage which ultimately produced two sons and four daughters for the poet. Finally, and probably most important in terms of his literary work, Du Fu met Li Bo in 744.

Following the Daoist tradition, Li Bo, who was ten years Du Fu's senior, had become a "withdrawn" poet after his banishment from the court. As such, he represented a viewpoint opposite to that of Du Fu concerning a literate man's obligations to Chinese society at that time. Du Fu's poetry exhibits his grappling with these contending views. He was sometimes attracted to the simple lifestyle of Li Bo, but the Confucian ethic under which Du Fu had been reared persevered, and he returned to the capital in 746, eleven years after his first attempt, to repeat the test for an official position. He failed again; this time, according to the historians, one of the emperor's officials was afraid that new appointees to the bureaucracy would weaken the latter's power in the court, so he saw to it that everyone who took the examination failed. The frustration and humiliation resulting from this second failure to pass the examination, perhaps heightened by the fact that his younger brother had passed the examination earlier, did not seem to deter Du Fu from his goal of securing an official post. Although he was forced to move outside the capital with his family and to rely on support from friends and relatives to survive, Du Fu seemingly resolved to gain an official position through another route, this time by ingratiating himself with important people who could aid his quest.

Wei Ji was one such person. As an adviser to the emperor, he was in a position to help Du Fu when the occasion arose. Du Fu was also well acquainted with Prince Li Jin, a pleasure-loving, undisciplined figure who was an embarrassment to the court. The prince had a great appreciation for literature, however, and after Du Fu wrote several poems dealing with "The Eight Immortals of the Wine Cup," as the prince and his coterie were called, the prince took a special liking to the poet. Because of these friendships, Du Fu's name was heard around the court, and when he wrote the "Three Great Ceremonies" poems, their excellence and their laudatory treatment of the emperor engendered imperial recognition and favor. A third examination for an official position ensued as a result. Whether Du Fu passed or failed this one was of little consequence; finally, at the age of forty-four, he was given an official position by imperial decree. (Li Bo's position with the court had also been established by imperial decree because he had refused to take the civil-service exam as a matter of principle.) Ironically, Du Fu refused the position. It apparently involved moving to a distant western district, and because the position required him to be a part of the police administration, it would also have involved beating people for infractions of the law, something Du Fu was not inclined to do. The poet's refusal found some sympathy in the court, and he was appointed instead to the heir apparent's household. Thus, the years 755 and 756 stand as pivotal ones in Du Fu's life: He received his first official position in the government after many years of struggle, and strangely enough, he gave up that position because he rapidly grew to dislike the servile aspects of the job. Amid all this, the An Lushan Rebellion began.

For the remainder of his life, Du Fu was one of the many who endured the misfortunes of this war. When the rebellion began in 756, the emperor was forced to flee the capital, as did Du Fu. The latter's poems from that period depict the many defeats of the imperial army. Once he had established his family in the relative safety of Fuzhou in the north, Du Fu set out to join the Traveling Palace of the displaced emperor, but he was captured by rebel forces and taken back to the capital, which they occupied. Held by the rebels for several months, he finally escaped and joined the Traveling Palace as a censor, an official responsible for reminding the emperor of matters which required his attention. During this period, Du Fu did not hear from his family for more than a year, and he wrote possibly the most famous poem in Chinese literature, a love poem to his wife and children entitled "Moonlit Night."

The capital was retaken the next year, 757, and Du Fu was reunited with his family. His "Journey North" describes the effects of the war on the Chinese people and countryside, as well as his homecoming to his family. With the government reestablished in the capital, Du Fu returned there with his family for official service. This period of service was also short-lived; he once again grew tired of the bureaucratic life and its constraints. Floods and the war had devastated the countryside around the capital, so Du Fu took his family west to flee the war and to find food. The war, however, also spread to the west, and as a result, Du Fu once again shifted his family, this time southward to Zhengdu, five hundred miles from the fighting.

The time he spent in the south has been labeled Du Fu's "thatched hut" period. This was something of a pastoral period in his life, during which he seemed to emulate Li Bo and the Daoist ethic to some degree. The war, however, persisted both in the countryside and in Du Fu's poems. The rebellion finally spread even to the south, and Du Fu was forced to leave his thatched hut in 765. He spent the remaining five years of his life in restless travel, cataloging in poetry his journeys and the events he witnessed. Du Fu, "the Master," died in 770, at the age of fifty-eight, as he traveled the Xiang River looking for a haven from the ill health and ill times which had beset him.

Analysis

Du Fu's poetry deals with a multitude of concerns and events. His verses express the moments of self-doubt and frustration which plagued the poet, such as when he failed the civil-service examinations or when he became increasingly afflicted by physical ailments later in life, referring to himself in one verse as an "emaciated horse." Du Fu's poems also deal with painting and the other arts, and they often employ allusions to outstanding figures in China's literary and political past to comment on contemporary conditions. It is, however, in his poems addressed to family and friends and in his nature poems that the substance and depth of his verse can be most clearly seen.

Among Du Fu's finest poems are those which express his love for friends and family. Poems addressed to friends constituted both a literary and a social convention in China during the Tang period. In literate society, men sought one another for friendship and intellectual companionship, and poems of the "address and answer" variety were often composed by the poet. Several examples occur in the poems which Du Fu wrote either to or about Li Bo, his fellow poet. After the two met in 744, they traveled together extensively, and a firm bond, both personal and scholarly, was established between them. In one poem commemorating the two poets' excursion to visit a fellow writer, Du Fu explained his feeling toward Li Bo: "I love my Lord as young brother loves elder brother/ . . . Hand in hand we daily walk together." In "A Winter Day," Du Fu writes that "Since early dawn I have thought only of you [Li Bo]," thoughts which may have been both pleasant and painful for Du Fu as he grappled with the question of whether he wanted to continue his quest for a governmental position or follow Li Bo's example and become a "withdrawn" poet. Du Fu also highly praised Li Bo's verses. In a later poem, "the Master" laments the fact that Li Bo has become unstable, but he also rejoices in the gift of Li Bo's talent: "My thoughts are only of love for his talent./ Brilliant are his thousand poems."

The concern and admiration which Du Fu felt and expressed poetically were not directed solely to other poets. Many of his poems of this type were addressed to longtime friends. "Zeng Wei ba chu shi" ("For Wei Ba, in Retirement") is one example which not only expresses Du Fu's friendship for Wei Ba but also describes the life stages the two have passed through together. The poet comments on how briefly their youth lasted, observing that "Though in those days you were not married/ Suddenly sons and daughters troop in." The two friends have not seen each other for twenty years, "both our heads have become grizzled," and Du Fu knows that the next day will separate them again. He is elated, however, by the "sense of acquaintance" his friend revives in him, and the poet captures that sense in his verse.

"Moonlit Night"

Du Fu was separated from his family several times, sometimes by the war, sometimes by economic conditions. His most famous poem, "Moonlit Night," expresses his deep concern for his wife as "In her chamber she alone looks out/ . . . In the sweet night her cloud-like tresses are damp/ In the clear moonlight her jade-like arms are cold." The poet wonders how long it will be before ". . . we two nestle against those unfilled curtains/ With the moon displaying the dried tear-stains of us both?" Essentially a love poem for the poet's wife, "Moonlit Night" was an unconventional work in its time. Wives in ancient China were seen primarily as pieces of reproductive machinery, with no intellectual capabilities. A poet might lavish great sentiment in verse on a male companion, but tender thoughts concerning a wife were rarely expressed in poetry.

"THE RIVER BY OUR VILLAGE"

In true classical fashion, Du Fu was also a nature poet. He could portray nature in an idyllic vein, as in "The River by Our Village," in which the poet describes how "Clear waters wind around our village/ With long summer days full of loveliness/ Fluttering in and out from the house beams the swallows play/ Waterfowl disport together as everlasting lovers." These lines reflect the contentment of Du Fu's pastoral or "thatched hut" period; he ends the poem by asking: "What more could I wish for?"

"THE WINDING RIVER"

While many of Du Fu's nature poems are distinguished by their vivid evocation of landscapes and wildlife for their own sake, he also treats nature symbolically. In "The Winding River," falling blossoms signify the changing of the seasons and cause the poet to ". . . grieve to see petals flying/ Away in the wind. . . ." This evidence of mutability engenders further reflection; as the poet watches "Butterflies going deeper and deeper/ In amongst the flowers, dragon-flies/ Skimming and flicking over the water," he is reminded that "Wind, light, and time ever revolve," that the only constant factor in life is change. In turn, the poet is led to reflect on the inconsequential and often futile nature of his and other men's ambitions: ". . . why should I be lured/ By transient rank and honours?" Nature instructs him ". . . to live/ Along with her" in a rich and full harmony rather than existing in the pale semblance of living which men have created for themselves.

Because of the range of his sympathy, Du Fu has been compared to William Shakespeare: Both were able to encompass in their works the whole teeming life of their times. Although Du Fu's declaration "In poetry I have exhausted human topics" may seem an overstatement, his many poems and their varied concerns seem almost to justify such a claim.

BIBLIOGRAPHY

Chou, Eva Shan. *Reconsidering Tu Fu*. 1995. Reprint. New York: Cambridge University Press, 2006. Chou examines the styles and techniques of Du Fu's poetry as well as his literary legacy. Contains some translations of poems. Bibliography and index.

Davis, A. R. *Tu Fu*. New York: Twayne, 1971. General and concise, addressing simply the often complicated problems of form and theme.

Du Fu. *The Selected Poems of Du Fu*. Translated by Burton Watson. New York: Columbia University Press, 2002. A collection of Du Fu's poems, translated into English by a noted specialist on China. The introduction provides a great deal of biological and background information.

_____. *The Selected Poems of Tu Fu*. Translated by David Hinton. New York: New Directions, 1989. A collection of Du Fu's poetic works, translated into English.

Hawkes, David. *A Little Primer of Tu Fu*. Oxford, England: Clarendon Press, 1967. Written for readers who know little Chinese. The volume contains the texts of thirty-five of Du Fu's poems in Chinese characters and Pinyin romanization, with descriptions in English of titles, subjects, and poetic forms followed by exegeses and translations. Can be employed as a very useful textbook.

Hung, William. *Tu Fu: China's Greatest Poet*. New York: Russell and Russell, 1969. The most valuable study in English. Clear and highly readable, it includes a volume of notes and incorporates translations of 374 poems.

McCraw, David R. *Du Fu's Laments from the South*. Honolulu: University of Hawaii Press, 1992. An examination of Du Fu's travels in Sichuan and his poetic output. Bibliography and indexes.

Pine, Red, trans. *Poems of the Masters: China's Classic Anthology of T'ang and Sung Dynasty Verse*. Port Townsend, Wash.: Copper Canyon Press, 2003. A collection of poetry from the Tang and Song Dynasties that includes the work of Du Fu. Indexes.

Seaton, J. P., and James Cryer, trans. *Bright Moon, Perching Bird: Poems by Li Po and Tu Fu*. Scranton, Pa.: Harper & Row, 1987. This work, part of the Wesleyan Poetry in Translation series, features the works of Li Bo and Du Fu, two Tang poets. Provides some information on Tang Dynasty poetry.

Seth, Vikram, trans. *Three Chinese Poets: Translations of Poems by Wang Wei, Li Bai, and Du Fu*. Boston: Faber and Faber, 1992. A collection of poems by Du Fu, Li Bo, and Wang Wei. Commentary provides useful information.

Kenneth A. Howe

RALPH WALDO EMERSON

Born: Boston, Massachusetts; May 25, 1803
Died: Concord, Massachusetts; April 27, 1882

PRINCIPAL POETRY
Poems, 1847
May-Day and Other Pieces, 1867
Selected Poems, 1876

OTHER LITERARY FORMS

Ralph Waldo Emerson's *The Journals of Ralph Waldo Emerson* (1909-1914), written over a period of fifty-five years (1820-1875), have been edited in ten volumes by E. W. Emerson and W. E. Forbes. Ralph L. Rusk edited *The Letters of Ralph Waldo Emerson* in six volumes (1939). Emerson was a noted lecturer in his day, although many of his addresses and speeches were not collected until after his death. These appear in three posthumous volumes—*Lectures and Biographical Sketches* (1884), *Miscellanies* (1884), and *Natural History of Intellect* (1893)—which were published as part of a centenary edition (1903-1904). A volume of Emerson's *Uncollected Writings: Essays, Addresses, Poems, Reviews, and Letters* was published in 1912. A sixteen-volume edition of journals and miscellaneous papers was published between 1960 and 1982.

ACHIEVEMENTS

Although Ralph Waldo Emerson's poetry was but a small part of his overall literary output, he thought of himself as very much a poet—even in his essays and lectures. He began writing poetry early in childhood and, at the age of nine, composed some verses on the Sabbath. At Harvard, he was elected class poet and was asked to write the annual Phi Beta Kappa poem in 1834. This interest in poetry continued throughout his long career.

During his lifetime, he published two small volumes of poetry, *Poems* and *May-Day and Other Pieces*, which were later collected in one volume for the centenary edition of his works. Altogether, the centenary volume contains some 170 poems, of which perhaps only several dozen are noteworthy.

Although Emerson produced a comparatively small amount of poetry and an even smaller number of first-rate poems, he stands as a major influence on the subsequent course of American poetry. As scholar, critic, and poet, Emerson was the first to define the distinctive qualities of American verse. His broad and exalted concept of the poet—as prophet, oracle, visionary, and seer—was shaped by his Romantic idealism. "I am more of a poet than anything else," he once wrote, although as much of his poetry is

Ralph Waldo Emerson
(Library of Congress)

found in his journals and essays as in the poems themselves. In *An Oration Delivered Before the Phi Beta Kappa Society, Cambridge* (1837; better known as *The American Scholar*), he called for a distinctive American poetry, and in his essay "The Poet," he provided the theoretical framework for American poetics. Scornful of imitation, he demanded freshness and originality from his verse, even though he did not always achieve in practice what he sought in theory. Rejecting the derivative verse of the Hartford wits and the sentimental versifiers of his day, he sought an original style and flavor for an American poetry close to the native grain. The form of his poetry was, as F. I. Carpenter argues (*Emerson Handbook*, 1953), the logical result of his insistence on self-reliance, while its content was shaped by his Romantic idealism. Thus his cumulative influence on American poetry is greater than his verse alone might imply.

Expression mattered more than form in poetry, according to Emerson. If he was not the completely inspirational poet called for in his essays, that may have been more a matter of temperament than of any flaw in his sense of the kind of poetry that a democratic culture would produce. In fact, his comments often closely parallel those of

Alexis de Tocqueville on the nature of poetry in America. Both men agreed that the poetry of a democratic culture would embrace the facts of ordinary experience rather than celebrate epic themes. It would be a poetry of enumeration rather than elevation, of fact rather than eloquence; indeed, the democratic poet would have to struggle for eloquence, for poetry of the commonplace can easily become flat or prosaic. Even Emerson's own best verse often seems uneven, with memorable lines interspersed with mediocre ones.

Part of the problem with Emerson's poetry arose from his methods of composition. Writing poetry was not for him a smooth, continuous act of composition, nor did he have a set formula for composition, as Edgar Allan Poe advocated in "The Philosophy of Composition." Instead, he trusted inspiration to allow the form of the poem to be determined by its subject matter. This "organic" theory of composition shapes many of Emerson's best poems, including "The Snow-Storm," "Hamatraya," "Days," and "Ode." These poems avoid a fixed metrical or stanzaic structure and allow the sense of each line to dictate its poetic form. Emerson clearly composed by the line rather than by the stanza or paragraph, in both his poetry and prose, and this self-contained quality often gives his work a gnomic or orphic tone.

Although some of his poems appear to be fragmentary, they are not unfinished. They lack smoothness or polish because Emerson was not a lyrical but a visionary, oracular poet. He valued poetry as a philosophy or attitude toward life rather than simply as a formal linguistic structure or an artistic form. "The poet is the sayer, the namer, and represents beauty," he observed in "The Poet." With Percy Bysshe Shelley he believed that the poet was the visionary who would make people whole and teach them to see anew. "Poets are thus liberating gods," Emerson concluded, because "they are free, and they make free." Poetry is simply the most concentrated expression of the poetic vision, which all people are capable of sharing.

Thus Emerson's poems seek to accomplish what the essays announce. His poems attempt to reestablish the primal relationship between humans and nature that he sought as a substitute for revelation. Emerson prized the poet as an innovator, a namer, and a language maker who could interpret the oracles of nature. In its derivation from nature, all language, he felt, was fossil poetry. "Always the seer is a sayer," he announced in his Harvard Divinity School address, and through the vision of the poet "we come to look at the world with new eyes."

Of the defects in Emerson's poetry, the chief is perhaps that Emerson's muse sees rather than sings. Because his lines are orphic and self-contained, they sometimes seem flat and discontinuous. Individual lines stand out in otherwise undistinguished poems. Nor do his lines always scan or flow smoothly, since Emerson was virtually tone-deaf. In "The Poet," he rejects fixed poetic form in favor of a freer, more open verse. For Emerson, democratic poetry would be composed with variable line and meter, with form subordinated to expression. The poet in a democracy is thus a "representative man," chanting the poetry of the common, the ordinary, and the low. Although Emerson pointed the way, it took Walt Whitman to master this new style of American poetry with his first edition of *Leaves of Grass* (1855), which Emerson promptly recognized and praised for its originality. Whitman thus became the poet whom Emerson had called for in *The American Scholar*; American poetry had come of age.

Biography

Born in Boston on May 25, 1803, Ralph Waldo Emerson was the second of five sons in the family of William Emerson and Ruth Emerson. His father was a noted Unitarian minister of old New England stock whose sudden death in 1811 left the family to struggle in genteel poverty. Although left without means, Emerson's mother and his aunt, Mary Moody Emerson, were energetic and resourceful women who managed to survive by taking in boarders, accepting the charity of relatives, and teaching their boys the New England values of thrift, hard work, and mutual assistance within the family. Frail as a child, Emerson attended Boston Latin School and Harvard, where he graduated without distinction in 1821. Since their mother was determined that her children would receive a decent education, each of her sons taught after graduation to help the others through school. Thus Emerson taught for several years at his brother's private school for women before he decided to enter divinity school. His family's high thinking and plain living taught young Emerson self-reliance and a deep respect for books and learning.

With his father and step-grandfather, the Reverend Ezra Ripley of Concord, as models, Emerson returned to Harvard to prepare for the ministry. After two years of intermittent study at the Divinity School, Emerson was licensed to preach in the Unitarian Church. He was forced to postpone further studies, however, and to travel south during the winter of 1826 because of poor health. The next two years saw him preaching occasionally and serving as a substitute pastor. One such call brought him to Concord, New Hampshire, where he met his future wife, Ellen Louisa Tucker. After his ordination in March, 1829, Emerson married Tucker and accepted a call as minister of the Second Church, Boston, where his father had also served. The position and salary were good, and Emerson was prepared to settle into a respectable career as a Boston Unitarian clergyman. Unfortunately his wife was frail, and within a year and a half, she died of tuberculosis. Grief-stricken, Emerson found it difficult to continue with his duties as pastor and resigned from the pulpit six months after his wife's death. Private doubts had assailed him, and he found he could no longer administer the Lord's Supper in good conscience. His congregation would not allow him to dispense with the rite, so his resignation was reluctantly accepted.

With a small settlement from his wife's legacy, he sailed for Europe in December, 1832, to regain his health and try to find a new vocation. During his winter in Italy, he admired the art treasures in Florence and Rome. There he met the American sculptor Horatio Greenough and the English writer Walter Savage Landor. The following spring, Emerson continued his tour through Switzerland and into France. Paris charmed him with its splendid museums and gardens, and he admired the natural history exhibits at the Jardin des Plantes. Crossing to England by August, he met Samuel Taylor Coleridge in London, then traveled north to visit Thomas Carlyle in Craigenputtock and William Wordsworth at Rydal Mount. His meeting with Carlyle resulted in a lifelong friendship.

After returning to Boston in 1833, Emerson gradually settled into a new routine of study, lecturing, and writing, filling an occasional pulpit on Sundays, and assembling ideas in his journals for his essay on "Nature." Lydia Jackson, a young woman from Plymouth, New Hampshire, heard Emerson preach in Boston and became infatuated with him. The young widower returned her admiration, although he frankly confessed that he felt none of the deep affection he had cherished for his first wife. During their engagement he renamed her "Lidian" in their correspondence because he disliked the name Lydia. She accepted the change without demur. Within a year, they were married and settled in a house on the Boston Post Road near the Old Manse of Grandfather Ripley. Emerson was now thirty-two and about to begin his life's work.

The next decade marked Emerson's intellectual maturity. *Nature* was completed and published as a small volume in 1836. In its elaborate series of correspondences between humans and nature, Emerson established the foundations of his idealistic philosophy. "Why should not we also enjoy an original relation to the universe?" he asked. Humans could seek revelations firsthand from nature, rather than having them handed down through tradition. A year later, Emerson gave an address before the Harvard Phi Beta Kappa Society, an event that Oliver Wendell Holmes later called "our intellectual Declaration of Independence." In his address, which is best known as *The American Scholar*, Emerson called for a distinctively American style of letters, free from European influences. Invited in 1838 to speak before the graduating class of Harvard Divinity School, Emerson affirmed in his address that the true measure of religion resided within the individual, not in institutional or historical Christianity. If everyone had equal access to the Divine Spirit, then inner experience was all that was needed to validate religious truth. For this daring pronouncement, he was attacked by Harvard President Andrews Norton and others for espousing "the latest form of infidelity." In a sense, each of these important essays was an extension of Emerson's basic doctrine of self-reliance, applied to philosophy, culture, and religion.

His self-reliance served him equally well in personal life, even as family losses haunted him, almost as if to test his hard-won equanimity and sense of purpose. Besides losing his first wife, Ellen, Emerson saw two of his brothers die and a third become so feeble-minded that he had to be institutionalized. Worst of all, his first-born and beloved son Waldo died in 1841 of scarlet fever at the age of six. Emerson's melioristic philosophy saw him through these losses, although in his journals he later chided himself for not feeling his son's death more deeply. Despite the hurt he felt, his New England reserve would not allow him to yield easily to grief or despair. Nor would he dwell in darkness while there was still light to be found.

During these years, Emerson found Concord a congenial home. He established a warm and stimulating circle of friends there and enjoyed the intellectual company of Nathaniel Hawthorne, Henry David Thoreau, and Bronson Alcott. As his fame as a lecturer and writer grew, he attracted a wider set of admirers, including Margaret Fuller, who often visited to share enthusiasms and transcendental conversations. Emerson even edited *The Dial* for a short time in 1842, but for the most part he remained aloof from, although sympathetic to, the transcendentalist movement that he had so largely inspired. His manner at times was even offhand. When asked for a definition of transcendentalism, he simply replied, "Idealism in 1842." When George Ripley invited him to join the Brook Farm Community in 1840, Emerson politely declined. Reform, he believed, had to begin with the individual. Thoreau later rebuked him for not taking a firmer stand on the fugitive slave issue, but Emerson was by nature apolitical and skeptical of partisan causes. His serenity was too hard-won to be sacrificed, no matter how worthy the cause.

So instead he continued to lecture and write, and his essays touched an entire generation of American writers. Thoreau, Whitman, and Emily Dickinson responded enthusiastically to the appeal of Emerson's thought, while even Hawthorne and Herman Melville, although rejecting it, still felt compelled to acknowledge his intellectual presence. Lecture tours took him repeatedly to the Midwest and to England and Scotland for a second time in 1847-1848. Harvard awarded him an honorary degree in 1866 and elected him overseer the following year. His alma mater also invited him to deliver a series of lectures on his philosophy in 1869-1870. When Emerson's home in Concord burned in 1877, friends sent him on a third visit to Europe and Egypt, accompanied by his daughter Ellen, while the house and study were rebuilt with funds from admirers. He spent his last few years in Concord quietly and died in the spring of 1882. Of his life, it can be said that perhaps more than any of his contemporaries, he embodied the qualities of the American spirit—its frankness, idealism, optimism, and self-confidence. For the American writer of his age, all things were possible. If, finally, he was as much prophet as poet, that may be because of the power of his vision as well as its lyrical intensity, a power that suffused his prose and was concentrated in his poems.

Analysis

Ralph Waldo Emerson's poetic achievement is greater than the range of his individual poems might suggest. Although perhaps only a handful of his poems attain undisputed greatness, others are rich in implication despite their occasional lapses, saved by a memorable line or phrase. As a cultural critic and poetic innovator, moreover, Emerson has had an immense influence through his essays and poetry in suggesting an appropriate style and method for subsequent American poets. He tried to become the poet he called for in *The American Scholar*, and to a degree, his poems reflect those democratic precepts. Determined to find distinctively American art forms, he began with expression— not form—and evolved the forms of his poems through their expression. Inspired by the "organic aesthetic" of the American sculptor Horatio Greenough, whose studio in Rome he visited in 1833, Emerson abandoned traditional poetic structure for a loose iambic meter and a variable (though often octosyllabic) line. Instead of following a rigid external form, the poem would take its form from its particular content and expression. This was the freedom Emerson sought for a "democratic" poetry.

Emerson's best poetry is thus marked by two qualities: organic form and a vernacular style; his less successful pieces, such as "The Sphinx," are too often cryptic and diffuse. These strengths and weaknesses both derive from his attempt to unite philosophical ideas and lyricism within a symbolic form in which the image would evoke its deeper meaning. "I am born a poet," he wrote to his fiancé, Jackson, "of a low class without doubt, yet a poet. That is my vocation. My singing, to be sure, is very 'husky,' and is for the most part in prose. Still I am a poet in the sense of a perceiver and dear lover of the harmonies that are in the soul and in matter, and specially of the correspondence between these and those." Correspondence, then, is what Emerson sought in his poetry, based on his theory of language as intermediary between humans and nature.

In "The Poet," Emerson announced that "it is not metres, but metre-making argument that makes a poem." His representative American poet would be a namer and enumerator, not a rhymer or versifier. The poet would take his inspiration from the coarse vigor of American vernacular speech and in turn reinvigorate poetic language by tracing root metaphors back to their origins in ordinary experience. He would avoid stilted or artificial poetic diction in favor of ordinary speech. This meant sacrificing sound to sense, however, since Emerson's "metre-making arguments" were more often gnomic than lyrical. As a result, his poems are as spare as their native landscape. They are muted and understated rather than rhapsodic, and—with the exception of his Orientalism—tempered and homey in their subject matter, since Emerson was more of an innovator in style than in substance. Emerson's "Merlin" provides perhaps the best definition of what he sought in his poetry:

> Thy trivial harp will never please
> Or fill my craving ear;
> Its chords should ring as blows the breeze,
> Free, peremptory, clear.

Emerson's poems fall into several distinct categories, the most obvious being his nature poems; his philosophical or meditative poems, which often echo the essays; his autobiographical verse; and his occasional pieces. Sometimes these categories may overlap, but the "organic" aesthetic and colloquial tone mark them as distinctly Emersonian. Two of his most frequently anthologized pieces, "Days" and "The Snow-Storm," will serve to illustrate his poetic style.

"Days"

"Days" has been called the most perfect of Emerson's poems, and while there is a satisfying completeness about the poem, it resolves less than might appear at first reading. The poem deals with what was for Emerson the continuing problem of vocation or calling. How could he justify his apparent idleness in a work-oriented culture? "Days" thus contains something of a self-rebuke, cast in terms of an Oriental procession of Days, personified as daughters of Time, who pass through the poet's garden bringing various gifts, the riches of life, which the poet too hastily rejects in favor of a "few herbs and apples," emblematic of the contemplative life. The Day scorns his choice, presumably because he has squandered his time in contemplation rather than having measured his ambition against worthier goals. The Oriental imagery employed here transforms a commonplace theme into a memorable poem, although the poet never responds to the implied criticism of his life; nor does he identify the "morning wishes" that have been abandoned for the more sedate and domestic "herbs and apples," although these images do suggest meanings beyond themselves.

"The Problem"

A thematically related poem is "The Problem," in which Emerson tries to justify his reasons for leaving the ministry, which he respects and admires but cannot serve. Perhaps because he was more poet than priest, Emerson preferred the direct inspiration of the artist to the inherited truths of religion, or it may have been that, as a romantic, he found more inspiration in nature than in Scripture. The third stanza of "The Problem" contains one of the clearest articulations of Emerson's "organic" aesthetic, of form emerging from expression, in the image of the artist who "builded better than he knew." The temples of nature "art might obey, but not surpass."

"The Snow-Storm"

This organic theory of art reached its fullest expression in "The Snow-Storm," which still offers the best example in Emerson's poetry of form following function, and human artistry imitating that of nature. Here the poem merges with what it describes. The first stanza announces the arrival of the storm, and the second stanza evokes the "frolic architecture" of the snow and the human architectural forms that it anticipates. Nature freely creates and humans imitate through art. Wind and snow form myriad natural forms that humans can only "mimic in slow structures" of stone. As the wind-sculpted snowdrifts create beauty from the materials at hand, the poem rounds on itself in the poet's implicit admiration of nature's work.

"Hamatraya"

One of the most intriguing of Emerson's poems is "Hamatraya," which contains an attack on Yankee land-greed and acquisitiveness, cast as a Hindu meditation on the impermanence of all corporeal things. In "Hamatraya," the crass materialism of his countrymen evokes Emerson's serenely idealistic response. No one finally owns the land, he asserts, and to pretend so is to be deceived. The land will outlive successive masters, all of whom boast of owning it. In the enduring cycle of things, they are all finally returned to the earth they claimed to possess. Emerson uses dramatic form and the lyrical "Earth-Song" as an effective counterpoint to the blunt materialism of the first two stanzas. His theme of all things returning unto themselves finds its appropriate metaphor in the organic (and Hindu) cycle of life. Hindu cosmology and natural ecology complement each other in Emerson's critique of the pretensions of private land-ownership.

"Brahma"

Another of Emerson's Oriental poems, his popular "Brahma," is notable for its blend of Eastern and Western thought. Here Emerson assumes the perspective of God or Brahma in presenting his theme of the divine relativity and continuity of life. Just as Krishna, "the Red Slayer," and his victim are merged in the unity of Brahma, so all other opposites are reconciled in the ultimate unity of the universe. This paradoxical logic appealed to Emerson as a way of presenting his monistic philosophy in poetic terms. The poem owes much to Emerson's study of the *Bhagavadgītā* (c. 200 B.C.E.-200 C.E.; *The Bhagavad Gita*, 1785) and other Oriental scriptures, the first stanza of "Brahma" being in fact a close parallel to the Hindu text. The smooth regularity of Emerson's ballad stanzas also helps to offset the exotic quality of the Hindu allusions and the novelty of the poem's theme.

"Uriel"

Religious myth is also present in "Uriel," which Robert Frost called "the greatest Western poem yet." Even if Frost's praise is overstated, this is still one of Emerson's most profound and complex poems. Again it deals with the reconciliation of opposites, this time in the proposed relativity of good and evil. Borrowing the theme of the primal revolt against God by the rebellious archangels, Emerson uses the figure of the angel Uriel as the prototype of the advanced thinker misunderstood or rejected by others. Uriel represents the artist as the rebel or prophet bearing unwelcome words, roles that Emerson no doubt identified with himself and the hostile reception given *An Address Delivered Before the Senior Class in Divinity College, Cambridge . . .* (1838; better known as *The Divinity School Address*) by the Harvard theological faculty. Uriel's words, "Line in nature is not found;/ Unit and universe are round; In vain produced, all rays return;/ Evil will bless, and ice will burn," speak with particular force to the modern age, in which discoveries in theoretical physics and astronomy seem to have confirmed Emerson's intuitions about the relativity of matter and energy and the nature of the physical universe.

"Each and All"

Emerson's monistic philosophy also appears in "Each and All," in which the poem suggests that beauty cannot be divorced from its context or setting without losing part of its original appeal. The peasant, sparrow, seashell, and maid must each be appreciated in the proper aesthetic context, as part of a greater unity. Beauty cannot be possessed, Emerson argues, without destroying it. The theme of "Each and All" perhaps echoes section 3 on beauty of his essay *Nature*, in which Emerson observes that "the standard of beauty is the entire circuit of natural forms—the totality of nature. . . . Nothing is quite beautiful alone; nothing but is beautiful in the whole. A single object is only so far beautiful as it suggests this universal grace." The poem "Each and All" gives a more concentrated and lyrical expression to this apprehension of aesthetic unity. The poetic images lend grace and specificity to the philosophical concept of the beauty inherent in unity.

"Give All to Love"

Emerson's fondness for paradoxical logic and the union of apparent opposites appears in yet another poem, "Give All to Love," which initially appears to falter on the contradiction between yielding to love and retaining one's individuality. The first three stanzas counsel a wholehearted surrender to the impulse of love, while the fourth stanza cautions the lover to remain "free as an Arab." The final two stanzas resolve this dilemma by affirming that the lovers may cherish joys apart without compromising their love for each other, since the purest love is that which is free from jealousy or possessiveness. Emerson reconciles the demands of love and those of self-reliance by idealizing the love relationship. Some commentators have even suggested that Emerson envisions a Neoplatonic ladder or hierarchy of love, from the Physical, to the Romantic, to the Ideal or Platonic—a relationship that in fact Emerson described in another poem titled "Initial, Daemonic, and Celestial Love"—but the theme of "Give All to Love" seems to be simply to love fully without surrendering one's ego or identity. The last two lines of the poem, "When half-gods go,/ The Gods arrive," are often quoted out of context because of their aphoristic quality.

"Threnody"

A poem that has led some readers to charge Emerson with coldheartedness or lack of feeling is "Threnody," his lament for the loss of his beloved son Waldo, who died of scarlet fever at the age of six. Waldo, the first child of his second marriage, died suddenly in January, 1842. Emerson was devastated by grief, yet he seems in the poem to berate himself for his inability to sustain his grief. In his journals, Emerson freely expressed his bitterness and grief, and he gradually transcribed these feelings into the moving pastoral elegy for his son. "Threnody," literally a death-song or lamentation, contains a mixture of commonplace and idealized pastoral images that demonstrate Emerson's ability to work within classical conventions and to ameliorate his grief through his doctrine of compensation. Some of the most moving lines in the poem describe the speaker's recollection of the child's "daily haunts" and unused toys, although these realistic details are later muted by the pathetic fallacy of external nature joining the poet in mourning the loss of his son.

"THE RHODORA"

Emerson's muse most often turned to nature for inspiration, so it is no accident that his nature poems contain some of his best work. "The Rhodora" is an early poem in which Emerson's attention to sharp and precise details of his New England landscape stands out against his otherwise generalized and formal poetic style. The first eight lines of the poem, in which Emerson describes finding the rhodora, a northern azalea-like flower, blooming in the woods early in May of the New England spring, before other plants have put out their foliage, seem incomparably the best. Unfortunately, the second half of the poem shifts from specific nature imagery to a generalized homily on the beauty of the rhodora, cast in formal poetic diction. Here Emerson's impulse to draw moralistic lessons from nature reminds us of another famous early nineteenth century American poem, William Cullen Bryant's "To a Waterfowl." This division within "The Rhodora" illustrates some of Emerson's difficulties in breaking away from the outmoded style and conventions of eighteenth century English landscape poetry to find an appropriate vernacular style for American nature poetry. Here the subject matter is distinctly American, but the style— the poem's manner of seeing and feeling—is still partially derivative.

"THE HUMBLE BEE"

"The Humble Bee" is a more interesting poem in some respects, in that Emerson uses a form adequate to his expression—a tight octosyllabic line and rhymed couplets—to evoke through both sound and sense the meandering flight of the bumble bee. As the poem unfolds, the bee gradually becomes a figure for the poet intoxicated by nature. Some of the poem's conceits may seem quaint to modern taste, but "The Humble Bee" is innovative in its use of terse expression and symbolic form. Its style anticipates the elliptical language and abbreviated form of Dickinson's poetry.

"WOODNOTES"

"Woodnotes" is a long and somewhat prosy two-part narrative poem that appears to be extracted from Emerson's journals. Part 1 introduces the transcendental nature lover ("A Forest Seer") in terms perhaps reminiscent of Thoreau, and part 2 describes the reciprocal harmony between humans and nature, in which each is fully realized through the other. The vagueness of part 2 perhaps illustrates Emerson's difficulty in capturing transcendental rapture in specific poetic language.

"Concord Hymn"

"Ode" ("Inscribed to W. H. Channing") and "Concord Hymn" are both occasional poems that otherwise differ markedly in style and technique. "Concord Hymn" is a traditional patriotic poem in four ballad stanzas that Emerson composed to be sung at the placing of a stone obelisk on July 4, 1837, to commemorate the Battle of Concord, fought on April 19, 1775, on land later belonging to the Reverend Ezra Ripley. The lines of the first stanza, now so well known that they are part of American national folklore, demonstrate that Emerson could easily master traditional verse forms when he chose to do so:

> By the rude bridge that arched the flood,
> Their flag to April's breeze unfurled,
> Here once the embattled farmers stood,
> And fired the shot heard round the world.

The images of the "bridge" and the "flood" in the first stanza ripen imperceptibly into metaphor in the poem's implied theme that the Battle of Concord provided the impetus for the American Revolutionary War.

"Ode"

Emerson's "Ode" is a much more unconventional piece, written in terse, variable lines, usually of two or three stresses, and touching on the dominant social and political issues of the day—the Mexican War, the Fugitive Slave Law of 1850, the threat of secession in the South, and radical abolitionism in the North. This open form was perhaps best suited to Emerson's oracular style that aimed to leave a few memorable lines with the reader. His angry muse berates Daniel Webster for having compromised his principles by voting for the Fugitive Slave Law, and it denounces those materialistic interests, in both the North and the South, that would profit from wage or bond slavery. Emerson's lines "Things are in the saddle,/ And ride mankind" aptly express his misgivings about the drift of American affairs that seemed to be leading toward a civil war. His taut lines seem to chant their warning like a Greek chorus, foreseeing the inevitable but being helpless to intervene. By the 1850's Emerson had become an increasingly outspoken opponent of the Fugitive Slave Law, and on occasion risked his personal safety in speaking before hostile crowds.

Legacy

Despite his commitment to a new American poetry based on common diction and ordinary speech, Emerson's poetry never quite fulfilled the promise of his call, in *The American Scholar* and "The Poet," for a new poetics. Emerson wanted to do for American poetry what Wordsworth had accomplished for English lyrical poetry, to free it from the constraints of an artificial and dead tradition of sensibility and feeling. However, he was not as consistent or as thoroughgoing a poetic innovator as the Wordsworth of the "Preface" to the second edition of *Lyrical Ballads* (1800), who both announced and carried out his proposed revision of the existing neoclassical poetic diction, nor did he apply his theory to his poetic composition as skillfully as Wordsworth did. Emerson could envision a new poetics but he could not sustain in his poetry a genuine American vernacular tradition. That had to wait for Whitman and Dickinson. Perhaps Emerson was too much the philosopher ever to realize fully the poetic innovations that he sought, but even with their flaws, his poems retain a freshness and vitality lacking in contemporaries such as Henry Wadsworth Longfellow and James Russell Lowell, who were probably more accomplished versifiers. Emerson's greatness resides in the originality of his vision of a future American poetry, free and distinct from European models. It can be found in the grace of his essays and the insights of his journals, and it appears in those select poems in which he was able to match vision and purpose, innovation and accomplishment. His "Saadi" was no less a poet for the restraint of his harp.

OTHER MAJOR WORKS

NONFICTION: *Nature*, 1836; *An Oration Delivered Before the Phi Beta Kappa Society, Cambridge*, 1837 (better known as *The American Scholar*); *An Address Delivered Before the Senior Class in Divinity College, Cambridge . . .* , 1838 (better known as *The Divinity School Address*); *Essays: First Series*, 1841; *Essays: Second Series*, 1844; *Orations, Lectures and Addresses*, 1844; *Addresses and Lectures*, 1849; *Representative Men: Seven Lectures*, 1850; *English Traits*, 1856; *The Conduct of Life*, 1860; *Representative of Life*, 1860; *Society and Solitude*, 1870; *Works and Days*, 1870; *Letters and Social Aims*, 1875; *Lectures and Biographical Sketches*, 1884; *Miscellanies*, 1884; *Natural History of Intellect*, 1893; *The Journals of Ralph Waldo Emerson*, 1909-1914 (10 volumes; E. W. Emerson and W. E. Forbes, editors); *The Letters of Ralph Waldo Emerson*, 1939 (6 volumes; Ralph L. Rusk, editor); *The Journals and Miscellaneous Notebooks*, 1960-1982 (16 volumes); *Emerson in His Journals*, 1982 (Joel Porte, editor); *Political Writings*, 2008 (Kenneth Sacks, editor).

EDITED TEXT: *Parnassus*, 1874.

MISCELLANEOUS: *Uncollected Writings: Essays, Addresses, Poems, Reviews, and Letters*, 1912.

BIBLIOGRAPHY

Bosco, Ronald A., and Joel Myerson, eds. *Ralph Waldo Emerson: A Documentary Volume*. Vol. 351 in *Dictionary of Literary Biography*. Detroit: Gale/ Cengage Learning, 2010. Provides primary source documents, including reviews and assessments, concerning Emerson and his works by contemporaries and by persons writing after his death.

Buell, Lawrence. *Emerson*. Cambridge, Mass.: Belknap Press, 2003. A thorough and admiring biography that presents Emerson as an international figure.

Gougeon, Len. *Emerson and Eros: The Making of a Cultural Hero*. Albany: State University of New York Press, 2009. Argues that, for Emerson, Eros is the essential cosmic force that joins humanity and the universe, and that Emerson's writings are filled with this dynamic spirit.

Myerson, Joel, ed. *A Historical Guide to Ralph Waldo Emerson*. New York: Oxford University Press, 2000. A collection of essays that provide an extended biographical study of Emerson. Later chapters study his concept of individualism, nature and natural science, religion, antislavery, and women's rights.

Porte, Joel, and Saundra Morris, eds. *The Cambridge Companion to Ralph Waldo Emerson*. New York: Cambridge University Press, 1999. Provides a critical introduction to Emerson's work through interpretations of his writing and analysis of his influence and cultural significance. Includes a comprehensive chronology and bibliography.

Schreiner, Samuel Agnew. *The Concord Quartet: Alcott, Emerson, Hawthorne, Thoreau, and the Friendship That Freed the American Mind*. Hoboken, N.J.: John Wiley & Sons, 2006. Examines the relationship among Emerson, Henry David Thoreau, Nathaniel Hawthorne, and Bronson Alcott. Sheds light on the mind behind Emerson's poetry.

Waynem, Tiffany K. *Critical Companion to Ralph Waldo Emerson: A Literary Reference to His Life and Work*. New York: Facts On File, 2010. Contains a biography of Emerson, an alphabetical list of his works, and a chronology.

York, Maurice, and Rick Spaulding. *Ralph Waldo Emerson: The Infinitude of the Private Man—A Biography*. Chicago: Wrightwood Press, 2008. A thorough biography with a chronology and selected bibliography. Describes the reaction of Emerson to Walt Whitman and his writing of "The Poet."

Andrew J. Angyal

ROBERT FROST

Born: San Francisco, California; March 26, 1874
Died: Boston, Massachusetts; January 29, 1963

PRINCIPAL POETRY
A Boy's Will, 1913
North of Boston, 1914
Mountain Interval, 1916
New Hampshire: A Poem with Notes and Grace Notes, 1923
Selected Poems, 1923
West-Running Brook, 1928
Collected Poems, 1930
A Further Range, 1936
Collected Poems, 1939
A Witness Tree, 1942
A Masque of Reason, 1945
A Masque of Mercy, 1947
Steeple Bush, 1947
Complete Poems, 1949
How Not to Be King, 1951
In the Clearing, 1962
The Poetry of Robert Frost, 1969

OTHER LITERARY FORMS

Although the majority of Robert Frost's published work is poetry, it is worth noting that he published a one-act play titled *A Way Out*, in 1929. By this point in his career, Frost had established himself as a fine narrative poet capable of both monologue and dialogue within the poetic narrative mode and with a strong visual mind capable of creating powerful dramatic situations. Although Frost never made a serious effort to adapt these dramatic strengths to the stage, much of his poetic success lies with his sense of stage and dramatic persona. His only other literary publications include letters, particularly to his friend Louis Untermeyer, and lectures in which he discusses in detail his own work and poetic theory. He recorded many of his poems on records and film.

ACHIEVEMENTS

Perhaps the most successful of American poets, Robert Frost reached a large and diversified readership almost immediately after the publication of *North of Boston*. He sustained both popular and critical acclaim throughout his entire career, which spanned

Robert Frost
(Library of Congress)

fifty years and ended with his death in 1963, shortly after the publication of his last collection, *In the Clearing*. He is the only writer to have won the Pulitzer Prize in poetry four times (in 1924 for *New Hampshire*, in 1931 for the first *Collected Poems*, in 1937 for *A Further Range*, and in 1943 for *A Witness Tree*). He was nominated for the Nobel Prize in 1950 on publication of the *Complete Poems* but did not receive it, perhaps because the two preceding Nobel Prizes had been awarded to Americans: T. S. Eliot in 1948 and William Faulkner in 1949. Frost earned other awards, such as the Russell Loines Award (1931), the Gold Medal for Poetry from the American Academy of Arts and Letters (1939), the Frost Medal from the Poetry Society of America (1941), an Academy of American Poets Fellowship (1953), and the Bollingen Prize for Poetry (1963). He served as the consultant in poetry (poet laureate) to the Library of Congress from 1958 to 1959 and was appointed poet laureate of Vermont in 1961.

Few American poets have laid claim to both an enormous critical and popular reputation. Much of Frost's contribution to American literature came from his ability to speak in poetic but plain language to both common people and scholars and to observe ordinary occurrences with irony and wit. If modern American poetry began with Walt

Whitman and Emily Dickinson and evolved through Edgar Lee Masters, Robinson Jeffers, and Edwin Arlington Robinson, Frost's poetry is the culmination, combining all elements of poetic craft and modern themes. Frost liberated American poets by proving the potential success of traditional forms, even during a period when form was giving way to free verse under the influence of T. S. Eliot and Ezra Pound.

Frost's most important contribution may be as the model for a clearly identifiable twentieth century American poet. Unlike the expatriate Americans, Frost never lost touch with American persistence, folk humor, plain speech, and attachment to the land. His pragmatic, clever intelligence never became pedantic, never abstract, condescending, or introverted, but remained full of mischief and horseplay. In both his poetry and his public image, although his private life was different, Frost embodied the American ideals of rugged gentleness, quiet reflection, and an unconquerable spirit. His poetry is compassionate without falling into sentimentality, and positive without being naïve.

Biography

A native of New Hampshire and a graduate of Harvard University, Robert Lee Frost's father, William Prescott Frost, moved to San Francisco in 1873 to escape post-Civil War bitterness against the South. Shortly before his untimely death at thirty-five, William Prescott requested that he be buried in New England. Fulfilling this request, Robert, his sister Jeanie Florence, and their mother accompanied the casket across the country to Massachusetts. Because they could not afford the return trip, the Frosts settled in Salem, New Hampshire, when Robert was eleven years old. In 1892, Robert Frost graduated as co-valedictorian from Lawrence High School and entered Dartmouth College to study law. He dropped out, however, before completing his first semester, spending the following two years working at odd jobs and writing poetry. In 1894, he published his first poem, "My Butterfly," and became engaged to Elinor White, with whom he had shared the valedictorian honor. After his marriage in 1895, Frost helped his mother run a small private school, studied for two years at Harvard, then moved to Derry, New Hampshire, for a life of farming. Between 1900 and 1905, Frost raised poultry and wrote most of the poems that would constitute his first two volumes; after 1905, he taught school in Plymouth, New Hampshire, and in 1912, he sailed for England with Elinor and his two children, where he collected and published *A Boy's Will* and *North of Boston*. By the time the Frosts returned to New York in 1915, *North of Boston* had become an enormous critical and popular success, and Frost spent the next year, and indeed most of his life, in the limelight giving readings and lectures.

Because Frost is so strongly identified as a New England poet whose poems are inextricably rooted in the land of New Hampshire and Vermont, readers expect a high correlation between the events of his life and the resultant poetry. Although Frost certainly invested most of his life in New England, there is a surprising dichotomy between his biography and his poetic themes. His family life was tragic because premature death beset many of its members. His father died of tuberculosis, his mother of cancer. He lost his sister, two of his children died in infancy, his married daughter died in childbirth, and his son committed suicide. While being operated on for cancer, his wife died of a heart attack. In spite of his long wait for recognition and the private disasters that befell him, however, Frost's poetry is free from bitterness and from any direct personal references. Instead of writing about his own experiences, as so many modern American poets have done, Frost wrote about the process of discovery and the relationship between people and their surroundings.

Frost's particular world was New England, but his landscapes are metaphorical, not specific; his speech universal, not regional; and his themes archetypal, not autobiographical. His official biographer, Lawrance Thompson, unveiled many shocking characteristics of Frost's personality—including jealousy and vindictiveness—but, much to Frost's credit, his art rises above these frailties and speaks not of pettiness but of deep matters of the heart.

Analysis

The most distinctive characteristic of Robert Frost's work is elusiveness. Frost operates on so many levels that to interpret his poems confidently on a single level frequently causes the reader to misunderstand them completely. This elusiveness makes Frost one of the most interesting and continually intriguing American poets. He teaches the joys of discovering what lies beneath the veil, and readers grow to appreciate how he has cleverly masked what seems so intuitively obvious.

The veils themselves are constructed of technical devices such as symbol, rhyme, stanzation, imagery, and dramatic situation, and they are rooted in language play, which Frost uses to effect sleight-of-hand tricks. He is a magician whose devices are so artful that readers usually cannot see how he transforms one theme into another; they may be delighted with the effect, yet they cannot help wondering how they have been tricked so completely.

Because Frost's poems operate on so many levels, it is possible for almost everyone to find his or her own beliefs about life reflected in Frost's poetry. Optimists can argue that Frost understands the complexities of life while still affirming humanity's ability to make creative choices that determine its future. Realists can argue that Frost is not an optimist, although, having acknowledged that doubt is more prevalent than faith, he still derives pleasure from the process of living life in the present. Skeptics can point out Frost's irony, noting that he affirms nothing but the dualities and contradictions of life and human nature. Each type of reader has interpreted Frost correctly; one must consider all levels of Frost's poems before being certain of any particular meaning. Because Frost writes about familiar experiences in what appears to be conversational language, the overwhelming impulse is to accept what he says at face value.

The fact that most readers seem to see their own beliefs reflected in Frost's poetry certainly accounts for his popular success, but this point also raises some serious questions about his poetic achievement. If his poems advance no universal truths, Frost may well be accused of having no philosophy—of being too vague and complex for any clear interpretation to be derived from his works. "Stopping by Woods on a Snowy Evening" is only one of many examples of a poem that has been read with many contradictory interpretations. Readers have variously explained its meaning, ranging from the serenity of a snowy night to the virtues of duty to the lure of death to self-mockery. A critic who reads Frost moralistically, believing that "Stopping by Woods on a Snowy Evening" is a lesson about keeping promises, has fallen into Frost's trap. Readers must be exceedingly careful not to impose their own ideas on the poems or to blindly accept any interpretations.

The place to begin an explication of Frost's poetry is with the narrative persona and dramatic situation, for it is here that Frost draws the reader into the poems and begins his illusions. Only a few of his poems have no dramatic context—most of his celebrated ones do, such as "Mending Wall," "Two Tramps in Mud Time," "Death of the Hired Man," "West-Running Brook," "Tree at My Window," and "Two Look at Two"—and except for such very short lyrical poems as "Nothing Gold Can Stay," the dramatic context offers the surest chance of discovering Frost's themes.

"After Apple-Picking"

In "After Apple-Picking," for example, a great deal can be established about the dramatic situation, the dramatic moment, and the narrative persona. The reader knows that the narrator has been harvesting apples, perhaps in great numbers, and that he is now "done" with apple-picking. He has collected his apples in barrels, one of which remains unfilled, and the narrator speculates that there may be a few applies left unpicked, although he does not know for certain. His ladder, long and two-pointed, is in the tree where he has left it, and it points "toward heaven still."

In the first six lines, Frost has already begun his sleight of hand by introducing some facts within the dramatic situation that seem extraneous to the poem's development. For example, why does he describe a "two-pointed" ladder when it does not make any difference what kind of ladder it is as long as the narrator can reach the apples with it? Why does he say that it is "sticking" toward heaven? These details of course help to bring the poem alive, but as part of the dramatic situation they add implications far beyond their descriptive use. Heaven is not simply a direction; if it were, Frost could have said "skyward," or not said anything at all since it is obvious that a ladder that sticks through a tree must be pointing up. The empty barrel is similarly suggestive: Readers want to know whether it is empty because somebody miscalculated the number of barrels needed, whether the narrator simply quit before the job was "done," or whether there is a more sinister suggestion that something that should have been filled is empty. Both the ladder and the barrel are facts within the dramatic situation, but they are more than simple details because they raise questions that fall outside the realm of the poem. Readers should be careful to recognize that these questions arise only if they wish to read the ladder and barrel as suggestive. Clearly, however, Frost did not place them in the poem by accident, and therefore they are important. The same kind of suggestiveness can be found in phrases throughout the poem: "winter sleep," "pane of glass," "my dreaming," "cellar bin," "rumbling sound," "cider-apple heap," "woodchuck," and "human sleep."

Complicating the dramatic moment, the narrator tells some things about himself that help to explain why he has left the barrel empty. Readers know that the time is late fall because it is the end of apple-picking season and the beginning of winter sleep. Readers also know that the narrator is tired as he remembers visions that he saw "this morning through a pane of glass" and as he recognizes what form his dreaming is about to take. The morning world of "hoary grass" was strange to him, and as the ice pane melted, the narrator intentionally let it fall and break. Now, at the end of the day, he is embarking on a nightmare of apples; his ladder sways precariously as the boughs bend. He is no longer safe in the apple tree where he had once been certain of his purpose; now, it is the source of his fears. Too many apples "rumble" into the cellar, a place beneath the earth, in the opposite to that direction in which the ladder is pointing. What worries the narrator most is that some of the good apples "not bruised or spiked" will end up in the "cider-apple heap," a place that offends the narrator's sense of justice. Just as readers want to know why the barrel was left unfilled, the narrator asks why good apples that he let fall by accident are sent to the heap. If readers can understand why he is so troubled by this, they will know a great deal more about the poem's meaning.

With his typical magic, however, Frost sets the reader up to accept the easy explanation as he tempts him to explain the narrator's anxieties merely as a fear of failure to do his job properly. Frost has planted a host of potentially misleading elements that encourage conventional interpretations. The ladder, with its image of outstretched arms, implores heaven, perhaps even suggesting Jacob's ladder. Because apples have such a strong traditional association with the story of the Garden of Eden, one might also conclude that apples represent the narrator's fall into mortal existence—his banishment from the grace of God. He has not, himself, sinned but carries the burden of Original Sin, and even though he has done the best he can with his life—he has dutifully picked apples until the very end—he is still plagued by nightmares. He knows that he has let slip from his grasp some apples that went undeservedly to the cider-apple heap; it is he who has condemned them to unworthy destruction by the apple grinder, and it occurs to him that his destiny might be similar to one of the good apples that is banished to destruction by chance. The narrator, then, is plagued by two doubts: The first is his own failure to fulfill all his earthly obligations, knowing that time is running out for him ("essence of winter sleep is on the air"); the second is a fear that there is no ultimate mercy—that fallen humans like fallen apples are disposed of indiscriminately. The hoary world he saw through the pane of glass (with its biblical allusion: "For now we see through a glass, darkly; but then face to face") was the image of life and death, and of his own mortality.

Frost has gone to a great deal of trouble to establish this as the proper reading: The narrator is frightened by the thought of death because he is uncertain whether he has satisfied his earthly duties. A simple moralistic conclusion might be that people should work harder before finding themselves, like the narrator, on the verge of death without salvation. Frost first offered the reader those suggestive objects; then presented a narrator filled with visions, dreams, and sleep; and finally produced a dozen highly recognizable and traditional biblical symbols. Why should not "After Apple-Picking" (and "Stopping by Woods on a Snowy Evening," for that matter) be interpreted as a poem about the virtues of steadfastness and singleness of purpose? Yet, one cannot read the poem only at that level; Frost has effected a sleight of hand. Any good magician must continually remind the audience that this is not reality; it is, indeed, a magic show where they have come to be fooled. If Frost wants readers to catch on, he has to provide some means for them to spot the trickery. With Frost's poetry, the price of admission to the magic show is high, and there are no easy explanations as to how the trick is performed, but Frost usually plays fair and gives the reader important clues.

One of the clues in "After Apple-Picking" is the use of personal pronouns. In line 16, and throughout the poem, the narrator continually refers to himself as "I," but in line 37 he shifts to say "one" ("one can see what will trouble this sleep of mine"). He could have said "*I* can see," but there is that deliberate shift to "one," who can be no one else but the reader, and Frost might as well have said "you" can see. All along, the reader has been thinking that the narrator is troubled about his sleep because he is unprepared for death, but now he begins to suspect that this interpretation is incorrect. "This sleep of *mine*" is not the sleep the reader originally understood, and the narrator corrects the misconception by adding, "whatever sleep it is." The reader believed it was death, and for good reason: Again tricked into it, the reader has fallen into the poem's message.

The "one" who can see the narrator's sleep is not the reader but the woodchuck who could "say" whether "it's like his long sleep or just some human sleep." In reality, the woodchuck could not *say* anything, nor could the woodchuck fear death because of any failure to fulfill religious obligations. The narrator can speak of and fear death, unsure of salvation, but not the woodchuck. Even more trickily, the narrator projects or imagines what the woodchuck's long sleep is ("as I describe its coming on"); so readers have the woodchuck, who cannot possess human vision, telling the narrator only what the narrator imagines and ascribes to the animal. It is through imagination that humans conceive death, just as readers have used their imagination to create the symbols in the poem. So moments of life may be misinterpreted to create concepts of death. For Frost, human imagination is the trickster, not death, and humans often use it to torment themselves about a mortality that they have fabricated.

THEME OF EARTHLY EXISTENCE

This theme of "After Apple-Picking" reflects Frost's larger worldview and helps to account for the frequent misreading of his poems. Even though "After Apple-Picking" seems to be concerned with death, Christian fate, redemption, and the virtuous life—abstract ideas about the afterlife—Frost is much more concerned with earthly existence. He seldom speaks of anywhere else, and when he does, it is always in terms of how one is on Earth. Frost neither believes nor disbelieves in religious or philosophical abstractions; yet, time and again, readers insist that he is promoting one view or the other. Frost's code, both in his art and in his public life, is an appreciation of wit and irony; Frost the magician is also the most appreciative audience of life's magic show, and it is important to remember that when there is a strong presence of a narrative persona, the poem is most likely to turn ironic. Frost is most ironic toward himself, and he becomes most poignant when he sees that he has become his own victim in the magic show. In "Birches," for example, the narrator is searching for connections that he does not fully understand, while in "At Woodward's Gardens," a remarkably similar poem, the narrator is more amused by a much too clever comparison between people and monkeys. By comparing these two poems, readers have an illustration of how, when the narrator is aloof and haughty, and when he is able to be more of an observer than a participant, the irony is weakened. When the narrator is as much the audience as the magician, however, the poems reverse themselves as the narrator, himself, comes to appreciate life's sleight of hand.

DRAMATIC SITUATION AND NARRATIVE PERSONA

Many of Frost's most popular and critically acclaimed poems employ what might be called "sleight of tongue." Notice how, when the narrator in "After Apple-Picking" says "this sleep of *mine*," he is also saying "this sleep of *mind*"; in "Tree at My Window," when the narrator says "not all their *light tongues* could be profound," he is referring not only to an image of leaves blowing on the tree but also to the process of photosynthesis that nourishes the plant. In his celebrated sonnet "Design," Frost mixes a set of provocative objects (spider web, delicate white flower, moth) within a dramatic situation, and for twelve lines asks a traditional poetic question that in traditional sonnet fashion will be answered in the couplet. Instead of giving an answer, however, Frost proffers another question that is keyed to the various uses of the parts of speech and the equivocal meanings of the words "design" and "appall." Similarly, in "Stopping by Woods on a Snowy Evening," Frost establishes a dramatic situation with an involved narrator, offers a solution to the dramatic question in line 15 ("And miles to go before I sleep"), then reverses the entire tone of the poem by repeating the line to give it a different meaning.

In the longer poems, dramatic situation and narrative persona are the important elements of irony, while in the shorter poems rhyme and stanzation provide the clues. The poems written in couplets are more playful and bemused than they are ironic because, in the cynical twentieth century, it was difficult for poets to sustain through couplets the solemnity that irony demands. A single couplet or triplet judiciously placed can create exactly the right ironic effect, but an entire poem in couplets tends toward ridicule rather than the reverse. Knowing this, Frost works to overcome the effect, but his couplet poems tend to reflect longing or sadness and are, in fact, more sincere than ironic. Curiously, some of the most ironic poems are those that use triple and quadruple rhyme schemes, such as "Stopping by Woods on a Snowy Evening" and "After Apple-Picking." The least ironic are those with an *abcb* structure; these poems present such personal and impossible questions that no answer is acceptable, and thus there is no irony. The impossibility of his question allows the narrator to be distanced from the dramatic tension, and the absence of personal involvement reduces the narrator's commitment to discovery. Comparing "Stopping by Woods on a Snowy Evening" to "Come In," two very similar poems, the reader can see that the rhyme scheme of "Come In" does not permit as strong a potential for a shift in tone as does the *aaba* of "Stopping by Woods on a Snowy Evening." The locked third line in the *aaba* form allows the narrator much less chance of escaping, and because the fourth line returns the poem to the first two, the narrator must turn internally to the poem for a resolution.

More adaptable to irony than the *abcb* stanzation are the alternating quatrains, octaves, and sonnets, but these are more openly philosophical and convey a sense of pleasant discovery rather than deep involvement. The narrator feels good about his discovery, as in "Two Tramps in Mud Time" and "Design," and these poems tend to contain elements of irony without making any final ironic statement. The forms in which Frost is most consistently ironic are stanzas with framed segments (such as *abba, abca, abbba, aaba*). In the longer, rhymed poems, such as "The Grindstone" and "After Apple-Picking," and in the four-line strophic poems, such as "Stopping by Woods on a Snowy Evening" and "Choose Something Like a Star," the ironic tone is strong, especially when Frost begins shortening lines, as in "Fire and Ice," and altering the number of syllables per line. Without ever reading the poem, one could speculate that "After Apple-Picking" is ironic because of the framed segments (such as the opening six lines), enjambment, shortened lines (line 2 following the long first line, and lines 14 and 16), and the double and triple rhymes (lines 5-6 and lines 14-16, for example). With this combination of techniques, there is little doubt that one cannot accept the poem at face value.

More important than the technical devices for discovering Frost's irony and major themes is the presence of "opposites," which set up patterns of reversal. Frost frequently presents "pairs" of contrasting personas, ideas, images, or symbols, such as in "Tree at My Window," where man faces nature with only a curtain between; in "Two Look at Two," where identical pairs confront each other; in "West-Running Brook," "Home Burial," and "Death of the Hired Man," where husband and wife take opposite views; in

"Two Tramps in Mud Time," where the narrator faces the lumberjacks in a confrontation of vocation and avocation; and perhaps most famously in "Mending Wall," where narrator and neighbor, pine and apple trees, civilized man and savage, father and son, light and dark, ego and alter ego square off against each other with yet another barrier—the wall—between them.

"Mending Wall"

Most of the "opposite" poems use some kind of physical barrier to identify territory, and the wall in "Mending Wall" has been consciously constructed in violation of nature that "doesn't love the wall." To the narrator, the wall serves no useful purpose and is only an annoying reminder of his neighbor's foolish platitudes and the inability of the neighbors to communicate except once a year at spring mending time. Before the narrator built a wall, he would want to know what he "was walling in or walling out," but there is a more important question implied: If there were no wall, would he and his neighbor still be opposites? Because the narrator knows that the answer is "yes," and because he is deliberately antagonistic ("Spring is the mischief in me, and I wonder if I could put a notion in his head"), the presence of the wall is a purely academic argument for the narrator. The wall is unnatural—nature wants it down and topples it every winter—just as the wife in "West-Running Brook" thinks it is unnatural that the brook runs west instead of east like all the other country brooks. Fred, her husband, however, knows that there is a more important issue: not one of "opposites" or dualities but one of "contraries." He says that "our life runs down in sending up the clock" and extends this comparison to the sun, which runs down in sending up the brook. The ultimate question is, What sends up the sun? What happens when the water flings backward on itself in a movement toward the source? There is something sending up the sun, something that does not love a wall. The persistence of "unnatural" barriers, like the wall, the brook, the apples, and the curtain in "Tree at My Window," reminds the narrator that he cannot explain the existence of contraries any more than his neighbor can explain why good fences make good neighbors, but he does know that in contraries lie the secrets of living; that through the self-conscious process of witnessing contraries one is mot likely to discover one's own life's forces rather than any profound secrets of life.

Unlike the English Romantic poets and "nature poets" with whom he is frequently compared, Frost does not look to nature for an affirmation of life, for solace, or for a road to self-discovery. For Frost, people are alone in the world, unable to answer questions about God and death but having some control over their earthly destiny. For Frost, who is not a fatalist or a determinist, who believes things happen neither for good nor evil but simply occur, who does not fear death nor embrace promises of heaven, the only way is "to go by contraries," making creative choices, accepting paradoxes, questioning walls and brooks.

Through wit and irony, people can remind themselves that much of their fallibility is self-induced; that they trick themselves and then despair when they think their manufactured illusions have become reality. They have not. Good fences do not necessarily make good neighbors; brooks do not wave at human beings in any annunciation; death does not come as a thrush, or a snowy night, or a spider.

"FIRE AND ICE"

In "Fire and Ice," the entire doctrine of "opposites" and irony is at work, and this poem, perhaps most directly of all his work, illustrates Frost's themes and techniques. Arranged as a single stanza of nine lines (in framed segments), the poem establishes the opposites of fire and ice, hot and cold, and love and hate, and centers on the middle (fifth) line of the poem. Fire is presented in the first four lines, ice in the last four. The center line asks, "But *if* it had to perish twice," and that becomes the ironic key. Whether the world will be destroyed a second time makes no difference to Frost's narrator; it is a moot question reserved for the gullible reader who interprets "After Apple-Picking" as a Christian manifesto. Frost is much more concerned with the power of hate, an opposite of love, which he says "will suffice," but one must not be tricked by that simple explanation either, to conclude that humankind is beset by hate any more than it is pursued by death. It "would suffice," if readers wanted it to, just as the woodchuck "would say" if he were asked, but the world does not have to "perish twice" except as one fears destruction, and readers do not have to ask the woodchuck, and one does not have to stoop to hate. "Some say the world will end in fire," but not Frost.

During an age when the thrust of literature has been to question illusion and reality, and to lament the lonely plight and desperation of the isolated person in an overwhelming universe, Frost presents a more positive vision, rooted in the American search for the good life. Human beings may struggle to discover their tormented spirit, but they are also capable of creative choices and of accepting contraries and uncertainties. Frost delights in the mysteries of life without being burdened by debilitating responsibilities for them, and while human beings might not become the conquerors of the universe, neither are they suppressed by it, and in that Frost rejoices.

OTHER MAJOR WORKS

PLAY: *A Way Out*, pb. 1929 (one act).

NONFICTION: *The Letters of Robert Frost to Louis Untermeyer*, 1963 (with commentary by Untermeyer); *The Record of a Friendship*, 1963 (Margaret Bartlett, editor); *Selected Letters of Robert Frost*, 1964 (Lawrance Thompson, editor); *Selected Prose*, 1966 (Hyde Cox and Edward C. Lathem, editors); *The Notebooks of Robert Frost*, 2006 (Robert Faggen, editor); *The Collected Prose of Robert Frost*, 2007 (Mark Richardson, editor).

Bibliography

Burnshaw, Stanley. *Robert Frost Himself*. New York: George Braziller, 1986. Written by a personal friend of Frost, this biography is in part an attempt to redress the balance skewed in the definitive Lawrance Roger Thompson work. Includes a chronology, extensive notes, an accurate index, and a revealing collection of illustrations.

Dickstein, Morris, ed. *Robert Frost*. Pasadena, Calif.: Salem Press, 2009. A collection of essays that examine topics such as Frost's legacy and his relationship with modernist poetics.

Faggen, Robert. *The Cambridge Introduction to Robert Frost*. New York: Cambridge University Press, 2008. Examines the literary traditions that shaped Frost's work as well as the poet's legacy. Discusses the controversies surrounding Frost criticism and the portrayals of his life.

_____, ed. *The Cambridge Companion to Robert Frost*. New York: Cambridge University Press, 2001. A collection of essays on Frost's art and thought, including controversies concerning his life and his reinvention of poetic conventions.

Gerber, Philip L. *Robert Frost*. Rev. ed. Boston: Twayne, 1982. Begins with an objective biographical overview and follows with substantial chapters on technique, themes, theories, and accomplishments. Includes chronology, extensive notes and references, select bibliography, and index.

Meyers, Jeffrey. *Robert Frost: A Biography*. Boston: Houghton Mifflin, 1996. Shapes a long life into a vivacious character study based on the conflicts that seemed to drive Frost as well as do him damage. Includes bibliographical references and index.

Parini, Jay. *Robert Frost: A Life*. New York: Henry Holt, 1999. Parini spent twenty years researching this volume, which delves into Frost's psyche and how he dealt with family tragedy and depression and examines his poetry in depth.

Potter, James L. *The Robert Frost Handbook*. University Park: Pennsylvania State University Press, 1980. A basic and widely used resource on Frost, this work is indispensable for both first readers and scholars. Contains chronologies of both life and works, guides to various approaches to the poems, discussions of various literary and cultural contexts, and technical analyses, as well as a complete annotated bibliography and an index.

Pritchard, William H. *Frost: A Literary Life Reconsidered*. New York: Oxford University Press, 1984. This measured, sophisticated, detailed approach to Frost's life and work is another attempt to correct Thompson's view. Unlike many scholarly biographies, this one is good for browsing and enjoyable for the general reader. Includes full notes and an index.

Stanlis, Peter J. *Robert Frost: The Poet as Philosopher*. Wilmington, Del.: ISI Books, 2007. Examines Frost's poetry from the standpoint of his philosophy, focusing on dualism.

Walton Beacham

THOMAS HARDY

Born: Higher Bockhampton, Dorset, England; June 2, 1840
Died: Dorchester, Dorset, England; January 11, 1928

PRINCIPAL POETRY
Wessex Poems, and Other Verses, 1898
Poems of the Past and Present, 1901
Time's Laughingstocks, and Other Verses, 1909
Satires of Circumstance, 1914
Selected Poems of Thomas Hardy, 1916
Moments of Vision and Miscellaneous Verses, 1917
Late Lyrics and Earlier, 1922
Human Shows, Far Phantasies, Songs, and Trifles, 1925
Winter Words in Various Moods and Metres, 1928
Collected Poems of Thomas Hardy, 1943
The Complete Poetical Works, 1982-1985 (3 volumes; Samuel Hynes, editor)

OTHER LITERARY FORMS

Besides his eight substantial volumes of poetry, Thomas Hardy published fourteen novels, four collections of short stories, two long verse plays, and a variety of essays, prefaces, and nonfiction prose. Although Hardy directed before his death that his letters, notebooks, and private papers be burned, much interesting material has survived in addition to that preserved in *The Early Life of Thomas Hardy* (1928) and *The Later Years of Thomas Hardy* (1930), both of which were dictated by Hardy himself to his wife, Florence Hardy. A definitive seven-volume edition of Hardy's letters (1978-1988) was edited by Richard Little Purdy and Michael Millgate. In addition, Ernest Brennecke has edited *Life and Art* (1925). *An Indiscretion in the Life of an Heiress* appeared serially in 1878 and as a book in 1934; it is a story based on scenes from Hardy's rejected first novel, *The Poor Man and the Lady*, which he later destroyed.

ACHIEVEMENTS

Although Thomas Hardy's poetic reputation has grown steadily since his death, critics seem unable to agree on the exact nature of his poetic achievement or even on a list of his best poems. Aside from a small group of frequently anthologized pieces, the bulk of Hardy's poetry goes unread. Part of the problem is the immense amount of his verse—nearly a thousand poems in eight substantial volumes. The other problem is the inevitable comparison between his poetry and his fiction and the tendency to prefer one or the

Thomas Hardy
(Library of Congress)

other, instead of seeking continuities in his work. This is an unavoidable problem with a poet-novelist, particularly with a novelist as accomplished as Hardy, whose fiction is better known than his poetry.

Hardy began his career as a novelist rather than as a poet. He turned to poetry later in life, publishing little before 1898. Here, however, chronology can be misleading. Hardy began composing verse early in life and continued to write poetry throughout the years when he was publishing his Wessex novels and tales. To a certain extent, economic pressures early led him to relegate poetry to a secondary place in his career. Once he had abandoned architecture, he turned to fiction to earn a livelihood. Had the means been available to him, he might have remained primarily a poet.

Yet even during his most productive years as a novelist, Hardy was putting aside verse that he would later publish. Sometimes these poems develop a lyrical twist to a scene or episode given fuller treatment in his novels, as in the case of "Tess's Lament," "In a Wood," or "At Casterbridge Fair." Moreover, Hardy was a lyrical prose stylist as well as a contemplative or meditative poet. The genres were fluid to him, and he moved easily from one to the other. Florence Hardy wrote in *The Later Years of Thomas Hardy* that "he had mostly aimed at keeping his narratives close to natural life and as near to poetry in their subjects as the conditions would allow, and had often regretted that these conditions would not let him keep them nearer still." Indeed, the same themes often appear in both the poems and the fiction: the capriciousness of fate, the cruelty of missed opportunities, and the large role of chance, accident, and contingency in human affairs.

Nor does chronology help much in understanding Hardy's development as a poet, since his verse shows only subtle variations in theme, subject matter, style, or treatment over more than six decades. There is a timeless quality in his verse, both early and late, with no discernible falling off in his creative power even in the late poems. Between 1898 and 1928, Hardy published eight volumes of lyrical poetry and two lengthy verse plays, which—even without the prior achievement of his fiction—would have made for an impressive literary career. That his poetry appeared after midcareer is a tribute to Hardy's undiminished creative imagination, especially when one remembers that the bulk of his poetry was published after he was sixty, with more than half of his lyrical poetry appearing after he turned seventy-four. *The Dynasts: A Drama of the Napoleonic Wars* (pb. 1903, 1906, 1908, 1910) alone would have been a major accomplishment for a writer of his age. For his last volume, *Winter Words in Various Moods and Metres*, published posthumously, he wrote an unused preface in which he boasted that he was the only English poet to bring out a new volume of verse on a birthday so late in life. His ambition was "to have some poem or poems in a good anthology like the Golden Treasury." Thus the poems, though they are the work of a lifetime, are in their final form the product of Hardy's late career.

Yet these poems are not the serene and mellow harvest of a successful literary career. Hardy turned to poetry in mid-career after the hostile critical reception of *Jude the Obscure* (1895); after that, he resolved to write no more novels. Instead, his poems extend and concentrate the often bitter and fatalistic tone and mood of his fiction. His verse reflects the weariness and discouragement of his Wessex characters, who have faced the worst that life can offer and cherish no illusions about what the future may bring. Many deal with love entanglements and marital difficulties. Others are cynical poems about human failings or brooding meditations on aging, loss, and death. Even his nature poems are elegiac in tone, presenting a Darwinian view of harsh competition for survival in a brutal and indifferent world. One critic has remarked that Hardy's vision reflects "his sense of the irreconcilable disparity between the way things ought to be and the way they are: the failure of the universe to answer man's need for order."

Although Hardy may have lacked the buoyant optimism of Robert Browning or the sturdy faith of Alfred, Lord Tennyson, there is no lack of emotional depth in his poems. Hardy had an instinctive sense of the emotional basis of all good poetry. Temperamentally, he found the Wordsworthian formula of "emotion recollected in tranquillity" a continual source of creative inspiration. He had a keen emotional memory, and even late in life, he could recall the poignancy of incidents that had occurred a half century earlier.

His range of topics may have been limited to a purview of Wessex, but he selected his poetic incidents or anecdotes on the basis of their emotional appeal and concentrated on evoking the essence of a mood or feeling. His wife recalled his remark that "poetry is emotion put into measure. The emotion must come by nature, but the measure can be acquired by art."

Hardy served his apprenticeship in Gothic architecture, and the same careful attention to detail that marked his church designs is evident in his subtle metrical variations. Although he experimented with a variety of stanzaic forms—the villanelle, triolet, and sapphic—he was partial to the ballad form and the common measure of hymn stanzas. He affected simplicity in his verse, favoring a subtle irregularity and practicing "the art of concealing art." Florence Hardy wrote:

> He knew that in architecture cunning irregularity is of enormous worth, and it is obvious that he carried on into his verse, perhaps in part unconsciously, the gothic art-principle in which he had been trained—the principle of spontaneity, found in mouldings, tracery, and such like—resulting in the "unforseen" . . . character of his metres and stanzas, that of stress rather than of syllable, poetic texture rather than poetic veneer.

Hardy is thus paradoxically the last of the great Victorians and the first of the moderns—at once traditional in style and modern in thought, attitude, and feeling. He laments the passing of the timeless relation of the countryman to the soil in his native Wessex and anticipates the confusion and bewilderment of the characters in his poems, who think in new ways but continue to feel in the old ways. Like Robert Frost, he writes of a diminished world, in which science has undercut traditional ways of thinking and believing. He shares much with the Georgian poets, who were younger than himself; their subdued lyricism, their dread of the Great War, their nostalgic pastoralism, and their sense of undefined loss and privation. What is unique in his vision is the compassion that he expresses for the victims of this changed world: his deep sense of their human plight and their loss of traditional sources of consolation. Hardy described himself once as less of a doubter or agnostic than "churchy" in an old-fashioned way: a person for whom the traditional sources of faith had disappeared yet who dreamed of "giving liturgical form to modern ideas." It is ironic that, when asked late in life whether he would have chosen the same career again, Hardy replied that he would rather have been "a small architect in a country town," so deep was his love of church architecture and the grace and ornateness of the gothic style.

Biography

Thomas Hardy was born on June 2, 1840, in a rambling, seven-room cottage in Higher Bockhampton, on the edge of Bockhampton Heath, near Dorchester. He was the eldest of four children, with a sister, Mary, born in 1841, a brother, Henry, in 1851, and a sister, Kate, in 1856. His father, also named Thomas, was a master builder and mason with a love of church music and violin playing, and his mother Jemima (née Hand) Hardy was a handsome, energetic woman of country stock who loved books and reading. At birth, their first child was so frail that he was supposed dead; but an attending nurse rescued the baby, and his mother and aunt nursed him back to health, although Thomas remained a small, delicate child, physically immature in appearance until well into adulthood. Despite his frail appearance, Thomas was a vigorous, active boy who relished village life and freely roamed the heath behind his home. As a child, he so enjoyed the country dance tunes and melodies his father played that he was given a toy accordion at the age of four and was taught to play the fiddle as soon as he could finger the strings. The Church of England service strongly moved him and sometimes on wet Sunday mornings he would enact the service at home, wrapping himself in a tablecloth and reading the morning prayer to his cousin and grandmother, who pretended to be the congregation.

At the age of eight, Hardy began his schooling at the local school in Bockhampton, recently established by the lady of the manor. The boy was a quick pupil, and after a year, he was transferred to Isaac Last's Nonconformist Latin School near Bockhampton. There he continued until the age of sixteen, when he was apprenticed to the ecclesiastical architect John Hicks. During this time, he played at country dances with his father and uncle and taught Sunday school at the local parish. After his formal schooling ended, Hardy continued to study Latin and Greek with his fellow apprentices. Hardy also began writing verses about this time, being especially impressed with the regional dialect poetry of the Reverend William Barnes, a Dorset poet. After continuing his apprenticeship in church architecture for almost six years, Hardy finally left Bockhampton for London at the age of twenty-one.

In the spring of 1862, Hardy arrived in London with two letters of introduction in his pocket, having decided to continue his study of architecture there. Through good fortune, he found temporary work with a London friend of Hicks, who was able to recommend Hardy to the noted ecclesiastical architect John Blomfield, with whom Hardy began work as an assistant in the drawing-office. Hardy persevered in his architectural training, and within a year he won a prize offered by the Royal Institute of British Architects for his essay on the uses of glazed bricks and terra cotta in modern architecture. Blomfield's office was within walking distance of the National Gallery, and Hardy soon began spending his lunch hours there, studying one painting carefully each day. He especially admired the landscapes of J. M. W. Turner and the Flemish masters.

Work was light under Blomfield, and young Hardy found time to write his first sketch, "How I Built Myself a House," which he published in *Chambers's Journal* in 1865. He also continued writing poetry during this time, although little of his juvenilia has survived. In the evenings, he continued his education at King's College in London, studying French. For a brief time, he even considered applying to Cambridge to study for the ministry, but he gave up the idea as impractical.

The confinement of life in London gradually sapped Hardy's health, and within five years, he was advised to return to Bockhampton to recuperate. There he assisted his former employer John Hicks with church restorations and soon regained his health. With time on his hands, Hardy turned to fiction and began working on his first novel, *The Poor Man and the Lady*. In 1870, he sent the manuscript to a London publisher, whose editor, George Meredith, praised the young writer but urged him to try something else with more plot ingenuity and suspense. This Hardy did, and ten months later finished his second novel, *Desperate Remedies*, which unfortunately was also initially rejected before it was published in 1871.

In the meantime, Hicks had sold his firm to another architect, G. R. Crickmay, who engaged Hardy to complete some church restorations in Cornwall. Hardy moved with the firm to Weymouth and, in March, 1870, set off to Cornwall to inspect a dilapidated gothic church at St. Juliot. There he met Emma Gifford, the young sister-in-law of the rector, who was eventually to become his first wife. At this time Hardy was already engaged to his cousin Tryphena Sparks, a young schoolteacher, but their engagement was broken after he met Gifford.

Although Hardy did complete his supervision of the church restoration at St. Juliot, his interest was gradually shifting from architecture to literature, and he began writing fiction in earnest. *Under the Greenwood Tree* was published in 1872, followed by *A Pair of Blue Eyes* (1872-1873) and *Far From the Madding Crowd* (1874). He was now sure enough of his future to marry Gifford in London on September 17, 1874, and after their honeymoon in France, he settled down to begin *The Return of the Native* (1878).

The next ten years saw the publication of five more novels and a number of short stories, strengthening his reputation as a major writer. He also continued to write poetry but withheld most of it from publication until after 1897. As their means grew, the Hardys moved back to Dorchester and built their permanent home, Max Gate. Hardy began making notes for an epic treatment of the Napoleonic Wars, eventually to become *The Dynasts*. Unfortunately, the Hardys had no children. This may have put a strain on their marriage, for although Emma Hardy continued to serve as her husband's secretary, making fair copies of his manuscripts for publication, she gradually drew apart from him and became embittered, perhaps resenting his success. Their marriage became a cold formality of two people living in separate rooms and seeing each other only at meals. The difficulties of this first marriage may have been reflected in the bleakness of Hardy's outlook.

After the Hardys moved into Max Gate in June, 1885, he embarked on his last decade of fiction writing. This period saw the publication of another five novels and approximately fifty short stories. *The Mayor of Casterbridge* (1886) was followed by *The Woodlanders* (1886-1887), *Tess of the D'Urbervilles* (1891), *Jude the Obscure*, and *The Well-Beloved* (1897). The multivolume edition of the Wessex novels also appeared in 1895-1896. During this time, Hardy was writing virtually a novel a year.

Hardy had ventured to treat new material in *Jude the Obscure*, and the uniformly hostile critical reception accorded the novel led him to put aside fiction after 1897 and embark on a second literary career as a poet. For the next thirty-one years, he would write only poetry. During that time, he published eight volumes of poetry, at least some of it early work, and the epic-drama *The Dynasts*. Hardy began to be recognized as a major English writer and received a number of awards, including honorary degrees from Aberdeen, Cambridge, and Oxford.

Emma Hardy died at Max Gate on November 27, 1912, and during his bereavement, Hardy visited the scenes of their courtship. Two years later, he married Florence Emily Dugdale, a young admirer who had served as his personal secretary after his wife's death. By this time, he was universally recognized as the last great Victorian writer and the preeminent English man of letters, although his lack of reputation abroad prevented him from receiving a Nobel Prize. Despite personal misgivings, he spoke out patriotically for England during World War I. After the war, he lived quietly with his second wife at Max Gate during the last decade of his life. In 1923, he published a second verse play, *The Famous Tragedy of the Queen of Cornwall*, based on the romance of Tristan and Iseult. After a brief illness, Hardy died on January 11, 1928. His heart was buried in the grave of his first wife in their parish churchyard in Stinsford, and his ashes were installed in the Poets' Corner, Westminster Abbey. After his death, Florence Hardy published a two-volume biography that her husband had dictated to her. She died on October 17, 1937.

Analysis

More than one critic has called the lyrics in *Satires of Circumstance* Thomas Hardy's finest achievement, although his most notable poems are probably distributed evenly among his eight volumes. Since there was no period of peak creative achievement for him—rather, a steady accumulation of poems over a long and productive career—the reader must search among the collected verse for those poems in which Hardy's style, vision, and subject matter coincide in a memorable work. Given the strength and originality of his vision, it is difficult to speak of influences on Hardy's poetry, although in many respects he carries forward the Romantic tradition of William Wordsworth and Percy Bysshe Shelley and the homey realism of George Crabbe. An obscure Dorset poet, William Barnes, whose poetry Hardy edited in 1908, may have first introduced him to the possibilities of writing regional poetry. Barnes was a clergyman and philologist with a keen interest in local dialects who introduced vivid scenes of Wessex life into his verse. Hardy read and admired Algernon Charles Swinburne and paid tribute to him on numerous occasions, notably in "A Singer Asleep," although his influence on Hardy appears to have been slight. Hardy's poetry is perhaps most akin in tone and spirit to Wordsworth's pastoral lyrics and odes, particularly "Michael," although Hardy's characters often lack the simple heroism and nobility of spirit of Wordsworth's protagonists.

WESSEX POEMS, AND OTHER VERSES

The appearance of Hardy's first volume of poetry, *Wessex Poems, and Other Verses*, was greeted by the critics with scarcely more understanding than that which had been accorded to *Jude the Obscure*. The fifty-one selections are a mixture of lyrics, sonnets, and ballads illustrated by the poet with thirty-one "Sketches of Their Scenes," designed to accompany the poems. The volume includes five historical poems in a ballad sequence about the Napoleonic Wars that anticipate *The Dynasts*; a series of four "She, To Him" love sonnets written in the Shakespearean manner; a number of lyrics on disillusioned love, of which "Neutral Tones" is probably the best; and a set of meditative nature poems, including the sonnet "Hap" and "Nature's Questioning." An additional group of lyrics enlarges on scenes from the novels, including the lovely "In a Wood," which echoes a nature description from *The Woodlanders*, and "The Ivy Wife," a figurative portrait of a possessive wife that borrows its metaphor from a description in that same novel.

"Neutral Tones" is the most frequently anthologized of Hardy's *Wessex Poems, and Other Verses*, and deservedly so. This four-quatrain lyric, rhyming *abba*, employs a series of muted winter images and a pond-side meeting to describe the death of a love affair. The implied confession by the beloved that she is no longer in love creates the dramatic occasion, and although the pronoun employed is "we," the point of view is clearly that of the forsaken lover. The poem possesses that haunting quality of a painful moment forever etched on one's memory: The colorless imagery of the setting suggests an impressionistic painting of two lovers meeting against a dreary December landscape in which nature's barrenness ("starving sod," "greyish leaves") serves as a counterpoint to the death of love. Even the negations of Hardy's poetic syntax combine with the winter imagery and the bitter dramatic occasion to sustain the mood of "Neutral Tones." This poignant lyric about the failure of a love relationship was written, interestingly enough, just before Hardy's engagement to his cousin Tryphena Sparks was broken, perhaps because he discovered her infatuation with his friend Horace Maule. This theme of love's betrayal is of course also found often in Hardy's novels, although it achieves greater intensity and concentration in poems such as "Neutral Tones."

"Hap," a sonnet about the forces that shape events unpredictably, records Hardy's troubled response to evolutionary theory, with its view of natural selection operating impartially, without purpose or direction. The speaker would prefer a personalized universe, even with "some Vengeful god," who wills and controls the course of events, rather than "Crass Casualty," "dicing Time," and "These purblind doomsters" who mete out bliss and pain alike without reason. "Hap" is thematically related to "Nature's Questioning," which implies that the author of the universe is "some Vast Imbecility" unconscious of human pains. This poem was so often quoted against him as evidence of his alleged atheism and hostility to religion that Hardy finally decided to write a preface for his second volume explaining that his poems taken individually did not necessarily reflect his personal philosophy. He later restated this disavowal in the preface to *Winter Words in Various Moods and Metres*; still, many of his poems did seem to invite speculation about his personal views. "Heiress and Architect," for example, is a philosophical allegory cast in terms of a dialogue between two speakers representing romantic and realistic views of life. The heiress finds her elaborate plans diminished in each succeeding stanza as she submits them to the cold scrutiny of the architect. Her house designs progressively shrink in this allegory of human dreams crushed by realities, a theme familiar to Hardy's novels.

POEMS OF THE PAST AND PRESENT

Hardy's second volume, *Poems of the Past and Present*, comprising a hundred poems, is nearly twice as long as *Wessex Poems, and Other Verses*. Two major sections include "War Poems," dealing with the Boer War, and "Poems of Pilgrimage," about notable historical and literary shrines in Italy and Switzerland, where the Hardys had traveled in the spring of 1882; a third section was composed of "Miscellaneous Poems." The "War Poems" record Hardy's deep reservations about British imperialism and the cost of war to ordinary men; "Drummer Hodge" is about a boy drafted from Dorset and fated to lie after his death under southern constellations. Among the "Miscellaneous Poems," "The Last Chrysanthemum" and "The Darkling Thrush" are incomparably the best. The first describes a perennial blooming out of season, into the winter, past the time when it should have flowered. This curious natural event becomes the occasion for a lyrical meditation on the mysteries of growth and change that regulate the life of each organism. Hardy continues the English tradition of the nature lyric, although in a much more subdued form than, for example, Wordsworth's "I Wandered Lonely as a Cloud." Instead of drawing inspiration from a simple vernal scene, Hardy records a more complex response to a post-Darwinian natural world that can no longer be identified with a beneficent Creator. In the final stanza of "The Last Chrysanthemum," however, he seems unwilling to discard entirely the notion of a deliberate, shaping purpose, even though the poem's affirmation is tentative at best.

This metaphor of unseasonableness is carried forward in "The Darkling Thrush," perhaps Hardy's finest lyric. Here tone, mood, theme, subject, and setting coincide to shape a nearly flawless meditation on the dawning of a new century. Hardy's thrush is his solitary singer, the projection of the speaker's hopes and the spirit of his age, which in the midst of a bleak winter landscape, an image of the times, finds reason to fling his song against the gathering darkness of the coming age. Hardy employs the traditional formula of the romantic inspirational lyric: the speaker's despondency, the corresponding gloom of the natural landscape, then the sudden change of mood within the lyric, in this case in the third octave, after the glimpse of a seemingly trivial natural event, the sight of a single thrush singing in a copse against the winter twilight. Yet this poem does not achieve the triumphant resolution of Percy Bysshe Shelley's "To a Sky-lark" or

John Keats's "Ode to a Nightingale"; instead, the concluding octave is curiously equivocal, even subversive of traditional consolations. The speaker still finds little cause for rejoicing; he simply pauses to marvel at the anomaly of the thrush's song against so bleak a setting. There is something so casual and disarming about the country setting, with the speaker leaning musingly on a "coppice gate" and quietly reflecting on the starkness of the December landscape, that readers may at first miss the implicit irony in his response to the thrush's "caroling." Was it merely an illusion to find cause for hope in the bird's song? The poem's deliberate ambiguity resists any easy interpretation, but it would be unlike Hardy to offer glib reassurances.

Time's Laughingstocks, and Other Verses

Time's Laughingstocks, and Other Verses includes ninety-four poems in four groupings: "Time's Laughingstocks," "More Love Lyrics," "A Set of Country Songs," and "Pieces Occasional and Various." Most of the selections are rustic character sketches and ballads of uneven quality, although Hardy considered one of the ballads, "A Trampwoman's Tragedy," to be perhaps "his most successful poem." It is a country tale of jealousy, murder, and a hanging that leaves the speaker alone in the world, without her "fancy-man," to haunt the hills and moors in which the deeds took place.

Satires of Circumstance

Satires of Circumstance continues the pattern of Hardy's earlier volumes of poetry, with 106 poems in four sections: "Lyrics and Reveries," comprising religious and philosophic meditations; "Poems of 1912-13," recollections of his courtship of Emma Gifford; "Miscellaneous Pieces"; and "Satires of Circumstance in Fifteen Glimpses." Two of the poems in the first section, "Channel Firing" and "The Convergence of the Twain," are among his most popular poems. Written three months before the outbreak of World War I, "Channel Firing" contains an ironic premonition of the impending conflict. The poem is narrated from the point of view of the dead in their coffins in a country churchyard, suddenly awakened by the "great guns" at sea. The nine stanzas in common measure present an ironic view of the futility and inevitability of war, with even God unable to prevent the ensuing bloodshed. All he can do is to reassure the frightened souls that "judgment-hour" is not at hand; the noise comes only from the naval guns practicing in the English Channel off the Dorset Coast.

Hardy wrote "The Convergence of the Twain" to commemorate the sinking of the luxury liner *Titanic* on April 14-15, 1912, after the ship collided with an iceberg on its maiden voyage across the Atlantic. He uses eleven stanzas of triplet rhyme with an extended third line to develop the theme and counterpoint of the human vanity ("Pride of Life") that boasted of building an unsinkable ship and "The Immanent Will" that prepared an iceberg to meet it by "paths coincident" on the night they were fated to collide. A retrospective narration in the first five stanzas pictures the sunken ship with its jewels and elegant furnishings now the home of grotesque sea-worms and "moon-eyed fishes." The final six stanzas recount the inevitable steps toward the final encounter as the two "mates"—ship and iceberg—move inexorably toward each other. A grim determinism seems to stalk this symbol of human arrogance and pride as the ship that even God "could not sink" goes down on its first voyage.

After the death of his first wife, Hardy wrote a series of elegies to Emma Gifford in his "Poems of 1912-13." The best of these may be "Voices," with its poignant recall of his first impressions of her as a young woman in Cornwall, its haunting dactylic tetrameters, and its lovely refrain. Here also Hardy projects much of his sadness and regret for their embittered relationship later in their marriage and for the series of misunderstandings that drove them apart. In "The Voice," he tries to recapture the joy of his earliest memories of his wife as she was during their courtship.

Perhaps the harshest portrait in *Satires of Circumstance* is Hardy's depiction of the hypocritical clergyman, who, "In Church," is discovered after the service by one of his Bible students, practicing before a mirror the flourishes and gestures that "had moved the congregation so."

MOMENTS OF VISION AND MISCELLANEOUS VERSES

Moments of Vision and Miscellaneous Verses, with 159 poems, is Hardy's largest volume, including a substantial body of reflective personal poems and an additional seventeen selections about World War I titled "Poems of War and Patriotism." Several of these lyrics are worth mentioning: "Heredity," with its glimpse of family traits that leap from generation to generation; "The Oxen," a frequently anthologized poem narrating a common folk legend about how the barnyard animals were said to kneel in adoration of the nativity on Christmas Eve; "For Life I Had Never Cared Greatly," a confession of Hardy's personal disillusionment; and "In Time of 'The Breaking of Nations,'" about how life, work, and love continue despite the ravages of war.

LATER POETRY

Two more volumes were yet to appear during Hardy's lifetime. Now in his eighties, he published *Late Lyrics and Earlier*, a collection of 151 lyrical incidents and impressions; three years later *Human Shows, Far Phantasies, Songs, and Trifles* appeared, with 152 poems. His last volume, *Winter Words in Various Moods and Metres*, was published posthumously by Florence Hardy. There is a sameness about these late poems that makes it difficult to select particular ones for discussion. A few show sparks of creative novelty, but many are recapitulations of earlier themes or material gleaned from notebooks or recollections during the time that Hardy was dictating his two-volume biography to his wife.

In *Late Lyrics and Earlier*, "A Drizzling Easter Morning" records a skeptic's response to the Easter resurrection on a day when rain falls and rural life continues unabated. "Christmas: 1924" from *Winter Words in Various Moods and Metres* draws a stark contrast between humankind's perennial hopes for peace on Earth and its use of poison gas in modern warfare; "He Never Expected Much" sums up the poet's personal philosophy; and "He Resolves to Say No More" expresses a tired old man's farewell to life, in which he refuses to offer any last words of insight. Perhaps this mood simply reflected his age and illness, but Hardy's last poem lacks the resoluteness of, for example, William Butler Yeats's "Under Ben Bulben."

THE DYNASTS

At one time, *The Dynasts* was hailed as Hardy's major achievement, although critics have since revised their judgment of this massive verse drama, "in three parts, nineteen acts, and one hundred and thirty scenes," of the Napoleonic Wars. Hardy subtitled his work "A Drama of the Napoleonic Wars," although he meant to glorify the British role in checking the French emperor's dynastic ambitions. In the play, he presents an allegorical view of history as a relentless, deterministic pageant in which human beings, mere automatons, enact the designs of the Immanent Will. Ever since his youth, Hardy had been planning a literary project involving the Napoleonic Wars, although he was unsure what form the work would eventually take. The final epic-drama, which he undertook in his sixties, is conceived on the grand scale of Shelley's *Prometheus Unbound: A Lyrical Drama in Four Acts* (pb. 1820), with the historical sweep of Leo Tolstoy's *War and Peace* (1865-1869), and though the work is unevenly executed, in places flawed by excessive allegory, and perhaps even inaccessible to the modern reader, it contains many impressive scenes.

From his early plans for an "*Iliad* of Europe from 1789 to 1815," Hardy evolved a dramatic form flexible enough to allow rapid panoramic shifts in scene that traced the paths of marching armies across the map of Europe and recorded the plots and intrigues of Napoleon as he schemed to strengthen his military domination. A chorus of Spirits or Phantom Intelligences introduce and conclude the scenes and interweave their comments with the human action below. What is most impressive, however, is Hardy's historical knowledge of the Napoleonic period, combined with his innate repugnance for war and his deep compassion for the victims of the clash of nations. His controlling vision, here and throughout his poetry, was of the continuity and sameness of the human spirit everywhere. As he observed about *The Dynasts*: "The human race [is] to be shown as one great network or tissue which quivers in every part when one point is shaken, like a spider's web if touched."

OTHER MAJOR WORKS

LONG FICTION: *Desperate Remedies*, 1871; *Under the Greenwood Tree*, 1872; *A Pair of Blue Eyes*, 1872-1873; *Far from the Madding Crowd*, 1874; *The Hand of Ethelberta*, 1875-1876; *An Indiscretion in the Life of an Heiress*, 1878 (serial), 1934 (book); *The Return of the Native*, 1878; *The Trumpet-Major*, 1880; *A Laodicean*, 1880-1881; *Two on a Tower*, 1882; *The Mayor of Casterbridge*, 1886; *The Woodlanders*, 1886-1887; *Tess of the D'Urbervilles*, 1891; *Jude the Obscure*, 1895; *The Well-Beloved*, 1897.

SHORT FICTION: *Wessex Tales*, 1888; *A Group of Noble Dames*, 1891; *Life's Little Ironies*, 1894; *A Changed Man, The Waiting Supper, and Other Tales*, 1913; *The Complete Short Stories*, 1989 (Desmond Hawkins, editor).

PLAYS: *The Dynasts: A Drama of the Napoleonic Wars*, pb. 1903, 1906, 1908, 1910 (verse drama); *The Famous Tragedy of the Queen of Cornwall*, pr., pb. 1923 (one act).

NONFICTION: *Life and Art*, 1925 (Ernest Brennecke, editor); *The Early Life of Thomas Hardy*, 1928; *The Later Years of Thomas Hardy*, 1930; *Personal Writings*, 1966 (Harold Orel, editor); *The Collected Letters of Thomas Hardy*, 1978-1988 (7 volumes; Richard Little Purdy and Michael Millgate, editors).

BIBLIOGRAPHY

Armstrong, Tim. *Haunted Hardy: Poetry, History, Memory*. New York: Palgrave, 2000. An attempt to elevate Hardy as poet within the Western tradition.

Gibson, James. *Thomas Hardy*. New York: St. Martin's Press, 1996. An introductory guide to Hardy's art, focusing on how Hardy used his own experience in his writing and tracing his development from fiction back to his first love, poetry.

Kramer, Dale, ed. *The Cambridge Companion to Thomas Hardy*. New York: Cambridge University Press, 1999. An essential introduction and general overview of all Hardy's work and specific demonstrations of Hardy's ideas and literary skills. Individual essays explore Hardy's biography, aesthetics, and the impact on his work of developments in science, religion, and philosophy in the late nineteenth century. The volume also contains a detailed chronology of Hardy's life.

Lanzano, Ellen Anne. *Hardy: The Temporal Poetics*. New York: Peter Lang, 1999. An examination of Hardy's poetics in the light of the temporal context out of which he wrote more than nine hundred poems. To a large extent, Hardy's struggle with the forms of time is a record of the nineteenth century engagement with the relationship of consciousness to the new science and the loss of traditional beliefs.

Mallett, Phillip, ed. *The Achievement of Thomas Hardy*. New York: St. Martin's Press, 2000. A study of the literary achievements of Hardy that also examines his depiction of Wessex. Bibliography and index.

Maynard, Katherine Kearney. *Thomas Hardy's Tragic Poetry: The Lyrics and "The Dynasts."* Iowa City: University of Iowa Press, 1991. This study examines the question of tragic literature's vitality in a secular age and explores the philosophical underpinnings of Hardy's tragic vision in his lyric poetry and in *The Dynasts*. It also examines Hardy's efforts within the context of nineteenth century poetry.

Millgate, Michael. *Thomas Hardy: A Biography Revisited*. New York: Oxford University Press, 2004. This biography enhances and replaces Millgate's 1982 biography, considered to be one of the best and most scholarly Hardy biographies available.

Page, Norman, ed. *Oxford Reader's Companion to Hardy*. New York: Oxford University Press, 2000. An encyclopedia devoted to the life and literary works of Hardy. Bibliography.

Ray, Martin, ed. *Thomas Hardy Remembered*. London: Ashgate, 2007. A collection of interviews with Hardy and recollections of him by his friends and acquaintances offer readers a fresh perspective on the writer. Also contains observations by Hardy on his writing and his contemporaries' opinions about his life.

Tomalin, Claire. *Thomas Hardy*. New York: Penguin, 2007. This thorough and finely written biography by a respected Hardy scholar illuminates the poet's drive to indict the malice, neglect, and ignorance of his fellow human creatures. Tomalin nicely brings Hardy's poetry to the fore in discussing aspects of his life that are apparent in his literary works.

Andrew J. Angyal

GERARD MANLEY HOPKINS

Born: Stratford, England; July 28, 1844
Died: Dublin, Ireland; June 8, 1889

PRINCIPAL POETRY
Poems of Gerard Manley Hopkins, Now First Published, with Notes by Robert Bridges, 1918
Poems of Gerard Manley Hopkins, 1930, 1948, 1967
The Poetical Works of Gerard Manley Hopkins, 1990

OTHER LITERARY FORMS

Gerard Manley Hopkins's letters and papers were published in six volumes that appeared between 1935 and 1959: *The Letters of Gerard Manley Hopkins to Robert Bridges* (1935, 1955; C. C. Abbott, editor), *The Correspondence of Gerard Manley Hopkins and Richard Watson Dixon* (1935, 1955; Abbott, editor), *The Notebooks and Papers of Gerard Manley Hopkins* (1937; Humphry House, editor), *Further Letters of Gerard Manley Hopkins* (1938, 1956; Abbott, editor), *The Journals and Papers of Gerard Manley Hopkins* (1959; House and Graham Storey, editors), and *The Sermons and Devotional Writings of Gerard Manley Hopkins* (1959; Christopher Devlin, editor). A selection of letters from the three volumes edited by Abbott, *Gerard Manley Hopkins: Selected Letters*, was published in 1990. Edited by Catherine Phillips, the letters include many analyses of the work of other poets and artists; they also reveal his bouts of "melancholy," or depression, and implicitly show his internal struggles between his religion and his work as a poet. In addition to the published material, there are significant unpublished lecture notes and documents by Hopkins at the Bodleian Library and the Campion Hall Library at Oxford University.

ACHIEVEMENTS

Although Gerard Manley Hopkins saw almost none of his writings published in his lifetime, he is generally credited with being one of the founders of modern poetry and a major influence on the development of modernism in art. Many of his letters reflect a sense of failure and frustration. "The Wreck of the *Deutschland*," which he considered to be his most important poem, was rejected by the Jesuit magazine *The Month*. As a professor of classical languages and literature, he was not a productive, publishing scholar. As a priest, his sermons and theological writing did not find popular success. Yet in 1918, some thirty years after his death, his friend Robert Bridges published a collection of his poems. By 1930, when the second edition of this volume appeared, Hopkins had begun to attract the attention of major theoreticians of modernism: Herbert

Gerard Manley Hopkins
(Library of Congress)

Read, William Empson, I. A. Richards, and F. R. Leavis. They acclaimed Hopkins as a powerful revolutionary force in poetry. Interest in his poetry led scholars to unearth his scattered letters and papers. Here, too, modern readers found revolutionary concepts: inscape, instress, sprung rhythm, underthought/overthought, counterpoint. Since about 1930, an enormous amount of scholarly analysis has combed through Hopkins's poetry and prose, establishing beyond doubt that he is one of the three or four most influential forces in modern English literature.

Biography

Gerard Manley Hopkins was the first of eight children born to Manley Hopkins, a successful marine insurance agent who wrote poetry and technical books. The family was closely knit and artistic. Two of Hopkins's brothers became professional artists, and Hopkins's papers contain many pencil sketches showing his own talent for drawing. He was devoted to his youngest sister, Grace, who was an accomplished musician, and he tried to learn several musical instruments as well as counterpoint and musical composition. The family was devoutly Anglican in religion. When Hopkins was eight years old, they moved from the London suburb of Stratford (Essex) to the more fashionable and affluent Hampstead on the north edge of the city.

From 1854 to 1863, Hopkins attended Highgate Grammar School. Richard Watson Dixon, a young teacher there, later became one of Hopkins's main literary associates. Hopkins studied Latin and Greek intensively, winning the Governor's Gold Medal for Latin Verse, as well as the Headmaster's Poetry Prize in 1860 for his English poem "The Escorial." His school years seem to have been somewhat stormy, marked by the bittersweet joy of schoolboy friendships and the excitement of a keen mind mastering the intricacies of Greek, Latin, and English poetry. He was such a brilliant student that he won the Balliol College Exhibition, or scholarship prize. Balliol was reputed to be the leading college for classical studies at Oxford University in the 1860's. Hopkins attended Balliol from April, 1863, until June, 1867, studying "Classical Greats," the philosophy, literature, and language of ancient Greece and Rome. The first year of this curriculum required rigorous study of the structure of the Latin and Greek languages. This linguistic study terminated with a very demanding examination, in which Hopkins earned a grade of "first" in December, 1864. The remaining years of his program involved the study of the philosophy and literature of ancient writers in their original tongues, concluding with the final honors examination. Hopkins concluded his B.A. (Hons.) with a "first" in June, 1867. A double first in "Classical Greats" is a remarkable accomplishment. Benjamin Jowett, the Master of Balliol and himself a famous classical scholar, called Hopkins "The Star of Balliol" and all who knew him at this period predicted a brilliant career for him. Hopkins loved Oxford—its landscapes and personalities, the life of culture and keen intellectual striving—and always looked back to his college days with nostalgia. His schoolmate there was Robert Bridges, who was to be his lifelong friend and correspondent.

These years were not peaceful, however, for the promising young scholar and poet. The colleges of Oxford University were then religious institutions. Only Anglicans could enroll as students or teach there. For some thirty years before Hopkins entered Balliol, Oxford University had been rocked by the Oxford Movement. A number of its illustrious teachers had questioned the very basis of the Anglican Church, the way in which the Church of England could claim to be independent of the Roman Catholic Church. Many of the leading figures of the Oxford Movement had felt compelled to leave Oxford and the Church of England and to convert to Roman Catholicism. Among the converts was Cardinal John Henry Newman, whose *Apologia pro Vita Sua*, or history of his conversion from the Anglican to the Roman Church, was published in 1864, the year Hopkins was preparing for his Moderations at Balliol. To follow Newman's lead meant to give up hope of an academic career at Oxford, and perhaps even the hope of completing his B.A. Nevertheless, by 1866 Hopkins was convinced that the only true church was the Roman. In October, 1866, he was received into the Roman Catholic Church by Newman himself. It is hard for modern readers to imagine the pain and dislocation this decision caused Hopkins. His family letters reveal the anguish of his father, who believed that his son's immortal soul was lost, not merely his temporal career. Hopkins was estranged from his family to some degree ever after his momentous conversion. After he had completed his B.A. at Oxford, Hopkins taught in 1867 at Newman's Oratory School, a Roman Catholic grammar school near Birmingham. There he decided to enter a religious order. In May, 1868, he burned all manuscripts of his poems, thinking that poetry was not a fit occupation for a seriously religious person. Fortunately, some of his early writing survived in copies he had given to Robert Bridges. He wrote no further poetry until "The Wreck of the *Deutschland*."

In the summer of 1867, he went on a walking tour of Switzerland. In that September, he entered the Jesuit Novitiate, Manresa House, London, for the first two years of rigorous spiritual training to become a Jesuit priest. There he followed the regime of the *Ejercicios espirituales* (1548; *The Spiritual Exercises*, 1736) of Saint Ignatius of Loyola (1491-1556), taking vows of poverty, chastity, and obedience. From 1870 to 1873, he studied philosophy at St. Mary's Hall, Stonyhurst, in the North of England. Although Hopkins had been a brilliant student of classical philosophy at Oxford, he seems not to have pleased his Jesuit superiors so well. Perhaps part of the problem was an independence of mind that could be disconcerting. At Stonyhurst, he first read the medieval philosopher John Duns Scotus, who had an unusually strong influence on Hopkins. He then returned to Manresa House for a year as professor of rhetoric. From 1874 to 1878, he studied theology at St. Bueno's College in Wales. There he began to write poetry again when he heard of the wreck of a German ship, the *Deutschland*, and the death of five Catholic nuns aboard.

It is the custom in the Jesuit order to move priests from one location to another frequently and to try them out in a variety of posts. In the next few years, Hopkins tried many different kinds of religious work without remarkable success. He was assigned to preach in the fashionable Farm Street Church in London's West End, but he was not a charismatic or crowd-pleasing performer. Parish work in the Liverpool slums left him depressed and exhausted. When he was assigned temporarily to the Catholic parish church in Oxford, he seemed to have had trouble getting along with his superior. Finally, he was appointed professor of Greek and Latin literature at University College, Dublin, Ireland. He held this post until his death in 1889. The Catholic population of Ireland at that time was in near-revolt against English oppression. Hopkins felt a conflict between his English patriotism and his Catholic sympathies. Although he had been a brilliant student as a young man, the University College duties gave him little opportunity to do gratifying scholarly work. Much of his time was spent in the drudgery of external examinations, grading papers of hundreds of students he had never taught. His lectures were attended by only a handful of students. He projected massive books for himself to write, but never was able to put them together. In this period, he wrote many sonnets that show spiritual desolation, unhappiness, and alienation. He died of typhoid in 1889 at the age of forty-five. Not until a generation later did the literary world recognize his genius.

ANALYSIS

In 1875, a number of Roman Catholic religious people had been driven out of Germany by the Falck Laws. In the winter of that year, five exiled nuns took passage on the *Deutschland*, which ran aground in a snowstorm near the Kentish shore of England. The ship gradually broke up in the high seas and many lives were lost, including those of the nuns. Their bodies were brought to England for solemn funeral ceremonies and the whole affair was widely reported in the newspapers. At this time, Gerard Manley Hopkins was studying theology at St. Bueno's College in Wales. He read the reports in the press, and many details in his poem reflect the newspapers' accounts. He seems especially to have noticed the report that, as passengers were being swept off the deck into the icy seas by towering waves, the tallest of the five nuns rose up above the others just before her death and cried out for Christ to come quickly to her. Hopkins discussed this fearful catastrophe with his rector, who suggested that someone should write a poem about it. Taking that hint as a command, Hopkins broke his self-imposed poetic silence and began to write again. The experience of the tall nun at her moment of death captured his imagination. How frightening and cruel it must have been to be on the deck of the shattered ship! Yet she was a faithful Catholic servant of God. How could God torment her so? What did she mean when she cried out for Christ to come to her as the fatal waves beat down on her?

"THE WRECK OF THE DEUTSCHLAND"

"The Wreck of the *Deutschland*" is a very difficult poem. Unlike the smooth sentences of Tennyson's *In Memoriam* (1850), for example, Hopkins's elegy is contorted, broken, sometimes opaque. When Robert Bridges published the first volume of Hopkins's poems in 1918, he warned readers that "The Wreck of the *Deutschland*" was like a great dragon lying at the gate to discourage readers from going on to other, more accessible poems by Hopkins. The thread of the occasion, however, can be traced in the text. The dedication of the poem to the memory of five Franciscan nuns exiled by the Falck Laws drowned between midnight and morning of December 7, 1875, gives the reader a point of reference. If readers skip to stanza 12, the story goes ahead, following newspaper accounts of the events reasonably clearly. Stanza 12 relates that some two hundred passengers sailed from Bremen bound for the United States, never guessing that a fourth of them would drown. Stanza 13 explains how the *Deutschland* sailed into the wintry storm. Stanzas 14 and 15 tell how the ship hit a sandbank and people began to drown. Stanza 16 depicts an act of heroism in which a sailor tries to rescue a woman, but is killed; his body dangles on a rope for hours before the eyes of the sufferers. Stanzas 17 through 23 are about the tall nun. In stanza 24, the poet contrasts his own comfortable setting under a safe roof in Wales with that of the nuns who were in their death struggle on the stormy sea. He has no pain, no trial, but the tall nun is dying at that very moment. Rising up in the midst of death and destruction, she calls, "O Christ, Christ, come quickly." Stanzas 25 through 35 contemplate that scene and ask, "What did she mean?" when she called out. What was the total meaning of her agony and life? The poem therefore can be divided into three sections: Stanzas 1 to 10 constitute a prologue or invocation, stanzas 11 through 25 depict the agony of the shipwreck and the tall nun, and stanzas 25 through 35 contemplate the meaning of that event. The middle section, describing the shipwreck and the tall nun's cry, is reasonably clear. Difficult details in this section are mostly explained in the notes to the revised fourth edition of *Poems of Gerard Manley Hopkins*. There are some additional perspectives, however, which are helpful in grasping the total work.

"The Wreck of the *Deutschland*" is related to the Jesuit contemplative "composition of place" and "application of the senses." As a member of the Society of Jesus, Hopkins's daily life and devotions were shaped by the *Ejercicios espirituales* (1548; *The Spiritual Exercises*, 1736) of Saint Ignatius of Loyola. Moreover, at certain times in his career, he withdrew from the world to perform the spiritual exercises in month-long retreats of an extremely rigorous nature. One objective of the spiritual exercises is to induce an immediate, overwhelming sense of the presence of divinity in our world. The contemplative is directed by the *Spiritual Exercises* to employ the technique of "composition." For example, to get a sharper sense of the divine presence, one might contemplate the birth of Christ. First one must imagine, or compose, the scene of the Nativity in all possible detail and precision. When Christ was born, how large was the room; what animals were in the stable; where was the holy family; were they seated or standing; what was the manger like? The imagination embodies or composes the scene. The contemplative then applies his five senses systematically to the composition. What did it look like, sound like, smell like, feel like, and taste like? Such a projection of the contemplative into the very situation induces a very powerful awareness of the religious experience. "The Wreck of the *Deutschland*" is similar to such a contemplative exercise. Hopkins is trying to experience the religious truth of the nuns's sacrifice. The middle of his poem is a composition of the scene where the tall nun died. It is constructed systematically to apply the five senses. Stanza 28 depicts the struggle of the poet to put himself in the nun's place, to feel what she felt, to suffer as she suffered, to believe as she believed. At her death, she saw her Master, Christ the King. The poet tries to participate in her experience. The poem should be read in comparison with other poems of the religious meditative tradition—for example, the poetry of George Herbert, Richard Crashaw, and Henry Vaughan. Louis L. Martz in *The Poetry of Meditation: A Study in English Religious Literature of the Seventeenth Century* (1962) is the best introduction to this aspect of Hopkins's work.

COMPLEXITIES OF SPRUNG RHYTHM

In addition to the religious complexities of the poem, there are aesthetic complexities. Hopkins claimed to have discovered a new poetic form, "sprung rhythm," which he employed in "The Wreck of the *Deutschland*." Despite intense scholarly investigation of Hopkins's metrics, there is no clear agreement as to what he means by "sprung rhythm." "The Wreck of the *Deutschland*" contains thirty-five stanzas, each with eight lines of varying length. If one counts the syllables in each line, or if one counts only the accented syllables in each line, there is a rough agreement in the length of a particular line in each of the stanzas. For example, line 1 has four or five syllables in almost all stanzas. Line 8 is much longer than line 1 in all stanzas. What makes lines of varying length metrical?

It is sometimes thought that Hopkins was isolated in the Jesuit order and did not know what he was doing when he created unusual poetic forms. That is absurd, for he was a professor of classical literature and in correspondence with leading literary scholars. The best way to look at sprung rhythm is to see what Hopkins's associates thought about meter. Robert Bridges, his college friend and lifelong correspondent, studied the iambic pentameter of Milton and wrote a major book on the prosody of Milton. Bridges thought that Milton built his lines out of iambic feet, units of two syllables with the second syllable pronounced more loudly than the first. An iambic pentameter line therefore had five iambic feet, or ten syllables with the even-positioned syllables stressed more loudly than the odd-positioned ones. Lines in Miltonic pentameter that do not fit this pattern follow a few simple variations defined by Bridges. Bridges's study appears to be accurate for Milton, but clearly Hopkins is not writing poetry of this sort. The number of unstressed syllables differs widely in his lines, a condition that Bridges shows never occurs in Milton.

Another of Hopkins's correspondents, Coventry Patmore, was a leading popular Catholic poet who wrote a study of English metrics based on time, similar to the prosody of hymns. Hopkins's sprung rhythm seems more consistent with such a musical time-based pattern than with the accentual-syllabic pattern of Milton as defined by Bridges. Hopkins, as a professor of classical languages, knew the advanced linguistic work going on in that area. Greek poetry was thought to be quantitative, based on the length of vowel sounds. As a schoolboy, Hopkins had to practice translating an English passage first into Latin, then into Greek poetry, arranging the long and short vowels into acceptable feet. (Some of his Latin and Greek poetry is collected in *Poems of Gerard Manley Hopkins*.) Modern readers are not often trained to understand these models in classical languages and so do not appreciate how important they are to Hopkins's patterns in English verse. In Hopkins's unpublished papers, there are lines of Greek poetry interlined by drafts of his English poems, sometimes with arrows and doodles matching up the English and Greek phrases. It seems possible that Hopkins based his distinctive rhythms on Greek models, especially the odes of Pindar. Essentially, however, the key to sprung rhythm remains to be discovered.

PRIEST VS. POET

"The Wreck of the *Deutschland*" was submitted to the Jesuit magazine *The Month* and, after some delay, rejected for publication. Hopkins said that they "dared not" print it, although there is no need to imagine a dark conspiracy among the Jesuit authorities to silence Hopkins. It is likely that the editors of *The Month* simply found "The Wreck of the *Deutschland*" baffling in form and content. The rejection dramatizes, however, a peculiar condition in Hopkins's life. His unquestionable genius for poetry found almost no encouragement in his immediate surroundings as a Jesuit priest. His poetry is, of course, shaped by Roman Catholic imagery and is mainly devotional in nature. Without his Church and his priestly calling, he never could have written his poems. On the other hand, what he wrote was largely unappreciated by his closest associates. Ironically, this highly religious poet became famous in the twentieth century because of the praise of readers who were frequently anti-Roman Catholic. There was a central anguish in Hopkins's life, a conflict between his priestly duties and his artistic creativity. Many scholars have tried to explain how Hopkins's poetry and his priesthood fit together. Roman Catholic critics usually tend to say that the Catholic faith made Hopkins a great writer. Readers who are hostile to Catholicism tend to think that Hopkins was a serious writer in spite of extreme discouragements and restraints placed on him by his faith. The truth is probably somewhere in the middle. If Hopkins had not been severely troubled, he would have had little motivation to write. His poems show all the commonplaces of religious imagery found in much less powerful Catholic poets, such as his friend Coventry Patmore. Hopkins rises above the average religious versifier because of his origial genius, yet this originality is what the Jesuit editors of *The Month* did not understand.

"THE WINDHOVER"

Stung by the criticism of his major poem, not only by the Jesuit editors but also by his friend Robert Bridges, Hopkins never again tried to write something so long and elaborate. He retreated into the most traditional form in English prosody, the sonnet. After "The Wreck of the *Deutschland*," Hopkins's most famous work is the sonnet "The Windhover." More has been written about these fourteen lines than about any other piece of poetry of comparable length in English. All of Hopkins's sonnets are related to the Petrarchan model, but he alters the tradition to fit his peculiar genius. The poem employs line-end rhymes *abba abba cdcdcd*. In addition to the repetition of sound at the end of each line, there is also thickly interwoven alliteration and assonance within each line. This internal rhyme is related to the *cynghanedd* or consonant chime of Welsh poetry. Hopkins tried to learn Welsh when he was a student at St. Bueno's College in Wales and he actually wrote a bit of Welsh poetry in the form called *cywydd*. The meter of "The Windhover" is the so-called sprung rhythm, allowing great variation in the length of lines. The Petrarchan sonnet uses its rhyme scheme to define two parts of the poem: *abba abba* is the octave or exposition in the opening eight lines, *cdcdcd* is the sestet or commentary in the concluding six lines. Hopkins explained in his letters that the essence of a sonnet is balance and proportion. The octave asserts a situation or condition and then a surprising commentary comes back in the sestet to reply to the octave. Since the sestet has only six lines, it must be correspondingly "sharper" or more forceful if it is to balance the initial statement. The key to the sonnet is this proportion. Hopkins wrote some sonnets longer than the usual fourteen lines and a few shorter, "curtail" or cut-short, sonnets. In all his sonnets, however, he maintains the proportion of octave to sestet, eight to six, and forces the shorter conclusion to a higher pitch of intensity.

In its octave, "The Windhover" describes the flight of a hawk of a kind commonly used in falconry or hunting circling against the dawn sky. The sestet begins with the description of the hawk diving, plummeting earthward, as it "buckles." The sure, steady circling of the hawk in the octave is astonishing, but the sudden buckling downward is even more thrilling. It is beautiful and breathtaking. In the sestet, the increased beauty of the hawk as it dives is compared to a plough made to shine as it is driven through sandy soil, and to an ember coated with ashes that sparkles when it falls and breaks.

"The Windhover" illustrates one of the key terms in Hopkins's aesthetic vocabulary: "inscape," a word he coined for the inner nature of a thing that distinguishes it from everything else in creation. Hopkins's reading of Franciscan philosopher John Duns Scotus is pertinent to his concept of inscape. *Qualis* in Latin means "what." When people look at the qualities of things, they examine what these things have in common with other members of their class. The qualities of a good racing horse are those features that it has in common with other good horses. Duns Scotus imagines that there is an opposite to quality. *Haec* means "this" in Latin. Duns Scotus coins the word *haecceitas*, the "thisness" of a thing, which sets it apart from everything else, making it unique and different—the principle of individuation. Hopkins frequently celebrates the rare, unusual, or unique in nature. He turns away from the universal quality and toward the individual. The octave of "The Windhover" can be seen as the poet's description of a natural event: the flight and dive of a falcon. In that movement, he seeks to find the inscape, the innermost shape as evidence of God's presence in the created world. He tries to see into the form of the thing, to find what makes it original, unique, special, strange, striking. Like the sacrifice of the tall nun in "The Wreck of the *Deutschland*," the act of the hawk is "composed" so as to be the object for a religious meditation.

Paradoxically, the only way to grasp the unique inscape of a thing is to compare it with something else. The tension of this paradox is evident in the striking, surprising comparisons that Hopkins employs in "The Windhover," comparing the dive of a hawk with a plough shining in use and a burning coal sparkling as it collapses. The poem says that these three events are comparable or analogous in that in each case when the object buckles it becomes brighter and more glorious. When the hawk buckles in its dive, it is a thousandfold more lovely than in its stately circling. When the rusty plough buckles to its work, the abrasion of the sandy soil makes the ploughshare shine in use. When the ash crumbles or buckles, its inner brightness shows through the gray, outer ash-coating. Hopkins gave "The Windhover" the dedication, "To Christ Our Lord." The Jesuit order sees itself as the chivalry or the Knights of Christ. Ignatius advises the novice to buckle on the armor of Christ. To become a Jesuit, to buckle on the armor of a true Christian knight, is the proper and glorious activity of a man who would follow his nature, or unique calling. In like manner, a hawk follows its true nature, it is what it was made to be, when it sails in the wind and dives. A plough was made to work the earth, a coal to burn, and these things do what they were intended to do when they buckle. The activity of buckling may be painful or dangerous, but it produces glory, brilliance, grace, and beauty. The discipline of accepting the vows of the Jesuits may be painful in some earthly way, but it brings the glory of Christ's service. Christ, too, accepted the pain and duty of his earthly incarnation. He was buckled to the cross. He did what he had to do and so was brought to glory through pain and humiliation. The structure of "The Windhover" appears to be a set of analogies or comparisons all coming together in the word "buckle." Such a strucure is also to be found in the odes of the Greek poet Pindar, which Hopkins studied intensely in school. Pindar's poems praise a great athlete or hero by linking together a series of seeming digressions in one key image or figure, sometimes called a "constellation," such as the "golden lyre," a "beacon fire," a "horse," or a "tree." Hopkins's poetry unites the Christian tradition of anagogical interpretation of the created world and the classical Greek tradition of the Pindaric ode.

THE SONNET FORM

Most of Hopkins's shorter poems are sonnets, yet within the confines of this form, Hopkins displays great originality in his metrical structure, his repetition of sound in alliteration and internal rhyme, and his changes in the length of the sonnet while maintaining the crucial eight-to-six proportion of the octave/sestet division. Like the form of the sonnet, the subjects of most of Hopkins's poems are extremely traditional: elation at the sight of some particular bit of nature; personal dejection, desolation, and despair; celebration of the inner worth of an outwardly ordinary human being. These three topics are commonplaces of Romantic and post-Romantic literature. Hopkins's originality lies in treating these subjects with unusual power and perception. Romantic poets such as William Wordsworth and Percy Bysshe Shelley often looked at nature and said that they felt their hearts leap up to behold the beauty of spring or autumn. For Hopkins, every little corner of nature was evidence of the divine presence of God. His Christianity reinforces the Romantic sentiment. The confluence of the Romantic and the Christian tradition produces unusually powerful statements.

Consider, for example, the sonnet "Hurrahing in Harvest." Like "The Windhover," this poem is an Italian sonnet, rhymed *abba abba cdcdcd*. Lines 6 and 7 end with an unusual rhyme device. "Saviour" is rhymed with the next line, but in order to hear the complete rhyme, one must continue to the "r" sound that begins line eight: "gave you a/ Rapturous." This extended rhyme is common in Hopkins and illustrates his predilection for unusual twists within the framework of rigid traditional expectations. The subjects of "The Windhover" and "Hurrahing in Harvest" are also similar. In both poems, the speaker looks up at the sky and finds nature breathtakingly beautiful. "Hurrahing in Harvest" declares that the summer is now ending. The stooks, or shocks of bundled grain, are now stacked in the fields. The technical and regional term stooks is characteristic of Hopkins's vocabulary. The word is not commonly known, but it is exact. The speaker looks up at the autumnal skies and sees the clouds. With the bold verbal comparisons that the poet prefers, he compares the skies to "wind-walks"—they are like alleyways for the winds. The clouds are like "silk-sacks"; they are soft, dainty, and luxurious. The movement of the clouds across the sky is like "mealdrift" or flour pouring across the heavens. In that soft, flowing beauty, the speaker walks and lifts up his eyes. He sees the glory of the natural scene and then recognizes that beyond the heavens, behind all the created universe, there stands the Savior. He at first rejoices in the sheer beauty of nature, but such earthly beauty leads him to the unspeakable inner beauty of Christ's immediate presence in the natural world. In the sestet, the speaker sees the azure hills of autumn as strong as the shoulder of a stallion, majestic and sweet with flowers, like the shoulder of God bearing the creation in all its glory. The speaker realizes that all this is here for him to see, and the realization makes his heart leap up as if it had wings; his spirit hurls heavenward.

NATURE SONNETS

Hopkins wrote many poems celebrating nature in sonnet form. "God's Grandeur" states in the octave that the grandeur of God's creating has been obscured by the Industrial Revolution, trade and toil. The sestet replies that there is a spark of freshness deep in nature that will spring up like the sun at dawn because God broods over Earth like a bird over its egg. "The Starlight Night" begins with a powerful octave describing the beauty of the stars in the night sky. The sestet replies that the stars are like a picket fence separating us from heaven through which we can glimpse a bit of what is on the other side. "Spring" typically gives an excited picture of the juice and joy of the earth stirring in springtime and compares it to the youthful, primal goodness of children, a hint of sinless Eden.

"PIED BEAUTY"

"Pied Beauty" is one of Hopkins's most important philosophical poems on nature. It reflects his study of Duns Scotus and his notion of inscape. The poem is a "curtail" or cut-short sonnet, only ten and a fraction lines long. Hopkins explained that this poem maintained the eight-to-six ratio, which he felt was the key to the sonnet form. The exposition, which occupies the first six lines, states that God is especially to be praised for the irregular, dappled, serviceable parts of creation. The sestet generalizes that whatever is contradictory, strange, or changeable originates in God.

In Platonic thought, a material thing is beautiful insofar as it approaches its unchanging ideal. For example, a beautiful circle is one that approaches—as nearly as possible in our world—the perfection of an ideal circle. Because the things of the world are always struggling to become like their perfect forms, the material world is always changing. It is sometimes called the mutable world of "becoming." The ideal world cannot change, however, because when something is perfect, any change would make it imperfect. The world of Platonic ideals is therefore unchanging. It is sometimes called the world of permanent "being."

"Pied Beauty" makes a striking statement about the nature of beauty. It asserts that things are not beautiful because they approach the perfect type, but because they are various, changing, contradictory. Hopkins seems to be praising the very aspect of the material world that Platonic philosophy connects with degeneration and decay. Somehow God, who is perfect and unchanging, has fathered a universe of imperfection, contradiction, and decay. Nevertheless, this created world reflects his praise: Duns Scotus maintained that God's perfection must be manifest somehow in the constant change and variety of his creation.

"Duns Scotus's Oxford"

Hopkins's admiration for Duns Scotus is expressed in "Duns Scotus's Oxford," which combines the nature-sonnet and the celebration of a famous man. Its octave depicts the ancient university town of Oxford. The sestet comments that this was the very city that Duns Scotus knew when the subtle doctor taught there in the thirteenth century. Now Hopkins finds Scotus to have the best insight into philosophical problems, even more comforting to him than Greek philosophers such as Plato, or Italian philosophers such as Saint Thomas Aquinas. All the nature sonnets give an extremely sharp picture of some relatively common event or situation in nature: a hawk in flight, the landscape of Oxford, the rebirth of the countryside in springtime, the clouds and fields of autumn. The poet reflects on the source of all this beauty. The scene itself uplifts his spirits, but the awareness of God's creative force glimpsed behind the material world brings even more elation.

The heroic sonnet

A second group of poems is in the tradition of the heroic sonnet. These poems examine a person's life and define what is noteworthy in an ordinary man's career. "The Lantern Out of Doors" is typical. The octave tells of seeing a lantern moving at night. There must be someone behind that light, but he is so far off that he passes in the darkness and all that can be seen is a little spark. Humans have trouble knowing other people, and they all die. The sestet replies that Christ knows every person; Christ is the first and last friend of every human.

"Felix Randal," one of Hopkins's best sonnets, is about a blacksmith who fell ill and died. The once powerful man wasted away, but he finally came to accept Christ. Paradoxically, in the weakness of his death he became more blessed than in the pagan power he was so proud of in the days when he forged and fitted horseshoes with his fellow workers.

"The Soldier," "Tom's Garland: Upon the Unemployed," and "Harry Ploughman" all fit into the category of poems celebrating the inner worth of ordinary people. Perhaps the pattern of this kind of sonnet is best displayed in "In Honour of Saint Alphonsus Rodriguez: Laybrother of the Society of Jesus." Alphonsus Rodriguez performed no noble deeds. For forty years, however, he faithfully carried out his duty and filled his station as doorkeeper. It is not his exploits, but his humanity, that Hopkins celebrates. Humility, obedience, and simple faith have their reward. The poem is in the tradition of Milton's theme of the faithful Christians: "They also serve who only stand and wait."

SONNETS OF TERROR

The third major theme of Hopkins's sonnets is spiritual desolation and terror. These poems constitute the dark, opposite side of Hopkins's view of reality. In the nature poems, the poet looks at some part of the created universe and feels that God is in every corner of the world. His joy, already aroused by the pure beauty of nature, rises to an ecstatic pitch when he realizes that God is behind it all. The poems of desolation, sometimes called the "terrible sonnets," on the other hand, imagine a world without God—all joy, freshness, and promise withdrawn. They depict the dark night of the soul.

Many readers think that these poems are directly autobiographical, indicating that Hopkins in the last years of his life was devastated by despair. This view is probably not sound. The sonnet is a highly dramatized form; sonnets are traditionally constructed like little plays. Thus the speaker of one of William Shakespeare's sonnets is no more Shakespeare, the man himself, than is Macbeth or Hamlet, and the persona or mask through which a sonneteer speaks is not to be confused with the real author. *The Spiritual Exercises* of Saint Ignatius, moreover, follows a spiritual progression that every Jesuit would imitate in his retreats and private worship. In a long retreat, lasting about a month, the exercitant is called on to drive himself gradually into a state of extreme desolation into which a renewed sense of God's presence finally bursts like Easter into the dormant world.

The sonnets of terror may be as artificial as Elizabethan love sonnets. They may be, to some degree, virtuoso exercises in imagining a world devoid of spirituality and hope. The real feelings of Hopkins may be quite separate from the imagined feelings of the persona who speaks these sonnets. On the other hand, one can hardly imagine that Hopkins could write these poems unless there were some wrenching personal feelings motivating his creative act.

The sonnets of terror appeal to readers today because they mirror a cosmic despair or alienation. The feeling that modern humans are strangers in a strange land, that they are alienated from the profit of their own productivity, that they are caught in a meaningless or absurd activity like Sisyphus rolling his stone endlessly up a mountain in Hell, is extremely widespread. It is doubtful that Hopkins felt alienated in exactly this way. His religious belief promised him a future life and salvation. When he speaks of despair, it is always hypothetical: Think how unbearable life would be if there were not hope.

"Carrion Comfort"

"Carrion Comfort," among the best of Hopkins's dark sonnets, considers despair, which is itself a sin, depicting the struggle of the Christian with his own conscience. It begins a series of six sonnets of unusual power that treat the struggle of the soul. These poems should be read in sequence: (1) "Carrion Comfort," (2) "No Worst, There Is None," (3) "To Seem a Stranger Lies My Lot," (4) "I Wake and Feel the Fell of Dark, Not Day," (5) "Patience, Hard Thing" and (6) "My Own Heart Let Me Have More Pity On." Read in sequence, these sonnets constitute a short psychodrama or morality play.

The Christian speaker confronts his own doubt, weakness, and unworth, and is terrified of God. In five scenes, he is seen writhing and twisting in mental contortions of guilt and terror. At the conclusion of "My Own Heart Let Me Have More Pity On," the sestet provides the dramatic release, as God's smile breaks through, like sunlight on a mountain guiding the traveler. This sonnet sequence corresponds to the progress of the seeker through the final stages of his spiritual exercises. The same progress of the mind, through terror to elation at the Resurrection, is outlined in "That Nature Is a Heraclitean Fire and of the Comfort of the Resurrection." The first segment of this poem looks at the changing natural world. Like a bonfire, everything around humans is changing, decaying, being consumed. Humans seem so pitifully weak and vulnerable among these flames. The only hope is Christ's promise of salvation, which comes to humans like a beacon. People will pass through the fire and, even when all else is destroyed, their souls will endure like immortal diamonds.

Hopkins's vocabulary

A striking characteristic of Hopkins's poetry is his rich vocabulary. As he sought to find the inscape or unique form in the created universe, he also attempted to find in language the original, spare, strange, exactly right word. He was one of the best trained linguists of his age, working at the research level in Latin and Greek, while studying Anglo-Saxon and Welsh. His notes and journals show him repeatedly developing elaborate etymologies of words. He belonged to a widespread movement in the Victorian era, spearheaded by Robert Bridges and his Society for Pure English, which glorified the archaic elements in modern English. In his notes, he records dialect words and the special words used by workers for their tools or by country people for plants and animals. This attention to the texture of language pours forth in his poetry in an unusually rich, eccentric vocabulary.

Legacy

Despite the orthodoxy of his religious views, Hopkins is known as one of the founders of modernism in literature. He is frequently compared with Walt Whitman, Emily Dickinson, and the French Symbolist poets as a great revolutionary who rebelled against the sterile forms of Victorian verse and brought a new urgency, freshness, and seriousness to poetry. He revolutionized the very basis of English meter with his experiments in sprung rhythm. He revitalized the bold metaphor in the manner of the English Metaphysical poets. He created a whole new lexicon, a poetic vocabulary constructed from dialect, archaic, technical, and coined words.

The critics who initially praised his work in the 1920's and 1930's tended to see him as a cultural primitive, a man isolated from the corruption of society and so able to return to a state of nature and get to the core of language more easily than writers such as Alfred, Lord Tennyson, who seemed corrupted by false traditions. Although Hopkins was undoubtedly a great innovator, he was certainly not a cultural primitive. He was a highly trained professor of Latin and Greek language and literature. In addition to his "Double First in Greats" from Oxford University, he undertook years of rigorous philosophical and theological training with the Society of Jesus. He was at the center of a group of correspondents who were as powerful intellectually as any group found in his era: Bridges, Dixon, Patmore, and other less frequent scholarly correspondents.

Hopkins was not a naïve writer; on the contrary, he was an extremely sophisticated writer. His poetry is revolutionary, not because he was ignorant of tradition, but because he brought together many powerful threads of tradition: the contemplative practice of the *Spiritual Exercises*, with their "composition of place" and "application of the senses"; the conventions of the Petrarchan sonnet; the complicated metrical studies of Bridges, Patmore, and the classical scholars; the classical philosophical background of Oxford University; and the medieval thought of the Jesuit schools, especially of John Duns Scotus. These traditions met, and sometimes conflicted sharply, in Hopkins. From that confluence of traditions he gave modern readers the unique gift of his poems.

Other major works

NONFICTION: *The Correspondence of Gerard Manley Hopkins and Richard Watson Dixon*, 1935, 1955 (C. C. Abbott, editor); *The Letters of Gerard Manley Hopkins to Robert Bridges*, 1935, 1955 (Abbott, editor); *The Notebooks and Papers of Gerard Manley Hopkins*, 1937 (Humphry House, editor); *Further Letters of Gerard Manley Hopkins*, 1938, 1956 (Abbott, editor); *The Journals and Papers of Gerard Manley Hopkins*, 1959 (House and Graham Storey, editors); *The Sermons and Devotional Writings of Gerard Manley Hopkins*, 1959 (Christopher Devlin, editor); *Gerard Manley Hopkins: Selected Letters*, 1990.

BIBLIOGRAPHY

Bloom, Harold, ed. *Gerard Manley Hopkins*. New York: Chelsea House, 1986. Includes a number of significant essays on Hopkins, chronology, a bibliography, and index.

Brown, Daniel. *Gerard Manley Hopkins*. Tavistock, England: Northcote House/British Council, 2004. A biography of Hopkins that examines his life in relation to his poetic works and themes.

_____. *Hopkins' Idealism: Philosophy, Physics, Poetry*. New York: Oxford University Press, 1997. Offers new readings of some of Hopkins's best-known poems and is the first full-length study of Hopkins's largely unpublished Oxford undergraduate essays and notes on philosophy and mechanics.

Feeney, Joseph J. *The Playfulness of Gerard Manley Hopkins*. Burlington, Vt.: Ashgate, 2008. Feeney examines the poetry of Hopkins, from the early period to the late, looking at his sense of humor and playfulness.

MacKenzie, Norman H. *Excursions in Hopkins*. Philadelphia: Saint Joseph's University Press, 2007. Examines the poetry of Hopkins in detail. Includes two chapters on "The Wreck of the *Deutschland*."

_____. *A Reader's Guide to Gerard Manley Hopkins*. 2d ed. Philadelphia: Saint Joseph's University Press, 2007. This guide provides information about Hopkins that helps readers interpret his poetry.

Mariani, Paul. *Gerard Manley Hopkins: A Life*. New York: Viking, 2008. Mariani, a poet, integrates Hopkins's spiritual and literary life to portray the life and works of Hopkins.

Milward, Peter. *A Lifetime with Hopkins*. Ann Arbor, Mich.: Sapientia Press, 2005. Jesuit priest and literary scholar Milward looks at Hopkins's views on God, nature, the self, and people, and examines his place in literary tradition.

White, Norman. *Hopkins: A Literary Biography*. New York: Oxford University Press, 1992. This massive biography traces the life, career, and religious struggles of the brilliant but profoundly alienated Victorian poet.

Wimsatt, James I. *Hopkins's Poetics of Speech Sound: Sprung Rhythm, Lettering, Inscape*. Buffalo, N.Y.: University of Toronto Press, 2006. The author examines the poetic techniques used by Hopkins, including sprung rhythm, lettering, and inscape.

Todd K. Bender

MATSUO BASHŌ

Born: Ueno, Iga Province, Japan; 1644
Died: Ōsaka, Japan; October 12, 1694
Also known as: Matsuo Kinsaku

PRINCIPAL POETRY
Sarumino, 1691 (*Monkey's Raincoat*, 1973)
Bashō's Haiku: Selected Poems by Matsuo Bashō, 2004
Haikai shichibu-shū, n.d.

OTHER LITERARY FORMS

The literary works of Matsuo Bashō (mah-tsew-oh bah-shoh) are difficult to classify, even for those acquainted with Japanese literary history. Bashō is popularly known as the greatest of all haiku poets, although the literary form was not defined and named until two hundred years after his death. Modern collections labeled "Bashō's *haiku*" are generally bits and pieces taken from his travel journals and *renku* (linked poems). In a sense, all Bashō's literary works are broader and more complex than the seventeen-syllable haiku for which he is remembered. The seven major anthologies of his school, listed above, contain *hokku* (opening verses) and *renku* composed by Bashō and his disciples, as well as an occasional prose piece. Besides *hokku* and *renku*, Bashō is known for his *haibun*, a combination of terse prose and seventeen-syllable *hokku* generally describing his pilgrimages to famous sites in Japan. His best-known travel journals include *Nozarashi kikō* (1687; *The Records of a Weather-Exposed Skeleton*, 1966), *Oku no hosomichi* (1694; *The Narrow Road to the Deep North*, 1933), *Oi no kobumi* (1709; *The Records of a Travel-Worn Satchel*, 1966), and *Sarashina kikō* (1704; *A Visit to Sarashina Village*, 1957). Bashō's conversations on poetry were preserved by disciples, and his surviving letters, numbering more than a hundred, are treasured today.

ACHIEVEMENTS

Matsuo Bashō is the favorite poet of Japan and one of the only poets of Asia whose verses are known popularly in the West. It is paradoxical that this complex poet whose profundity continues to tease the minds of Japan's greatest literary critics is read and recited by schoolchildren in many lands. Although technically he never wrote a haiku, Bashō serves as a model for many children, East and West, writing their first verses as haiku. The wedding of simplicity and profundity that characterizes Bashō's work provides a true measure of his stature as a poet.

The continuing popularity of Bashō in his homeland, a country where laymen pride themselves on being aesthetic critics, is itself an extraordinary tribute to his work. Japanese still make pilgrimages to the stone monuments marking the stopping places on his journeys. Many recite his verses when they hear a frog splash, smell plum blossoms on a mountain trail, or hear a cicada's shrill voice. Thanks in no small part to his work, many average citizens of Japan still write poetry, hang scrolls containing verse, and read the poetry column in Japan's daily newspapers.

In an age when aristocrats were the arbiters of taste, setting the complex rules for the writing of *waka* and *renga*, the chief poetic forms of Japan, Bashō devoted himself to *haikai*, an informal style of poetry celebrating the seasons of nature and the round of ordinary life among peasants and merchants. Without Bashō, *haikai* was in danger of sliding into slavish imitation of aristocratic canons or of degenerating into a display of vulgarity, coarse humor, and puns. Bashō democratized literature in Japan, and through literature, he helped democratize Japanese aesthetics. Bringing to bear his own sensitivity to the nature mysticism of Chinese Daoism and the radical sacramentalization of the ordinary in Zen Buddhism, he created a poetry of breadth and depth for the Japanese populace. As he observes in one of his *hokku*: "The beginning of art:/ Songs sung by those planting rice/ In the back country."

More specifically, Bashō's achievements in literature led to the maturing of three forms: the *hokku*, the *haikai no renga* (informal linked verse), and the *haibun*. Devoting a lifetime of effort to *hokku*, those seventeen-syllable verses intended as openings for linked poems, Bashō prepared the form for its modern independence as haiku. Working tirelessly with disciples in Japan's cities and countryside, Bashō infused a sense of the shared spirit of poetry that led to Japan's greatest *renku*, perhaps the high point of *za no geijutsu* (group art) in the history of world literature. Finally, his mastery of the combination of prose and poetry in travel journals set a new standard for the form the Japanese call *haibun*.

Describing himself in one of his *haibun*, *The Records of a Travel-Worn Satchel*, Bashō suggested a further unity, the unity of all arts when sounded to their depths, and the unity of art with nature, a philosophy that has given Japan its unique character:

> Finally, this poet, incapable as he is, has bound himself to the thin line of poetry. One and the same thread runs through the *waka* of Saigyō, *renga* of Sōgi, paintings of Sesshū, and tea ceremony of Riky. What the arts hold in common is a devotion to nature and companionship with the four seasons.

Biography

Centuries of warfare among the lords and samurai of Japan's chief clans came to an end when Tokugawa Ieyasu established a military dictatorship, the Shogunate, about 1600. With a Tokugawa shogun established in the thriving merchant city of Edo (modern-day Tokyo) and a ceremonial imperial court in ancient Kyoto, Japan officially closed its doors to the outside world in 1638. Such was the setting in which Matsuo

Matsuo Bashō

Bashō was born as Matsuo Munefusa in 1644 at Ueno in Iga province, only thirty miles from the imperial palace in Kyoto and two hundred miles from the powerful shogun in Edo.

Bashō was one of several children born to Matsuo Yozaemon, a minor samurai nominally in the service of the Tōdō family that ruled the Ueno area. Bashō's father had limited means and probably provided for his family by farming and giving lessons in calligraphy. At about age twelve, perhaps the year his father died, Bashō entered the service of the Tōdō family as a study companion to one of the Tōdō heirs, Yoshitada, a youth two years his senior with a bent toward poetry. A genuine friendship with Yoshitada encouraged young Bashō in the study of poetry and gave him access to one of the leading teachers of the day, Kitamura Kigin (1624-1705). When Yoshitada died suddenly in 1666, Bashō, only twenty-two years of age, lost both a friend and a patron. He apparently remained in the area of Ueno and Kyoto, devoting himself to poetry in the *haikai* style of the Teitoku school favored by his teacher Kigin. Pursuing a career as a poet, by 1672, he had published at his own expense *Kai-ōi* (seashell game), a collection of humorous verses by local poets that he matched and commented upon as poet-teacher. Some scholars believe that during this period, Bashō entered a relationship with a woman later known by her religious name, Jutei, and perhaps fathered children by her, but other scholars have dismissed this as pure speculation.

In 1672, at age twenty-eight, Bashō established himself in the bustling city of Edo, where his reputation as *haikai* poet and teacher increased. In 1680, he published *Tōsei montei dokugin nijū kasen* (twenty *kasen* by Tōsei's pupils), a collection of thirty-six-link *renku*. That year, he settled in a hut on the outskirts of Edo, next to which one of his disciples planted a *bashō*. In time, the poet's residence became known as the *Bashō-an* (banana-plant hut), and his students began to address him as "Master Bashō." Thus was born the nickname by which he was known for the rest of his life.

Bashō's early poetry was influenced by the Teitoku or Teimon style of *haikai*, using clever literary allusions and wordplay. In Edo, he came under the influence of the Danrin school, which explored greater freedom in theme and diction and demonstrated genuine interest in the life of the merchants and laborers of Edo. By about 1681, his own style, called *shōfū*, had begun to emerge, as evidenced in his *hokku* describing a crow on a withered branch in autumn twilight. Bashō also began practicing meditation under the direction of a Zen priest, Butchō (1642-1715).

In the fall of 1684, Bashō put on the robes of a Buddhist priest and began a series of pilgrimages over the roads and rugged mountain trails of Japan to perfect the new ideal of his art, *sabi* (solitariness). The final twelve years of his life were given largely to strenuous travel, the perfecting of the *haibun*-style travel journal, and sessions with disciples along the way who responded to his teaching and joined him in the art of *haikai no renga*, the linking of verses to produce *renku*. By 1686, he had written his most famous verse, describing the contrast of an old pond and a frog's splash, and by 1689, he had taken the difficult inland journey that led to the height of *haibun* art, *The Narrow Road to the Deep North*. Near the end of his life, to the chagrin of some of his disciples, Bashō had begun to advocate a new principle for the writing of *haikai*: *karumi* (lightness), a focus on the ordinary and unadorned.

During a final trip to Ueno and Ōsaka to preach *karumi* and to patch up a quarrel among his disciples, Bashō's strength failed and an old illness flared up; he dictated a final verse from his deathbed: "Ill on the journey/ My dreams going round and round/ Over withered fields."

Analysis

At a time when many *haikai* poets wrote hundreds of verses during a single night's linked-poetry session, Matsuo Bashō's lifetime accumulation of barely a thousand seventeen-syllable *hokku* is indicative of the seriousness with which he took his art. Constantly struggling with each of these verses, Bashō established a standard of craftsmanship and profundity that would later lead to *hokku*'s independent status as haiku.

The *hokku* often singled out as Bashō's first masterpiece is his crow verse of 1681: "On a withered branch/ A crow settles itself down—/ Autumn evening." The stark tableau of a black branch against the darkened sky is broken by the sudden movement of a crow alighting. Here, timelessness and the momentary meet, and as they merge, the wider and deeper cycle of nature's seasonal pattern is revealed. The darkness of branch, crow, and autumn nightfall interpenetrate, suggesting the Japanese aesthetic qualities called *wabi* (poverty) and *sabi* (solitude).

Themes

What the poet has not said is as significant as his choice of theme. The traditional aristocratic themes of Japanese court poetry, the scented love notes, koto music, and tear-drenched sleeves of *waka* are absent. Bashō reaches back to the themes and cadences of the great Tang Dynasty poets of China, Du Fu and Li Bo, to lend universality to his verse. The monochromes of the great Chan masters are suggested by the black branch and crow, and perhaps the *hokku* itself suggests the Chinese poetic topic, "shivering crow in leafless tree." The merging of all in the mystery of darkness suggests Bashō's reading preferences: Daoism's Zhuangzi (Chuang-tzu) and Japan's poet-priests Saigyō and Sōgi. The rhythm and repetition of sounds, lost in English translation, witness Bashō's careful craftsmanship in the crow verse: *kare* (withered), *karasu* (crow), *aki no kure* (autumn evening).

Frog verses

One of Bashō's Edo disciples, Senka, compiled a *haikai* matching of verses on the subject "frog" in 1686, *Kawazu awase* (frog contest). Bashō provided the opening verse, or *hokku*, the most famous of all his works: "An age-old pond—/ A frog leaps into it/ Splash goes the water." The presence of *kawazu* (frog), a *kigo* (season word), tells the reader that it is spring. The poet sees the still surface of a murky pond, probably an ancient pond edged by rocks and reeds designed centuries earlier by some Zen priest as a setting for a temple. A sudden splash shatters the stillness of the pond, and in that disruption a new awareness of the eternal is sealed on the consciousness. Asian philosophy's yin-yang complementarity is revealed in the relation of stillness to sound, and the Daoist theme of a void from which momentary forms of life emerge and to which they return is celebrated. The consummate demonstration of just how much can be suggested in a few words constitutes Bashō's principal contribution to the *hokku* and suggests the Asian "one-corner philosophy": Sensitivity to the smallest creature or the briefest moment within the cycle of nature provides a gateway to the motion and meaning of the entire universe. In the words of Zen Buddhism, "The mountains, trees, and grasses are the Buddha."

ZEN AND DAOISM

Bashō's training in Zen Buddhist meditation and his donning the robes of a Buddhist priest for his travels might suggest that the key concept of Buddhism, *sunyata* (emptiness), would find expression in his verses. It is significant that many of Bashō's *hokku* focus not on a presence but rather on an "absence," a creative emptiness that suggests "pure potentiality." He writes of a skylark "clinging to nothing at all," of Mount Fuji "disappearing in mist," of flowers "without names," and of "a road empty of travelers." The Daoist void and Buddhist emptiness are expressed in the aesthetic quality Japanese call *yūgen* (mysterious vagueness), a quality of the *hokku* akin to the vacant spaces in a Zen scroll painting.

KARUMI

In 1693, just a year before his death, Bashō "shut his gate" for a time, refusing all visitors. When he opened the gate again to his disciples, he began teaching a further development of *haikai* poetry, the principle of *karumi* (lightness). Even close disciples had misgivings and uncertainties about this principle to which the poet devoted his final year. Moving beyond *wabi, sabi*, and *yūgen*, Bashō sought a return to some primal simplicity in the ordinariness of life, simplicity beyond both technical excellence and poetic response to the past. He wrote of a "sick wild duck/ falling in the cold of night," of "salted fish" in a street market, of a "white-haired/ graveyard visit," a "motionless cloud," and "autumn chill." The experience of eternity was no longer simply intensified by the momentary; for Bashō, it had become incarnate in the unadorned ordinariness of life.

THE ART OF HAIKAI

Modern interest in Bashō's art has generally focused on the *hokku*. Bashō himself, however, believed the art of *haikai* was to be found less in isolated verses than in cooperative effort of a like-minded school of poets involved in "sequence composition," and apparently he felt his greatest achievements occurred in this area: "Among my disciples many are as gifted as I am in writing *hokku*. But this old man knows the true spirit of *haikai*." The art of *haikai*, or *haikai no renga*, is so foreign to Western experience that appreciation of its merits and of Bashō's contribution is especially difficult.

The *waka* was the chief poetic form of the Japanese from prehistory through the thirteenth century. The special possession of the aristocracy at court, short *waka* called *tanka* were sometimes created by two persons, one composing the upper seventeen syllables and another responding with the lower fourteen. When *tanka* rules became too confining, some poets began to compose *renga* (linked verses) of a *haikai* (informal) or *mushin* (frivolous) sort. *Renga* soon became adopted by the court and developed its own *ushin* (serious) rules, and so by the sixteenth century a *haikai no renga* movement sought to democratize the form again.

Bashō, an artist of *haikai no renga*, sought to keep the form open to creative contact with everyday life, yet sought also to transcend common wordplay and vulgarities. His cooperative poetic efforts with four Nagoya merchants in *Fuyu no hi* (a winter's day) and with sixteen disciples in a hundred-verse sequence called *Hatsu kaishi* (*First Manuscript Page*), culminating in a series of thirty-six-link *renku* collected in *Monkey's Raincoat*. Using the rules regarding season sequences and moon and flower verses with freedom yet sensitivity, he advocated linking alternate seventeen-syllable and fourteen-syllable verses through the principle of *nioi* (fragrance), a vague but effective sense of atmosphere and mood conveyed by one poet and verse to another.

"In the City"

A *renku* in thirty-six verses titled "Ichinaka wa" ("In the City") appears in *Monkey's Raincoat*. Its opening verse (*hokku*) is by the poet Bonchō, who introduces the "heavy odor of things" in the city and uses the seasonal words "summer moon." Bashō responds with the answering verse (*waki*), describing voices in the night at "gate after gate." They repeat, "It is hot, so hot." From there, a third poet shifts the scene to a rice paddy, Bonchō continues with a verse describing a farmer's "smoked sardine" meal, and Bashō adds a link that pictures himself as a visitor to this poor farm neighborhood, where "they don't even recognize money." Within the next half dozen verses, a young girl's religious experience is described, the season shifts to winter, and Bashō introduces an aged peasant who "can only suck the bones of fish." Sounds and word associations linking one verse to another are so subtle that even experienced *haikai* poets disagree in their analysis, though not in their high evaluation of the *renku*.

Perhaps the greatest facet of Bashō's art, linked poetry written cooperatively through a shared "fragrance," is largely closed to the Western reader, though a good *renku* translation and commentary may be of some aid. Those familiar with Western chamber music may detect similarities, as themes pass from one player to another, exciting changes in tempo and mood are introduced, and one instrument modulates to support the contribution of another.

THE NARROW ROAD TO THE DEEP NORTH

Finally, it should be noted that some critics view neither the *hokku* nor the *haikai no renga* as the height of Bashō's art. They would view his travel journals, culminating in *The Narrow Road to the Deep North*, as the epitome of his creative efforts.

In *The Narrow Road to the Deep North*, widely regarded as one of the finest works in all Japanese literature, the pilgrim-poet seeks to mature his art by hiking to those sites of beauty and history that inspired Saigyō and other poet-priests of the past. Taking arduous trails both to the inner country of Japan and the inner reaches of his own art, Bashō weaves prose and poetry into a record of a pilgrimage of the Japanese spirit as it responds to the history and beauty of the homeland. The famous opening declares that "moon and sun are eternal travelers," and bids the reader to join in the journey. Bashō describes famous sites and views at Matsushima, Hiraizumi, and Kisagata, pausing to muse over ruined castles and ancient battlefields:

> The summer grasses—
> For courageous warriors
> The aftermath of dreams.

In a land ruled by powerful military shoguns who had closed Japan to all outside contacts, such musings in the spirit of the great T'ang poets of China made this travel journal an act of courage and a proclamation that art cannot be confined by political borders. Allusions to Chinese poetry and philosophy, Japanese history and aesthetics, are woven together in such a complex tapestry that, once again, the Western reader is in need of a superior translation and a helpful commentary, but the treasures to be discovered are worth the effort.

Bashō, the poet whose verses are loved by children yet challenge the best efforts of mature scholars, spent his life in pilgrimage for his art and died on the road. In *The Narrow Road to the Deep North*, he sums up the relevance of his wanderings in a few simple words, identifying his readers as pilgrims, too: "For each day is a journey, and the journey itself is home."

OTHER MAJOR WORKS

NONFICTION: *Nozarashi kikō*, 1687 (travel; *The Records of a Weather-Exposed Skeleton*, 1966); *Oku no hosomichi*, 1694 (travel; *The Narrow Road to the Deep North*, 1933); *Sarashina kikō*, 1704 (travel; *A Visit to Sarashina Village*, 1966); *Oi no kobumi*, 1709 (travel; *The Records of a Travel-Worn Satchel*, 1966).

MISCELLANEOUS: *The Essential Bashō*, 1999.

Bibliography

Aitken, Robert. *A Zen Wave: Bashō's Haiku and Zen.* New York: Weatherhill, 1978. One of the few studies of Bashō by a Western roshi, or master teacher of Zen. This overview evaluates the poet's work in the context of Zen philosophy, offering the claim that Bashō's haiku transcend mere nature poetry and instead serve as a way of presenting fundamental religious truths about mind, nature, and cosmos.

Caws, Mary Ann, ed. *Textual Analysis: Some Readers Reading.* New York: Modern Language Association of America, 1986. Earl Miner's chapter on Bashō has as its main thesis that Bashō has not been known in the West as he would have wished to be known. The focus of his discussion is the fact that the Western concept of mimesis, what is real and what is fiction, differs from its Eastern counterpart, opening the way to misunderstanding.

Hamill, Sam, trans. *The Essential Bashō.* Boston: Shambhala, 1999. The introduction to this work represents Bashō as a consummate writer. In this work, religious issues are significantly downplayed. Instead Hamill presents his subject as a poetic and philosophical wanderer: someone engaged in a lifelong process of literary experimentation and discovery. Particularly fascinating is the overview of Bashō's transformation from a highly derivative stylist to a powerfully original poet.

Qiu, Peipei. *Basho and the Dao: The Zhuangzi and the Transformation of Haikai.* Honolulu: University of Hawaii Press, 2005. Examines the relationship between Daoism and Bashō's poetry. Contains considerable discussion of themes and influences.

Shirane, Haruo. *Traces of Dreams: Landscape, Cultural Memory, and the Poetry of Bashō.* Stanford, Calif.: Stanford University Press, 1998. This work puts the poet in the position of cultural conservationist, arguing that Bashō's poems drew on deeply held concepts of nature.

Ueda, Makoto. *Matsuo Bashō.* New York: Twayne, 1970. This study offers a brief biography as well as general perspectives on the author's major works. In addition to the expected focus on haiku, it treats Bashō's *renku* (long, collaboratively written poems) and prose works.

_____, ed. *Bashō and His Interpreters: Selected Hokku with Commentary.* Stanford, Calif.: Stanford University Press, 1992. This work is a chronologically organized anthology of Bashō's poems, each accompanied by the original Japanese text (transliterated into Western characters) and literal translations. Although this anthology offers little new insight into Bashō's life or interpretations of his work, this volume does demonstrate the tremendous influence of translation on the written word.

Cliff Edwards

W. S. MERWIN

Born: New York, New York; September 30, 1927

PRINCIPAL POETRY
A Mask for Janus, 1952
The Dancing Bears, 1954
Green with Beasts, 1956
The Drunk in the Furnace, 1960
The Moving Target, 1963
The Lice, 1967
Animae, 1969
The Carrier of Ladders, 1970
Writings to an Unfinished Accompaniment, 1973
The First Four Books of Poems, 1975
The Compass Flower, 1977
Feathers from the Hill, 1978
Finding the Islands, 1982
Opening the Hand, 1983
Koa, 1988
The Rain in the Trees, 1988
Selected Poems, 1988
The Second Four Books of Poems, 1993
Travels, 1993
The Vixen, 1996
Flower and Hand: Poems, 1977-1983, 1997
The Folding Cliffs: A Narrtive, 1998
The River Sound, 1999
The Pupil, 2001
Migration: New and Selected Poems, 2005
Present Company, 2005
The Shadow of Sirius, 2008

OTHER LITERARY FORMS

A talented translator, W. S. Merwin has translated numerous works including *The Poem of the Cid* (1959), Persius's *Satires* (1961), *The Song of Roland* (1963), *Voices*, by Antonio Porchia (1969, 1988), *Transparence of the World*, by Jean Follain (1969), Dante's *Purgatorio* (2000), and poetry by Pablo Neruda and Osip Mandelstam. He has also written plays: *Rumpelstiltskin*, produced by the British Broadcasting Corporation

(BBC) in 1951; *Pageant of Cain*, produced by BBC Third Programme in 1952; and *Huckleberry Finn*, produced by BBC television, 1953. *Darkling Child* was produced in London by Arts Theatre in 1956, *Favor Island* was produced by Poet's Theatre in Cambridge, Massachusetts, in 1957, and *The Gilded West* was produced in 1961 in Coventry, England, by the Belgrade Theatre. Merwin's prose works include *The Miner's Pale Children* (1970), *Unframed Originals* (1982), *Regions of Memory: Uncollected Prose, 1949-1982* (1987, edited by Cary Nelson), *The Lost Upland* (1992), *The Ends of the Earth: Essays* (2004), and *Summer Doorways: A Memoir* (2005).

Achievements

W. S. Merwin received early recognition for his poetry with the selection in 1952 of *A Mask for Janus* for publication in the Yale Series of Younger Poets, and he went on to receive many grants, fellowships, and awards. He won two Pulitzer Prizes, for *The Carrier of Ladders* (1971) and *The Shadow of Sirius* (2009). He was the recipient of a Kenyon Review Fellowship (1954), a National Institute of Arts and Letters Award (1957), an Arts Council of Great Britain bursary (1957), a Rabinowitz Research Fellowship (1961), a Ford Foundation Grant (1964), a Rockefeller grant (1969), the Academy of American Poets Fellowship (1973), and a National Endowment for the Arts Grant (1978). His many awards and honors include the Bess Hokin Prize (1962), the Chapelbrook Award (1966), the Harriet Monroe Memorial Prize from *Poetry* magazine (1967), a PEN Translation Prize for *Selected Translations, 1948-1968* (1969), the Shelley Memorial Award (1974), a Bollingen Prize (1979), the Governor's Award for Literature of the State of Hawaii (1987), and the Aiken Taylor Award in Modern American Poetry (1990). In 1994, he received the Lenore Marshall Poetry Prize for *Travels*, the Theodore Roethke Prize from *Poetry Northwest*, the Wallace Stevens Award, and the Lila Wallace-*Reader's Digest* Writers' Award. He won the Ruth Lilly Poetry Prize (1998), the Gold Medal for poetry from the American Academy of Arts and Letters (2003), the Harold Morton Landon Translation Award (2003), the Lannan Lifetime Achievement Award (2004), the National Book Award for *Migration* (2005), and the Bobbitt National Prize for *Present Company* (2006). He was elected a member of the American Academy of Arts and Letters in 1972 and was a special bicentennial consultant (poet laureate) to the Library of Congress along with poets Rita Dove and Louise Glück in 1999-2000. He served as chancellor for the Academy of American Poets from 1998 to 2000. In 2010, Merwin was named poet laureate consultant in poetry to the Library of Congress.

Biography

William Stanley Merwin was born in New York City on September 30, 1927, and grew up in Union City, New Jersey (where his father was a Presbyterian minister), and in Scranton, Pennsylvania. From his own account, his parents were strict and rather cheerless. His earliest poems, written as a child, were austere hymns for his father. He received his bachelor's degree in English from Princeton University in 1947. In 1947, he married Dorothy Jeanne Ferry, the secretary to a Princeton physicist. While at Princeton, he was befriended by the critic R. P. Blackmur and became very interested in the work of Ezra Pound. Like Pound, he was a student of romance languages and began to value translation as a means of remaking poetry in English. As a student, he even grew a beard in imitation of Pound and eventually went to visit Pound at St. Elizabeths Hospital. In 1949, he followed Pound's example and left the United States to become an expatriate. His sojourn was to last some seven years. From 1949 to 1951, he worked as a tutor in France and Portugal. In 1950, he lived in Mallorca, Spain, where he was tutor to Robert Graves's son, William. Graves's interest in myth became one important influence on the younger poet. In Europe, he met Dido Milroy, whom he married in 1954; they would separate in 1968. After that he made his living for several years by translating from French, Spanish, Latin, and Portuguese. From 1951 through 1953, he worked as translator for the BBC's Third Programme. During 1956 and 1957, Merwin was playwright-in-residence for the Poets' Theatre in Cambridge, Massachusetts, and in 1962, he served as poetry editor for *The Nation*. He was an associate at the Théâtre de la Cité in Lyons, France, during 1964-1965. In 1971, he won a Pulitzer Prize for his collection *The Carrier of Ladders*.

In 1976, Merwin moved to Hawaii to study Buddhism. There he met Paula Schwartz; they were married in 1983. Merwin has made Maui his home base, traveling to the mainland United States to lecture and give readings. He has become an ecological advocate, lending his support to Hawaii's environmental movement.

Analysis

The achievement of W. S. Merwin is both impressive and distinctive. His body of work encompasses a wide range of literary genres and includes poetry, plays, translations, and prose. His development as a poet has spanned great literary distances, from the early formalism of *A Mask for Janus* to the spare, simple language and openness of the verse form he refined in *The Lice*. His poetry has often displayed a prosaic, almost conversational quality, as in "Questions to Tourists Stopped by a Pineapple Field," from *Opening the Hand*.

Although Merwin himself has carefully avoided making in-depth comments or pronouncements about his poetry and has not engaged in the often fussy critical debate that has shadowed his career, his work continues to show evidence that the exploration of the power and enigmatic nature of language is one of his great concerns. His many remarkable translations have perhaps been a stimulating influence on his own innovations of poetic form. In moving away from the rather mannered style of his early verse with its reliance on myth, rhyme, and punctuation to a poetry of silence and absence, Merwin, according to Sandra McPherson, began "researching the erasures of the universe."

Beginning with his first book of poetry, *A Mask for Janus*, Merwin has explored how language structures and creates experience. He has also been devoted to myth, or mythmaking, as a way of making sense of experience. While experimenting with language and myth, he has examined the possibilities of developing poetic forms suited to expressing what language can reveal about the mind and existence. In his search, Merwin has had rich resources to draw from, such as the other languages of his many translations and his firm grounding in earlier poetic traditions. His background led him first to master orthodox forms and later to move beyond them.

His devotion to poetry and his life as a wandering poet have given him a folk hero's aura. Being of the generation that began writing in the 1940's and 1950's, he had his poetic roots in more classically influenced, technically controlled verse forms. His disaffection with the formal poetic styles of his predecessors was shared by other poets of his generation such as James Wright and Robert Bly. What he had to say required new ways of communicating, new vessels that would journey toward new realms of perception. By immersing himself in the literature of other cultures, both as a student of languages and as a translator, Merwin has been able to bring a sense of the archetypal source of all poetic expression to his work. His ability to look at a tree and describe the space between its leaves may be unique among contemporary poets. Merwin has referred to his poems as houses that he makes out of virtually anything and everything he can find. These houses made of words are places where the reader can enter and experience "the echo of everything that has ever/ been spoken."

A Mask for Janus

Published in 1952, *A Mask for Janus* used myth and traditional prosodic forms to explore such themes as the birth-death cycle and the isolated self. In "Meng Tzu's Song," the speaker meditates on concerns of identity and solitude:

> How can I know, now forty
> Years have shuffled my shoulders,
> Whether my mind is steady
> Or quakes as the wind stirs?

At first reading, this poem has the flavor of a translation. Ed Folsom, writing in *W. S. Merwin: Essays on the Poetry* (1987), notes that while the verse in *A Mask for Janus* was seen by some critics as an example of traditional craftsmanship, it was also stiff at times, wordy, and overwrought. In recalling and using the structures and tonalities of a more formal poetry, however, Merwin was able to develop his mastery of those elements and earn his release from them.

The Dancing Bears

Merwin continued his use of myth and the narrative form in *The Dancing Bears*. In "East of the Sun and West of the Moon," Merwin uses the myth of Psyche and Cupid to explore the problem of identity. Through language that is often elegant and precisely shaped into neat thirteen-line stanzas, he offers clues to the enigma of inner and outer reality. In what may be read as a clarifying statement, Merwin reveals his belief that "all metaphor . . . is magic," and "all magic is but metaphor." Here, he employs his magic to explore the hidden realms of being.

THE DRUNK IN THE FURNACE

The preoccupation with myth and a formal, poetic style followed in his next two works, *Green with Beasts* and *The Drunk in the Furnace*. However, there is also a strange new energy working as Merwin begins moving away from Greco-Roman myths and toward the creation of his own.

In "The *Portland* Going Out" (from *The Drunk in the Furnace*), the apparent randomness of the disaster that strikes a passing ship recalls to the poet the mystery of life and death and thus of existence itself. The *Portland* had passed close by the poet's ship on its way out of the harbor to an ill-fated rendezvous with a storm, where it put "all of disaster between us: a gulf/ Beyond reckoning." This glimpse into the abyss works ironically as a reaffirmation of life.

There are several other poems in this collection that revolve around images of the sea. Alice N. Benston, writing in *Poets in Progress* (1962), calls the sea the "perfect symbol for Merwin." The duality inherent in the sea as both life-giver and symbol of nature's indifference to humanity provides Merwin with a metaphor for the unknown.

The poems in *The Drunk in the Furnace* take some other new and significant directions. For example, several examine the poet's youth and the family members who helped shape his early experiences. These poems are not reverential but sober, almost bitter reflections on his memories of "faded rooms," his grandfather left alone to die in a nursing home, and his grandmother's failure to see her worst sins as she reminisces about her life. The sarcastic tone of "Grandfather in the Old Men's Home" seems directed at the society in which Merwin was brought up—a society that he would later reject.

The family poems in *The Drunk in the Furnace* and others such as "Home for Thanksgiving" and "A Letter from Gussie" in *The Moving Target* allowed Merwin to explore his past further before turning away to begin a new journey. It is as if these poems generate and voice his realization and declaration that he will no longer be bound by the expectations of the culture into which he was born. Nor will he recognize any longer the restraints of the poetic forms that served as his early models.

THE LICE

The new style toward which Merwin was moving in *The Moving Target* emerges more fully realized in *The Lice*. Here he abandons narrative, adopts open forms, and eliminates punctuation:

> The nights disappear like bruises but nothing is healed
> The dead go away like bruises
> The blood vanishes into the poisoned farmlands
> Pain the horizon
> Remains

With *The Lice*, in effect, Merwin leaves the shore, lifts off the launching pad, and enters a new realm where the poem becomes the vessel for voyages toward "nameless stars." While numerous critics have pointed to the overall negativism and pessimism of *The Lice*, hope is undeniably evident in the very act of poetic discovery, as Merwin sheds his skin and emerges as something born not only "to survive," but indeed "to live."

In *The Lice* lie keys to an understanding of the work that will follow. The stark, even dumbfounding silences in a poem such as "December Among the Vanished"—in which "the old snow gets up and moves taking its/ Birds with it"—attract Merwin away from a world that seems to be in the process of self-destruction and toward a new, strange sensibility. A new spareness, a new simplicity and immediacy inform these poems. Gone are the earlier elaborate, formal structures. According to Ed Folsom and Cary Nelson in their introduction to *W. S. Merwin: Essays on the Poetry*, Merwin had begun to lose, at this stage, his faith in language and for a time was not even sure he could write words to articulate experience. In an interview with Edward Hirsch in 1987, Merwin explained how he came to distrust language, believing that experience cannot be articulated.

The Lice also reveals a new, more serious concern with the deadly corrosiveness of politics and the wanton destruction of the environment by greedy corporations. Behind the poet's initial anger and numbing frustration over mass environmental destruction, however, is a recognition of the potential for other responses to Earth's tragedy. He listens carefully, trying to hear the hidden voices in nature. These voices, and the voices emanating from his inner self, offer the possibility of discovering new consciousness—new poems—as long as he does not allow his anger to deafen him or the state of the world to distract him.

In listening for these other voices, the poet remains open to the discovery not only of the world but also of himself. In "For a Coming Extinction," he asks the reader to join voices with "the sea cows the Great Auks the gorillas" and, using the speech of innocents, to testify to the inherent significance of all life.

THE CARRIER OF LADDERS

A new tone emerges in Merwin's poetry in *The Carrier of Ladders*, which was awarded the Pulitzer Prize in 1971. The tone is one of rebirth and reaffirmation. Thus far he has stared into the dark night of his disillusionment with a world corrupted by human beings and has seen only his own reflection. However much he regrets the alienation that such a vision brought forth, he realizes at this stage that to live and create he must seek the renewal of his own spirit. To do so, the poet will have to step into the darkness, the unknown, and accept both what is there and what is not there. In "Words from a Totem Animal," Merwin writes,

> My eyes are waiting for me
> in the dusk
> they are still closed
> they have been waiting a long time
> and I am feeling my way toward them

The language and form of *The Carrier of Ladders* are perfectly suited to the poet's task of trying to see things with new eyes. This poetry is less judgmental and more open to the experiences of being alive. The simplicity of the diction, and the clear, fresh immediacy of tone draw the reader into the poems. There the poet waits, "standing in dry air" and "for no reason"—praying simply that his words may be clear.

NATURE

During the 1970's, Merwin continued his search for oneness with nature and the knowledge of self such a quest promises. The childlike innocence achieved in the poems of *The Carrier of Ladders* continues to characterize much of the poetry in *Writings to an Unfinished Accompaniment*, *The Compass Flower*, and *Finding the Islands*. Scattered throughout these books are references to the sea, fish, owls, dogs, cows, stones, mountains, clouds, the moon, and the stars. In "Gift" (*Writings to an Unfinished Accompaniment*), Merwin comes to realize that the revelation he seeks must be found through trust in what is given to him. An almost mystical stillness resides in these poems, as if one could hear the "sound of inner stone."

OPENING THE HAND

With *Opening the Hand*, Merwin looks outward toward more familiar landscapes and situations and fixes his hermetic gaze on them. In a poem about the death of his father, told as through a dream, the poet hallucinates images that seem to haunt him like ominous premonitions. His concern with ecology is also evident in this collection. In "Shaving Without a Mirror," he seems to be waking up from a night outdoors, listening for forest voices. The awe he feels, and his urge to surrender to the experience of being alone in the wilderness, confirms his sense of the interrelatedness of all things, a sense that first emerged in *The Lice*.

"What Is Modern" is a poem charged with irony. Merwin comments on the American culture's ridiculous preoccupation with defining modernity. An undeniable sense of humor and a refreshing looseness characterize the poem: "is the first/ tree that comes/ to mind modern/ does it have modern leaves." While grounded in the particular, the recognizable and commonplace, the poetry of *Opening the Hand* still achieves the same obsidian polish of earlier poems whose spare diction and muteness gave an ethereal rather than concrete quality to things.

The Rain in the Trees

The Rain in the Trees combines many of the qualities in the work of the 1960's and 1970's, while continuing Merwin's experiments in style and form. The subjects include his family, nature, travel, John Keats, language, the Statue of Liberty, Hawaii, and love. In such diversity of subjects come surprise and freshness. The poems mirror his wanderings and his restlessness in pursuit of the ineffable.

In "Empty Water," Merwin uses incantatory speech to invoke the spirit of a toad whose eyes were "fashioned of the most/ precious of metals." He chants for the toad's return:

>come back
>believer in shade
>believer in silence and elegance
>believer in ferns
>believer in patience
>believer in the rain

A joy in the primal unity and the inherent beauty of all life is evident throughout *The Rain in the Trees*. In "Waking to the Rain," the poet wakes from a dream "of harmony" to find rain creating the one sound that reveals the silence that surrounds him.

Travels

Travels shows Merwin continuing to experiment with syllabic lines and formal structures of his own devising. As the title suggests, the themes are varied, as are the locales. Meditations on his parents are among the most successful poems collected here, but what seem most fresh are the narratives that deal with historical figures: "Rimbaud's Piano," "The Blind Seer of Ambon," and "The Real World of Manuel Cordova" are likely to become classics of this kind of poem.

The Vixen

The Vixen, with its uniformity of style, can be read almost as a book-length poem. At once lyrical, narrative, and meditative, these pieces portray the landscapes and the people of the region in southwest France that Merwin knows so well and that are the subject of his *The Lost Upland*. Merwin's long, unpunctuated breaths of sinuous syntax wrap around line ends, twisting corners of thought and emotion in mesmerizing ways. Many of these pieces are quite short, and, though separately titled, they blend into one another to form a large, richly embroidered tapestry of sensation and a prayer-like celebration of interaction with place.

The Folding Cliffs

More clearly designed as a book-length poem, *The Folding Cliffs* is a sustained historical narrative about the exploitation of nineteenth century Hawaii. It is a major act of homage to that place that has been Merwin's home since 1976. Though many poems in his earlier collections deal with damage to Hawaii's ecosystems and to its culture, this poem serves as a capstone to Merwin's efforts. It is another in his ongoing testimonies to the experience of loss.

The River Sound

Loss remains a theme, as well, in *The River Sound*, a fascinating if somewhat demanding collection that demonstrates Merwin's great vitality as he moves into old age. Stylistically, it is more varied that any of Merwin's other collections, as if, having tried it all, he can now pull from his long experience whatever suits the matter at hand. Although most of the poems here are short, there are three long ones that center and focus the book. "Testimony," with its 229 eight-line stanzas rhyming (though not mechanically) *ababbcbc*, is an ambitious memoir in verse, ranging back over key experiences and people in Merwin's life. "Lament for the Makers," set in fifty-two tidy couplet quatrains, is his tribute to fellow poets now gone. "Suite in the Key of Forgetting" is more associative, conjuring various states of absence and loss.

The Pupil

Hawaii and memories of his boyhood on the Atlantic coast take a backseat in *The Pupil*. Instead Merwin turns his poetic eye toward astronomy and the night sky, which allow for reflections on mortality, transience, and the void, delivered in Merwin's familiar fluid sentences. One poem remembers "the year of the well of darkness/ overflowing with no/ moon and no stars"; others portray "the darkness thinking the light" or "the white moments that had traveled so long." Other disparate themes are explored, including government-sponsored torture of bears in Pakistan and 1998's homophobic beating death of Matthew Shepherd in Wyoming.

Present Company

Present Company is a collection of 101 poems that address topics ranging from the prosaic to the profound. Many touch on the act of writing, which the elderly Merwin knows intimately well, and many others reflect on the constant changes that are a fact of old age. The poems are often stark in their portrayals—as if time has stripped away the concealing punctuation and metaphoric language in which younger poets indulge—but they are rarely brutal. Rather, Merwin's voice has become almost gentle in its reflective observation of long-deceased people and distant places. As in earlier works, Merwin embraces a delicacy of touch that demands the full attention of the reader. "To a Falling Leaf in Winter," for example, is a poem that takes a common symbol of the passage of time in the natural world—a falling leaf—and imbues it with a fresh viewpoint. Rather than watching the "fall" with ambivalence or fear, the poet looks on the appearance of winter with a calm assurance that he has intentionally not been fully mindful of the passage of his own years. "To Forgetting," as another example, describes the loss of memory as a rather desired state of affairs. The poet wistfully recalls the quiet vacuity of early life because he finds that his memories are increasingly interfering with the peaceful enjoyment of the physical pleasures inherent in a good meal, a stimulating conversation, or the view of a pretty face. All of these experiences end up reminding him of people and places that have long since ceased to be—a situation that makes his life seem fraught with sadness and defined by loss.

Migration

Merwin was born in Scranton, Pennsylvania, but has spent his old age in the appropriately named town of Haiku. Given the vast geographical distance of Merwin's beginnings and endings, it should be no surprise that one of his later collections of verse should be named *Migration*. Merwin selected verses from fifteen of his previous volumes for *Migration*, seeking to make a collection that would be diverse in both topic and form. *Migration* is also a volume that celebrates Merwin's mastery of unstructured verse. Few poets have had poetic careers as long as that of Merwin, which makes the creation of a comprehensive collection of verse particularly challenging. On one hand, there is a vast and comprehensive range of poems to choose from; on the other, coming to any final decision on which works are to be included and which works are to be left out is a painful exercise in economy of scale. So many of Merwin's poems seem to engage in an intertextual dialogue that one hates to exclude any of them. The archaic forms of his earliest verse—lines that suggest the epic poetry of William Butler Yeats—are succeeded with increasingly spare, image-dependent lines that lack punctuation and traditional language, but there remains a consistency of purpose—the examination of one's conscience and one's definitions of self—within both types of poetry. For example, "For the Anniversary of My Death," Merwin moves outside linear time to be able to perceive the past and the future with equal clarity. Like Merlin, the wizard trapped in a crystal prison by his former student Morgan le Fay, Merwin's omniscient view is both a gift and a curse. He occupies every moment of his existence equally and is equally appalled and entranced by what he sees before him.

The Shadow of Sirius

Even in his eighties, Merwin's poetic vision never seems to falter. *The Shadow of Sirius*, which earned Merwin his second Pulitzer Prize, demonstrates the ever-present agility of his trademark deft handling of free verse. Old age and mortality, once things to be feared, are studied with a kind of breathless intensity. "Still Morning," for example, relates the tireless flight of birds who are so accustomed to the support of myriad breezes and currents that they have ceased to notice their movement in space. Aging is a similar process, Merwin notes, as he travels time without allowing its passage to dim the ecstasy of his journey. Merwin recalls the formation of his childhood self with the sharpness of a much younger man, but his analyses have a greater depth and sensitivity tempered by the perspective that only intervening decades of self-reflection could provide. One of the ironies of Merwin's half-century of poetic work has been that his penchant for spinning multiple interpretations of a memory's significance has been developed into a finely honed skill by his actual longevity. Merwin is not only a poet shaped by memory, but also a poet who has much memory yet to shape. The simplicity of the form and structure of the poems in *The Shadow of Sirius* belies a thematic complexity that surprised even the poet himself. The poems came together easily, betraying connections that Merwin described as almost taking shape unconsciously. For the creator of *A Mask for Janus*, an unseen secondary persona that underlies a deceptively open form is nothing new. Paradoxically, Merwin can appear to lay his themes out before one like an open book while still concealing a deeper meaning under the deceptively simple images.

OTHER MAJOR WORKS
SHORT FICTION: *The Miner's Pale Children*, 1970; *Houses and Travellers*, 1977; *The Lost Upland*, 1992.
PLAYS: *Darkling Child*, pr. 1956; *Favor Island*, pr. 1957; *The Gilded Nest*, pr. 1961.
TELEPLAY: *Huckleberry Finn*, 1953.
RADIO PLAYS: *Rumpelstiltskin*, 1951; *Pageant of Cain*, 1952.
NONFICTION: *Unframed Originals*, 1982; *Regions of Memory: Uncollected Prose, 1949-1982*, 1987 (Cary Nelson, editor); *The Ends of the Earth: Essays*, 2004; *Summer Doorways: A Memoir*, 2005.
TRANSLATIONS: *The Poem of the Cid*, 1959; *Satires*, 1961 (of Persius); *Spanish Ballads*, 1961; *The Song of Roland*, 1963; *Selected Translations, 1948-1968*, 1968; *Products of the Perfected Civilization: Selected Writings of Chamfort*, 1969 (of Sébastian Roch Nicolas Chamfort); *Transparence of the World*, 1969 (of Jean Follain); *Twenty Love Poems and a Song of Despair*, 1969 (of Pablo Neruda); *Voices*, 1969, 1988 (of Antonio Porchia); *Asian Figures*, 1973 (of various Asian pieces); *Selected Poems*, 1973, 1989 (of Osip Mandelstam; with Clarence Brown); *Iphigenia at Aulis*, 1978 (of Euripides; with George E. Dimock, Jr.); *Selected Translations, 1968-1978*, 1979; *Four French Plays*, 1985; *From the Spanish Morning*, 1985 (of Spanish ballads, Lope de Rueda's prose play *Eufemia*, and *Vida de Lazarillo de Tormes*); *Vertical Poetry*, 1988 (of Roberto Juarroz); *East Window: The Asian Translations*, 1998; *Purgatorio*, 2000 (of Dante); *The Life of Lazarillo de Tormes: His Fortunes and Adversities*, 2005; *Spanish Ballads*, 2008.

Bibliography

Byers, Thomas B. *What I Cannot Say: Self, Word, and World in Whitman, Stevens, and Merwin*. Urbana: University of Illinois Press, 1989. Byers's chapter on Merwin, "W. S. Merwin: A Description of Darkness," focuses primarily on *The Lice* and attempts to define Merwin's place in the American poetic tradition descended from Ralph Waldo Emerson and Walt Whitman. According to Byers, Merwin sees, as Stevens did, the self as inevitably isolated, even though his poetics recognize the need to see oneself as related to other people and other things in order to become more ecologically aware. Includes notes, a bibliography, and an index.

Christhilf, Mark. *W. S. Merwin, the Mythmaker*. Columbia: University of Missouri Press, 1986. Christhilf discusses Merwin's contributions to the postmodernist movement (with *The Moving Target*) and his assumed role of mythmaker, noting that the poet became ambivalent toward this role in the 1980's. In a useful discussion, Christhilf traces the mythmaking concern in American poetry across four decades.

Davis, Cheri. *W. S. Merwin*. Boston: Twayne, 1981. This study makes the poetry and prose of Merwin accessible to the reader new to his work. While well aware of the variety in Merwin's writing, Davis attempts to reveal what gives it unity. She examines his attitudes toward language and silence, his concern for animals and ecology, and his beliefs about poetry and nothingness. Chapters 1 through 5 look at his books of poetry, from *A Mask for Janus* through *The Compass Flower*. Chapter 6 discusses the prose poetry of *The Miner's Pale Children* and *Houses and Travellers*.

Felsteiner, John. *Can Poetry Save the Earth? A Field Guide to Nature Poems*. New Haven, Conn.: Yale University Press, 2009. Contains a chapter "W. S. Merwin's Motion of Mind," which deals with Merwin's concern for the environment.

Frazier, Jane. *From Origin to Ecology: Nature and the Poetry of W. S. Merwin*. Madison, N.J.: Fairleigh Dickinson University Press, 1999. An anlysis of images of nature in Merwin's poetry. Includes bibliographical references and an index.

Hix, H. L. *Understanding W. S. Merwin*. Columbia: University of South Carolina Press, 1997. Hix argues that despite its reputation for difficulty, Merwin's verse is clear and direct. Close readings of Merwin's verse reveal the emergence of such dominant themes as apocalypse, ecology, society, and place.

Nelson, Cary, and Ed Folsom, eds. *W. S. Merwin: Essays on the Poetry*. Urbana: University of Illinois Press, 1987. The editors provide a good introductory essay, comparing Merwin to Ezra Pound (both students of romance languages), William Carlos Williams, and Wallace Stevens. William H. Rueckert's notes are a help to readers of *The Lice*, and Folsom discusses Merwin's change in style beginning with *The Compass Flower*. Includes comprehensive bibliographies, full notes, and a thorough index.

O'Driscoll, Bill. "Legendary Poet W. S. Merwin Returns to Pittsburgh." Review of *Mi-

gration. CP: Pittsburgh City Paper, November 9, 2006, p. C1. O'Driscoll's review is particularly interesting because it highlights the return of the western Pennsylvanian poet to the regions of his youth. O'Driscoll celebrates Merwin as a poet of "silence" and find the poet's reserve to echo the quiet ruminations of generations of Pennsylvanian pacifists and environmentalists.

Scigaj, Leonard M. *Sustainable Poetry: Four American Ecopoets.* Lexington: University Press of Kentucky, 1999. The chapter on Merwin traces how the poet's initial "poetics of absence" has slowly transformed "into an ecological poetics of wakefulness." Scigaj connects Merwin's growing understanding of stressed ecosystems to his aesthetic experimentation.

Francis Poole; Philip K. Jason; Sarah Hilbert
Updated by Julia M. Meyers

MAY SWENSON

Born: Logan, Utah; May 28, 1919
Died: Ocean View, Delaware; December 4, 1989

PRINCIPAL POETRY
Another Animal, 1954
A Cage of Spines, 1958
To Mix with Time: New and Selected Poems, 1963
Half Sun Half Sleep, 1967
Iconographs, 1970
New and Selected Things Taking Place, 1978
In Other Words, 1987
The Love Poems of May Swenson, 1991
Nature: Poems Old and New, 1994
May Out West: Poems of May Swenson, 1996
The Complete Love Poems of May Swenson, 2003

OTHER LITERARY FORMS

May Swenson's forays away from poetry included short fiction, drama, and criticism. A number of her short stories have appeared in magazines and anthologies. A play, *The Floor*, was produced in New York in 1966 and published a year later. Her best-known critical essay, "The Experience of Poetry in a Scientific Age," appeared in *Poets on Poetry* (1966). She also wrote the introduction to the 1962 Collier edition of Edgar Lee Masters's *Spoon River Anthology*.

Several books for young people have expanded the audience for Swenson's poetry. *Poems to Solve* (1966), *More Poems to Solve* (1971), and *The Complete Poems to Solve* (1993) are selections of her riddle poems. For still younger children, there is *The Guess and Spell Coloring Book* (1976). Many poets owe a heavy debt to their childhoods, and few have discharged that debt more gratefully or delightfully. As a child, Swenson learned from her immigrant parents the language that she would later render into English in *Windows and Stones: Selected Poems by Tomas Tranströmer* (1972), a translation (with Leif Sjöberg) for which she won the International Poetry Forum Translation Medal. She recorded her own poems on both the Folkways and the Caedmon labels.

ACHIEVEMENTS

As traditional as she was inventive, as alliteratively Anglo-Saxon as she was typographically contemporary, May Swenson was well respected among twentieth century

American poets. Her thirty-five-year career was an ongoing celebration of language wed to life-as-it-is. Her sharp-eyed curiosity led her to address a broader and more diverse range of subjects than did many of her contemporaries: She was rural and urban, scientific and mythic, innocent and worldly, and, sometimes, even literary, and she could be any number of these within the same poem. Once she fixed her attention on something, she had a remarkable gift for letting that object of her curiosity find its voice and for allowing the poem to determine its own form. No poet wrote more perceptively or persuasively about birds—or about astronauts.

Swenson was a member of the American Academy of Arts and Letters (1970-1989) and a chancellor of the Academy of American Poets from 1980 to her death. She was awarded grants and fellowships by a number of agencies and organizations, including the Ford, Rockefeller, and Guggenheim Foundations, and the National Endowment for the Arts. She received a National Institute of Arts and Letters Award in 1960, the Shelley Memorial Award in 1968, and the Academy of American Poets Fellowship in 1979. In 1981, she shared with fellow poet Howard Nemerov the prestigious Bollingen Prize in Poetry, in recognition of her collection *New and Selected Things Taking Place*. She also served as a judge for the Lamont Poetry Selection of the Academy of American Poets and for the National Book Awards. Her frequent readings and visiting professorships at a number of colleges and universities enhanced her contribution to American letters.

Biography

The daughter of Swedish immigrants, Anne Thilda May Swenson grew up in Logan, Utah, a small college town. Her parents had left behind both their native land and their Lutheran faith to follow the teachings of the Mormon Church, which Swenson came to reject in spite of (or perhaps because of) her strict upbringing among the Latter-day Saints. As the oldest daughter in a large family, she learned early to value solitude, and at the age of thirteen, alone with her father's typewriter, she pecked out with two fingers a short piece she had written. When she looked at the resultant shape of the words on the page, she said, "This is a poem"; her life's work had begun.

Swenson's father taught woodworking and carpentry at Utah State University, which at the time was known as Utah State Agricultural College. Swenson studied English and art there and received her B.A. degree in 1939. She then worked as a reporter for a Salt Lake City newspaper, but after about a year, she made her break with home and family and moved to New York's Greenwich Village. Before gaining recognition as a poet, she worked at a variety of office jobs and, after a few years, began publishing in various magazines, including *Poetry* and *The New Yorker*. In 1954, a selection of her poems was chosen to appear with the work of two other poets (Harry Duncan and Murray Noss) in the first volume of Scribner's *Poets of Today* series. Within the next few years, she began the round of fellowships, residencies, and visiting professorships that sustained her for the rest of her career. Among her more notable positions and appointments were the editorship of New Directions Press, 1959-1966; positions as poet-in-residence at Purdue University, 1966-1967, at the University of North Carolina at Greensboro, 1968-1969 and 1975, at Lethbridge University in the Canadian province of Alberta, 1970, and at the University of California, Riverside, 1973; she also held a position on the staff of the Bread Loaf Writers' Conference, 1976. In addition, she spent time at the Yaddo and MacDowell colonies, sojourned in Europe, and traveled widely in the United States, giving readings and teaching. From 1970 until her death in 1989, Swenson and her longtime friend and companion, Rozanne Knudson, made their home in what Swenson called an "Adirondack shack" in Sea Cliff, New York, on Long Island Sound.

ANALYSIS

In his introduction to the first volume of the *Poets of Today* series, John Hall Wheelock assessed the task of the contemporary poet as one of rediscovery and revelation, in which a world gone stale must be renewed: "A poem gives the world back to the maker of the poem, in all its original strangeness, the shock of its first surprise. It is capable of doing the same for the rest of us." That volume included May Swenson's first book-length collection of poems, *Another Animal*. In the thirty-five years to follow, no voice in contemporary poetry showed more commitment to that task of poetic revelation and renewal. Although she was often spoken of as a nature poet, Swenson was as adept at celebrating the skyline of Brooklyn as a quiet wood. She was equally at home with astronauts and angels, with swans and subways. If she could bring her senses to bear upon a subject, it was the stuff of poetry.

ANOTHER ANIMAL

Swenson's verse can be classified as poetry of the senses—especially of and for the eye. A good starting point for a consideration of her work is "Horses in Central Park," a celebration of light, color, and texture: "Colors of horses like leaves or stones/ or wealthy textures/ liquors of light." A horse is not, at first glance, very much like a leaf or a stone, but Swenson always looks past that first glance to something more. The alliteration in the third line is only a mild example of her wordplay, which ranges from pure Anglo-Saxon to latter-day E. E. Cummings. Everything works together; the poem introduces a liquid tone, the sense suggests intoxication. What follows is no mere catalog of horses, but the play of light and words put through their paces. There is an autumnal truth, a lean horse the color of "sere October," fall cantering through fall. The procession continues, as "mole-gray back" and a "dappled haunch" pass by, along with "fox-red bay/ and buckskin blond as wheat." The reader takes in all the richness of the harvest and of October's light, distilled into the colors and liquid movements of horses. One need only witness the "Sober chestnut burnished/ by his sweat/ to veined and glowing oak" to let one's eyes at last convince the mind of what it may have shied away from at the poem's opening. Not only does this comparison of horse to oak leaf work but also could not be better. This effortless rhetoric of the senses distinguishes Swenson's verse. One cannot believe everything one sees or hears, she seems to say, but one had better believe in it.

ICONOGRAPHS

Swenson's verse is variously described as fierce, fresh, inquisitive, innovative, and sensuous. Her frequent experimentation with the physical appearance of her poems, however, has caused such adjectives to alight in the wrong places. Though she had dealt from the start in unorthodox punctuation, spacing, and typographic arrangements, Swenson's experiments in this direction culminated in *Iconographs*. This collection of shaped poems—"image-writing," as she described them—is mistakenly referred to by some as concrete poetry. Swenson makes it clear in an afterword that the poems were all finished down to the last word before being arranged into shapes that would enhance the words. In visual terms, the poems are the paintings, the shapes only frames. Thus, a poem on a José de Rivera mobile twists and turns on the page. In a poem called "The Blue Bottle," the words outline the shape of a bottle; in "How Everything Happens," a poem written after close observation of how ocean waves gather, break, and recede, the lines of the poem gather, break, and recede in a visual variation on the poem's message. Such devices are certainly consistent with Swenson's belief that words are, among other things, objects, and that a poem is itself an object, to be encountered by the eye and its companion senses, not merely by the intellect. These shaped poems are innovative enough in their appearance before they are even read, but it is not in their shapes that they succeed as poetry. When these or any of Swenson's poems succeed, it is because of an absolute sureness of touch and rightness of language.

Her images are at times startling, but they work upon the senses and emotions in such a way that readers cannot help giving in to their aptness and inevitability. In "The Garden at St. John's," a mother caresses her baby, whose hair is "as soft as soft/ as down as the down in the wingpits of angels." Any momentary hesitation over "wingpits" is lulled by the enchanting repetition of "soft" and "down," and the image rings, or rather, whispers, true. "Water Picture," the upside-down world reflected in the surface of a pond, would seem to be a conventional enough idea for a poem, but Swenson is not so interested in ideas as in things, and it is, indeed, the thing that finds expression here. Everyone has gazed into still water and watched the reflections, but when, in this poem, "A flag/ wags like a fishhook/ down there in the sky," when a swan bends to the surface to "kiss herself," and the "tree-limbs tangle, the bridge/ folds like a fan," one is there with a powerful immediacy.

RIDDLING POEMS

Again and again Swenson affirmed that the wonders of the world are too good merely to be described or talked about. They must be shared as directly as possible. Her mode of sharing experience was to involve herself completely in an experience, to "live into" the experience in order to express it. Thus, there is much more to poetry than the mere recording or labeling of experience. Some of Swenson's most successful poems came out of the avoidance of simply giving a name to an object. Many of these are her "riddling" poems, in which the object shared is never named, but only hinted at. One of her best known riddle poems is "By Morning":

> Some for everyone
> plenty
> and more coming
> Fresh   dainty   airily arriving
> everywhere at once.

As in most of Swenson's riddles, the clues reveal rather than obscure their answer. One need not read far into this particular poem to realize that it is about snow, but the real charm of the poem lies much deeper than the simple solution of the riddle. Systems of imagery are at work as "a gracious fleece" that spreads "like youth like wheat/ over the city." "Fleece" is picked up several lines down in the prediction that "Streets will be fields/ cars be fumbling sheep." "Youth" and "wheat" resolve themselves together at the poem's conclusion: "A deep bright harvest will be seeded/ in a night/ By morning we'll be children/ feeding on manna/ a new loaf on every doorsill." The avoidance of any explicit reference to snow is part of the poem's success, but the real strength of the piece is in the same rightness of expression that Swenson's work so consistently displays, right down to the use of extra space between certain words to vary the tempo, and, at times, the sense of a line.

THE SCIENCE POEMS

In her work of "living into" the world, Swenson explored one territory that many poets have avoided—science. She wrote poems on electronic sound patterns and on the deoxyribonucleic acid (DNA) molecule, as well as a number of poems on the U.S. space program. To one who can derive so much wonder from the ordinary and familiar, the astronaut is a wonderful figure, though not solemnly so. In "August 19, Pad 19," the astronaut waits in his cramped capsule, "Positioned for either breech birth/ or urn burial," anticipating the liftoff that will drag him "backward through 121 sunsets." Just before the mission is aborted on account of weather, he puts himself into an unheroic perspective:

> Never so impotent, so important.
> So naked, wrapped, equipped, and immobile,
> cared for by 5000 nurses.
> Let them siphon my urine to the nearest star.

The treatment is more playful than disrespectful. The fun is not at the astronaut's expense; on the contrary, he knows to what extent he is to be admired, to what extent to be pitied, yet asks for neither admiration nor pity. He is no longer so distant from humanity as he might have seemed in space, umbilicaled, "belted and bolted in" ten stories above the pad. As he gazes through the capsule's tiny window seeing "innocent drops of rain" and "Lightning's golden sneer," the reader can sneer right back with him; the same things that ruin simple Sunday picnics ruin his splendid plans as well.

NEW AND SELECTED THINGS TAKING PLACE

To say Swenson strove for variety in her work would not be quite accurate. Her variety came naturally; more often than not it came from within a poem. Once a poem had found its form, discovered its voice, and appeared in print, she rarely revised it. An apparent exception to this rule is the selection of formerly shaped poems that appear in *New and Selected Things Taking Place*, minus their iconographic frames. Probably this indicates that, having done as much as she cared to do with the iconographic poem, she chose to second-guess herself and present some of these in more conventional configurations.

A thorough study of this comprehensive collection reveals something else. Beginning with her early work, Swenson moved toward more conventional form in her poems; certainly her punctuation grew less experimental. Behind her later verses is a mature poet, more aware than ever of her considerable strengths and less willing to divert the reader's attention in any way from what she does best. One of the finest poems of her later years is "October." It speaks in hard, clear images of growing older gracefully. In one of the poem's seven sections:

> I sit with braided fingers
> and closed eyes
> in a span of late sunlight.
> The spokes are closing.
> It is fall: warm milk of light,
> though from an aging breast.

Here, many years after the dappled light of "Horses in Central Park," light keeps its liquid quality but is less intoxicating, a more nourishing, comforting distillate. In this "warm milk" of a later, mellower light, the watcher is moved to something like prayer, in spite of herself.

Swenson was not an intensely literary poet, conscious of working in a particular tradition. Certainly any poet who addressed herself so fully to "the thing" could be expected to feel a special kinship with such writers as Marianne Moore and Elizabeth Bishop. Swenson acknowledged that kinship, as well as a special feeling for another master of wordplay, Cummings. There are, as well, poets whom she considered "healthy to read," and they are rather a mixed bag—Theodore Roethke, Gerard Manley Hopkins, Emily Dickinson, Walt Whitman, and among Swenson's contemporaries, Richard Wilbur, Anthony Hecht, Anne Sexton, and James Merrill, but this is no matter of influence or imitation. Swenson acknowledged as much affinity with such visual artists as Georgia O'Keeffe and Marcel Duchamp as with any literary artist.

The poetry of others rarely moved her to song, and "literary" poems are rare among her works. Typically, a poem on Robert Frost, "R. F. at Bread Loaf His Hand Against a Tree," avoids the temptation to indulge in literary assessment and instead addresses Frost as part of the literal scene: "Companions he and the cross/ grained bark...." What might have been, in other hands, literary history in verse is rendered instead into an exuberant portrait in wordplay. For purposes of inspiration, Swenson was less likely to look to literature than to the newspaper, the zoo, *Scientific American*, a walk in the woods, or a ride on the subway.

IN OTHER WORDS

In this regard, Swenson's last volume of poems, *In Other Words*, is of a piece with her earlier work. Here are plenty of examples of Swenson's gift for discovering poetry taking place in unexpected places—a hospital blood test; the consignment of Charlie McCarthy, perhaps history's most famous ventriloquist's dummy, to the Smithsonian after the death of Edgar Bergen; and a magazine ad for a digital watch. In Swenson's hands, all are the stuff of poetry.

A package received in the mail prompts "A Thank-You Letter." For the package? No, for "the wonderful cord 174″ long" that bound the package. The poem ends with the narrator's cat entangled in the string, "having a wonderful puzzle-playtime." The narrator admits,

> . . . I haven't yet
>
> taken the sturdy paper off your package.
> I hardly feel I want to. The gift has been
> given! For which, thank you ever so much.

The process in this poem in many ways encapsulates Swenson's approach to poetry as a whole: Swenson's approach is eclectic in the very best sense, for "eclectic" means, at its root, not "to throw together" but "to pick out."

Because she picked and chose so well, because she was so much a part of the experiences that she made into poetry, and because her poems are so resistant to paraphrase and explication, her works are their own best commentary. "A Navajo Blanket" is a sort of guided tour of one of the "Eye-dazzlers the Indians weave." Having worked in from the edges over paths of brilliant colors,

> You can sleep at the center,
> attended by Sun that never fades, by Moon
> that cools. Then, slipping free of zigzag and
> hypnotic diamond, find your way out
> by the spirit trail, a faint Green thread that
> secretly crosses the border, where your mind
> is rinsed and returned to you like a white cup.

No matter what colors she worked in, what patterns she wove, Swenson was always careful to include that "faint Green thread" that was her perpetual wonder at things as they are. By following that thread, the reader can embrace the world, a world clean and new, good to look upon and good to hold.

Other major works

PLAY: *The Floor*, pr. 1966.

NONFICTION: *The Contemporary Poet as Artist and Critic*, 1964; "The Experience of Poetry in a Scientific Age," 1966; *Made with Words*, 1998 (Gardner McFall, editor).

TRANSLATION: *Windows and Stones: Selected Poems by Tomas Tranströmer*, 1972 (with Leif Sjöberg; of Tomas Tranströmer).

CHILDREN'S LITERATURE: *Poems to Solve*, 1966; *More Poems to Solve*, 1971; *The Guess and Spell Coloring Book*, 1976; *The Complete Poems to Solve*, 1993.

MISCELLANEOUS: *Dear Elizabeth: Five Poems and Three Letters to Elizabeth Bishop*, 2000.

Bibliography

Crumbley, Paul, and Patricia M. Gantt, eds. *Body My House: May Swenson's Work and Life*. Logan: Utah State University Press, 2006. A collection of critical essays that discuss many aspects of Swenson's life and work, including her nature poems, her explorations of sexuality, and her friendships with other writers.

Doty, Mark. "Queen Sweet Thrills: Reading May Swenson." *Yale Review* 88, no. 1 (January, 2000): 86-110. Doty discusses Swenson's work, describing how, over the course of her eleven books of poetry, the poet developed a dramatic dialogue between revelation and concealment.

Gould, Jean. *Modern American Women Poets*. New York: Dodd, Mead, 1984. Account of Swenson's life includes details of her childhood, the influence—or lack of influence—of her parents' Mormon faith, and her associations with other writers, especially Robert Frost and Elizabeth Bishop. Gould also explores Swenson's longtime relationship with teacher and children's author Rozanne Knudson.

Howard, Richard. *Alone with America*. New York: Atheneum, 1969. This book-length study of modern American poets includes a chapter on Swenson, "Turned Back to the Wild by Love." Howard provides a fine, detailed study of Swenson's poetics and technique, illustrated by dozens of examples from her early poems.

Salter, Mary Jo. "No Other Words." Review of *In Other Words*. *The New Republic* 201 (March 7, 1988): 40-41. This review of Swenson's last volume of poems offers a brief but perceptive discussion of her poetic strengths and limitations. Salter compares her work to that of poets as diverse as Elizabeth Bishop, Gerard Manley Hopkins, and George Herbert.

Stanford, Ann. "May Swenson: The Art of Perceiving." *Southern Review* 5 (Winter, 1969): 58-75. This essay treats Swenson as a master of observation and perception. Through numerous examples—drawn mostly from the poet's nature poems—Stanford explores Swenson's ability to surprise and delight the reader by observing the world from unexpected angles or by simply noticing and recording the easily overlooked detail.

Swenson, May. "An Interview with May Swenson: July 14, 1978." Interview by Karla Hammond. *Parnassus: Poetry in Review* 7 (Fall/Winter, 1978): 60-75. In this piece, Swenson talks in some detail on a range of subjects, from her childhood and education to her writing habits, her approach to poetry, and her admiration for such poets as Elizabeth Bishop and E. E. Cummings. Throughout, she illustrates the discussion with examples from her work.

Zona, Kirstin Hotelling. "A 'Dangerous Game of Change': Images of Desire in the Love Poems of May Swenson." *Twentieth Century Literature* 44, no. 2 (Summer, 1998): 219-241. Zona argues that Swenson's strategy of employing blatantly heterosexual or stereotypically gendered tropes is central to the relationship between sexuality and subjectivity that shapes her larger poetic.

Richard A. Eichwald

RABINDRANATH TAGORE

Born: Calcutta, India; May 7, 1861
Died: Calcutta, India; August 7, 1941
Also known as: Rabindranath Thakur

PRINCIPAL POETRY
 Saisab sangit, 1881
 Sandhya sangit, 1882
 Prabhat sangit, 1883
 Chabi o gan, 1884
 Kari o komal, 1887
 Mānashi, 1890
 Sonār tari, 1893 (*The Golden Boat*, 1932)
 Chitra, 1895
 Chaitāli, 1896
 Kanika, 1899
 Kalpana, 1900
 Katha o kahini, 1900
 Kshanikā, 1900
 Naivedya, 1901
 Sisu, 1903 (*The Crescent Moon*, 1913)
 Smaran, 1903
 Utsarga, 1904
 Kheya, 1905
 Gitānjali, 1910 (*Gitanjali Song Offerings*, 1912)
 The Gardener, 1913
 Gitali, 1914
 Balāka, 1916 (*A Flight of Swans*, 1955, 1962)
 Fruit-Gathering, 1916
 Gan, 1916
 Stray Birds, 1917
 Love's Gift, and Crossing, 1918
 Palataka, 1918 (*The Fugitive*, 1921)
 Lipika, 1922
 Poems, 1922
 Sisu bholanath, 1922
 The Curse at Farewell, 1924
 Prabahini, 1925

Purabi, 1925
Fifteen Poems, 1928
Fireflies, 1928
Mahuya, 1929
Sheaves: Poems and Songs, 1929
Banabani, 1931
The Child, 1931
Parisesh, 1932
Punascha, 1932
Vicitrita, 1933
Bithika, 1935
Ses saptak, 1935
Patraput, 1936, 1938 (English translation, 1969)
Syamali, 1936 (English translation, 1955)
Khapchada, 1937
Prantik, 1938
Senjuti, 1938
Navajatak, 1940
Rogsajya, 1940
Sanai, 1940
Arogya, 1941
Janmadine, 1941
Poems, 1942
Sesh lekha, 1942
The Herald of Spring, 1957
Wings of Death: The Last Poems, 1960
Devouring Love, 1961
A Bunch of Poems, 1966
One Hundred and One, 1967
Last Poems, 1973
Later Poems, 1974
Final Poems, 2001

OTHER LITERARY FORMS

Besides more than fifty collections of poetry, Rabindranath Tagore (tuh-GOHR) wrote thirteen novels, ten collections of short stories, more than sixty plays, and numerous volumes of literary criticism, letters, translations, reminiscences, lectures, sermons, travel sketches, philosophy, religion, and politics. In addition, he translated a considerable amount of his own work from its original Bengali into English.

Tagore's drama, which generally tends to be more lyric than dramatic, is best repre-

Rabindranath Tagore
(©The Nobel Foundation)

sented by *Visarjan* (pb. 1890; *Sacrifice*, 1917), *Chitrāngadā* (pb. 1892; *Chitra*, 1913), *Prayaschitta* (pr. 1909; atonement), *Rājā* (pb. 1910; *The King of the Dark Chamber*, 1914), *Dākghar* (pb. 1912; *Post Office*, 1914), and *Raktakarabi* (pb. 1924; *Red Oleanders*, 1925). Examples of later plays—*Muktadhārā* (pb. 1922; English translation, 1950), *Natir Pujā* (pb. 1926; *Worship of the Dancing Girl*, 1950), and *Chandālikā* (pr., pb. 1933; English translation, 1938)—were translated by Marjorie Sykes in *Three Plays* (pb. 1950).

Tagore's fiction, which also reflects his lyric bent, sometimes seems to prefigure the "open form." Including some of his best work, his short stories have been compared to those of Guy de Maupassant. Some of his short stories have been translated in *The Hungry Stones, and Other Stories* (1916), *Mashi, and Other Stories* (1918), and *The Runaway, and Other Stories* (1959). *Gora* (1910; English translation, 1924) is usually considered his best novel, but others of interest are *Chokher bāli* (1902; *Binodini*, 1959), *Ghare bāire* (1916; *Home and the World*, 1919), *Chaturanga* (1916; English translation, 1963), *Jogajog* (1929; cross currents), *Shesher kabita* (1929; *Farewell My Friend*, 1946), and *Dui bon* (1933; *Two Sisters*, 1945).

Tagore's nonfictional prose, some of which was originally written as lectures in English, is represented by *Jivansmriti* (1912; *My Reminiscences*, 1917), *Personality* (1917), *Nationalism* (1919), *Creative Unity* (1922), *The Religion of Man* (1931), and *Towards Universal Man* (1961).

Achievements

Few writers have achieved such fame as came to Rabindranath Tagore when he was awarded the 1913 Nobel Prize in Literature. The first Asian to receive the award, he was viewed in the West as the embodiment of Eastern mystical wisdom. Indian critics at the time, however, often attacked his work, usually for political reasons, even though he did more than any other writer to establish Bengali as a flexible literary language (he was experimenting with it to the end of his life). Perhaps needing money for the school he had established at Santiniketan, Tagore took advantage of his fame to churn out English translations. Although he admitted his limited skill in English, he was shrewd enough to satisfy the sentimental streak in his English-speaking audiences. The combination of modest skill and banality was devastating for his poetry. His so-called prose poems—usually paraphrases, though they occasionally break into Whitmanesque free verse—are noteworthy examples of what is lost in the translation of poetry. Eventually, these translations caught up with his reputation, which began sinking in the West about the time that graduates of Santiniketan began producing books on their *Gurudev*. One of these former students, Aurobindo Bose, has produced the best English translations of Tagore's poetry now available.

As Jane Addams (of Hull House) noted, Tagore was "at once a poet, a philosopher, a humanitarian, an educator," and as Hermann Hesse said, Tagore's reputation was built in part on "the rich heritage of ancient Indian philosophy." Similarly, Tagore's work reflects certain native literary traditions, such as Indian drama and the *Baul* folk songs, which are alien to the West. Finally, where his poetry is concerned, it should be borne in mind that Tagore was a songwriter (he composed about two thousand songs), that he set some of his poems to music, and that in Bengali his poetry has rich musical qualities—rhythm, rhyme, alliteration, assonance—that accompany the words, images, and ideas. All these factors must be carefully weighed in evaluating Tagore's overall achievement.

Otherwise, each individual work must be considered separately. Tagore wrote too much, so there is repetition and wide variation in quality, especially in his poetry. (Apparently he needed a critical audience off which to bounce his poems, but he found it neither in his Indian milieu nor in the adulatory West.) For example, the same period that produced *Gitanjali Song Offerings* and *A Flight of Swans* also produced the soppy poems in *The Crescent Moon*. Besides *Gitanjali Song Offerings* and *A Flight of Swans*, perhaps his finest works are the short stories translated in *The Hungry Stones, and Other Stories*. Readers of English would also do well to rediscover his lectures, wherein Tagore speaks for peace, internationalism, and understanding—themes prominent in his literary work.

Biography

Rabindranath Tagore was born into a wealthy, influential, and culturally active Brahmin family. The name Tagore is an English corruption of the title *Thakur* (that is, Brahmin), and the name Rabindranath means "lord of the sun" (*rabi* means "the sun"). Tagore's father was Maharishi (Great Sage) Devendranath Tagore, an important religious writer and leader of Brahmo Samaj (Society of God), a new monotheistic religion founded on a return to the Upanishads and progressive political ideas. A response both to orthodox Hinduism (characterized by idolatry, the caste system, suttee, and similar oppressive practices) and to Western culture (especially Christianity), the reformist Brahmo Samaj virtually defined the development of Tagore's own thought.

Despite his apparent advantages, Tagore, the youngest of fourteen children, had a difficult childhood. His father was involved with his activities as a maharishi, and Tagore's mother was sickly (she died when he was thirteen). The infant Rabi was turned over to the care of servants, who simplified their duties by confining him within rooms and chalk circles. He did not last long in any of the several schools he attended, consequently receiving little formal education. He was saved by his father and family activities. At the age of twelve, he accompanied his father, whom he idolized, on an extended journey to Santiniketan (his father's rural retreat, about one hundred miles west of Calcutta), Amritsar, and the Himalayas, where they lived in a mountain hut and where his father instructed him. On his return to Calcutta, the young Tagore gradually became involved in family activities.

The family was ostracized by orthodox Hindus, thus leaving the Tagores free to do as they pleased. As a result, the family home, Jorasanko Palace, was the cultural center of Calcutta, buzzing with more than a hundred inhabitants as well as a steady flow of distinguished visitors—reformist religious leaders, nationalist politicians, writers, artists, and musicians. The evenings were filled with musical performances, plays, readings, and discussions that lasted far into the night. Even the women were involved, further scandalizing the neighbors, who still practiced purdah (the formal seclusion of women from public view). The lively teenage Tagore plunged into this activity, contributing songs, readings, and critical observations. When, in 1877, the family started its own monthly magazine, *Bharati*, the sixteen-year-old Tagore helped edit it and was a main contributor. What better education could one find for Tagore the writer (not to mention Tagore the singer, songwriter, actor, critic, politician, philosopher, and artist)?

One more try at formal education occurred in 1878, when Tagore was sent to Great Britain to prepare to study law, first at a school in Brighton, then at University College, London. He continued to make contributions to *Bharati*, expressing his dislike for the British people and his love for British literature (especially William Shakespeare and the Romantics). After two years, Tagore returned home, and in 1883, a marriage was arranged for him with Mrinalini Devi (then only nine years old), whom he called Nalini. In 1891, they settled down in Shelidah, where Tagore's father assigned him to manage the family estates and where Tagore for the first time came into direct contact with the Indian countryside and peasant life. This period provided him with some of his best material for short stories. (For example, he rescued a tenant's wife who was being swept down a flooding river, but did she thank him? No, she was trying to commit suicide.) Sympathy for the conditions of peasant life also deepened his involvement in the growing Indian Nationalist movement, for which he wrote and made speeches. When the Nationalist movement eventually became violent, however, he broke off his involvement and withdrew to Santiniketan (which, appropriately, means "abode of peace"). Later, he would come to believe that nationalism is one of the great evils of the modern world.

In 1901, Tagore began his career as an educator, starting a school at Santiniketan. It is ironic, but understandable, that the dropout should become the educator; some of his five children were of school age, and, recalling his school experience, he had his own ideas about how to teach them. These ideas he put into practice at Santiniketan. He was also responding to the conditions around him, seeking to uplift his countrymen in a way that did not involve violence. Besides, there was always something of the teacher in Tagore, as shown by his campaign to enlighten first his own countrymen and later the West. The teacher comes out frequently (though indirectly) in his poetry, in which he sometimes seems to adopt the stance of the Great Sage. Above all, Tagore was interested in seeing certain ideas prevail, as proclaimed by the motto of Santiniketan: "Santam, sivam, advaitam" (peace, good, union).

The early years at Santiniketan were marred for Tagore by great personal loss: In 1902 his wife died, in 1904 his eldest daughter, in 1905 his father, and in 1907 his youngest son. However, the deepening process of meditating on these losses produced his best poetry, *Gitanjali Song Offerings* and *A Flight of Swans*. The school was also in constant need of money, which eventually required him to make several fund-raising and lecture trips to the United States, Great Britain, and the European Continent. These journeys established him as an ambassador to the West—a role he found much easier to fill after he won the 1913 Nobel Prize in Literature. Everywhere he went, he was received as the Great Sage, and he was awarded numerous honors (such as a British knighthood in 1915). He visited the Soviet Union and Japan, both of which he admired, but he criticized Communist suppression of individual rights and the militant nationalism of the Japanese. He was especially appalled by Japanese efforts to conquer China.

Tagore's last years were spent in traveling, in expanding the Santiniketan complex, in practicing a new art (painting), and in pointing the world toward peace. In 1922, he established Sriniketan (abode of grace), an institute for agriculture and rural reconstruction, and Visva-Bharati (universal voice), an international university for bringing the message of the East to the West. His paintings were exhibited in Europe to favorable reviews. He was disappointed in his work for peace, thinking that nations that had endured one world war would not want another. The 1930's were increasingly depressing for him, and he died in 1941, just as World War II was reaching its full incarnation.

ANALYSIS

The main theme of Rabindranath Tagore's poetry is the essential unity (or continuity) of all creation, which is also the main theme of the ancient Hindu Upanishads. Indeed, a brief summary of Hindu belief provides a useful introduction to Tagore's work. According to Hindu thought, the only absolute, unchanging, eternal thing is Brahman, the supreme being or world soul who forms the essence of everything. In living things, the essence of Brahman is known as Atman, or soul. Brahman operates through three aspects: Brahma, the creator; Siva, the destroyer; and Vishnu, the preserver or renewer. Brahma's work is finished, but Siva and Vishnu are necessary for change, and change is necessary so that living things may grow toward union with Brahman, a perfect, changeless state, nirvana. Few, if any, achieve nirvana in one lifetime, so reincarnation is necessary. In each successive incarnation, one improves one's status in the next through good karma or deeds (broadly interpreted as actions, thoughts, or faith).

The questions raised by Hindu belief may be ignored here (for example, why would Brahman create something imperfect in the first place?); so also may certain negative social implications (such as the potential for inaction, the caste system, and unconcern for the individual human life). Instead, what should be noticed is the positive emphasis of Hinduism, in contrast to Western thought as characterized by the old Germanic notion that everything is moving toward *Götterdämmerung*; the Christian emphasis on Original Sin, evil, and Hell; the masked versions of human sacrifice. It is the positive implications of Hindu belief that Tagore develops in his poetry. For example, his imagery—dwelling on sunrises and sunsets, flowers and their scents, songs and musical instruments, the beautiful deodar tree (*deodár* meaning "divine wood"), the majestic Himalayas—is a constant reminder that creation is charged with divinity: Beauty and majesty are concrete manifestations of Brahman. Change, natural disasters, and death are necessary for renewal, which will come. All people have divine souls, so they should tolerate, respect, and love one another. The advantaged should help the disadvantaged; thereby, they both rise toward Brahman. The individual should strive to live in such a way as to throw off impurities and achieve the essence of divinity within the self. The development of these and related themes can be traced throughout Tagore's oeuvre.

GITANJALI SONG OFFERINGS

Published in 1910, *Gitanjali Song Offerings* is Tagore's most popular work. The English edition, published in 1912, includes translations not only from the original *Gitānjali* but also from other collections, particularly *Naivedya* (offerings). As light work to keep his mind occupied, Tagore did the translations himself while he was convalescing from an illness at Shelidah and on board a ship for Great Britain. He showed them to British friends who wanted to read his work. They in turn showed the translations to William Butler Yeats, and the result was English publication followed by the 1913 Nobel Prize in Literature. Aware of the undistinguished quality of his translations,

Tagore himself could never understand why he was rash enough to do them or why they created such a sensation.

Sometimes compared to the Book of Psalms, *Gitanjali Song Offerings* explores the personal relationship between the poet and divinity. This divinity he calls Jivandevata, which he often translates as "Lord of my life" or "life of my life" but also refers to as "my God," "King," "Father," "Mother," "lover," "friend," and "innermost one." The range of terms here suggests the varied associations of Jivandevata and also the conventional metaphors Tagore generally uses to develop his relationship with Jivandevata. Perhaps the most numerous poems are those in which, like John Donne or Saint Teresa of Ávila, Tagore speaks of the deity as a lover with whom he longs to be united. In Song 60 (numbers refer to the English edition), Tagore varies the formula somewhat. He describes a woman who dwells in purdah within his heart. Many men have come asking for her, but none has seen her face, because she waits only for God. The woman represents the spark of divinity in Tagore which longs to be reunited with its source, and the purdah suggests its loneliness and purity. The divinity within inspires Tagore's songs and motivates him to lead a pure life, but he confesses that involvement in commonplace events sometimes creates a smoke screen that obscures the divinity within and without. The commonplace, however, also has its divinity. God is to be found not only in the temple but also with the workers in the fields. Because divinity runs through everything, even the metaphors that Tagore uses to describe God have an element of literal truth.

The most interesting poems in *Gitanjali Song Offerings* are a group dealing with death. Songs 86 and 87 are about a family member—probably the poet's wife—whom death has taken. Although heartbroken by her death, Tagore welcomes the visit of God's "servant" and "messenger," and seeking her in the oneness of the universe has brought Tagore closer to God. Thus reconciled, Tagore welcomes his own death as "the fulfillment of life." His dying will be like a bride meeting her bridegroom on the wedding night or like a feeding babe switching from the right breast to the left breast of its mother. Meanwhile, his soul is like "a flock of homesick cranes," on the wing day and night to reach "their mountain nests."

A FLIGHT OF SWANS

Perhaps Tagore's best work, *A Flight of Swans*, takes its title from the image on which *Gitanjali Song Offerings* ends. Thematically, *A Flight of Swans* also takes up where *Gitanjali Song Offerings* ends. Although *A Flight of Swans* continues to develop the personal relationship between the poet and divinity, there is a new emphasis on the impersonal workings of divinity throughout creation. The dual emphasis can be seen in the opening poem of the English edition, the title poem, wherein the flight of swans breaking the silence of the evening symbolizes not only the aspiration of the human soul but also the yearning of inanimate nature for "the Beyond." Even the mountains and deodar trees long to spread their wings like the "homeless bird" inside the breast of Tagore and "countless others." The images of movement and yearning here also serve to introduce the theme of change so prominent in *A Flight of Swans*.

For Tagore, the abstract notion of change is embodied in the dance of Siva, the destroyer, who is featured in several poems. Sometimes called Rudra (the terrible one), Siva brings violence, destruction, and death. To scholars of Sigmund Freud, Tagore's worship of Siva might sound like an Eastern version of the death wish, and his reveling in "the sea of pain" and "the sport of death" might repel squeamish readers. Nevertheless, there is a reason for Tagore's embrace of resounding agony. The dance of Siva purges the cosmological systems. It prevents the flow of "gross Matter" from backing up and putrefying, "renews and purifies" creation in "the bath of death," and speeds souls onward toward nirvana. The only thing which survives Siva's dance is immortal art, as represented by the Taj Mahal. Becoming Siva's partner, Tagore aligns himself with the young rather than the old, with the unknown rather than the known, with wandering rather than home, with movement rather than stagnancy.

With its focus on movement and change, on the cyclic nature of things, *A Flight of Swans* breathes the same spirit as Percy Bysshe Shelley's "Ode to the West Wind": If Siva comes, can Vishnu be far behind? Indeed, Tagore hoped that Vishnu, the preserver and renewer, would come soon. Tagore wrote *A Flight of Swans* at the outset of World War I, and the poems reflect his awareness of the war's catastrophic violence. Once the war started, he hoped that it would at least bring about some good results—that it would clean out the evils of the old world system and bring about a new order of peace and brotherhood.

PATRAPUT

Patraput means "a cup of leaves." The poems in this collection are the leaves shed by the poet's tree of life during his old age. *Patraput* is also a reminder that Tagore wrote poetry on subjects other than religion. He was a love poet, especially in his early career, a nature poet (*Banabani*) concentrating on trees and plants, and he even wrote a collection of humorous poems that he called *Khapchada* (a little offbeat). *Patraput* represents not only the mellowness of Tagore's old age but also the variety of his subjects. There are even a few love poems from the seventy-five-year-old poet.

Many of the poems in *Patraput* celebrate subtle effects. With humor and sensitivity, two poems (2 and 7) explore the idleness of holidays. At home by himself in the countryside (probably Santiniketan), the poet has trouble adjusting to doing nothing but feels himself better off than vacationers scrambling through railway stations. In the surrounding scenes of nature that Tagore pauses to observe, God provides him with a "change of air" and a visit to "the eternal ocean" for free. Meanwhile, he knows his "return ticket" will soon expire and he will have to return to the workaday world, "to return here from here itself." These two poems and others contain some attractive descriptions of nature. Another excellent example is Poem 9, which traces the coming and passing of a storm. A number of the poems also trace shifts of mood, from one season to another, from one time of day to another, from one scene to another. In some of these small effects, there are suggestions of bigger themes. For example, there are intimations of the poet's coming death ("return ticket") in the description, as though he is sinking slowly into the placid Indian countryside. The epiphany in Poem 1, where the poet climbs a mountaintop to see the sun setting on one hand and the moon rising on the other, is reminiscent of William Wordsworth's topping of Mount Snowdon in *The Prelude: Or, The Growth of a Poet's Mind* (1850).

Another interesting group of poems in *Patraput* consists of those containing social commentary. In Poem 6, Tagore urges the reader ("O thou hospitable") to invite in the destitute pilgrim so that the poor fellow can rise above his mere struggle for existence. In Poem 15, Tagore, himself ostracized when a child, identifies with the untouchables who are prohibited from entering temples, and with the itinerant *Baul* singers, who sing that God is "the Man of my heart." Like them, Tagore has no caste, no temple, no religion except the religion of Man. Poem 16 is a lament for Africa, ransacked for slaves by the purveyors of Christian "civilization." Their phony belief in religion is duplicated in the modern era by the militarists who seek Buddha's blessings for their killing (apparently a slap at Japanese aggression in Manchuria).

CRITICISM OF FORMAL RELIGION

As the unflattering references to Hindus, Christians, and Buddhists indicate, Tagore had no more enthusiasm for formal religion than he had for formal education. Nevertheless, along with such figures as Gerard Manley Hopkins and T. S. Eliot, Tagore is a leading religious poet of the modern era. The social commentary in *Patraput* marks the final stage of his spiritual journey. In *Gitanjali Song Offerings*, he is concerned with his personal fate, his individual relationship to God. In *A Flight of Swans*, he explores the impersonal workings of divinity through the terrible dance of Siva; and in *Patraput*, he shows that religious belief must ultimately be expressed through concern (and action) for one's fellow men. With his "religion of Man," Tagore ends up in a position very similar to Western Humanism, but it is a position that retains its ties to ancient religious belief, belief summed up in the teaching of the humble *Baul* singers that God is "the Man of my heart."

OTHER MAJOR WORKS

LONG FICTION: *Bau-Thakuranir Hat*, 1883; *Rajarshi*, 1887; *Chokher bāli*, 1902 (*Binodini*, 1959); *Naukadubi*, 1906 (*The Wreck*, 1921); *Gora*, 1910 (English translation, 1924); *Chaturanga*, 1916 (English translation, 1963); *Ghare bāire*, 1916 (*Home and the World*, 1919); *Jogajog*, 1929; *Shesher kabita*, 1929 (*Farewell My Friend*, 1946); *Dui bon*, 1933 (*Two Sisters*, 1945).

SHORT FICTION: *The Hungry Stones, and Other Stories*, 1916; *Mashi, and Other Stories*, 1918; *Stories from Tagore*, 1918; *Broken Ties, and Other Stories*, 1925; *The*

Runaway, and Other Stories, 1959; *Selected Short Stories*, 1991 (translated with an introduction by William Radice).

PLAYS: *Prakritir Pratishodh*, pb. 1884 (verse play; *Sanyasi: Or, The Ascetic*, 1917); *Rājā o Rāni*, pb. 1889 (verse play; *The King and the Queen*, 1918); *Visarjan*, pb. 1890 (verse play; based on his novel *Rajarshi; Sacrifice*, 1917); *Chitrāngadā*, pb. 1892 (verse play; *Chitra*, 1913); *Prayaschitta*, pr. 1909 (based on his novel *Bau-Thakuranir Hat*); *Rājā*, pb. 1910 (*The King of the Dark Chamber*, 1914); *Dākghar*, pb. 1912 (*The Post Office*, 1914); *Phālguni*, pb. 1916 (*The Cycle of Spring*, 1917); *Arupratan*, pb. 1920 (revision of his play *Rājā*); *Muktadhārā*, pb. 1922 (English translation, 1950); *Raktakarabi*, pb. 1924 (*Red Oleanders*, 1925); *Chirakumār Sabhā*, pb. 1926; *Natir Pujā*, pb. 1926 (*Worship of the Dancing Girl*, 1950); *Sesh Rakshā*, pb. 1928; *Paritrān*, pb. 1929 (revision of *Prayaschitta*); *Tapati*, pb. 1929 (revision of *Rājā o Rāni*); *Bānsari*, pb. 1933; *Chandālikā*, pr., pb. 1933 (English translation, 1938); *Nritya-natya Chitrāngadā*, pb. 1936 (revision of his play *Chitrāngadā*); *Nritya-natya Chandālikā*, pb. 1938 (revision of his play *Chandālikā*); *Three Plays*, 1950.

NONFICTION: *Jivansmriti*, 1912 (*My Reminiscences*, 1917); *Sadhana: The Realisation of Life*, 1913; *Nationalism*, 1917; *Personality*, 1917; *Glimpses of Bengal*, 1921; *Greater India*, 1921; *Creative Unity*, 1922; *Talks in China*, 1925; *Lectures and Addresses*, 1928; *Letters to a Friend*, 1928; *The Religion of Man*, 1931; *Mahatmaji and the Depressed Humanity*, 1932; *The Religion of an Artist*, 1933; *Man*, 1937; *Chhelebela*, 1940 (*My Boyhood Days*, 1940); *Sabhyatar Samkat*, 1941 (*Crisis in Civilization*, 1941); *Towards Universal Man*, 1961.

MISCELLANEOUS: *Collected Poems and Plays*, 1936; *A Tagore Reader*, 1961.

BIBLIOGRAPHY

Das Gupta, Uma. *Rabindranath Tagore: A Biography*. New York: Oxford University Press, 2004. A biography of Tagore, based largely on his letters, that reveals him as a poet and writer with a social conscience.

_____, ed. *The Oxford India Tagore: Selected Writings on Education and Nationalism*. New York: Oxford University Press, 2009. An examination of Tagore's views on education and nationalism and his relationship with Oxford.

Dutta Gupta, Reeta. *Rabindranath Tagore: The Poet Sublime*. New Delhi: Rupa, 2002. A biography that examines the life and works of Tagore, with emphasis on his poetry.

Ghosh, Dipali, comp. *Bengali Works of Rabindranath Tagore into English: A Bibliography*. Calcutta: Firma KLM, 2008. A bibliography of the works written by Tagore in Bengali and translated into English.

Ivbulis, Viktors. *Tagore: East and West Cultural Unity*. Calcutta: Rabindra Bharati University, 1999. The author looks at the influence of both the West and the East in Tagore's work. Bibliography.

Nandi, Sudhirakumara. *Art and Aesthetics of Rabindra Nath Tagore*. Calcutta: Asiatic Society, 1999. Nandi analyzes the Tagore's aesthetics as expressed in his writings. Bibliography and index.

Nandy, Ashis. *The Illegitimacy of Nationalism: Rabindranath Tagore and the Politics of Self*. New York: Oxford University Press, 1994. This study focuses on the political and social views of Tagore as demonstrated by his life and writings. Bibliography and index.

_____. *Return from Exile*. New York: Oxford University Press, 1998. An analysis of Tagore's political writing which puts him in the context of India's move in the 1920's toward nationalism. This, in turn, illuminates some of the philosophy and themes in his other writing.

Saha, Panchanan. *Tagore and USA*. Calcutta: Biswabiksha, 2009. An account of Tagore's life that focuses on his travels in the United States and relations with Americans.

Sen Gupta, Kalyan. *The Philosophy of Rabindranath Tagore*. Burlington, Vt.: Ashgate, 2005. A comprehensive introduction to Tagore's poetry and essays and the way they relate to his philosophy, politics and religion.

Harold Branam

EDWARD THOMAS

Born: London, England; March 3, 1878
Died: Arras, France; April 9, 1917

PRINCIPAL POETRY
Six Poems, 1916
Poems, 1917
Last Poems, 1918
Collected Poems, 1920, 1928
The Poetry of Edward Thomas, 1978

OTHER LITERARY FORMS

Although Edward Thomas is remembered today as a poet, throughout his working life, he supported himself and his family by writing various sorts of prose. He always considered himself to be a writer, and the lasting tragedy of his life was that he never seemed able, until the outbreak of World War I, to buy enough time to devote himself to the art of writing as he obviously wished to do. Ironically, the war in which he died also provided him with the structured, organized environment and the freedom from financial anxiety that enabled him to produce the work which has secured his reputation.

His entire prose opus runs to nearly forty volumes, most of which were published during his lifetime. The titles cover a variety of subjects. It is also possible to see what a remarkable volume of work he produced in the years 1911 to 1912, a productivity that culminated, after nine published works, in a breakdown in 1912. Although the prose work of Thomas is often dismissed as being unimportant, it is obvious from merely reading the titles where his main interests lay. Themes of nature and of the British countryside predominate, together with literary criticism.

In fact, Thomas was a remarkably perceptive literary critic. He was among the first reviewers to appreciate the work of Robert Frost, and he also recognized Ezra Pound's achievement in *Personae* (1909), which he reviewed in its first year of publication. When he began to write, he was heavily influenced by Walter Pater's code of aesthetics, his love of rhetoric, and his formality. He was later to have to work hard to rid his prose of those features, which he recognized as being alien to his own poetic voice.

ACHIEVEMENTS

In his poetry, Edward Thomas succeeded in realizing two ambitions, which another poet of nature set out as his aims more than a century earlier. In the preface to the *Lyrical Ballads* (1798), William Wordsworth stated that his intent in writing poetry was "to exalt and transfigure the natural and the common" and also to redefine the status of the poet so that he would become "a man speaking to men." Wordsworth's poetry received both acclaim and abuse when it first appeared and formed an expectation of poetry that continued until the end of the nineteenth century. By that time, the aesthetic movement had come to the fore, and poetry was well on its way, at the outbreak of World War I, toward suffocating itself with overblown rhetoric.

Thomas is not generally regarded as a war poet, being discussed more often in conjunction with Thomas Hardy and Walter de la Mare than with Wilfred Owen, Siegfried Sassoon, and Isaac Rosenberg. By combining his acute perceptions of both nature and political events, however, Thomas produced poetry in which evocations of place and detailed descriptions of nature become a metaphor for humanity's spiritual state. F. R. Leavis, writing in *New Bearings in English Poetry* (1932) made this observation: "He was exquisitely sincere and sensitive, and he succeeded in expressing in poetry a representative modern sensibility. It was an achievement of a very rare order, and he has not yet had the recognition he deserves." Thomas's poetry has become widely known, and he has become almost an establishment figure in the literature of the early twentieth century. It is a measure of his achievement that in returning to his slender *Collected Poems*, it is always possible to be stimulated and surprised by his work.

Biography

Edward Philip Thomas was born in London, the eldest of six boys. Both of his parents were Welsh, and Thomas always had an affinity with the principality, spending much time there during his childhood, although the landscapes of his poetry are predominantly those of the south of England. Thomas's father was a stern, unyielding man who had risen by his own efforts to a social position far above that which might be expected from his poor background. Having succeeded in elevating himself, he was naturally very ambitious for his eldest son, and Thomas received an excellent education, attending St. Paul's School, Hammersmith (as a contemporary of G. K. Chesterton and E. C. Bentley, among others), and going on from there to Jesus College, Oxford.

Shortly before going to Oxford, Thomas met Helen Noble; it was one of the momentous events in his life. Both he and Noble had very advanced ideas for their time; they were already lovers while Thomas was still an undergraduate. They discussed their future lives together and how they would bring up their children in accordance with Richard Jeffries's theories of freedom and the open-air life. Noble herself said, "We hated the thought of a legal contract. We felt our love was all the bond there ought to be, and that if that failed it was immoral to be bound together. We wanted our union to be free and spontaneous." In the spring of 1899, Noble discovered that she was pregnant and was rather appalled to discover that Edward himself, as well as her friends in the bohemian community in which she lived, thought that they should be married. Noble's family were shocked to learn of her pregnancy, insisting on a hurried marriage and refusing to help the young couple in any way. Thomas's family was more sympathetic, allowing

Noble to live with them and helping Thomas while he worked toward his degree.

Once he graduated, the need to earn money to support his family became pressing, and determined not to become submerged in the drudgery of an office job, Thomas solicited work from publishers. Until the time that he joined the Artists' Rifles, Thomas supported himself and his family by writing. They were always poor, and he often reproached himself bitterly because he had no regular source of income.

Writing became a chore to him, something to be done merely for the sake of the money. In 1912, he suffered a breakdown brought on by overwork. At about that time, also, he met Frost and formed a close friendship with the American poet. Thomas was among the first to appreciate Frost's poetry, and Frost encouraged Thomas to try his hand at writing poetry himself; Thomas gradually gained confidence in his ability to say what he wanted in poetry. When he was killed by a bombshell in the spring of 1917, what might have become a considerable voice in English poetry was tragically silenced.

Analysis

Perhaps the most notable feature of Edward Thomas's poetry, which strikes the reader immediately, is its characteristic quietness of tone and its unassertive, gentle quality. He is primarily a poet of the country, but through his descriptions of the English landscape, impressionistic and minutely observed, he also attempts to delineate some of the features of his own inner landscape.

As may be seen from the titles of the many books of prose that he wrote before beginning to write poetry at the behest of Frost, he was always deeply interested in nature and the land. Many of the fleeting observations in his poetry are drawn from his notebooks, in which he recorded such things as the first appearance of a spring blossom and the first sightings of various species of birds. In his prose, as opposed to the notebooks, his style was highly rhetorical, so that the keen observations that make his poetry so effective are lost in a plethora of adjectival excess. In one of his reviews, he wrote that "The important thing is not that a thing should be small, but that it should be intense and capable of unconsciously symbolic significance." In his poetry, by the acuity of his observation and the spareness and tautness of his language, he certainly achieves remarkable—if low-key—intensity. He also achieves, in his best work, an unforced symbolic resonance.

"As the Team's Head-Brass"

"As the Team's Head-Brass" is one of Thomas's most impressive achievements; at first reading, it may appear to be only an account of a rural dialogue between the poet and a man plowing a field. It begins with a reference to the plowman, and to some lovers who are seen disappearing into the wood behind the field being plowed. The lovers are not directly relevant to the substance of the poem, but they are an important detail. The poem begins and ends with a reference to them, and although they are in no sense representative of a Lawrentian "life-force," their presence in the poem does suggest the triumph of life and love over death and destruction. The very mention of the lovers reinforces the image of the plow horses "narrowing a yellow square of charlock"—that is, destroying the (living) weeds, that better life may grow.

"If we could see all all might seem good" says the plowman, and this seems to be Thomas's contention in this poem. The writing throughout is highly controlled, the structure of the poem reinforced with alliteration and internal rhyme—seeming to owe something to Gerard Manley Hopkins and ultimately even to the Welsh *cynghanedd* form, with the use of "fallen/fallow/plough/narrowing/yellow/charlock" all in four lines, and then later in the same opening section, "word/weather/war/scraping/share/screwed/furrow." Leavis observes that "we become aware of the inner life which the sensory impressions are notation for." This is particularly true of "As the Team's Head-Brass." The closing lines bring the whole poem together most succinctly—the lovers, forgotten since the opening lines, emerge from the wood; the horses begin to plow a new furrow; "for the last time I watched" says Thomas, and the reader must pause here to ask whether he means "for the last time on this particular occasion" or "for the last time ever." All the conversation in the poem has been about war, and in the last two lines come the words "crumble/topple/stumble," which, although used ostensibly with reference to the horses and the soil, may equally be taken to refer back to the fallen tree on which the poet is sitting, the plowman's workmate who has been killed in the war, the changing state of society, and the relentless passage of time.

"Adlestrop"

"As the Team's Head-Brass" is not typical of Thomas's work, however, for it is longer and much more detailed and elaborate than most of his poems. More typical of his work are poems such as "Tall Nettles" and "Adlestrop," which evoke the moment without attempting to do more than capture the unique quality of one particular place or one particular moment in time. "Adlestrop" is a poem much anthologized and much appreciated by those who love the English countryside. It has been described as the most famous of modern "place" poems, and yet it also seems to conjure up an almost sexual tension (perhaps by the use of the words "lonely fair"?) of a kind that is often implicit in such hot summer days. This is a sense of the poem that the contemporary poet Dannie Abse has obviously found, for he has written a poem titled "Not Adlestrop," in which the unspecified lady actually makes an appearance in a train going in the opposite direction. Abse's poem is something of a literary joke, but it does pinpoint an element of unresolved sexual tension in several of Thomas's poems. "Some Eyes Condemn," "Celandine," and "The Unknown" all seem to be worlds away in mood from "And You, Helen," a poem written for his wife.

"No One So Much as You"

The poignant "No One So Much as You," a kind of apologia for an imperfectly reciprocated love, was written for Mary Elizabeth Thomas, the poet's mother, although it has often been mistaken for a love poem to his wife. In either case it would seem that familiarity did not necessarily increase Thomas's love for his family—in fact, it was obvious, both from his despairing reaction to the news of his wife's second pregnancy and from his well-documented impatience with domestic life—that distance and mystery were important elements of attraction for him. Perhaps fortunately for all concerned, Thomas's dissatisfactions and unfulfilled longings seem to have made up only a very small part of his nature. Having come to poetry late, he wastes little time in cataloging regrets for what he might have been and concentrates mainly on what he was able to do best—that is, to capture his own impressions of English rural life and country landscapes and combine them in poetry with various insights into his own personality.

Affinity for country life

It would not be possible to offer a succinct analysis of Thomas's poetry without referring to his deeply felt patriotism. In *Edward Thomas: A Poet for His Country* (1978), Jan Marsh describes an incident that occurred soon after Thomas enlisted in the British army, although he was in fact over the usual age limit for enlistment. A friend asked the poet what he thought he was fighting for; Thomas bent down and picked up a pinch of earth and, letting it crumble through his fingers, answered, "Literally, for this."

This is the predominant impression that the reader carries away from an encounter with Thomas's poetry, for here is a sensitive, educated man who, despite his cultivation, is deeply attuned to the land. This affinity is particularly clear in the country people who inhabit Thomas's poetry, for they are always portrayed as being part of a long and noble tradition of rural life. Thomas does not romanticize his vision: He portrays the cruelties of nature as well as its beauties. A recurring image in his poetry is that of the gamekeeper's board, hung with trophies in an attempt to discourage other predators. Perhaps because he makes an honest attempt to describe the reality of country life without attempting to gloss over or soften its less attractive aspects, he succeeds superbly. Since his life, when his poetry was scarcely known, Thomas's work has become steadily more popular, so that he has become known as one of England's finest nature poets.

Other major works

NONFICTION: *The Woodland Life*, 1897; *Horae Solitariae*, 1902; *Oxford*, 1903; *Rose Acre Papers*, 1904; *Beautiful Wales*, 1905; *The Heart of England*, 1906; *Richard Jeffries*, 1909; *The South Country*, 1909; *Feminine Influence on the Poets*, 1910; *Rest and Unrest*, 1910; *Rose Acre Papers*, 1910; *Windsor Castle*, 1910; *Celtic Stories*, 1911; *The Isle of Wight*, 1911; *Light and Twilight*, 1911; *Maurice Maeterlinck*, 1911; *The Tenth Muse*, 1911; *Algernon Charles Swinburne*, 1912; *George Borrow: The Man and*

His Books, 1912; *Lafcadio Hearn*, 1912; *Norse Tales*, 1912; *The Country*, 1913; *The Happy-Go-Lucky Morgans*, 1913; *The Icknield Way*, 1913; *Walter Pater*, 1913; *In Pursuit of Spring*, 1914; *The Life of the Duke of Marlborough*, 1915; *A Literary Pilgrim in England*, 1917; *Cloud Castle, and Other Papers*, 1922; *Chosen Essays*, 1926; *Essays of Today and Yesterday*, 1926; *The Last Sheaf*, 1928; *The Childhood of Edward Thomas*, 1938; *The Prose of Edward Thomas*, 1948 (Roland Gant, editor); *Letters from Edward Thomas to Gordon Bottomley*, 1968; *Letters to America, 1914-1917*, 1978.

CHILDREN'S LITERATURE: *Four-and-Twenty-Blackbirds*, 1915.

BIBLIOGRAPHY

Cuthbertson, Guy, and Lucy Newlyn, eds. *Branch-Lines: Edward Thomas and Contemporary Poetry*. Chester Springs, Pa.: Dufour Editions, 2007. Contains essays on Thomas and poems by him and the poets he influenced.

Emeny, Richard, comp. *Edward Thomas, 1878-1917: Towards a Complete Checklist of His Publications*. Edited by Jeff Cooper. Blackburn, Lancashire, England: White Sheep Press, 2004. A bibliography of Thomas's numerous publications, from the poetry to the many prose writings.

Farjeon, Eleanor. *Edward Thomas: The Last Four Years*. Rev. ed. Foreword by P. J. Kavanagh. Edited by Anne Harvey. Stroud, Gloucestershire, England: Sutton, 2007. A double memoir that uses Thomas's letters and Farjeon's diaries to provide a candid account of their developing friendship. Offers a unique account of Thomas's development as a poet, including his meeting Robert Frost, whose encouragement led to Thomas's first poems. Thomas's letters describe his family, his friendships with other writers, and provides a detailed account of his experiences in World War I.

Frost, Robert, and Edward Thomas. *Elected Friends: Robert Frost and Edward Thomas to One Another*. Edited by Matthew Spencer. New York: Handsel Books, 2003. Contains the letters and poems that Frost and Thomas wrote to each other. Frost's influence helped Thomas develop as a poet.

Kirkham, Michael. *The Imagination of Edward Thomas*. New York: Cambridge University Press, 1986. Kirkham ignores chronology as he explores Thomas's imagination by identifying the characteristic style that is evidenced in his poetry. This extremely helpful book is augmented with a solid bibliography and an index.

Motion, Andrew. *The Poetry of Edward Thomas*. 1980. Reprint. London: Hogarth, 1991. Motion approaches Thomas's poetry as drawing from the Georgian tradition while anticipating the arrival of the modernists in content and in form. Motion examines the subtle style of Thomas and introduces him as an evolutionary poet.

Smith, Stan. *Edward Thomas*. London: Faber & Faber, 1986. Thomas is considered in this book as the "quintessential English poet," whose devotion to the rural countryside is reflected in his poetry. Presents several critical approaches. Helpful selected bibliography.

Thomas, R. George. *Edward Thomas: A Portrait*. 1985. Reprint. Oxford, England: Clarendon Press, 1987. This book provides rare insight into the life and work of Thomas by making use of letters, memoirs, and personal papers. Biographical in nature, and supported by an excellent bibliography, the book gives a solid foundation for the study of his prose and poetry.

Wiśniewski, Jacek. *Edward Thomas: A Mirror of England*. Newcastle upon Tyne, England: Cambridge Scholars, 2009. Critical analysis of the works of Thomas, whom the author finds to be representative of England.

Vivien Stableford

HENRY DAVID THOREAU

Born: Concord, Massachusetts; July 12, 1817
Died: Concord, Massachusetts; May 6, 1862

PRINCIPAL POETRY
Poems of Nature, 1895
Collected Poems of Henry Thoreau, 1943 (first critical edition)

OTHER LITERARY FORMS

Henry David Thoreau (thuh-ROH) published two books during his lifetime: *A Week on the Concord and Merrimack Rivers* (1849) and *Walden: Or, Life in the Woods* (1854). Three additional books edited by his sister Sophia and his friend William Ellery Channing were published soon after his death: a collection of his travel essays titled *Excursions* (1863), *The Maine Woods* (1864), and *Cape Cod* (1865). During his lifetime, Thoreau also published essays in various periodicals. They were generally of three kinds: travel essays such as "A Yankee in Canada," nature essays such as "Walking," and social and political essays such as "Life Without Principle" and "Civil Disobedience." Those essays are collected in the standard "Walden" edition of Thoreau's complete writings, and the best of them are generally available today in paperback collections. Thoreau also dabbled in translations and occasionally published in *The Dial* his translations of Greek and Roman poetry. Perhaps Thoreau's greatest literary work, however, is his journal, which he kept throughout most of his adult life and most of which is available in the last fourteen volumes of the "Walden" edition of his collected writings. A portion of the journal from 1840 to 1841 was omitted from the collected writings but was later edited and published by Perry Miller in *Consciousness in Concord* (1958). Also not included in the collected writings were portions of the journal dealing with Thoreau's first trip to Maine and portions that Thoreau himself cut out for use in his books. The Princeton University Press brought together Thoreau's journals in a more unified way in *Journal*, a seven-volume edition published between 1981 and 2002.

ACHIEVEMENTS

During his own lifetime, Henry David Thoreau met with only modest literary success. His early poems and essays published in *The Dial* were well known and appreciated in Transcendentalist circles but were generally unknown to popular audiences. As a lecturer, his talks were appreciated by the most liberal of his audiences but were generally found to be obscure or even dangerous by more conservative listeners. Thus, he had brief spurts of popularity as a lecturer, particularly in 1859 to 1860, but was not gener-

Henry David Thoreau
(Library of Congress)

ally popular on the lecture circuit. His first book, *A Week on the Concord and Merrimack Rivers*, was published in 1849 at his own expense in an edition of one thousand copies. It met with very little success; only 294 copies were sold or given away, while the remaining copies were finally shipped four years later to Thoreau himself, who sarcastically remarked in his journal, "I have now a library of nearly nine hundred volumes, over seven hundred of which I wrote myself: Is it not well that the author should behold the fruits of his labor?" Although *A Week on the Concord and Merrimack Rivers* carried an advertisement of the forthcoming publication of *Walden*, the failure of the first book prompted Thoreau to withhold publication of the later one until he could feel more certain of its success. After much revision, Thoreau published *Walden* in 1854. It met with generally favorable reviews and good sales, over seventeen hundred copies of an edition of two thousand being sold in the first year. By 1859, it was out of print, but it was reissued in a second edition shortly after Thoreau's death. *Walden* won

Thoreau some fame with general audiences and created a small but devoted number of disciples who would occasionally visit Thoreau in Concord or send him complimentary copies of books. After the success of *Walden*, Thoreau found it easier to publish his essays in the more popular periodicals, such as *Putnam's Magazine* and *The Atlantic Monthly*. In his last years, he also acquired some notoriety as an abolitionist through his impassioned lectures and essays on John Brown.

Thoreau's literary reputation has risen steadily since his death, his writings appealing primarily to two very different kinds of readers: those who see him as an escapist nature writer and those who see him as a political radical. As Michael Meyer suggests, his advice to people to simplify their lives and return to an appreciation of nature has had especially strong appeal in times of economic difficulty such as the 1920's and 1930's, and it has also served to cushion criticism of Thoreau in times such as the 1940's, when his political views seemed unpatriotic. In the twenty-first century, it is probably still his nature writing that appeals to most readers. His social and political views, particularly his concept of passive resistance expressed in his essay "Civil Disobedience," have periodically made their influence felt in the actions of major social and political reformers such as Mahatma Gandhi and Martin Luther King, Jr. Thoreau's popularity peaked in the 1960's when his nature writing and his political views simultaneously found an audience of young American rebels advocating retreat from urban ugliness and materialism and passive resistance to an unpopular war. Since the 1960's, his popularity has subsided somewhat, but he continues to be widely read, and his place among the great writers of American literature seems secure.

Biography

Henry David Thoreau (christened David Henry Thoreau) was born in Concord, Massachusetts, on July 12, 1817, the third of four children of John Thoreau and Cynthia Thoreau. His father was a quiet man whose seeming lack of ambition had led to a series of unsuccessful attempts to establish himself as a shopkeeper prior to his finally establishing a very successful pencil factory in Concord. His mother was an outgoing, talkative woman who took in boarders to supplement the family's income. Both parents were fond of nature and could often be seen taking the children picnicking in the Concord woods.

Thoreau received a good grammar school education at the Concord Academy and seems to have had an essentially pleasant and typical boyhood. He attended Harvard College from 1833 to 1837, taking time out during his junior year to recuperate from a prolonged illness and to supplement his income by teaching for several months in Canton, Massachusetts. Upon being graduated near the top of his class, he took a teaching job in the Concord public schools, but after a few weeks he resigned in protest over the school board's insistence that he use corporal punishment to discipline his students. Unable to find another position, Thoreau opened a private school of his own and was eventually joined by his older brother John. John's cheerful disposition together with Henry's high academic standards made the school very successful until it was closed in 1841 because of John's prolonged illness.

During these years as a teacher, Thoreau traveled to Maine, took, with his brother, the famous excursion on the Concord and Merrimack rivers that eventually became the subject of his first book, delivered his first lecture, and published his first essay and his first poetry in *The Dial*. Through one of his students, Edmund Sewall (whom he praises in one of his best-known poems, "Lately, Alas, I Knew a Gentle Boy") he met Ellen Sewall, the only woman to whom he seems to have been romantically attracted in any serious way. Ellen seems to have been the subject or recipient of a number of Thoreau's poems of 1839 and 1840, but his brother John was the more forward of the two in courting Ellen, and it was after John's proposal to Ellen had failed that Henry also proposed, only to be rejected as John had been.

After the closing of the school, Thoreau was invited to live with Ralph Waldo Emerson's family as a handyman; he stayed two years, during which time he continued to contribute to and occasionally help Emerson edit *The Dial*. In 1842, his brother John died suddenly of a tetanus infection, leaving Thoreau so devastated that he himself briefly exhibited psychosomatic symptoms of the disease. The following year, a brief stint as a tutor to William Emerson's family on Staten Island confirmed his prejudice against cities, so he returned to Concord, where in 1844, he and a companion accidentally set fire to the Concord Woods, thus earning some rather long-lasting ill will from some of his neighbors and some long-lasting damage to his reputation as a woodsman.

For several years, Thoreau had contemplated buying a house and some land of his own, but in 1845, he settled for permission from Emerson to use some land near Walden Pond to build his own cabin. He built a one-room cabin and moved in on July 4, thus declaring his intention to be free to work on his writing and on a personal experiment in economic self-reliance. He continued to use the cabin as his main residence for two years, during which time he wrote *A Week on the Concord and Merrimack Rivers* and much of *Walden*, raised beans, took a trip to the Maine Woods, and spent his famous night in the Concord jail for nonpayment of taxes. An invitation from Emerson to spend another year as a resident handyman finally prompted him to leave the pond in the fall of 1847, but he left with little regret, because, as he says in *Walden*, "I had several more lives to live, and I could not spare any more time for that one." The fruits of his stay at the pond finally began to appear in 1849, when *A Week on the Concord and Merrimack Rivers* and his essay on "Resistance to Civil Government" (later renamed "Civil Disobedience") were both published.

Throughout the 1840's, Thoreau had become increasingly interested in the natural sciences, and he began to spend much time gathering and measuring specimens, often at the expense of his writing, so that by 1851, he had reason to complain in his journal, "I feel that the character of my knowledge is from year to year becoming more distinct and scientific; that, in exchange for views as wide as heaven's scope, I am being narrowed down to the field of the microscope." His scientific and mechanical abilities had benefits for the family's pencil-making business, however, because in 1843 he had developed a more effective means of securing the graphite in the pencils and was later to improve the quality of pencils still further. Throughout his life he maintained of necessity an interest in the family business, although he seldom enjoyed having to take active part in it. His aversion to the routine of regular employment also applied to his surveying talents, which were called on by his neighbors increasingly after 1850. Although by 1851 Thoreau seems to have felt that life was passing him by without his having been able to achieve his goals, the publication of *Walden* in 1854 revived his self-esteem when the book sold well and brought a small but devoted group of admirers.

Throughout the 1850's, Thoreau made several excursions to Canada, the Maine Woods, and Cape Cod, which culminated in travel essays in popular periodicals. He also traveled to New Jersey and to Brooklyn, where he met Walt Whitman, with whom he was favorably impressed. Thoreau's admiration for Whitman's raw genius was surpassed only by his admiration for Brown, the abolitionist, whom he first met in 1857 and whose cause he vigorously supported in lectures and published essays.

In 1860, Thoreau caught a bad cold and eventually was diagnosed with tuberculosis. Advised to seek a different climate, Thoreau took a trip to Minnesota in 1861, a trip that provided him with some brief glimpses of "uncivilized" Indians but with no relief from his illness. After returning to Concord, his health continued to deteriorate, and he died at home on May 6, 1862.

Analysis

For Henry David Thoreau, the value of poetry lay not primarily in the poem itself, but in the act of writing the poem and in that act's influence on the poet's life. The importance of poetry to the poet is, as he says in *A Week on the Concord and Merrimack Rivers*, in "what he has become through his work." Since for the Transcendentalists life was superior to art, Thoreau could assert that "My life has been the poem I would have writ,/ But I could not both live and utter it." No art form could surpass God's act of creating nature or a person's act of shaping his or her own life. In his journal for 1840, Thoreau suggests that the best an artist can hope for is to equal nature, not to surpass it. The poet's job is to publish nature's truth accurately, and thus at times, verse seemed to him to be the best vehicle for publicizing nature because of its greater precision. By the mid-1840's, however, he had mostly abandoned verse and concluded that "Great prose, of equal elevation, commands our respect more than great verse, since it implies a more permanent and level height.... The poet often only makes an irruption ... but the prose writer has conquered ... and settled colonies." In 1851, he found it necessary to warn himself to beware "of youthful poetry, which is impotent." Another problem with poetry was that it was too artificial. One could not capture in words the rhythms of the wind or the birds. He found that "the music now runs before and then behind the sense, but is never coincident with it." One could make music, or one could make sense; Thoreau eventually preferred the latter.

Because of this ambiguous attitude toward the value of verse (he eventually came to speak of both good verse and good prose as "poetry"), Thoreau's poetry is seldom first-rate, and even at its best, it does not rival that of such contemporaries as Emily Dickinson and Whitman. Nevertheless, it is of significance to the modern reader, first, because it demonstrates vividly the problems that American poets faced in freeing themselves artistically from European influences, and second, because it provides some fresh insights, not available as fully in his prose, into some of the deepest problems of Thoreau's life, especially his attempts to cope with the problems of love and friendship and of his own role as an artist.

Thoreau could never quite free himself from imitating the great poets he admired to find a voice of his own. He mined his expert knowledge of Greek and Latin to write epigrams or odes (essentially Horatian in form) such as "Let Such Pure Hate Still Underprop," which is also reminiscent of the seventeenth century Metaphysical poets in its use of paradox. Indeed, it is the Metaphysicals to whom Thoreau seems to have turned most often as muses for his own poetry: the paradoxes, introspection, and elaborate conceits of John Donne or Andrew Marvell. At other times, one can find in Thoreau's verse the loose rhythms of John Skelton's near-doggerel dimeter, as in "The Old Marlborough Road," or the more graceful tetrameter couplets, which are Thoreau's most frequently used form and which, as critic Henry Wells suggests, can also be traced to the Metaphysicals. Finally, Thoreau frequently employs the three-part structure and tight stanza form of George Herbert's meditations. The stanza form of "I Am a Parcel of Vain Strivings Tied," for example, is clearly modeled on Herbert, while a poem such as "The Poet's Delay" has, as H. Grant Sampson suggests, the three-part meditative structure that moves from a particular scene in nature to the poet's awareness of the scene's wider implications, and finally to the poet's recognition of the scene's specific spiritual meaning for him.

THE INFLUENCE OF THE ROMANTIC POETS

Although Thoreau most frequently looked to the past for poetic models, he did admire some of the Romantic poets of his own day, particularly William Wordsworth. Thoreau's "I Knew a Man by Sight," for example, portrays a typical Wordsworthian rustic wanderer, while in Thoreau's unfortunate attempt at rhyme in the lines "Late in a wilderness/ I shared his mess" readers also see the glaring difference in poetic skill between the two poets. In "My Books I'd Fain Cast Off, I Cannot Read," Thoreau expresses a view of the superiority of nature to books, very much like that in Wordsworth's "Expostulation and Reply." In several other poems, he seems to echo Wordsworth's theories of human development. In "Manhood," for example, Thoreau presents the same view of the child as father of the man that Wordsworth presents in "Ode: Intimations of Immortality from Recollections of Early Childhood." In "Music," he also presents a view of a person's loss of youthful faculties and of compensation for that loss with adult wisdom similar to that presented by Wordsworth in "Lines Composed a Few Miles Above Tintern Abbey" and in *The Prelude: Or, The Growth of a Poet's Mind* (1850).

From this unlikely mixture of classical, Metaphysical, and Romantic influences, Thoreau apparently hoped to create a poetry that would express his own love of paradox, introspection, and nature, while creating a style both stately and rugged, at once elevated and natural. The task was, as Thoreau himself came to realize, impossible. It is also interesting to note, however, that Thoreau seems not to have looked to his own countrymen, except perhaps Emerson, for models. His diction and rhythms are most frequently traceable to European influence, and when he attempts to break free of that influence, he usually meets with only modest success or complete failure.

Because Thoreau's prose is generally more effective than his poetry, when he deals with a topic in both genres, the poetry is generally valuable primarily as a gloss on the prose. In "Wait Not Till Slaves Pronounce the Word," for example, Thoreau reminds the reader that slavery is as much a state of mind as an external condition: "Think not the tyrant sits afar/ In your own breasts ye have/ The District of Columbia/ And power to free the Slave." His statement in *Walden*, however, makes the same point more powerfully: "It is hard to have a Southern overseer; it is worse to have a Northern one; but worst of all when you are the slave driver of yourself." Some of Thoreau's nature poems do present some fresh minor insights into Thoreau's view of nature, but those poems that are of most value and interest in their own right are those that shed autobiographical light on some of his personal dilemmas either unexpressed or not expressed as well in his prose, particularly his attempt to find an ideal friendship and his attempt to meet the artistic goals he set for himself.

THE IDEAL OF FRIENDSHIP

Thoreau's ideal of friendship, expressed most fully in the "Wednesday" chapter of *A Week on the Concord and Merrimack Rivers*, is typically Transcendentalist in its insistence on paradox in human relationships. To Thoreau, friends were to be united with one another and yet separate. They were to love one another's strengths while at the same time hating one another's weaknesses, to be committed to one another and yet be free, to express their love and yet remain silent. They were to be equal, and yet he insists that only a friendship contracted with one's superior is worthwhile. Friendship, as he suggests in a manuscript poem titled "Friendship," was to combine truth, beauty, and goodness in a platonic spiritual oneness, symbolized in the poem by two oak trees that barely touch above the ground but are inseparably intertwined in their roots. Although he tends to overintellectualize this concept of friendship, Thoreau was quite in earnest in seeking it in his friends, especially after his college years when he was trying to define his own identity through those he cared about. The person who perhaps came closest to being the soul mate whom Thoreau sought was his brother John. Unfortunately, as is often the case with affection for relatives, Thoreau found that he could seldom express his love for John adequately. When John died, his only outlet was to pour out his affection in his writings by dedicating his first book to him and by writing a gently moving poem, "Brother Where Dost Thou Dwell."

Others who for a time seemed to realize his ideal were Edmund Sewall (one of his students) and Edmund's sister, Ellen. To Edmund, Thoreau wrote one of his best poems, "Lately, Alas, I Knew a Gentle Boy." In this poem, Edmund is described as one who effortlessly wins the love of all around him by his quiet virtue. Mutual respect between the poet and the boy leads them both to keep their love unexpressed, however, and they paradoxically find themselves "less acquainted than when first we met." The friendship thus slips away without being overtly expressed, and the poet is left to cherish only "that virtue which he is." Although this poem certainly has androgynous qualities and is sometimes used to suggest a youthful homosexuality in Thoreau, it seems wiser to take it for what it more obviously is: one of the clearest and most moving of Thoreau's expressions of the joys and frustrations of platonic love. His poems to Edmund's sister, Ellen, are similarly platonic in tone. In one poem ("Love"), for example, he describes himself and Ellen as a "double star" revolving "about one center." In "The Breeze's Invitation," he adds a pastoral touch, describing himself and Ellen as a carefree king and queen of a "peaceful little green." In such poems, the reader sees a Thoreau who, beneath the platonic and pastoral conventions, is a young man earnestly seeking affection—a young man much more vulnerable than the didactic prose philosophizer of *A Week on the Concord and Merrimack Rivers* or the self-confident chanticleer in *Walden*.

Artistic hopes

That same human vulnerability is also the most striking quality of those poems that deal with Thoreau's artistic goals. Aside from his journals, it is in his poems that Thoreau most fully reveals his artistic hopes and disappointments. Those hopes were a typically romantic mixture of active achievement and passive reception. On one hand, as he suggests in "The Hero," a man must contribute something new to his world; he must, as he says in *Walden*, "affect the quality of the day." On the other hand, he can achieve such results only if he is receptive to the inspiration of God through nature. Such inspiration at its most powerful culminates in the sort of mystical experience described by Thoreau in his poem "The Bluebirds," in which he describes his feelings as if "the heavens were all around,/ And the earth was all below" and as if he were a "waking thought—/ A something I hardly knew."

INSPIRATION

Such mystical experiences were the crucial source of the poet's action, whether in writing or in deeds; thus, as Paul O. Williams has demonstrated, much of Thoreau's poetry deals directly or indirectly with the subject of inspiration. The fullest and clearest treatment of the theme is in "Inspiration," a poem in which he describes having occasionally felt a godlike sensitivity to the world so powerful that he felt thoroughly reborn and ready to "fathom hell or climb to heaven." The poet's predicament, however, was that such pure inspiration could seldom be translated untainted into action, and it is this predicament which is at the heart of several of his best poems. In "Light-Winged Smoke, Icarian Bird," one of the most often reprinted and discussed of his poems, he cryptically describes himself as a flame and his poetry as the smoke that he sends heavenward to God. Unfortunately, as the smoke rises to God, it also blots out the truth of God's sun and negates the poet's purpose of clarifying that truth. Thoreau's point here, as Eberhard Alsen convincingly argues, is that even the "clear flame" of the poet is not pure enough to avoid misrepresenting God's truths. That sense of the human artist's limitations in a world of infinite wonder sometimes led Thoreau to feel that his life was being wasted, as in "The Poet's Delay," in which he expresses his fear that while nature's seasons progress into autumn and bear fruit, his own "spring does not begin." Elsewhere, however, as in "I Am a Parcel of Vain Strivings Tied," he consoles himself with a sacrificial satisfaction that his own failures will allow others to be more fruitful. If he is a parcel of picked flowers unable to produce further beauty, at least the other flowers can bloom more beautifully because his have been thinned out of the garden.

In such poems as these, one realizes that Thoreau sensed early what is quite clear when one surveys the body of his poetry: that verse was not the best vehicle for his thoughts but that it freed him to make his prose more powerful. He would have to wait until the publication of *Walden* to feel that the slow-paced seasons of his artistic life had truly begun to bear fruit. Nevertheless, his poetry served him both as a valuable testing ground for his ideas and as an outlet for some of his deepest private problems. It is also worth the modern reader's time because it provides an occasional peek behind the persona of his prose works and because it helps in understanding the dilemma of the Romantic artist, attempting to convey the ideal while being hindered by the very real limitations of human language—a problem that confronts many modern poets as well.

OTHER MAJOR WORKS

NONFICTION: "Civil Disobedience," 1849 (also known as "Resistance to Civil Government"); *A Week on the Concord and Merrimack Rivers*, 1849; *Walden: Or, Life in the Woods*, 1854; *Excursions*, 1863; *The Maine Woods*, 1864; *Cape Cod*, 1865; *Letters to Various Persons*, 1865 (Ralph Waldo Emerson, editor); *A Yankee in Canada, with Anti-Slavery and Reform Papers*, 1866; *Early Spring in Massachusetts*, 1881; *Summer*,

1884; *Winter*, 1888; *Autumn*, 1892; *Familiar Letters of Henry David Thoreau*, 1894 (F. B. Sanborn, editor); *Journal*, 1981-2002 (7 volumes); *Letters to a Spiritual Seeker*, 2004 (Bradley P. Dean, editor).

MISCELLANEOUS: *The Writings of Henry David Thoreau*, 1906 (20 volumes); *Collected Essays and Poems*, 2001.

BIBLIOGRAPHY

Cain, William E. *A Historical Guide to Henry David Thoreau*. New York: Oxford University Press, 2000. Historical and biographical context and treatment of Thoreau.

Hahn, Stephen. *On Thoreau*. Belmont, Calif.: Wadsworth, 2000. A concise study intended to assist a beginning student in understanding Thoreau's philosophy and thinking. Includes bibliographical references.

Kerting, Verena. *Henry David Thoreau's Aesthetics: A Modern Approach to the World*. New York: Peter Lang, 2006. Examines Thoreau's writings for his worldview and aesthetics.

McSweeney, Kerry. *The Language of the Senses: Sensory-Perceptual Dynamics in Wordsworth, Coleridge, Thoreau, Whitman, and Dickinson*. Montreal: McGill-Queen's University Press, 1998. Compares and contrasts the senses in the poetry of Thoreau, William Wordsworth, Samuel Taylor Coleridge, Walt Whitman, and Emily Dickinson.

Myerson, Joel, ed. *The Cambridge Companion to Henry David Thoreau*. 1995. Reprint. New York: Cambridge University Press, 2006. A guide to the works and to the biographical, historical, and literary contexts. Includes a chronology and further readings.

Richardson, Robert D. *Henry Thoreau: A Life of the Mind*. Berkeley: University of California Press, 1986. This study focuses primarily on the development of Thoreau's leading themes and the formulation of his working philosophy. Richardson offers clear accounts of some of the writer's complex theories. Provides notes, a bibliography, and an index.

Smith, Larry. *Thoreau's Lost Journal: Poems*. Toledo, Ohio: Westron Press, 2001. Smith concentrates on Thoreau's poetry as found in his journal.

Sullivan, Robert. *The Thoreau You Don't Know: What the Prophet of Environmentalism Really Meant*. New York: Collins, 2009. Although this work examines *Walden* more than the poetry, it presents a different perspective on Thoreau, one that suggests that the work was meant to be a communal work, an inspiration, rather than a reclusive work.

Tauber, Alfred I. *Henry David Thoreau and the Moral Agency of Knowing*. Berkeley: University of California Press, 2001. Tauber shows how Thoreau's metaphysics of self-knowing informed all that this multifaceted writer, thinker, and scientist did. A clear presentation of the man in the context of social and intellectual history.

Thoreau, Henry David. *I to Myself: An Annotated Selection from the Journal of Henry D. Thoreau*. Edited by Jeffrey S. Cramer. New Haven, Conn.: Yale University Press, 2007. This work offers selections from Thoreau's journals from 1837-1861. Includes comprehensive annotations that uncover allusions, provide biographical information, and offer word definitions.

Richard J. Schneider

JONES VERY

Born: Salem, Massachusetts; August 28, 1813
Died: Salem, Massachusetts; May 8, 1880

PRINCIPAL POETRY
Essays and Poems, 1839
Poems by Jones Very with an Introductory Memoir by William P. Andrews, 1883
Poems and Essays by Jones Very: Complete and Revised Edition, 1886
Poems and Essays by Jones Very: James Freeman Clarke's Enlarged Collection of 1886 Re-edited with a Thematic and Topical Index, 1965
Jones Very: Selected Poems, 1966
Jones Very: The Complete Poems, 1993

OTHER LITERARY FORMS

Jones Very (VEH-ree) wrote a few critical essays, the best of which were originally collected, along with a selection of his poetry, in *Essays and Poems*. Such essays as "Epic Poetry," "Hamlet," and "Shakespeare" have been particularly rich resources for biographers and literary critics interested in understanding Very's poetic goals and practices. Also, about 117 sermons survive in manuscript form, the results of his service as a supply minister for nearly four decades.

ACHIEVEMENTS

Both during his life and after, Jones Very's significance as a poet has generally been understood in relationship to the American Transcendentalist movement. Of particular importance to biographers and critics has been Very's connection to Ralph Waldo Emerson, Transcendentalism's chief spokesperson and writer. Certainly, Emerson's sponsorship of Very resulted in the only book-length publication of Very's poems during Very's lifetime, in 1839, a volume which Emerson edited and for which he made the necessary contacts with a publisher. For a very short period, during the years 1838 and 1839, Very seemed to Emerson and his associates to be the epitome of the American Transcendentalist poet linked to divinity, expressing intuitive insights and truths about the universe in pure and beautiful language.

Later biographers and literary critics have been able to observe that Very's connection to the Transcendentalists and Emerson was at best a mixed blessing. Although it resulted in early publication of his efforts, it also made it difficult to perceive that Very, at least for a short time, was a unique and powerfully mystical poet in his own right. Interestingly, many of the poems that Emerson chose not to include in his selection of poetry for Very's first publication are the ones that now seem most central and original. Since the majority of Very's poems are sonnets, he also has assumed importance as one of the most successful of America's writers of poetry in the sonnet form.

Biography

Jones Very was born in Salem, Massachusetts, in 1813 to a sea captain father and a strong-minded, highly independent, and somewhat atheistic mother. Very sailed with his father for nearly two years, beginning at age nine, but after his father's untimely death in 1824, Very attended school in Salem for three years, excelling as a scholar, until at age fourteen he left for employment in an auction room. He refused to give up his goal of enrolling at Harvard, however, and continued his self-education through extensive reading, eventually obtaining the help of a special tutor as well as securing employment as an assistant in a Latin school, preparing younger boys for entrance into college. During this time, his earliest, rather imitative poems began appearing in a local newspaper, the Salem *Observer*.

So advanced was Very in his scholarly ability that he was able to enter Harvard in February, 1834, as a second-term sophomore. His years at Harvard were crucial in Very's progress as a scholar, poet, and religious thinker. He distinguished himself as a student, eventually graduating second in his class in 1836 with particular expertise in Latin and Greek. He continued to write poetry, including the class songs for his sophomore and senior years, as well as poems imitative of William Wordsworth and William Cullen Bryant.

Most important, however, under the influence of some of his Unitarian teachers and classmates, he began to turn to religion in a serious way for the first time in his life, thus deviating radically from his mother's skepticism. Particularly in his senior year, he experienced what he called "a change of heart," becoming convinced "that all we have belongs to God and that we ought to have no *will* of our own." During the next two years, while staying on at Harvard as a tutor in Greek and a student at the Divinity School, he gave himself to the struggle of ridding himself of his own will and becoming perfectly conformed to the will of God working within him. His poetry writing more and more partook of this spiritual battle, centering on intense religious feelings and intuitions within the framework of the traditional Shakespearean sonnet form.

Very delivered a lyceum lecture on the subject of epic poetry in Salem in December of 1837. Elizabeth Palmer Peabody, a prominent Transcendentalist and reformer, attended this lecture and immediately recognized the uncommon promise of Very as a thinker. Knowing nothing of his poetry writing, she immediately set up a connection between Very and Ralph Waldo Emerson, which resulted in Very's lecturing at Concord in April of 1838. Very also began attending some of the so-called Transcendental Club meetings during the spring and summer of 1838. Emerson was much taken with Very's depth of thought and his insights into William Shakespeare and encouraged him to continue his writing about poetry, but Emerson, like Peabody, seems to have been unaware of Very's own poetic productions during these months.

Very's spiritual journey reached some sort of a high point in the fall of 1838, when he evidently experienced what he thought was the total replacement of his own will by the will of God. This perhaps mystical experience immediately resulted in his proclaiming to students and friends that the end of the world and Christ's Second Coming were occurring, as evidenced in Very's own new relationship with divinity. He claimed that the Holy Spirit was speaking through him, and he urged those who listened to experience this Second Coming through a similar banishing of their own wills. Such statements were upsetting to some students and brought the displeasure of the Harvard authorities. Very was sent home to Salem, where his similar proclamations to ministers and leaders regarding their need of repentance and reformation led to his being removed to the McLean Asylum in Charlestown as one who was perhaps insane.

Although Very was released from the hospital after a month, his newfound spiritual intensity continued to challenge his new Transcendentalist friends and Salem society. It was during this period of heightened spiritual feeling that Very's poetry began to flow rapidly from his pen, with more than three hundred sonnets produced during just over one year of religious exaltation from September, 1838, to the latter part of 1839. Emerson became aware of Very's poetry during this time and undertook the job of selecting and editing the poems that were collected in the small volume *Essays and Poems*.

Interestingly, the publication of the poems seemed to coincide with the decline of Very's religious intensity and with his return to a more mundane, albeit dedicated, religious life. For the next forty years, he lived in Salem with his siblings, never marrying but serving as a supply minister to Unitarian churches in the New England area, presenting sermons in the absence of the regular ministers. He continued to produce poetry, but not at the rate nor with the intensity and originality of the poems authored in 1838 and 1839. He died in 1880 in relative obscurity.

Analysis

During the course of his long poetic career, Jones Very wrote some 870 separate poems, many of them published in newspapers and magazines of his day, but only 65 appearing in the thin volume edited by Emerson in 1839. It is common for biographers and literary critics to separate the poems written by Very during his period of growing religious excitement in the late 1830's from the largely imitative poems written before that period and the competent but not strikingly intense poems written in the four decades after that period. It is the poetry of the so-called ecstatic period that most interested and challenged the Transcendentalists and has continued to impress readers in the various generations since. Although repetitious in themes and format, the sonnets from the religiously intense phase of Very's experience carry a certain power and originality markedly lacking in the poetry written before and after this period.

POEMS OF SPIRITUAL INTENSITY

During the late 1830's, poems poured from Very's pen, sometimes, according to Peabody, at the rate of one or two a day. Very, convinced that his will had been totally replaced by the will of divinity, believed that these sonnets were in essence not authored by him but rather were the words of God or the Holy Spirit. Written rapidly, seemingly without revision (how could one revise the words of God?), with little attention to formalities such as spelling and punctuation, the poems of this phase have presented serious editorial issues to editors from Emerson to the present. Yet, the lack of formality and polish helps to bring immediacy to the poems, the best of which seem particularly forceful in their expression of religious passion.

"The New Birth," a sonnet that seemingly recalls Very's intense feelings of change as a result of the key mystical experience in the fall of 1838 when he became convinced of the subjugation of his own will, nicely illustrates the power of Very's poetry during this period. The poem begins with the announcement that "'Tis a new life," followed by a vivid figure of how "thoughts" no longer "move" as before, "With slow uncertain steps," but now "In thronging haste" like "the viewless wind" (a traditional biblical image for the Holy Spirit) enter "fast pressing" through "The portals." Such a change has resulted because human "pride" (the will) has been "laid" in the "dust." The thoughts demand "utterance strong" (perhaps the writing of poetry as well as the face-to-face confrontation with teachers and friends), imaged as the sound of "Storm-lifted waves swift rushing to the shore" whose "thunders roar" "through the cave-worn rocks." The poem ends with the speaker in the poem ecstatically announcing as "a child of God" his new freedom, his awakening from "death's slumbers to eternity."

Most of the other sonnets written during this period of high religious feeling center on the traditional Christian themes of death, rebirth, the Second Coming, resurrection, and hope, often with figures and allusions highly dependent on biblical sources. Not all of them are successful, often being little more than paraphrases of Scripture.

However, some of them are very striking, perhaps the most interesting to modern readers being those poems in which the poet or the speaker in the poem assumes the voice of God or Christ, poems so stunningly transcendental in their linkage of humanity to divinity that they were not for the most part included by Emerson in the little volume published in 1839, perhaps because he feared the probable attacks of conservative Christians. For example, Christ seems to be the speaker in "I Am the Bread of Life," while God seems the central voice in "The Message." Even more complicated is a poem such as "Terror," which centers on the end of the world. The poem begins with the speaker as a seemingly human witness to end-time events: "Within the streets I hear no voices loud,/ They pass along with low, continuous cry." Yet by the end of the poem, the speaker has become God, who calls loudly to humans: "Repent! why do ye still uncertain stand,/ The kingdom of my son is nigh at hand!" Although this seemingly audacious commandeering of a divine voice is perfectly understandable, given Very's belief that his poems during this period were indeed the products of divine authorship, for the uninitiated reader such a mixture of the human and the divine is at minimum attention getting as well as a challenge to ordinary religious thinking.

EARLIER AND LATER POEMS

The largely imitative poems written before the late 1830's show a poet progressing in competence and often center on themes and didactic approaches typical of the early Romantic movement in England and the United States. Very's poems about nature, for example, usually focus first on some observable aspect of his surroundings, followed by overt linkage, often somewhat sentimentally, to an appropriate lesson. "The Wind-Flower" begins with the personification of this early spring blossom as one that "lookest up with meek, confiding eye/ Upon the clouded smile of April's face" and then praises the "faith" of this frail flower, willing to bloom with the threat of winter still around, as being "More glorious" than that of "Israel's wisest king" (Solomon). Such innocent "trust" is, the poem suggests, something humans can learn from, as the last line of the poem underscores, "A lesson taught by Him, who loved all human kind." Other nature poems of the early period which illustrate this tying of the observation of natural phenomena to religious and moral lessons include "The Robin" and "The Columbine."

Throughout the last four decades of his life, Very continued to write moralizing poems on nature as well as poems centering on the biblical themes characteristic of the sonnets composed during his ecstatic period of the late 1830's. He also turned to writing poems with links to the social and historical events of his time. Such poems show his poetic competence and his interest in current events but usually do not achieve anything like lasting artistic merit. His abolitionist stance is mirrored in the poem "The Fugitive Slaves," for example, while his reaction to the Civil War and Reconstruction can be seen in such poems as "Faith in the Time of War" and "National Unity." Very also penned the lyrics to numerous hymns during this final phase of his poetic career, including such relatively well-known examples as "Father, Thy Wonders Do Not Singly Stand" and "We Go Not on a Pilgrimage."

BIBLIOGRAPHY

Barlett, William Irving. *Jones Very: Emerson's "Brave Saint."* Durham, N.C.: Duke University Press, 1942. This first "modern" biographical and critical study of Very presents a balanced analysis of his life and poetry, and perhaps most important, publishes numerous poems heretofore uncollected, thus bringing to light some of the best poetry of Very written during his ecstatic period.

Clayton, Sarah Turner. *The Angelic Sins of Jones Very.* New York: Peter Lang, 1999. This full-length study of Very centers on a New Historicist approach to how readers in various decades have received and understood Very's poetry, from the time of the Transcendentalists to the present age. The book is particularly effective at bringing together an abundance of scholarly and critical responses to Very's poetry while illuminating how certain lasting qualities of Very's writing continue to fascinate readers.

Gittleman, Edwin. *Jones Very: The Effective Years, 1833-1840*. New York: Columbia University Press, 1967. This work presents an exhaustive treatment of Very's life and writing during the years of his religious awakening. Gittleman approaches Very's biography from a psychological perspective and asserts that Very's religious mania had its roots in family relationships.

Very, Jones. *Jones Very: Selected Poems*. Edited by Nathan Lyons. New Brunswick, N.J.: Rutgers University Press, 1966. Perhaps more important than the poems selected by Lyons are his considerations of Very's religious stance and his interpretations of key Very poems in the introduction to this work.

_____. *Jones Very: The Complete Poems*. Edited by Helen R. Deese. Athens: University of Georgia Press, 1993. Deese has provided an inestimable service for readers interested in Very's poetry by bringing together all the poems and editing them with an appropriate scholarly approach and apparatus. Of immense value, also, is her introduction to the volume, which covers Very as a person, thinker, and poet, perhaps the most concise and insightful review of the research on Very.

Delmer Davis

DAVID WAGONER

Born: Massillon, Ohio; June 5, 1926

PRINCIPAL POETRY
Dry Sun, Dry Wind, 1953
A Place to Stand, 1958
Poems, 1959
The Nesting Ground, 1963
Staying Alive, 1966
New and Selected Poems, 1969
Working Against Time, 1970
Riverbed, 1972
Sleeping in the Woods, 1974
A Guide to Dungeness Spit, 1975
Collected Poems, 1956-1976, 1976
Travelling Light, 1976
Who Shall Be the Sun?, 1978
In Broken Country, 1979
Landfall, 1981
First Light, 1983
Through the Forest: New and Selected Poems, 1977-1987, 1987
Walt Whitman Bathing, 1996
Traveling Light: Collected and New Poems, 1999
The House of Song, 2002
Good Morning and Good Night, 2005
A Map of the Night, 2008

OTHER LITERARY FORMS

Best known as a poet and novelist, David Wagoner (WAG-uh-nuhr) has also written plays—*An Eye for an Eye for an Eye* was produced in Seattle in 1973—as well as short fiction and essays. He edited and wrote the introduction to *Straw for the Fire: From the Notebooks of Theodore Roethke, 1943-1963* (1972).

ACHIEVEMENTS

It is possible that David Wagoner will be best remembered as one of the finest "nature" and "regional" poets of twentieth century America, and as one who has been instrumental in generating renewed interest in Native American lore. To categorize him so narrowly, however, does disservice to his versatility, and to the breadth of his talent and interests. Publishing steadily since the early 1950's, Wagoner has created a body of work that impresses not only for the number of volumes produced, but also for their quality. His novels have been praised for their energy and humor and in many cases for the immediacy of their Old West atmosphere. He received a Ford Fellowship for drama (1964), but it is as a poet that he has been most often honored: with a Guggenheim Fellowship (1956), a National Institute of Arts and Letters Grant (1967), and a National Endowment for the Arts Grant (1969). *Poetry* has awarded him its Morton Dauwen Zabel Prize (1967), its Oscar Blumenthal Prize (1974), its Eunice Tietjens Memorial Prize (1971), its Levinson Prize (1994), and its Union League Civic and Arts Poetry Prize (1997). *Sleeping in the Woods*, *Collected Poems, 1956-1976*, and *In Broken Country* were nominated for National Book Awards. He won Pushcart Prizes in 1979 and 1983. Wagoner served as a chancellor of the Academy of American Poets from 1978 to 1999, succeeding Robert Lowell. He received an Academy Award in literature (1987) from the American Academy of Arts and Letters. He was awarded the Ruth Lilly Poetry Prize (1991), the Ohioana Book Award (1997) for *Walt Whitman Bathing*, and two Washington State Book Awards in Poetry (2000, 2009).

Biography

David Russell Wagoner was born on June 5, 1926, in Massillon, Ohio, and was reared in Whiting, Indiana, the son of a steelworker. After receiving his B.A. degree from Pennsylvania State University in 1947 and his M.A. from Indiana University two years later, Wagoner began his teaching career at DePauw University, returning after a year to Pennsylvania State University. During this time, he was deeply influenced by Theodore Roethke, with whom he had studied as an undergraduate. In 1954, Roethke was instrumental in Wagoner's move to the University of Washington, where he taught until his retirement in 2002. X. J. Kennedy has speculated that perhaps "the most valuable service Roethke ever performed for Wagoner was to bring him to the Pacific Northwest and expose him to rain forests"—and to the culture of the Northwest Coast and Plateau Indians, one might add. Not only has Wagoner made use in his own poems of specific Native American myths and legends, but he has also absorbed the Indians' animistic spiritualism into his own philosophy. In the author's note to *Who Shall Be the Sun?*, he explains that Indians "did not place themselves above their organic and inorganic companions on earth but recognized with awe that they shared the planet as equals." Wagoner finds this equality "admirable and worthy of imitation," as much of his poetry indicates.

When not teaching, Wagoner has worked as a railroad section hand, a park police officer, and a short-order cook. He is a member of the Society of American Magicians. He served as editor of *Poetry Northwest* from 1966 until it ceased publication in 2002, and he has contributed poetry and commentary to a range of literary journals, including *Antioch Review*, *The Atlantic*, *Harvard Review*, *New England Review*, *Poetry*, and *Prairie Schooner*.

Analysis

Despite David Wagoner's accomplishments and honors, and despite the fact that his poems appear regularly in mass-circulation magazines such as *The New Yorker* and *The Atlantic*, as well as the literary quarterlies, he is generally regarded as one of the most underappreciated of American poets. His works, with the exception of "Staying Alive," had not been included in major poetry anthologies until the early twenty-first century, when his poems began appearing in collections such as *The Best American Poetry* (2003, 2004, 2005, 2006). There are several possible explanations for this. First, he lives in Seattle and has chosen as his primary subject matter the land and people of the Pacific Northwest—thus giving rise to the dismissive "regional" label. It is also possible that some of his own best qualities may work against him. His subject matter is anything but trendy; the reader searches his poems in vain for the issues of the day. The only explicit social comment one is likely to find is contained in a half dozen or so poems addressing the Weyerhaeuser Company, a logging firm, and its practice of clear-cutting three-mile swaths of virgin forest.

Perhaps the major problem, as X. J. Kennedy suggests, is Wagoner's very "readability." Much of his poetry seems, at least on first encounter, curiously unpoetic, even prosy. His unpretentious language and casual, conversational tone frequently combine with his sense of humor to create a deceptively simple surface for his complex and serious ideas. This simplicity does make the work accessible; on the other hand, it may actually encourage the casual or first-time reader to dismiss Wagoner's work as lightweight.

Even in his most alienated and melancholy early poems, Wagoner's wit continually asserts itself. He is fond of puns, palindromes, and other forms of wordplay, and makes frequent use of colloquialisms, folk sayings, clichés, non sequiturs, and other lunacies of ordinary speech, often twisting words or phrases in such a way that they take on startling new meanings. Still, it is not as a semantic magician that Wagoner should be remembered; there are not a great many "quotable" lines—in the sense of the exquisite image of dazzling insight to be isolated for admiration out of context—in his work. Wagoner is at least as much philosopher as poet, and his poems, effective as they are when looked at individually, together take on cumulative power and meaning. Outwardly dissimilar poems are often interrelated below the surface to a marked degree. The result is a coherent, explicitly delineated philosophy, a "way" of life based on acceptance, self-reliance, and a profound reverence for the natural world.

Those who insist on calling Wagoner a regional or nature poet are certainly correct, to a point. From his earliest collection on, his work has amply indicated a sensitivity to the landscape around him. Later poems, in particular, have been praised for their descriptive qualities. The same can be said of many writers, but the use to which Wagoner has put his rain forests, mountains, rivers, and coastlines is uniquely his own. His wilderness, with its unsentimental, uncompromising beauty, serves on one level as a conventional metaphor: the landscape, physical and spiritual, through which one travels on one's life journey. Rather than seeing rocks, trees, and animals, however, as separate entities to be reacted to—climbed over, caught and eaten, run from—Wagoner views the natural world as the medium through which humans can best learn to know themselves. Put another way, if one can accept one's place as a part of the ongoing natural processes of life, death, decay, and rebirth, one begins to "see things whole." It is this sense of wholeness, this appreciation for the interrelatedness of all the "organic and inorganic companions on earth" to which Wagoner invites his reader, as if to a feast.

The way to this ideal state involves an apparent paradox: To find oneself, one must first lose oneself, shedding the subject/object, mind/body, spirit/intellect dualities typical of "rational" Western thought. In "Staying Alive," a traveler lost in the woods is faced not only with problems of physical survival but also with "the problem of recognition," by anyone or anything external that might be looking for him, as well as recognition of his own true nature. Unable to make contact with others, the traveler is advised that "You should have a mirror/ With a tiny hole in the back . . ." that will reflect the sun and flash messages, that will reflect one's familiar physical image and that, because of the aperture, will also allow one to see through one's physical self to the wholeness of the surrounding natural world.

It is clear that, in Wagoner's view, modern industrial society has created too many wastelands and polluted waterways, and more than enough fragmented citizens such as "The Man from the Top of the Mind," with "the light bulb screwed into his head,/ The vacuum tube of his sex, the electric eye." This gleaming creature of pure intellect can "Bump through our mazes like a genius rat" but is incapable of any human emotion except destructive rage. On every level, it would appear, one has become estranged—from oneself, from others and from one's environment.

HANDBOOK POEMS

In place of this fragmentation and alienation, Wagoner offers synthesis: the ability to see and experience things whole. In a remarkable series of poems, he not only extends the offer but also provides an explicit, step-by-step guide—a Scouts' handbook or survival manual for the reader to follow.

Although these handbook poems span several volumes (from *Staying Alive* through *In Broken Country*), they are best read as a single group. All are similar in language and tone; all address an unnamed "you," offering advice for coping with problems that might arise on a wilderness trip. Should one find oneself lost, one need only remember that "Staying alive . . . is a matter of calming down." Further poems instruct one on what to do when "Breaking Camp," or "Meeting a Bear" ("try your meekest behavior,/ . . . eyes downcast"), even after "Being Shot" ("if you haven't fallen involuntarily, you may/ Volunteer now . . ."). In each case, "you," the reader, are put in touch—in most cases both literally and figuratively—with something that has previously seemed foreign or outside the realm of ordinary human experience. In other words, lack of sensitivity to natural processes results in estrangement and isolation. By becoming more receptive, and perhaps less "top of the mind" rational, one allows for the possibility of "rescue" in the form of new understanding.

Frequently, since they typically involve a stripping away of the ego, these new insights prove to be humbling. Traveling "From Here to There," one can see the destination easily, while the distance deceives and one is confused by mirages: "Water put out like fire, . . . flying islands,/ The unbalancing act of mountains upside down." The problem of recognition resurfaces; nothing is what it seems. There is nothing to do but keep slogging: "One Damn Thing After Another," until finally, having "shrugged off most illusions" you "find yourself" in a place "where nothing is the matter/ . . . asking one more lesson." Still harder to accept are the lessons that teach acquiescence in mortality; lessons that teach that even a violent death is as much a part of the life process as birth. In "Being Shot," one finds oneself helpless on the forest floor, "study[ing]/ At first hand . . . the symptoms of shock." With Wagoner's open and accepting life view, death is as natural and therefore as necessary as birth, and "To burrow deep, for a deep winter," as "Staying Alive" advises, will result, come spring, in a renewal of some kind, if only because—should one not survive—one's decaying body will provide nutrients with which to feed other forms of life.

A series of poems in the final section of *In Broken Country* provide a guide to survival in the desert rather than the forest. Similar in tone and intent to the earlier handbook poems, these divert from "The Right Direction" past "The Point of No Return," where ". . . from here on/ It will take more courage to turn than to keep going." The process is what matters.

The "you" in these poems is never identified. There is a strong sense that the reader is being addressed directly, as if he or she has enrolled in an Outward Bound course and is receiving a curious mix of practical and cryptic last-minute advice before setting out on a solo adventure. There is also a sense of the poet talking to himself, working his own way both from the industrialized northern Indiana of his youth to the rain forests of Washington, and, in a parallel journey, from a sense of alienation to one of harmony.

DRY SUN, DRY WIND

In *Dry Sun, Dry Wind*, Wagoner's first collection, his affinity with nature is already apparent, but no real contact seems possible. The poet remains isolated, seeing about him images of destruction ("sun carries death to leaves"), decay, and uncertainty ("last year's gully is this year's hill"). Time flies; memory is unable to delay it. The natural environment, blighted though it is, is "Too much to breathe, think, see" ("Warning"). In the early poems, the relationship between humans and nature—or humans and anything or anyone else—was generally one of conflict, an ongoing struggle for control resulting in disillusionment: a war, rather than a reconciliation, of opposites. "Progress" was often best achieved through violence to the land, and the stillness that in later works will open the way to enlightenment has precisely the opposite effect in early poems such as "Lull." Recognition, and, by extension, synthesis, are possible only when "the wind hums or wheels," creating movement, a kind of artificial life.

It is perhaps significant that none of the poems from this first volume has been included in any subsequent collection. The suggestion is that Wagoner quickly moved beyond these early efforts, struggling with his own problem of recognition as he searched for a true voice of his own. The major themes are there, often apparent only in their negative aspects, as, for example, the fragmentation and conflict that will yield in later poems to synthesis. In addition, there is at least one poem that deserves reading on its own merit.

"Sam the Aerialist" is "sick of walking." He wants to fly. Like the poet, like the trickster of Native American myth, like dreamers everywhere, he hungers for the impossible and yearns to exceed his natural bounds. In this, Sam is like most of the human race. His crime is not so much his desire to fly as it is his attitude, which is aggressive, self-serving, exploitative: Sam has a "lust for air" that is anything but properly reverent. The birds, therefore, instead of sharing their secrets with him, "have kept/ Far from his mind." "Birds are evil," Sam concludes,

> they fly
> Against the wind. How many have I pulled
> Apart . . .
> To learn the secret?

Sam learns by destroying. He lacks the empathy that could move him toward true understanding, and he remains isolated, cut off from his own nature as well as that around him.

Although he is never again referred to by name, there is a sense in which Sam the Aerialist's presence is felt throughout Wagoner's later poetry. He represents a kind of high-technology Everyman; his failings are the failings of society at large. He makes a stubborn but useful pupil. If such a one can absorb the early wisdom of "The Nesting Ground," that sometimes standing still will gain one more than flight; if he can follow where the handbook poems lead and lose himself in the discovery that there is a bottom as well as a top to his mind, then perhaps all is not lost. Certainly, there is an aspect of Sam in the "you" to whom the handbook poems speak.

"Seven Songs for an Old Voice"

Another step beyond specific survival lore in Wagoner's progress from alienation to harmony is represented by several groups of poems based on the mythology of the Northwest Coast and the Plateau Indians. Wagoner's interest in Native American culture is longstanding. "Talking to the Forest," included in *Staying Alive*, responds to a Skagit tribesman's statement: "When we can understand animals, we will know the change is halfway. When we can talk to the forest, we will know the change has come."

In *Riverbed*, "Old Man, Old Man" teaches that "Every secret is as near as your fingers."

It was in the 1974 collection *Sleeping in the Woods*, however, that the pivotal group, "Seven Songs for an Old Voice," first appeared. This Voice, still singing the ancient animistic wisdom as reverently as it did in the days before the Iron People (whites) arrived, offers hymns equally to Fire, which keeps enemies away, and to the Maker of Nightmares, who "eat[s] my sleep for . . . food." Other songs address death, the soul leaving the body and returning to it, and the First People, nonhumans who became rocks, animals, plants, and water when they learned of the coming of humankind. No matter what the subject, the tone is one of acceptance and awe. Death is part of life. Terrifying as they are, nightmares are not to be denied. The Voice promises to "drink what you bring me in my broken skull,/ The bitter water which once was sweet as morning."

WHO SHALL BE THE SUN?

These "Seven Songs for an Old Voice" are included in *Who Shall Be the Sun?* along with other previously collected poems, new groups of "Songs for the Dream-Catchers," "Songs of Only-One," "Songs of He-Catches-Nothing," and two groups of myths and legends—one each from the Plateau and Northwest Coast Indian tribes. Wagoner explains in his author's note that the myths and legends are retellings of existing stories. The songs are original works, but Wagoner stresses his debt to the Indians' spirit if not their words.

As Robert K. Cording points out, these Indian-lore poems allow Wagoner to blend several hitherto separate themes. For the Native American, the interrelationship of humans and nature has traditionally been a given, as has a belief in the power of various religious and quasi-religious rituals and practices that non-Indians might call magic. Magic, as a motif, appears fairly frequently in Wagoner's earlier work; in this collection, human beings "magically" converse with the spirits of the First People in the trees above them and the dust beneath their feet. It is not only the First People who are capable of such transformations. Animals also can take on human shapes; humans can put on different skins. In certain situations, the dead can return to earth and the living can cross in safety to the land of the dead. Magic here is more than sleight-of-hand and an Indian's dreams are tools more powerful than the technology of Sam the Aerialist, as the title poem shows. "Who Shall Be the Sun?" the People ask, and despite his apparent lack of suitability for the job, Snake's ability to dream, coupled with his seemly modesty, allows him to succeed where the assertive, egocentric Raven, Hawk, and Coyote (who can merely think) have failed.

"Who Shall Be the Sun?" and other poems in the myth and legend sections are written in a language that closely echoes the cadences of English prose translations of Indian legends with which the reader may be familiar. The song groups are distinct from one another, the tone and rhythm consistent with each singer's personality and the subject addressed. It should be noted that although the pervading attitude is one of reverence and peace, not all of these poems present such a harmonious picture. Coyote and Raven, classic tricksters, are as likely to cause harm with their pranks as they are to improve the lot of those they purport to help, as the Indian culture, like any other, has always had its share of misfits, liars, and thieves. There is disease, madness, and death, of course, as well as someone called Only-One, who, half-blinded by the beak of an injured heron he had attempted to heal, sees only halves of things. Scarred by smallpox, neither truly dead nor truly alive, Only-One is an isolated soul. He dances with Dead Man, and the half-girl he takes for his bride turns out to be the bird that blinded him.

IN BROKEN COUNTRY AND LANDFALL

Following *Who Shall Be the Sun?*, Wagoner returned to a more characteristic range of subjects. *In Broken Country* mixes poems about love, childhood memories, parents, poets (including a lovely elegy to Roethke), bums, and prisoners (Wagoner himself included). A dozen desert handbook poems are preceded by a series of self-parodying mock-handbook entries.

Landfall also covers a broad range, although a particularly strong unifying cord runs throughout. A number of the most moving poems are about making contact with one's past, not merely in the sense of looking back and remembering, but in trying for reconciliation with aspects of one's life that may have caused one pain. Over the years, Wagoner has written poems about his father—puttering around the house, building a wall—a pleasant-seeming man, drained by his job in the steel mill. A certain edgy ambivalence of tone in these poems has kept the elder Wagoner an insubstantial figure. "My Father's Garden" changes this, introducing the reader to a man who picked "flowers" for his family: "small gears and cogwheels/ With teeth like petals," found in the scrapheap he passed on his way to work, work which "melted" his mind to the point that all he retained of an education in the classics was enough Latin and Greek for crossword puzzles. Paired with this is "My Father's Ghost," an extraordinary piece based on a Midwestern folk saying and reminiscent in tone of the Indian songs. Having performed the proper rituals, the poet should be able to see his father's spirit; but the charms do not work. The room stays empty. It is necessary to "imagine him," then; "and dream him/ Returning unarmed, unharmed. Words, words. I hold/ My father's ghost in my arms in his dark doorway."

The final section, "A Sea Change," describes a journey with no destination, in which the poet and his wife leave forest, desert, and marsh behind and head out to sea. This sea voyage is more explicitly psychological than the handbook poems, but here, too, reconciliations take place. The travelers must come to terms with the unfamiliar element to which they have entrusted their lives; in doing so, they will discover that it is not so foreign as they thought. They must overcome their dread of the dimly seen monsters coiling in the depths. In doing so, they discover that the monsters never break through the "mirror" of the water's surface—suggesting, perhaps, that to accept one's demons as the Old Voice singer accepted nightmares and death is to rob them of much of their power. In contrast to Wagoner's explicitly instructive poems, the Sea Change group does not explain precisely by what means these primal fears are to be overcome or how other changes are to be brought about. At journey's end, "Landfall," the two travelers simply come "wallowing" ashore like their "hesitant helpless curious ancestors," having somehow been in touch with a past too dim for memory or rational understanding. On feet that "keep believing/ In the sea," they regain firm ground, asking, "Have we come home? Is this where we were born? . . . this place/ Where, again, we must learn to walk?"

Wagoner's own answer to this would be yes, over and over again, on all ground and in all weather, backward, on our hands, on water, and on air. Getting there means starting over; starting over means rebirth, renewal, a second chance to see things whole. In many ways, this is just what Wagoner has been doing throughout his career.

WALT WHITMAN BATHING

In *Walt Whitman Bathing*, Wagoner finds inspiration in American experience and landscape, translating it into stacked, searching clauses: "Above the river, over the broad hillside/ and down the slope in clusters and strewn throngs,/ cross-tangled and intermingled,/ wildflowers are blooming, seemingly all at once." Story and lyric take alternating turns at center stage, and his lines consistently find their breath—long and short, substantial and supple—as in "Mapmaking," from the compelling sequence on landscapes: "You fix your eyes on [landmarks], one at a time,/ And learn the hard way/ How hard it is to fabricate broken country."

The first half of the book consists of poems of nostalgic, personal reminiscence and public eulogies. He advises, in "In the Woods," that as "you" find "yourself" contemplating the trees,

> Now you may make yourself at home by doing without
> The pointless heroics of moving, by remaining
> Quiet, by holding still
> To take your place as they have taken theirs: by right
> Of discovery in this immanent domain,
> Simply by growing
> Accustomed to being here instead of nowhere.

The book's second half revisits many of Wagoner's familiar settings, themes, and stylistics: there is nature without trivial transcendence, flora and fauna, and verses heavy with pronouns, addressed to his ever-present and insistent "you." His insights run deep and are expressed with a soft-spoken directness intimately linked to his skepticism about humankind's role in the cosmos. Wagoner talks quietly with the reader—when not penned in the second-person singular, his poetry beckons the reader near—about the relativity of the self and about "Searching for more than you at the end of you."

Wagoner also presents moving poems about human affection, often set during his midwestern boyhood. "My Father Laughing in the Chicago Theater" memorably portrays "Two hundred and twenty horizontal pounds/ Of defensive lineman, of open-hearth melter" doubling over at the quips of vaudeville comics. Several poems also center on American Gothic-era memories (red-nosed cops, trained bears, boys who wear "nightgowns"), images kept from cliché by Wagoner's sure touch. Never folksy, the poems are plainspoken and display a formal virtuosity that allows Wagoner to penetrate beneath the surface, as when sketching his parents in three-stress lines: "They stand by the empty car,/ By the open driver's door,/ Waiting. The evening sun/ is glowing like pig-iron." The sum effect of the book is authoritative but detached, descriptive yet minimalistic.

TRAVELING LIGHT

Culling poems from forty-five years of published work, *Traveling Light*, a generous retrospective, calls on Wagoner's experiences of hiking and camping in mountain wilderness, comments on angst and paranoia based on his everyday urban existence, and provides a glimpse into his personal experience with literature, love, and death. His plain midwestern diction and even tone prevent him from moving into portentousness à la Carl Sandburg, whom he meets and raises stakes on in such poems as "A Day in the City" and "The Apotheosis of the Garbageman." With a nod to Robert Penn Warren, he masters the poetic sequence ("Landscapes" or "Traveling Light"), and in a series on his late father, a steel-mill worker, he colloquially recalls his own sympathetic gestures:

> I shook the dying and dead
> Ashes down through the grate
> And, with firetongs, hauled out clinkers
> Like the vertebrae of monsters.

THE HOUSE OF SONG

Poems in *The House of Song, Good Morning and Good Night*, and *A Map of the Night* carry forward Wagoner's extraordinary variety of poetic voices; his eye for significant concrete details; his ear for easy rhythms, deceptively prose-like but subtle in their placement of pauses and emphasis; his wit, manifested in puns, irony, and metaphor; and his themes of the integration of the self with nature, family, tradition, and the world.

In the title poem of *The House of Song*, a Gilbert Islander made a song out of his environment each year, taught his song to his community, and then sat silent "As the people became that song,/ As the whole village around him and around them/ Became the house of that song." Wagoner, like the Gilbert Island singer makes the world around him—around the reader—into poetry.

In "Arranging a Book of Poems" (from *Good Morning and Good Night*), Wagoner describes his care in ordering his poems, and in the first section of *The House of Song*, he moves from the house of song to the greater, mysterious, but enlightening world beyond song. "The Book of Moonlight" begins with a quotation from Wallace Stevens: "The Book of Moonlight is not written yet." Wagoner asks, "Why should we ever write it?" Our "illiterate fingers" cannot make sense of the mystery of its overflowing brightness.

"Elegy on the First Day of Spring" describes the flowers' struggle against the poor soil and the hard climate of Wagoner's mother's garden, paralleling her own later struggles with dementia, which erased even her recognition of her family, but let her still play and sing songs about flowers. Wagoner himself moved on to a place where flowers grow abundantly, where "The earth wants to make music," and where the sun can be ". . . as astonished as we are/ At everything we can still remember."

The last words of the last poem of *The House of Song*, written from a Native American point of view, bring the reader full circle from the collection's title poem: "We must become more than what is left of our bodies/ And will see and become what is always/ Rushing toward us and around us."

GOOD MORNING AND GOOD NIGHT

Good Morning and Good Night begins with Federico García Lorca dreaming a beautiful poem and awakening to hear it actually sung—as he discovers—by an illiterate street sweeper. Possessing the gift of literacy, García Lorca returns to his bed "To lie there stark awake as sleeplessly/ As a poet who'd been told he was immortal." The collection ends with a series of poems on the night and the morning, some of them ironic. The final poem, "At the Foot of the Mountain," set in the early morning, seems to have nothing to do with the night—actual or metaphoric—until the unexpected last word: at the end of the poem "you"—one of Wagoner's common subjects, here a reluctant climber—finally join other climbers in "their uninterrupted *chanting*" [emphasis added]. Perhaps, then, this too is not only a good morning but a good night poem and the climb a metaphor for mortality, seen as challenge, duty, and ritual.

This collection also contains several handbook poems, a set of which are military instructions, and a section of poems about poetry. In "Trying to Make Music," the poet confronts not only unsympathetic listeners but also his own self-doubts. In "Poetry in Motion," he questions whether poetry can ". . . move itself and more/ Than itself and not be here, flat on the page." In "A Date with the Muse," the poet finds the muse repeatedly unresponsive to his offers. However, in the metaphorical "On Being Asked to Discuss Poetic Theory," the poet describes finding snow falling in the mountains and following the snowmelt as it courses down to the ocean. Even if the white tops of the mountains disappear behind clouds, he knows that snow is falling again. Clouded in mystery, the sources of the poet's inspiration do not fail.

A Map of the Night

Many of the poems in *A Map of the Night* are companion pieces to poems previously published. For instance, "My Father's Dance" is a counterpart to "Elegy to the First Day of Spring" in *The House of Song*, "Thoreau and the Mud Turtle" and "Thoreau and the Quagmire" add to the set of Thoreau poems also in *The House of Song*, and several military "Handbook" poems extend those in *Good Morning and Good Night*.

Wagoner's wit is displayed in several poems: In "Trying to Write a Poem While the Couple in the Apartment Overhead Make Love," the rhythms of Wagoner's poem neatly match the rhythms of the subject. In "Attention" (a military "Handbook" poem), the typography of the short two-stress lines makes the poem stand at attention on the page. Wagoner's focus on decorum in this, as in all of his "Handbook" poems, tends to put readers in their places. In "On First Looking Through the Wrong End of the Telescope," a series of puns puts all humankind in its place.

This collection also includes "On a Glass of Ale Under a Reading Lamp," in which small flies, like the drinker, risk "... a desire/ ... to drink without drowning// to touch the good bitterness/ again, not knowing why." Another memorable poem is "On an Island," the protagonist of which, once again "you," is on a beach, with the sea on one side and a "dense interior" on the other. Here "you" must "... reconsider the unromantic agony/ of change without progress ... ," finding "... yourself/ beginning where you were and seeing/ what you tried your best to remember/ or dismiss and forget."

Wagoner's poetry is readily accessible, not overly formal, expressive, even emphatic, sometimes witty, sometimes metaphorical, and solidly based in concrete images. Wagoner continues to advance his worldview of humankind in harmony with the familial, social, and, above all, natural orders.

Other major works

LONG FICTION: *The Man in the Middle*, 1954, 1955; *Money, Money, Money*, 1955; *Rock*, 1958; *The Escape Artist*, 1965; *Baby, Come On Inside*, 1968; *Where Is My Wandering Boy Tonight?*, 1970; *The Road to Many a Wonder*, 1974; *Tracker*, 1975; *Whole Hog*, 1976; *The Hanging Garden*, 1980.

PLAY: *An Eye for an Eye for an Eye*, pr. 1973.

EDITED TEXTS: *Straw for the Fire: From the Notebooks of Theodore Roethke, 1943-1963*, 1972; *The Best American Poetry 2009*, 2009 (with David Lehman).

Bibliography

Boyers, Robert. "The Poetry of David Wagoner." Review of *Staying Alive*. *Kenyon Review* 32 (Spring, 1970): 176-181. An appreciative review noting that *Staying Alive* marks a turning point in Wagoner's development. Boyers states that from this point forward, Wagoner could claim to be a major figure in contemporary American poetry.

Durczak, Joanna. "David Wagoner: Instructor Against Instructors." *Treading Softly,*

Speaking Low: Contemporary American Poetry in the Didactic Mode. Lublin, Poland: Wydawnictwo Uniwersytetu, 1994. Uniquely useful as an extended analysis of Wagoner's "Handbook" poems.

Lieberman, Laurence. "David Wagoner: The Cold Speech of the Earth." In *Unassigned Frequencies: American Poetry in Review, 1964-1977.* Urbana: University of Illinois Press, 1977. Looks at how this poet maps out a topography through his choice of words and images. Compares the later poems with the earlier ones and cites the same imagination but with greater depth of vision. Offers strong, in-depth criticism of *Collected Poems, 1956-1976* and places Wagoner in the company of Walt Whitman, Robert Frost, Edgar Lee Masters, and William Stafford.

McFarland, Ronald E. *The World of David Wagoner.* Moscow: University of Idaho Press, 1997. Presents literary criticism and interpretation of Wagoner's writings and looks at the role of the American Midwest and Northwest in literature.

Peters, Robert. "Thirteen Ways of Looking at David Wagoner's New Poems." Review of *Landfall. Western Humanities Review* 35, no. 3 (Autumn, 1981): 267-272. A provocative review, unusual among commentaries on Wagoner's poetry in its stress on what Peters takes to be Wagoner's lack of imagination and risk-taking.

Waggoner, Hyatt H. *American Visionary Poetry.* Baton Rouge: Louisiana State University Press, 1982. Chapter 7, "Traveling Light," explores Wagoner's identity as a visionary poet through his nature poems. Examines Wagoner's portrayal of the wilderness and how he guards himself in his poems. A sympathetic critique that praises Wagoner's volume *The Nesting Ground.*

Wagoner, David. "David Wagoner." Interview by Nicholas O'Connell. In *At the Field's End: Interviews with Twenty Pacific Northwest Writers,* edited by O'Connell. Seattle: Madrona, 1987. The interviewer explores with Wagoner the subjects of his poems and how he has re-created the Northwest landscape on paper. Examines the structure and sense of rhythm in his poems. Of particular note is a discussion of *Who Shall Be the Sun?,* a collection of poems for which he received much praise.

_____. "David Wagoner." Interview by Sanford Pinsker. In *Three Pacific Northwest Poets: William Stafford, Richard Hugo, and David Wagoner.* Boston: Twayne, 1987. A useful and insightful introduction to Wagoner's poems, analyzing his choice of themes and techniques. Contains critical commentary on all of his major poems. Notes that among Wagoner's strengths is his "sense of the dramatic."

_____. "David Wagoner—Slightly Different Ways of Thinking: An Interview." Interview by Kate Gray. In *Page to Page: Retrospectives of Writers from the "Seattle Review,"* edited by Colleen J. McElroy. Seattle: University of Washington Press, 2006. An account of a wide-ranging interview, accompanied by photographs, a bibliography, and three poems by Wagoner.

Sara McAulay; Sarah Hilbert
Updated by David W. Cole

ALICE WALKER

Born: Eatonton, Georgia; February 9, 1944

PRINCIPAL POETRY
Once, 1968
Five Poems, 1972
Revolutionary Petunias, and Other Poems, 1973
Good Night, Willie Lee, I'll See You in the Morning, 1979
Horses Make a Landscape Look More Beautiful, 1984
Her Blue Body Everything We Know: Earthling Poems, 1965-1990 Complete, 1991
Absolute Trust in the Goodness of the Earth: New Poems, 2003
A Poem Traveled Down My Arm: Poems and Drawings, 2003

OTHER LITERARY FORMS

Although Alice Walker's poetry is cherished by her admirers, she is primarily known as a fiction writer. The novel *The Color Purple* (1982), generally regarded as her masterpiece, achieved both popular and critical success, winning the Pulitzer Prize and the National Book Award. The Steven Spielberg film of the same name, for which Walker acted as consultant, reached an immense international audience.

Other Walker fiction has received less attention. Her first novel, *The Third Life of Grange Copeland* (1970), depicts violence and family dysfunction among people psychologically maimed by racism. *Meridian* (1976) mirrors the Civil Rights movement, of which the youthful Walker was actively a part. Later novels, *The Temple of My Familiar* (1989), *Possessing the Secret of Joy* (1992), and *By the Light of My Father's Smile* (1998) have employed narrative as little more than a vehicle for ideas on racial and sexual exploitation, abuse of animals and the earth, and New Age spirituality. *In Love and Trouble: Stories of Black Women* (1973) and *You Can't Keep a Good Woman Down* (1981) revealed Walker to be one of the finest of late twentieth century American short-story writers. She also has written an occasional children's book (*To Hell with Dying*, 1988, is particularly notable) and several collections of essays (*In Search of Our Mothers' Gardens: Womanist Prose*, 1983, is the most lyrical) that present impassioned pleas for the causes Walker espouses.

ACHIEVEMENTS

At numerous colleges, as a teacher and writer-in-residence, Alice Walker established herself as a mentor, particularly to young African American women. Her crusades became international. To alert the world to the problem of female circumcision in Africa, she collaborated with an Anglo-Indian filmmaker on a book and film. She has been a voice for artistic freedom, defending her own controversial writings and those of others, such as Salman Rushdie. In her writings and later open lifestyle, she affirmed lesbian and bisexual experience. However, the accomplishment in which she took the most pride was her resurrection of the reputation of Zora Neale Hurston, a germinal African American anthropologist and novelist, whose books had gone out of print.

Walker won the Rosenthal Award of the National Institute of Arts and Letters for *In Love and Trouble* and received a Charles Merrill writing fellowship, a National Endowment for the Arts award, and a Guggenheim Fellowship. Her second book of poetry, *Revolutionary Petunias, and Other Poems*, received the Lillian Smith Award and was nominated for a National Book Award. Her highest acclaim came with the novel *The Color Purple*, for which she won the National Book Award and the 1983 Pulitzer Prize. She received the Fred Cody Award for lifetime achievement in 1990. Walker was inducted into the California Hall of Fame in 2006.

Biography

Alice Malsenior Walker was the youngest of eight children born to a Georgia sharecropper and his wife. Her father earned about three hundred dollars per year, while her mother, the stronger figure, supplemented the family income by working as a maid. Walker herself was a bright, confident child until an accident at age eight blinded her in one eye and temporarily marred her beauty. At this time, she established what was to become a lifelong pattern of savoring solitude and making the most of adversity. She started reading and writing poetry.

Because of her partial blindness and her outstanding high school record, Walker qualified for a special scholarship offered to disabled students by Spelman College, the prestigious black women's college in Atlanta. When she matriculated there in 1961, her neighbors raised the bus fare of seventy-five dollars to get her to Atlanta.

As a Spelman student, Walker was "moved to wakefulness" by the emerging Civil Rights movement. She took part in demonstrations downtown, which brought her into conflict with the conservative administration of the school. Finding the rules generally too restrictive and refreshed with her new consciousness, she secured a scholarship at Sarah Lawrence College in Bronxville, New York. She then felt closer to the real action that was changing the country. At Sarah Lawrence College, she came under the influence of the poet Muriel Rukeyser, who recognized her talent and arranged for her first publications. She also took a summer off for a trip to her "spiritual home," Africa. She returned depressed and pregnant, contemplated suicide for a time, but instead underwent an abortion and poured her emotions into poetry.

After graduation, Walker worked for a time in the New York City Welfare Department before returning to the South to write, teach, and promote voter registration. She married Melvyn Leventhal, a white Jew, and worked with him on desegregation legal cases and Head Start programs. Their child, Rebecca, was born during this highly productive period. By the time the marriage ended in 1976, Walker was already becoming recognized as a writer, though she did not become internationally famous until after the publication of *The Color Purple*.

Walker continued to write during the 1980's and 1990's, though never again achieving the acclaim or the notoriety that *The Color Purple* brought her. Critics complained of her stridency, the factual inaccuracies in her writings, and her tendency to turn her works of fiction into polemics. Many African Americans felt that her writings cast black society in a grim light. Walker moved to California and lived for several years with Robert Allen, the editor of *Black Scholar*. Times had changed; the motto was no longer "black and white together": marriages between Jews and African Americans were out, and black-black relationships were in.

Walker also became more alert to the problems women of color faced throughout the world. Taking a female partner, she decided to devote her time and talents to celebrating women and rectifying wrongs committed against them. In March of 2003, Walker was arrested for protesting the Iraq War. In 2009, Walker visited Gaza to promote peace and friendlier relations between Egypt and Israel. Walker has always encouraged awareness of important issues in her writing, but she has attracted attention to issues such as problems in the black culture, violence against women, and the ravages of war by personally participating in or protesting events about which she feels passionately.

Analysis

Alice Walker writes free verse, employing concrete images. She resorts to few of the conceits, the extended metaphors, the Latinate language, and other common conventions of poetry. Readers frequently say that her verses hardly seem like poetry at all; they resemble the conversation of a highly articulate, observant woman. Although her poetry often seems like prose, her fiction is highly poetic. The thoughts of Miss Celie, the first-person narrator of *The Color Purple*, would not have been out of place in a book of poetry. Boundaries between prose and poetry are minimal in the work of Walker. Her verse, like her prose, is always rhythmic; if she rhymes or alliterates, it seems to be by accident. The poetry appears so effortless that its precision, its choice of exact image or word to convey the nuance the poet wishes, is not immediately evident. Only close scrutiny reveals the skill with which this highly lettered poet has assimilated her influences, chiefly E. E. Cummings, Emily Dickinson, Robert Graves, Japanese haiku, Li Bo, Ovid, Zen epigrams, and William Carlos Williams.

Walker's poetry is personal and generally didactic, generated by events in her life, causes she has advocated, and injustices over which she has agonized. The reader feels that it is the message that counts, before realizing that the medium is part of the message. Several of her poems echo traumatic events in her own life, such as her abortion. She remembers the words her mother uttered over the casket of her father, and she makes a poem of them. Other poems recall ambivalent emotions of childhood: Sunday school lessons which, even then, were filled with discrepancies. Some poems deal with the creative process itself: She calls herself a medium through whom the Old Ones, formerly mute, find their voice at last.

Some readers are surprised to discover that Walker's poems are both mystical and socially revolutionary, one moment exuberant and the next reeking with despair. Her mysticism is tied to reverence for the earth, a sense of unity with all living creatures, a bond of sisterhood with women throughout the world, and a joyous celebration of the female principle in the divine. On the other hand, she may lament that injustice reigns in society: Poor black people toil so that white men may savor the jewels that adorn heads of state.

ONCE

Walker's first collection of poetry, *Once*, communicates her youthful impressions of Africa and her state of mind during her early travels there and the melancholy and thoughts of death and suicide she felt on her return to United States, where racism persisted. Perhaps the epigram from French philosopher Albert Camus, which prefaces the book, expresses its mood best: "Misery kept me from believing that all was well under the sun, and the sun taught me that history wasn't everything."

The title poem of the collection contains several loosely connected scenes of injustice in the American South, small black children run down by vans because "they were in the way," Jewish Civil Rights workers who cannot be cremated because their remains cannot be found, and finally a black child waving an American flag, but from "the very/ *tips/* of her/ fingers," an image perhaps of irony or perhaps of hope. There are meditations on white lovers—blond, Teutonic, golden—who dare kiss this poet who is "brown-er/ Than a jew." There are memories of black churches, where her mother shouts, her father snores, and she feels uncomfortable.

The most striking poem is certainly "African Images," an assortment of vignettes from the ancestral homeland: shy gazelles, the bluish peaks of Mount Kenya, the sound of elephants trumpeting, and rain forests with red orchids. However, even when viewed in the idealism of youth, Africa is not total paradise. The leg of a slain elephant is fashioned into an umbrella holder in a shop; a rhinoceros is killed so that its horn may be made into an aphrodisiac.

REVOLUTIONARY PETUNIAS, AND OTHER POEMS

Revolutionary Petunias, and Other Poems is divided into two parts. The first is titled "In These Dissenting Times . . . Surrounding Ground and Autobiography." She proposes to write "of the old men I knew/ And the young men/ I loved/ And of the gold toothed women/ Mighty of arm/ Who dragged us all/ To church." She writes also "To acknowledge our ancestors" with the awareness that "we did not make/ ourselves, that the line stretches/ all the way back, perhaps, to God; or/ to Gods." She recalls her baptism "dunked . . . in the creek," with "gooey . . . rotting leaves,/ a greenish mold floating." She was a slight figure, "All in white./ With God's mud ruining my snowy/ socks and his bullfrog spoors/ gluing up my face."

The last half of the collection, "Revolutionary Petunias . . . the Living Through," begins with yet another epigram from Camus, reminding the reader that there will come a time when revolutions, though not made by beauty, will discover the need for beauty. The poems, especially those referred to as "Crucifixions," become more anguished, more angered. Walker becomes skeptical of the doctrine of nonviolence, hinting that the time for more direct action may have come. The tone of the last poems in the collection may be expressed best by the opening lines to the verse Walker called "Rage." "In me, " she wrote, "there is a rage to defy/ the order of the stars/ despite their pretty patterns."

Good Night, Willie Lee, I'll See You in the Morning

Good Night, Willie Lee, I'll See You in the Morning expands on earlier themes and further exploits personal and family experiences for lessons in living. The title poem is perhaps the most moving and characteristic of the collection. Walker shared it again on May 22, 1995, in a commencement day speech delivered at Spelman College. As a lesson in forgiveness, she recalled the words her mother, who had much to endure and much to forgive, uttered above her father's casket. Her last words to the man with whom she had lived for so many years, beside whom she had labored in the fields, and with whom she had raised so many children were, "Good night, Willie Lee, I'll see you in the morning." This gentle instinctive act of her mother taught Walker the enduring lesson that "the healing of all our wounds is forgiveness/ that permits a promise/ of our return/ at the end."

Horses Make a Landscape Look More Beautiful

Horses Make a Landscape Look More Beautiful took its title from words of Lame Deer, an Indian seer who contemplated the gifts of the white man—chiefly whiskey and horses—and found the beauty of horses almost made her forget the whiskey. This thought establishes the tone of the collection. These are movement poems, but as always, they remain intensely personal and frequently elegiac. The poet seems herself to speak:

> I am the woman
> with the blessed
> dark skin
> I am the woman
> with teeth repaired
> I am the woman
> with the healing eye
> the ear that hears.

There is also lamentation for lost love:

> When I no longer have your heart
> I will not request your body
> your presence
> or even your polite conversation.
> I will go away to a far country
> separated from you by the sea
> —on which I cannot walk—
> and refrain even from sending
> letters
> describing my pain.

HER BLUE BODY EVERYTHING WE KNOW

Her Blue Body Everything We Know contains a selection of poems written between 1965 and 1990, along with a few new verses and revealing commentary. This collection includes poems from *Once*; *Revolutionary Petunias, and Other Poems*; *Good Night, Willie Lee, I'll See You in the Morning*; and *Horses Make a Landscape Look More Beautiful*. Walker provides readers with insights on the art of poetry (in poems such as "How Poems Are Made: A Discredited View" and "I Said to Poetry"). In her introduction to the final section of the collection, Walker relates how she once felt jealous of how musicians connect with their work and seem to be one with it, but that during career as a writer, she has learned that poets share a similar relationship with their poetry. Walker, a woman of passion, shows how her personal beliefs about Africa (in the first section of this collection, "African Images: Glimpses from a Tiger's Back"), multiracial relationships (in the poem "Johann"), and the pangs of love (in poems such as "Did This Happen to Your Mother? Did Your Sister Throw Up a Lot?") are intricately intertwined and evident in her poetic creations.

Walker calls the final section "We Have a Beautiful Mother: Previously Uncollected Poems." The poems in this section, including "Some Things I Like About My Triple Bloods," "If There Was Any Justice," "We Have a Map of the World," and "Telling," are deeply personal and challenge readers to think about boundaries between cultures, countries, and hearts.

ABSOLUTE TRUST IN THE GOODNESS OF THE EARTH

In the preface to *Absolute Trust in the Goodness of the Earth*, Walker confides that she thought that she had reached the end of her career as a poet and was at peace with this, but after the terrorist attacks of September, 11, 2001, on the United States, Walker found herself writing poems regularly. After the attacks, Walker feared imminent war, and her poems in this book reflect that anxiety, including pieces such as "Thousands of Feet Below You," "Not Children," and "Why War Is Never a Good Idea." The narrator of "Thousands of Feet Below You" mentions a boy, running away from the bombs of war, who eventually is shredded to pieces in a violent explosion. Walker shares similar feelings about the concept of war in "Not Children," in which she refers to war as a cowardly act and an event that the world can do without. The title of "Why War Is Never a Good Idea" is self-explanatory, the subtitle of which ("A Picture Poem for Children Blinded by War") emphasizes Walker's stance on the issue.

Walker also continuously challenges readers to think about race relations in the United States, and how they might be improved. For example, "Patriot" encourages readers to respect all Americans, no matter what their country of origin is (she mentions Middle Eastern men, American Indian men, and African women, in particular), because these people all combine to make and define the United States. "Projection" encourages readers to look beyond the stereotypes associated with certain ethnicities (such as Indians, Germans, and Arabs) and remember that, inside each person, exists an innocent child.

In the preface to *Absolute Trust in the Goodness of the Earth*, Walker also shares her interest in and admiration for the environment and plants in particular. These feelings about the natural world are represented clearly in the title of this collection, which praises the earth for its beauty and righteousness. Walker, like many writers, associates nature with an inherent sense of peace. Natural imagery abounds in this collection, appearing in poems such as "Even When I Walked Away," "Red Petals Sticking Out," "Inside My Rooms," and "The Tree." Walker's plant and flower images remind readers of her belief that humankind is deeply rooted in and connected to the earth.

A POEM TRAVELED DOWN MY ARM

In the introduction to *A Poem Traveled Down My Arm*, Walker explains that her publisher sent her blank pages to autograph; these pages would later be bound into copies of *Absolute Trust in the Goodness of the Earth* to save Walker time at forthcoming book signings. Tired of signing her own name so many times, Walker says that she suddenly started drawing little sketches on the pieces of paper. Soon, she was scrambling to keep up with writing down poems that sprang to mind, inspired by the images she had drawn. Walker feels this collection is strange when compared with her others, especially because she thought she was done writing poetry a few years earlier. Instead, she published two collections of poetry in a single year.

The poems in *A Poem Traveled Down My Arm* typically hover around ten words each. These succinct poetic creations address topics prevalent in the rest of Walker's canon, including love, peace, nature, and war. The untitled poems function almost like a series of proverbs, offering her readers advice about living a healthy spiritual life while respecting Earth and all of humanity.

OTHER MAJOR WORKS

LONG FICTION: *The Third Life of Grange Copeland*, 1970; *Meridian*, 1976; *The Color Purple*, 1982; *The Temple of My Familiar*, 1989; *Possessing the Secret of Joy*, 1992; *By the Light of My Father's Smile*, 1998; *Now Is the Time to Open Your Heart*, 2004.

SHORT FICTION: *In Love and Trouble: Stories of Black Women*, 1973; *You Can't Keep a Good Woman Down*, 1981; *The Complete Stories*, 1994; *Alice Walker Banned*, 1996 (stories and commentary).

NONFICTION: *In Search of Our Mothers' Gardens: Womanist Prose*, 1983; *Living by the Word: Selected Writings, 1973-1987*, 1988; *Warrior Marks: Female Genital Mutilation and the Sexual Blinding of Women*, 1993 (with Pratibha Parmar); *The Same River Twice: Honoring the Difficult*, 1996; *Anything We Love Can Be Saved: A Writer's Activism*, 1997; *The Way Forward Is with a Broken Heart*, 2000; *Sent by Earth: A Message from the Grandmother Spirit After the Attacks on the World Trade Center and Pentagon*, 2001; *We Are the Ones We Have Been Waiting For: Light in a Time of Darkness*, 2006; *The World Has Changed: Conversations with Alice Walker*, 2010 (Rudolph P. Byrd, editor).

CHILDREN'S LITERATURE: *Langston Hughes: American Poet*, 1974; *To Hell with Dying*, 1988; *Finding the Green Stone*, 1991; *There Is a Flower at the Tip of My Nose Smelling Me*, 2006; *Why War Is Never a Good Idea*, 2007.

EDITED TEXT: *I Love Myself When I Am Laughing . . . and Then Again When I Am Looking Mean and Impressive: A Zora Neale Hurston Reader*, 1979.

BIBLIOGRAPHY

Bates, Gerri. *Alice Walker: A Critical Companion*. Westport, Conn.: Greenwood Press, 2005. A well-crafted biography that discusses Walker's major works, tracing the themes of her novels to her life.

Bloom, Harold, ed. *Alice Walker*. New York: Chelsea House, 1989. An important collection of critical essays examining the fiction, poetry, and essays of Walker from a variety of perspectives. The fourteen essays, including Bloom's brief introduction, are arranged chronologically. Contains useful discussions of her first three novels, brief analyses of individual short stories, poems, and essays, and assessments of Walker's social and political views in connection with her works and other African American female authors. Chronology and bibliography.

Bloxham, Laura J. "Alice (Malsenior) Walker." In *Contemporary Fiction Writers of the South*, edited by Joseph M. Flora and Robert Bain. Westport, Conn.: Greenwood Press, 1993. A general introduction to Walker's "womanist" themes of oppression of black women and change through affirmation of self. Provides a brief summary and critique of previous criticism of Walker's work.

Gates, Henry Louis, Jr., and K. A. Appiah, eds. *Alice Walker: Critical Perspectives Past and Present.* New York: Amistad, 1993. Contains reviews of Walker's first five novels and critical analyses of several of her works of short and long fiction. Also includes two interviews with Walker, a chronology of her works, and an extensive bibliography of essays and texts.

Gentry, Tony. *Alice Walker.* New York: Chelsea House, 1993. Examines the life and work of Walker. Includes bibliographical references and index.

Lauret, Maria. *Alice Walker.* New York: St. Martin's Press, 2000. Provocative discussions of Walker's ideas on politics, race, feminism, and literary theory. Of special interest is the exploration of Walker's literary debt to Zora Neale Hurston, Virginia Woolf, and even Bessie Smith.

Simcikova, Karla. *To Live Fully, Here and Now: The Healing Vision in the Works of Alice Walker.* Lanham, Md.: Lexington Books, 2007. Simcikova focuses on Walker's spirituality, her relationship with nature, and how these beliefs and connections present themselves in her oeuvre of work.

Smith, Lindsey Claire. "Alice Walker's Eco-'Warriors.'" In *Indians, Environment, and Identity on the Borders of American Literature: From Faulkner and Morrison to Walker and Silko.* New York: Palgrave Macmillan, 2008. Smith analyzes boundaries delineating cultural, geographical, and racial differences in Walker's canon.

Walker, Rebecca. *Black, White, and Jewish: Autobiography of a Shifting Self.* New York: Riverhead, 2001. A self-indulgent but nevertheless insightful memoir by Alice Walker's daughter, Rebecca Walker. She describes herself as "a movement child," growing up torn between two families, two races, and two traditions, always in the shadow of an increasingly famous and absorbed mother.

White, Evelyn C. *Alice Walker: A Life.* New York: Norton, 2004. The life and accomplishments of Walker are chronicled in this biography through interviews with Walker, her family, and friends.

Allene Phy-Olsen
Updated by Karley K. Adney

WANG WEI

Born: District of Qi, Taiyuan Prefecture, Shanxi Province, China; 701
Died: Changan (now Xian), Jingzhao Prefecture, China; 761
Also known as: Wang Mojie; Wang Youcheng; Wang Yu-ch'eng

PRINCIPAL POETRY
Wang Wei: New Translations and Commentary, 1980 (Pauline Yu, translator)
Laughing Lost in the Mountains: The Poems of Wang Wei, 1991 (Willis Barnstone, Tony Barnstone, and Shu Haixin translators)
The Selected Poems of Wang Wei, 2006 (David Hinton, translator)

OTHER LITERARY FORMS

Although known primarily for his poetry, Wang Wei (wong way) was also the author of several important writings pertaining to various traditions in Tang Dynasty Buddhism, in particular his funeral inscription for the *stēlē* of the Sixth Chan (Zen) Patriarch, Huineng. In addition, Wang was an accomplished musician and painter, acquiring considerable renown for the latter talent after his death. No painting authentically attributable to him is extant, but numerous copies of several of his works were executed over a period of centuries. One of the best known of these is the long scroll depicting his country estate on the Wang River. From the Song Dynasty onward, when only copies of his works survived, he became glorified as the preeminent Chinese landscape painter, with his work honored as the prototype of *wen ren hua* (literati painting)—amateur rather than academic, intuitive and spontaneous rather than formalistic and literal.

ACHIEVEMENTS

Wang Wei is generally acknowledged to be one of the major poets of the Tang Dynasty (618-907), the most brilliant period in the long history of Chinese poetry; he was probably the most respected poet of his own time. In one of the many classificatory schemes of which traditional Chinese critics were particularly fond, he was labeled the "Poet Buddha," ranked with the two poets of the era who were to exceed him in fame, Li Bo, the "Poet Immortal," and Du Fu, the "Poet Sage." This appellation reflects Wang's association with Buddhism, which flourished in eighth century China, but it is important to note that very few of his poems are overtly doctrinal or identifiable solely with any one of the many traditions or lineages of Buddhism active during the Tang.

Like those of most men of letters of the time, Wang's life and works reflect a typically syncretic mentality, integrating yet exploring the conflicts among the goals and ideals of Confucian scholarship and commitment to public service, Daoist retreat and equanimity, and Buddhist devotion. Such issues, however, are not dealt with directly or at length in his works. His poetry relies on suggestion rather than direct statement, presenting apparently simple and precise visual imagery drawn from nature which proves elusive and evocative at the same time. He eschews definitive closure for open-endedness and irresolution, leaving the reader to attempt to resolve the unanswered questions of a poem. His best poems rarely include any direct expression of emotion and frequently suppress the poet's own subjective presence, yet this seeming impersonality has become the hallmark of a very personal style.

Because Wang's poems embody what Stephen Owen has called the artifice of simplicity, they were frequently imitated, both by the coterie of court contemporaries at whose center he stood and by later poets, followers of the "Wang Wei school." Although many of the imitators were able to replicate the witty understatement, the stark imagery, and the enigmatic closure of Wang's work, none—by general critical agreement—succeeded in probing to the same extent depths of emotion and meaning beneath a deceptively artless surface.

Biography

Wang Wei (also known by his cognomen, Wang Mojie, and his courtesy name, Wang Youcheng) was the eldest child of a prominent family in Shanxi Province. He became known for his precocious poetic, musical, and artistic talents and was well received by aristocratic patrons of the arts in the two capital cities of the empire. After placing first in his provincial examinations at the age of nineteen, Wang went on to pass the most literary of the three main types of imperial civil-service examinations in 721, one of the thirty-eight successful candidates that year. (Typically, only 1-2 percent of the thousands of candidates recommended each year for this highly competitive examination would pass.) He received the *jinshi* (presented scholar) degree and began his slow but steady rise through government ranks.

Like all Chinese scholar-bureaucrats, Wang moved from post to post and to various parts of the empire, most of which appear in his poetry. From his position as a court secretary of music in the western capital of Changan, he was sent to the east in Shandong (720's), back to the capital (734), to the northwest frontier (737), south to the Yangzi River area (740), and back to the capital (742). His career was interrupted at intervals by temporary losses of favor, factional intrigues, and various infractions, the most serious of which was his collaboration—though forced—in the puppet government of the rebel general An Lushan, whose armies overran the capitals and forced Emperor Xuanzong into exile from 755 to 757. Only the intercession of Wang's younger brother, Wang Jin, who had fought valorously with the loyalist forces, secured a pardon for the poet in 758. The next year, he attained the high-ranking sinecure of *shangshu youcheng* (undersecretary of state) and is thus frequently referred to as Wang Youcheng. In this respect, his career differed markedly from that of his two most famous poet contemporaries, Li Bo and Du Fu, neither of whom passed the imperial examinations or enjoyed Wang's considerable family connections. Unlike them, Wang never suffered severe financial hardship (despite the posing of some of his poems), maintaining a relatively secure position in the social and cultural center of what was later to be perceived as the golden age of the Tang Dynasty itself, the reign of Emperor Xuanzong (713-755).

The date of Wang's marriage has not been recorded, nor the number and names of any children he may have had. His wife died around 730, however, and Wang remained celibate thereafter—somewhat unusual for the times and an index of his devotion to Buddhist principles. It was in fact around the time of his wife's death that he began a serious study of Buddhism. In addition to the several essays and inscriptions connected with issues and figures in Tang Buddhism that are included in Wang's collected works, the most illuminating evidence of his religious commitment is his choice of cognomen, Mojie. Combined with his given name, Wei, these syllables form the Chinese transliteration (Weimojie) of one of the Buddha's best-known contemporaries, Vimalakīrti, said to have preached a sutra that became especially popular in China, not only for its doctrines but also because he himself remained a layman throughout his life. Vimalakīrti also espoused such central Confucian social ideals as filial piety and loyalty to the ruler and demonstrated to the Chinese that the good Buddhist did not necessarily have to leave his family and retreat to a monastery.

This example was an important one for Wang, for his religious beliefs never led him to abjure totally his political and social relationships. Popular legend has long held Wang to have been but a reluctant bureaucrat, and his poetry speaks frequently of a desire for reclusion. Wang did spend much of his time on retreat in various locations, particularly at his country estate at Lantian on the Wang River, which he acquired around 750 and where he eventually built a monastery. All the same, he remained officially in office until his death.

Analysis

The poems of Wang Wei were first collected by his brother, Wang Jin, at imperial request and presented to the throne in 763. The number of poems that can be attributed definitively to him is small—371, compared with the thousand or more each of Li Bo and Du Fu. The official dynastic history records his brother as telling the emperor that there were once ten times that many, the rest having been lost during the turmoil of the An Lushan Rebellion.

Whatever the case, the poems for which Wang is best remembered have fostered an image of him as a private, contemplative, self-effacing observer of the natural scene. In fact, however, despite references in several poems to his solitude behind his "closed gate" at home, many of his poems were inspired by social occasions—visits from or to friends, journeys of fellow bureaucrats to distant posts, his own departures to new offices—and by official occasions as well. Wang was a highly successful court poet, the master of a graceful, formally regulated style whose patterns had been perfected during the seventh century.

The ability to write poetry on any occasion was expected of all government officials and was in fact tested on the civil-service examination. Several of Wang's poems bear witness by their titles to having been written "to imperial command" on some formal court occasion—an outing to the country, an important birthday, the construction of a new building, the presentation of some gift—and often "harmonize respectfully" with the rhymes of a model poem composed by the emperor himself. Most of these poems were written in a heptasyllabic eight-line form with rigidly regulated rules of tone, parallelism, and rhyme. Poets in attendance would vie with one another to complete their poems first, and there was often some official evaluation of literary quality. Other poems in Wang's corpus arose out of less formally decorous contexts but reveal nevertheless the demands on the Tang poet to be able to respond to the stimulus of an occasion in an apparently spontaneous and sincere, appropriate, economical, and witty manner.

"Lady Xi"

A good example of Wang's mastery of the literary and contextual demands of the poem written on command is his early work "Xi furen" ("Lady Xi"). He is said to have composed this poem at the age of twenty (nineteen by Western reckoning), when he was preparing for the imperial examination and in residence at the court of the emperor's half brother, Li Xian, prince of Ning. It is one of several poems in Wang's collection for which was noted his supposed age at composition—unverifiable, but attesting the recognition of his early prowess. An anecdote recorded in a collection of stories attached to poems compiled in the ninth century provides the necessary explanation of the background of the poem. The prince, it seems, had been attracted by the wife of a pastry vendor and had purchased her as his concubine. After a year had passed, he asked her if she still thought of her husband, but she did not reply. The prince then summoned the vendor, and when his wife saw him, her eyes filled with tears. Ten or so people were present at the time, including Wang, and their patron commanded them to write a poem on the subject. Wang's quatrain was the first completed, and everyone else agreed that none better could be written. The prince then returned the pastry vendor's wife to her husband.

In the poem itself, there are, surprisingly, no overt references to the couple in question. The first two lines express a simple and general denial—that loves of the past can be forgotten because of present affections. The last two lines conclude with an allusion, but not to the pastry vendor and his wife; they refer to a text, a story in the Zuo commentary on the "Spring and Autumn Annals" (722-481 B.C.E.) of the *Chunqiu* (sixth to fifth century B.C.E.), one of the Confucian classics. There it is recorded that the king of Chu defeated the ruler of Xi and took the latter's wife as his own. Though she bore him children, Lady Xi never spoke to her new spouse, and when finally asked why, she is said to have answered: "I am but one woman, yet it has been my fate to serve two husbands. Although I have been unable to die, how should I dare to speak?"

This poem illustrates concisely Wang's typical "artifice of simplicity," his ability to charge the briefest of poems—twenty syllables in all—with a considerable burden. Typically, denials open and close the poem, revealing Wang's penchant for the open-ended quality of negation as opposed to assertion. What could have been a merely sentimental episode becomes dignified here through the link made to the moral dilemma of a historical ruler's wife and by the poet's choice not to mention the contemporary protagonists at all. Typically effective, also, is the poet's refusal to make any direct comment. Understatement and allusion work hand in hand here to make a point that is no less clear for not being stated explicitly.

THE WANG RIVER COLLECTION

These same methods of indirection and evocation, of using objects and events to suggest something lying beneath the surface, distinguish Wang's most famous poems, his limpid and apparently selfless depictions of natural scenes. These works are not, as a rule, devoid of people, and much of their impersonal quality derives simply from the general tendency of the classical Chinese language to avoid the use of subjective pronouns and to remain uninflected for person, tense, number, gender, and case. Wang does, however, exploit the inherent potential of the language to create indeterminate or multiple meanings more than do most other traditional poets. This is true, for example, of several poems in his well-known sequence, the Wang River collection. As Wang's preface explains, this group of twenty pentasyllabic quatrains, each of which names a site on Wang's country estate, was written in the company of one of his closest friends, a minor official named Pei Di (born 716). Pei wrote twenty poems to match those of his host, and these are also included in standard collections of Wang's poetry.

As Owen has noted in his history of poetry in the High Tang, Wang's quatrains as a whole probably represent his most significant contribution to generic development, particularly because of his substitution of enigmatic understatement for the epigrammatic closure more common at the time. The Wang River collection is informed by some of the key modes of consciousness of the poet's entire oeuvre: an emphasis on perceptual and cognitive limitations, a transcendence of temporal and spatial distinctions, and a sense of the harmony of the individual and nature. This is especially true of the fifth and probably most famous poem in the sequence, "Lu zhai" ("Deer Park").

"DEER PARK"

This poem exemplifies typical quatrain form, narrowing its focus from the massiveness of a mountain to a ray of the setting sun entering a mossy grove. Each line presents a perception that is qualified or amplified by the next. What is given in the first line as an "empty mountain," where no people are seen, reverberates with echoes of human voices in the second line. Whether these echoes signify that other people are actually present on the mountain at some distance or are intended metaphorically, to suggest the poet's memories of friends in an altogether different location, however, remains unspecified. The third line places the plot in a specific place and time—toward sunset, when "returning" (*fan*) light sends a "reflected" (also *fan*) glow through an opening into a glade. The fourth line suggests that the poet has been in the grove that same morning, or perhaps all day, and thus knows that the light is shining on the blue-green moss "again."

More than a brief nature poem, "Deer Park" links keenly observed and deceptively simple perceptions with far-ranging Buddhist implications. Scholar Marsha L. Wagner has made some important observations about the title: that "Deer Park" was the name of the site near Benares where the Buddha preached his first sermon after becoming enlightened, that it was an alternate name for the monastery Wang built on his Wang River estate, and that the deer not caught in a trap was a conventional Buddhist symbol for the recluse. Within the poem itself, the crucial word is *kong* (empty), on which hinges more than the question about the unpopulated state of the mountain. *Kong* is also the translation of the Sanskrit word *śūnyatā*, which was a key term in the Buddhist traditions with which Wang was familiar, denoting the illusory or "empty" nature of all reality and the ultimate reality, therefore, of "emptiness." *Kong* is one of the most frequently recurring words in Wang's poetic vocabulary—translated sometimes as "empty," at other times meaning "merely" or "in vain," in each case with the same powerful resonance. Moreover, the vision of the light entering the grove, the counterpart of beams of moonlight in other poems, provides a concrete image of the experience of enlightenment itself. The poem as a whole, then, encapsulates key Buddhist notions about the nature of reality and human perception of it.

"Deer Park" provides a good example of how Wang suggests religious and philosophical doctrines and attitudes in an indirect manner. Even in poems that treat Buddhist subjects more directly, doctrinal elements are generally merely implicit. Many of his accounts of journeys to monasteries, for example, are by convention metaphorical from the outset: Since temples were frequently located high in the mountains, visiting them required an effort that represented the physical counterpart to the progress toward enlightenment. Several of Wang's poems on this topic emphasize the spiritual implications of the physical ascent, among which "Guo Xiangji si" ("Visiting the Temple of Gathered Fragrance") is particularly well known.

"Visiting the Temple of Gathered Fragrance"

Wang opens "Visiting the Temple of Gathered Fragrance" with a profession of ignorance. He does not "know" the temple, and this at once suggests several possibilities: He does not know of its existence, of its location, or of its significance—or perhaps he has discarded a rational, cognitive kind of "knowing" for an intuitive, nondifferentiating awareness more conducive to true spiritual knowledge. In any event, this special kind of ignorance sets the tone for the description of the journey up the mountain, each stage of which contains images of extreme ambiguity and vagueness. The second line speaks of "entering cloudy peaks," but the verb can refer either to the action of the speaker or to the location of the monastery, thus deliberately blurring the distinction between the traveler and his destination, or subject and object. The obscurity of these cloudy peaks is frequently associated in Wang's poetry with temples and transcendent realms and suggests the inadequacy of merely sensuous perception on such a journey of the spirit.

The poem continues to reinforce this sense of linguistic and perceptual ambiguity. The phrase "paths without people" in the third line can also be read as "no paths for people," thus further suggesting the speaker's venture into unknown territory, untraveled by others; this experience must be undertaken in absolute solitude. This sense of mystery is evoked again in the question of the following line: "Where is the bell?" As in the opening couplet, Wang reveals here a distrust of visual perception and purely intellectual cognition. Presumably the sound of a bell from somewhere deep in the mountains confirms the existence of the monastery, at least, if not its precise location. Has he heard the bell himself, though? He does not say. Thus, he must continue his ascent without the comforting knowledge of where he is or where he is going.

In the third couplet, the images appear to be more concrete than those in the preceding lines, but they are in fact equally ambiguous. In each line of the third couplet, the verb can be read either actively or passively, suggesting that the processes occurring cannot be subjected to rational analysis; they can be apprehended only intuitively as one total experience in which subject and object are indistinguishable. Furthermore, Wang's diction also undermines the sensuous precision of the couplet. Rather than focusing on the concreteness of the nouns—"stream" and "sun"—he speaks of the former's "sound" and the latter's "color," so that in each case he is describing an abstraction rather than a concrete object.

The final couplet of the poem in no way diminishes the mysterious quality of the journey. Wang has reached a pond—perhaps at the monastery, though he does not say—whose bends and curves continue to recall the winding paths of other spiritual journeys. What does it mean for the pond to be "empty"? Is it dried up, deserted, illusory, or an image of ultimate reality? In the last line, Wang simply presents a process without specifying the subject or the precise nature of the object. The "peaceful meditation" may be that of a monk from the temple or the poet himself, or it may not refer to an individual at all but rather to an intangible atmosphere of the place. The "poison dragons" tamed by the meditation are traditionally interpreted as passions or illusions that may stand in the way of enlightenment, and many possible sources in Buddhist texts have been suggested. They are controlled and not eliminated, present by virtue of their very mention, thus suggesting Wang's awareness, in this poem, at least, of the effort required to attain the tranquil and selfless union with the world that, in so many of his poems, he seems to possess.

This harmony is one that transcends boundaries between subject and object and those of language as well; hence Wang's reliance on understatement and what he does not say. One well-known poem, however, flirts briefly with the possibility that perhaps words are not inadequate after all. "Chou Chang shaofu" ("In Response to Vice-Magistrate Chang") opens quite discursively with an observation that occurs frequently in Wang's poetry on the contrast between past and present priorities. The profession that only age has enabled him wisely to reject worldly involvement is familiar also to readers of the poetry of Tao Qian, the poet of the past with whom Wang most strongly identified and in whose eighth century revival he played an instrumental role. Like Tao Qian, who left office early on matters of principle, Wang claims also to be rejecting the "long-range plans" associated with governmental policy. He now "only" (or "emptily"—*kong* again) knows "to return to the old forest," and the word "return" recalls the importance of the same word for Tao Qian, who employed it frequently for the implications it possessed in early Daoist literature of getting back to one's original nature, uncorrupted by civilization and its trappings.

The third couplet of "Visiting the Temple of Gathered Fragrance" provides images of Wang's newfound freedom. Pine winds blow loose the belt of his robe, and the moon provides congenial companionship as he plays the zither, the instrument traditionally associated with scholar-recluses. The penultimate line turns to a question posed by the addressee of the poem and suggests that Wang will finally put into words the wisdom he has gained, the "reasons for success and failure" or the "principles of universal change." His response in the last line, however, provides no easy answer, only an enigmatic image of a fisherman's song that can be read in a number of ways.

In the first place, the last line in the third couplet may be regarded as a nonanswer in the tradition of the Chan or Zen koan, by means of which a Buddhist master attempts to bring a student to enlightenment by answering a rational question with a non sequitur, thus jolting the latter out of conventional, logical, categorical modes of thinking, and liberating his mind to facilitate a sudden, intuitive realization of truth. Wang's answer, then, would deliberately bear no relationship to Chang's query, seeking instead to reject such cognitive concerns or indeed denying the validity of his question.

There is a second possibility. Because the fisherman, along with the woodcutter, was a favorite Daoist figure representing the rustic, unselfconscious life in harmony with nature, this final line may be read as a simple suggestion to change to follow the example of such recluses and escape from official life to the freedom and serenity of country living. This is a realm, moreover, where the vicissitudes of the world and such distinctions as failure and success will have no meaning.

A third interpretation of the line hinges on a possible reference to a specific fisherman's song, the "Yufu" ("Fisherman"), included in the southern anthology, the *Chu ci* (songs of Chu), compiled during the Han Dynasty. In the earlier poem, a wise fisherman converses with the fourth century B.C.E. poet Qu Yuan, who had been a loyal minister to the king of Chu and committed to the Confucian ideal of service but who was slandered by others at court and banished. He remained self-righteous about his inflexible moral purity and later chose suicide rather than compromise his principles. In this song, when Qu Yuan meets the fisherman, he explains the reasons behind his exile; the fisherman suggests that it might have been more circumspect to adapt to the circumstances, but Qu Yuan insists that he would rather drown than do so. The fisherman departs with a gentle mocking reply, singing that if the waters are clean, he will wash his hat-strings in them, and if they are dirty, he will wash his feet. Unlike the self-righteous Qu Yuan, the fisherman can adjust to the conditions he finds and paradoxically remains freer of their influence. Ultimately, perhaps, he realizes that, when seen from a higher perspective, the waters are all the same.

If Wang's use of this allusion is to be granted, then he is certainly affirming the kind of unifying vision and transcendence of distinctions that underlies his poetry as a whole. Perhaps the more important point, however, is Wang's failure to allow a definitive resolution to the question at all. The conclusion to this poem, as to so many of his poems, is purposely inconclusive and open-ended, leaving the reader to puzzle out what answers there may be.

BIBLIOGRAPHY

Chou, Shan. "Beginning with Images in the Nature Poetry of Wang Wei." *Harvard Journal of Asiatic Studies* 42 (June, 1982): 117-137. Chou proposes that the solution to the problem of meaning in Wang's nature poetry is to be found in understanding the Buddhist influence.

Owen, Stephen. "Wang Wei: The Artifice of Simplicity." In *The Great Age of Chinese Poetry: The High T'ang*. New Haven, Conn.: Yale University Press, 1981. Owen supplies an excellent short overview of Wang as poetic technician and relates the poet's work to his life and historical context.

Wagner, Marsha L. *Wang Wei*. Boston: Twayne, 1982. Part of the Twayne World Authors series, this scholarly, well-written account of Wang's life provides a balanced, perceptive appraisal of his contributions as poet, painter, and government official. Includes fine translations.

Wang Wei. *Laughing Lost in the Mountains: Poems of Wang Wei*. Translated by Tony Barnstone, Willis Barnstone, and Xu Haixin. Hanover, N.H.: University Press of New England, 1991. Excellent translation of 171 poems. The critical introduction, "The Ecstasy of Stillness," by the Barnstones provides insights into these poems.

_____. *The Poetry of Wang Wei: New Translations and Commentary*. Translated by Pauline Yu. Bloomington: Indiana University Press, 1980. This study provides excellent, scholarly translations and notes as well as knowing critical appraisals of Wang's poems.

_____. *The Selected Poems of Wang Wei*. Translated by David Hinton. New York: New Directions, 2006. A translation of Wang's poems, with an introduction providing critical analysis and a biography.

Wang Wei, Li Bo, and Du Fu. *Three Chinese Poets: Translations of Poems by Wang Wei, Li Bai, and Du Fu*. Translated by Vikram Seth. Boston: Faber and Faber, 1992. A collection of poems by Wang, Du Fu, and Li Bo. Commentary by translator Seth provides useful information.

Weinberger, Eliot. *Nineteen Ways of Looking at Wang Wei*. Mount Kisco, N.Y.: Moyer Bell, 1987. This short book offers insights into the art of translating Chinese poems. Includes commentary by both Weinberger and writer Octavio Paz.

Yang, Jingqing. *The Chan Interpretations of Wang Wei's Poetry: A Critical Review*. Hong Kong: Chinese University Press, 2007. Looks at Chan (Zen) Buddhism and how it relates to Wang's poetry.

Young, David, trans. *Five T'ang Poets: Wang Wei, Li Po, Tu Fu, Li Ho, Li Shang-yin*. Oberlin, Ohio: Oberlin College Press, 1990. Provides an opportunity for appreciating Wang along with contemporary poets during the Tang Dynasty.

Pauline Yu

PHILLIS WHEATLEY

Born: West Coast of Africa (possibly the Senegal-Gambia region); 1753(?)
Died: Boston, Massachusetts; December 5, 1784

PRINCIPAL POETRY
Poems on Various Subjects, Religious and Moral, 1773
The Poems of Phillis Wheatley, 1966, 1989 (Julian D. Mason, Jr., editor)

OTHER LITERARY FORMS

Phillis Wheatley's cultivation of the letter as a literary form is attested by her inclusion of the titles of several letters in each of her proposals for future volumes subsequent to the publication of her *Poems on Various Subjects, Religious and Moral* (1773). Regrettably, none of these proposals provoked enough response to secure publication of any new volumes. Scholars continue to discover both poems and letters that Wheatley names in these proposals. The letters mentioned in them are addressed to such noted persons as William Legge, second earl of Dartmouth; Selina Hastings, countess of Huntingdon; Benjamin Rush; and George Washington. They display a graceful style and articulate some of Wheatley's strongest protestations in support of the cause of American independence and in condemnation of Christian hypocrisy regarding slavery.

ACHIEVEMENTS

From the time of Phillis Wheatley's first published piece to the present day, controversy has surrounded the life and work of America's first black poet and only its second published woman poet, after Anne Bradstreet. Few poets of any age have been so scornfully maligned, so passionately defended, so fervently celebrated, and so patronizingly tolerated. However, during the years of her young adulthood, Wheatley was the toast of England and the colonies. For years before she attempted to find a Boston publisher for her poems, she had published numerous elegies commemorating the deaths of many of the city's most prominent citizens. In 1770, she wrote her most famous and most often-reprinted elegy, on the death of "the voice of the Great Awakening," George Whitefield, chaplain to the countess of Huntingdon, who was one of the leading benefactors of the Methodist evangelical movement in England and the colonies.

Not finding Boston to be in sympathy with her 1772 proposal for a volume, Wheatley found substantial support the following year in the countess of Huntingdon, whose interest had been stirred by the young poet's noble tribute to her chaplain. Subsequently, Wheatley was sent to London, ostensibly for her health; this trip curiously accords, however, with the very weeks that her book was being printed. It is likely that she proofread the galleys herself. At any rate, she was much sought after among the intellec-

Phillis Wheatley
(Library of Congress)

tual, literary set of London, and Sir Brook Watson, who was to become Lord Mayor of London within a year, presented her with a copy of John Milton's *Paradise Lost* (1667, 1674) in folio. The earl of Dartmouth, who was at the time secretary of state for the colonies and president of the board of Trade and Foreign Plantations, gave her a copy of Tobias Smollett's *Don Quixote* (1755), a translation of Miguel de Cervantes's *El ingenioso hidalgo don Quixote de la Mancha* (1605, 1615; *The History of the Valorous and Wittie Knight-Errant, Don Quixote of the Mancha*, 1612-1620; better known as *Don Quixote de la Mancha*). Benjamin Franklin, to whom she would later inscribe her second book of poetry (never published), has even recorded that, while in London briefly, he called on Wheatley to see whether "there were any service I could do her."

In the opening pages of her 1773 volume appears a letter of authentication of Wheatley's authorship, which is signed by still another of the signatories of the Declaration of Independence, John Hancock. Added to the list of attesters are other outstanding Bostonians, including Thomas Hutchinson, then governor of Massachusetts, and James Bowdoin, one of the founders of Bowdoin College. Later, during the early months of the American Revolution, Wheatley wrote a poem in praise of General Washington, "To His Excellency General Washington." As a result, she received an invitation to visit the general at his headquarters, and her poem was published by Tom Paine in *The Pennsylvania Magazine*. John Paul Jones, who also appreciated Wheatley's celebration of freedom, even asked one of his officers to secure him a copy of her *Poems on Various Subjects, Religious and Moral*.

Nevertheless, she did not continue to enjoy such fame. A country ravaged by war has little time, finally, for poetry, and Wheatley regrettably, perhaps tragically, faced the rejection of two more proposals for a volume of new poems. Thwarted by the vicissitudes of war and poverty, Wheatley died from complications resulting from childbirth. Even so, her poetry has survived and is now considered to be among the best of its period produced in America or in England. It is just beginning to be recognized that, contrary to the opinion of those who would dispose of Wheatley as a mere imitator, she produced sophisticated, original poems whose creative theories of the imagination and the sublime anticipate the Romantic movement.

Biography

The known details of Phillis Wheatley's life are few. According to her master, John Wheatley of Boston, she "was brought from Africa to America in the Year 1761, between Seven and Eight Years of Age [sic]." Her parents were apparently sun-worshipers, for she is supposed to have recalled to her white captors that she remembered seeing her mother pouring out water to the sun every morning. If such be the case, it would help to explain why the sun is predominant as an image in her poetry.

Her life with the Wheatleys, John and Susanna and their two children, the twins Mary and Nathaniel, was probably not too demanding for one whose disposition toward asthma (brought on or no doubt exacerbated by the horrible "middle passage") greatly weakened her. The Wheatleys' son attended Harvard, so it is likely that Nathaniel served as the eager young girl's Latin tutor. At any rate, it is certain that Wheatley knew Latin well; her translation of the Niobe episode from Ovid's *Metamorphoses* (c. 8 C.E.; English translation, 1567), book 6, displays a learned knowledge and appreciation of the Latin original. Wheatley's classical learning is evident throughout her poetry, which is thick with allusions to ancient historical and mythological figures.

The turning point of Wheatley's career, not only as an author but also as a human being, came when her *Poems on Various Subjects, Religious and Moral* was published in London in 1773. After she returned from England, having been recalled because of Susanna Wheatley's worsening illness, she was manumitted sometime during September, 1773. It is probable that Wheatley was freed because of the severe censure that some English reviewers of her *Poems on Various Subjects, Religious and Moral* had directed at the owners of a learned author who "still remained a slave." At this very point, however, the poet's fortunes began a slow decline. In 1778, at the height of the war and after the deaths of both John and Susanna Wheatley, she married John Peters, a black man of some learning who failed to rescue the poet from poverty.

Wheatley died alone and unattended in a hovel somewhere in the back streets of the Boston slums in 1784, truly an ignominious end for one who had enjoyed such favor. She was preceded in death by two of her children, as well as by the third, to whom she had just given birth. She was at most only thirty-one years old. Given Wheatley's vision of the world "Oppress'd with woes, a painful endless train," it should not be surprising that her most frequently adopted poetic form is the elegy, in which she always celebrates death as the achievement of ultimate freedom—suggesting the thanatos-eros (desire for death) motif of Romanticism.

ANALYSIS

Beginning in the 1970's, Phillis Wheatley began to receive the attention she deserves. George McMichael and others, editors of the influential two-volume *Anthology of American Literature* (1974, 1980), observe that she and Philip Freneau were "the most important poets" of America's Revolutionary War era. To be sure, one of the major subjects of her poetry is the American struggle for independence. Temporal freedom is not her only subject, however; she is also much concerned with the quest for spiritual freedom. Consequently, the elegy, in which she celebrates the Christian rewards of eternal life and absolute freedom after death, is her favorite poetic form. In addition, she delights in describing God's creation of nature's splendors and sometimes appears to enjoy the beauties of nature for their own sake and not simply as acts of God's providence. It is in "On Imagination," however, that Wheatley waxes most eloquent; in this poem, perhaps her most important single work, she articulates a theory of the imagination that strikingly anticipates that of Samuel Taylor Coleridge. Indeed, Wheatley's affinities with Romanticism, which run throughout her poetry, may come to be seen as her surest claim to a place in literary history.

Such an approach to this early American poet contradicts the widespread critical view that Wheatley was a highly derivative poet, inextricably mired in the neoclassical tradition. Her preference for the heroic couplet, one of the hallmarks of neoclassicism, has deceived many into immediately classifying her as neoclassical. One must recall, however, that Lord Byron also had a passion for the couplet. Surely, then, one must not be satisfied with a cursory glance at Wheatley's adoption of the heroic couplet; one must go on to explore the content of her poetry.

POLITICAL POEMS

Her political poems document major incidents of the American struggle for independence. In 1768, she wrote "To the King's Most Excellent Majesty on His Repealing the American Stamp Act." When it appeared, much revised, in *Poems on Various Subjects, Religious and Moral*, the poet diplomatically deleted the last two lines of the original, which read, "When wars came on [against George] the proudest rebel fled/ God thunder'd fury on their guilty head." By that time, the threat of the King's retaliation did not seem so forbidding nor the injustice of rebellion against him so grave.

"America," a poem probably written about the same time but published more than two hundred years later, admonishes Britain to treat "americus," the British child, with more deference. According to the poem, the child, now a growing seat of "Liberty," is no mere adorer of an overwhelming "Majesty," but has acquired strength of his own: "Fearing his strength which she [Britain] undoubted knew/ She laid some taxes on her darling son." Recognizing her mistake, "great Britannia" promised to lift the burden, but the promise proved only "seeming Sympathy and Love." Now the Child "weeps afresh to feel this Iron chain." The urge to draw an analogy here between the poem's "Iron chain" and Wheatley's own predicament is irresistible; while America longs for its own independence, Wheatley no doubt yearns for hers.

The year 1770 marked the beginning of armed resistance against Britain. Wheatley chronicles such resistance in two poems, the second of which is now lost. The first, "On the Death of Mr. Snider Murder'd by Richardson," appeared initially along with "America." The poem tells how Ebenezer Richardson, an informer on American traders involved in circumventing British taxation, found his home surrounded on the evening of February 22, 1770, by an angry mob of colonial sympathizers. Much alarmed, Richardson emerged from his house armed with a musket and fired indiscriminately into the mob, killing the eleven- or twelve-year-old son of Snider, a poor German colonist. Wheatley calls young Christopher Snider, of whose death Richardson was later found guilty in a trial by jury, "the first martyr for the common good," rather than those men killed less than two weeks later in the Boston Massacre. The poem's fine closing couplet suggests that even those not in sympathy with the quest for freedom can grasp the nobility of that quest and are made indignant by its sacrifice: "With Secret rage fair freedom's foes beneath/ See in thy corse ev'n Majesty in Death."

Wheatley does not, however, ignore the Boston Massacre. In a proposal for a volume which was to have been published in Boston in 1772, she lists, among twenty-seven titles of poems (the 1773 volume had thirty-nine), "On the Affray in King Street, on the Evening of the 5th of March." This title, naming the time and place of the massacre, suggests that the poet probably celebrated the martyrdom of Crispus Attucks, the first black to lose his life in the American struggle, along with the deaths of two whites. Regrettably, the poem has not yet been recovered. Even so, the title alone confirms Wheatley's continued recording of America's struggle for freedom. This concern shifted in tone from obedient praise for the British regime to supplicatory admonition and then to guarded defiance. Since she finally found a publisher not in Boston but in London, she prudently omitted "America" and the poems about Snider and the Boston Massacre from her 1773 volume.

She chose to include, however, a poem dedicated to the earl of Dartmouth, who was appointed secretary of state for the colonies in August, 1772. In this poem, "To the Right Honourable William, Earl of Dartmouth, His Majesty's Principal Secretary of State for

North America," she gives the earl extravagant praise as one who will lay to rest "hatred faction." She knew of the earl's reputation as a humanitarian through the London contacts of her mistress, Susanna. When the earl proved to support oppressive British policies, the poet's expectations were not realized; within four years of the poem's date, America had declared its independence. Since her optimism was undaunted by foreknowledge, Wheatley wrote a poem that was even more laudatory than "To The King's Most Excellent Majesty on His Repealing the American Stamp Act." Perhaps she was not totally convinced, however; the poem contains some unusually bold passages for a colonist who is also both a woman and a slave.

For example, she remarks that, with Dartmouth's secretaryship, America need no longer "dread the iron chain,/ Which wanton *Tyranny* with lawless hand/ Had made, and with it meant t'enslave the land." Once again Wheatley uses the slave metaphor of the iron chain. Quite clearly she also accuses the Crown of "wanton *Tyranny*," which it had wielded illegally and with the basest of motives—to reduce the colonies to the inhuman condition of slave states. Here rebellious defiance, no longer guarded, is unmistakable; the tone matches that of the Declaration of Independence. It is a mystery how these lines could have gone unnoticed in the London reviews, all of them positive, of her 1773 volume. Perhaps the reviewers were too bedazzled by the "improbability" that a black woman could produce such a volume to take the content of her poetry seriously.

In this poem, Wheatley also presents a rare autobiographical portrait describing the manner in which she was taken from her native Africa. The manuscript version of this passage is more spontaneous and direct than the more formally correct one printed in the 1773 volume and thus is closer to the poet's true feelings. It was "Seeming cruel fate" that snatched her "from Afric's fancy'd happy seat." Fate here is only apparently cruel, since her capture has enabled her to become a Christian; the young poet's piety resounds throughout her poetry and letters. Her days in her native land were, nevertheless, happy ones, and her abduction at the hands of ruthless slavers doubtless left behind inconsolable parents. Such a bitter memory of the circumstances of her abduction fully qualifies her to "deplore the day/ When Britons weep beneath Tyrannic sway"; the later version reads: "And can I then but pray/ Others may never feel tyrannic sway?" Besides toning down the diction, this passage alters her statement to a question and replaces "Britons" with the neutral "others." The question might suggest uncertainty, but it more probably reflects the author's polite deportment toward a London audience. Since, in the earlier version, she believed Dartmouth to be sympathetic with her cause, she had no reason to exercise deference toward him; she thought she could be frank. The shift from "Britons" to "others" provokes a more compelling explanation. In the fall of 1772, Wheatley could still think of herself as a British subject. Later, however, after rejoicing that the earl's administration had given way to restive disillusionment, perhaps the poet was less certain about her citizenship.

Three years after the publication of her 1773 volume, Wheatley unabashedly celebrated the opposition to the "tyrannic sway" of Britain in "To His Excellency General Washington," newly appointed commander in chief of the Continental Army; the war of ideas had become one of arms. In this piece, which is more a paean to freedom than a eulogy to Washington, she describes freedom as "divinely fair,/ Olive and laurel bind her golden hair"; yet "She flashes dreadful in refulgent arms." The poet accents this image of martial glory with an epic simile, comparing the American forces to the power of the fierce king of the winds:

> As when Eolus heaven's fair face deforms,
> Enwrapp'd in tempest and a night of storms;
> Astonish'd ocean feels the wild uproar,
> The refluent surges beat the sounding shore.

For the young poet, America is now "The land of freedom's heaven-defended race!" While the eyes of the world's nations are fixed "on the scales,/ For in their hopes Columbia's arm prevails," the poet records Britain's regret over her loss: "Ah! cruel blindness to Columbia's state!/ Lament thy thirst of boundless power too late." The temper of this couplet is in keeping with Wheatley's earlier attitudes toward oppression. The piece closes as the poet urges Washington to pursue his objective with the knowledge that virtue is on his side. If he allows the fair goddess Freedom to be his guide, Washington will surely emerge not only as the leader of a victorious army but also as the head of the newly established state.

In Wheatley's last political poem, "freedom's heaven-defended race" has won its battle. Written in 1784 within a year after the Treaty of Paris, "Liberty and Peace" is a demonstrative celebration of American independence. British tyranny, the agent of American oppression, has now been taught to fear "americus" her child, "And newborn *Rome* shall give *Britannia* Law." Wheatley concludes this piece with two pleasing couplets in praise of America, whose future is assured by heaven's approval:

> Auspicious Heaven shall fill with favoring Gales,
> Where e'er *Columbia* spreads her swelling Sails:
> To every Realm shall *Peace* her Charms display,
> And Heavenly *Freedom* spread her golden Ray.

Personified as Peace and Freedom, Columbia (America) will act as a world emissary, an emanating force like the rays of the sun. In this last couplet, Wheatley has captured, perhaps for the first time in poetry, America's ideal mission to the rest of the world.

The fact that Wheatley so energetically proclaims America's success in the political arena certainly attests her sympathies—not with the neoclassic obsession never to challenge the established order nor to breach the rules of political and social decorum—but with the Romantic notion that a people who find themselves unable to accept a present, unsatisfactory government have the right to change that government, even if such a change can be accomplished only through armed revolt. The American Revolution against Britain was the first successful such revolt and was one of the sparks of the French Revolution. Wheatley's steadfast literary participation in the American Revolution clearly aligns her with such politically active English Romantic poets as Percy Bysshe Shelley and Lord Byron.

THE ELEGIES

In her elegies, on the other hand, Wheatley displays her devotion to spiritual freedom. As do her political poems, her elegies exalt specific occasions, the deaths of people usually known to her within the social and religious community of the poet's Old South Congregational Church of Boston. As do her poems on political events, however, her elegies exceed the boundaries of occasional verse. The early, but most famous of her elegies, "On the Death of the Rev. Mr. George Whitefield, 1770," both illustrates the general structure in which she cast all seventeen of her extant elegies and indicates her recurring ideological concerns.

Wheatley's elegies conform for the most part to the Puritan funeral elegy. They include two major divisions: First comes the portrait, in which the poet pictures the life of the subject; then follows the exhortation, encouraging the reader to seek the heavenly rewards gained by the subject in death. The portrait usually comprises three biographical steps: vocation or conversion; sanctification, or evidence of good works; and glorification, or joyous treatment of the deceased's reception into heaven. Wheatley's elegy on Whitefield surprisingly opens with the glorification of the Great Awakener, already in heaven and occupying his "immortal throne." She celebrates the minister's conversion or vocation in an alliterative line as "The greatest gift that ev'n a God can give." Of course, she writes many lines describing the good works of a man wholly devoted to the winning of souls during the seven visits he made to America during and after the period of the Great Awakening.

Whitefield died in Newburyport, Massachusetts, on September 30, 1770, having left Boston only a week or so before, where he had apparently lodged with the Wheatley family. Indeed, the young poet of sixteen or seventeen appears to recollect from personal experience when she observes that the minister "long'd to see *America* excel" and "charg'd its youth that ev'ry grace divine/ Should with full lustre in their conduct shine." She also seizes this opportunity to proclaim to the world Whitefield's assertion that even Africans would find Jesus of Nazareth an "*Impartial Saviour*." The poem closes with a ten-line exhortation to the living to aspire toward Whitefield's example: "Let ev'ry heart to this bright vision rise."

As one can see, Wheatley's elegies are not sad affairs; quite to the contrary, they enact joyful occasions after which deceased believers may hope to unite, as she states in "On the Death of the Rev. Dr. Sewell, 1769," with "Great God, incomprehensible, unknown/ By sense." Although people's senses may limit their firsthand acquaintance with God, these same senses do enable them to learn about God, especially about God's works in nature. The poem in the extant Wheatley canon that most pointedly addresses God's works in nature is "Thoughts on the Works of Providence." This poem of 131 lines opens with a 10-line invocation to the "Celestial muse," resembling Milton's heavenly muse of *Paradise Lost*.

Identifying God as the force behind planetary movement, she writes, "Ador'd [is] the God that whirls surrounding spheres" which rotate ceaselessly about "the monarch of the earth and skies." From this sublime image she moves to yet another: "'Let there be light,' he said: from his profound/ Old chaos heard and trembled at the sound." It should not go unremarked that Wheatley could, indeed, find much in nature to foster her belief, but little in the mundane world of ordinary humans to sustain her spiritually. The frequency of nature imagery but the relative lack of scenes drawn from human society (with the exception of her political poems, and even these are occasions for abstract departures into the investigation of political ideologies) probably reflects the poet's insecurity and uncertainty about a world which first made her a slave and then gave her, at best, only second-class citizenship.

In "An Hymn to the Morning," one of her most lyrical poems, Wheatley interprets the morn (recall her mother's morning ritual of pouring out water to the rising sun) as the source of poetic afflatus or inspiration. The speaker of the poem, Wheatley herself, first perceives the light of the rising sun as a reflection in the eye of one of the "feather'd race." After she hears the song of the bird that welcomes the day, she turns to find the source of melody and sees the bird "Dart the bright eye, and shake the painted plume." Here the poet captures with great precision the bird's rapid eye movement. The bird, archetypal symbol of poetic song, has received the dawn's warm rays that stimulate him to sing. When the poet turns to discover the source of melody, however, what she sees first is not Aurora, the dawning sun, but Aurora the stimulus of song reflected within the "bright eye" of the bird.

In the next stanza, the poet identifies the dawn as the ultimate source of poetic inspiration when she remarks that the sun has awakened Calliope, here the personification of inspiration, while her sisters, the other Muses, "fan the pleasing fire" of the stimulus to create. Hence both the song of the bird and the light reflected in its eye have instructed her to acknowledge the source of the bird's melody; for she aspires to sing with the same pleasing fire that animates the song of the bird. Like many of the Romantics who followed her, Wheatley perceives nature both as a means to know ultimate freedom and as an inspiration to create, to make art.

It is in her superlative poem, "On Imagination," however, that Wheatley most forcefully brings both aspirations, to know God and to create fine poetry, into clear focus. To the young black poet, the imagination was sufficiently important to demand from her pen a fifty-three-line poem. The piece opens with this four-line apostrophe:

> Thy various works, imperial queen, we see,
> How bright their forms! how deck'd with pomp by thee!
> Thy wond'rous acts in beauteous order stand,
> And all attest how potent is thine hand.

Clearly, Wheatley's imagination is a regal presence in full control of her poetic world, a world in which her "wond'rous acts" of creation stand in harmony, capturing a "beauteous order." These acts themselves testify to the queen's creative power. Following a four-line invocation to the Muse, however, the poet distinguishes the imagination from its subordinate fancy:

> Now, here, now there, the roving Fancy flies;
> Till some lov'd object strikes her wand'ring eyes,
> Whose silken fetters all the senses bind,
> And soft captivity involves the mind.

Unlike the controlled, harmonious imagination, the subordinate fancy flies about here and there, searching for some appropriate and desired object worthy of setting into motion the creative powers of her superior.

FANCY AND MEMORY

In "Thoughts on the Works of Providence," the poet describes the psychology of sleep in similar fashion. Having entered the world of dreams, the mind discovers a realm where "ideas range/ Licentious and unbounded o'er the plains/ Where Fancy's queen in giddy triumph reigns." Wheatley maintains that in sleep the imagination, once again "Fancy's queen," creates worlds that lack the "beauteous order" of the poet sitting before a writing desk; nevertheless, these dreamworlds provoke memorable images. In "On Recollection," Wheatley describes the memory as the repository on which the mind draws to create its dreams. What may be "long-forgotten," the memory "calls from night" and "plays before the fancy's sight." By analogy, Wheatley maintains, the memory provides the poet "ample treasure" from her "secret stores" to create poetry: "in her pomp of images display'd,/ To the high-raptur'd poet gives her aid." "On Recollection" asserts a strong affinity between the poet's memory, analogous to the world of dreams, and the fancy, the associative faculty subordinate to the imagination. Recollection for Wheatley functions as the poet's storehouse of images, while the fancy channels the force of the imagination through its associative powers. Both the memory and the fancy, then, serve the imagination.

Wheatley's description of fancy and memory departs markedly from what eighteenth century aestheticians, including John Locke and Joseph Addison, generally understood as the imagination. The faculty of mind that they termed "imagination" Wheatley relegates to recollection (memory) and fancy. Her description of recollection and fancy closely parallels Coleridge's in the famous thirteenth chapter of *Biographia*

Literaria (1817), where he states that fancy "is indeed no other than a mode of Memory emancipated from the order of time and space." Wheatley's identification of the fancy as roving "Now here, now there" whose movement is analogous to the dream state, where "ideas range/ Licentious and unbounded," certainly frees it from the limits of time and space. Coleridge further limits the fancy to the capacity of choice. "But equally with the ordinary memory," he insists, "the Fancy must receive all its materials ready made from the law of association." Like Coleridge's, Wheatley's fancy exercises choice by association as it finally settles on "some lov'd object."

If fancy and memory are the imagination's subordinates, then how does the imagination function in the poet's creative process? Following her description of fancy in "On Imagination," Wheatley details the role the imagination plays in her poetry. According to her, the power of the imagination enables her to soar "through air to find the bright abode,/ Th' empyreal palace of the thund'ring God." The central focus of her poetry remains contemplation of God. Foreshadowing William Wordsworth's "winds that will be howling at all hours," Wheatley exclaims that on the wings of the imagination she "can surpass the wind/ And leave the rolling universe behind." In the realm of the imagination, the poet can "with new worlds amaze th' unbounded soul."

Immediately following this arresting line, Wheatley illustrates in a ten-line stanza the power of the imagination to create new worlds. Even though winter and the "frozen deeps" prevail in the real world, the imagination can take one out of unpleasant reality and build a pleasant, mythic world of fragrant flowers and verdant groves where "Fair Flora" spreads "her fragrant reign," where Sylvanus crowns the forest with leaves, and where "Show'rs may descend, and dews their gems disclose,/ And nectar sparkle on the blooming rose." Such is the power of imagination to promote poetic creation and to release one from an unsatisfactory world. Unfortunately, like reality's painful intrusion on the delicate, unsustainable song of John Keats's immortal bird, gelid winter and its severe "northern tempests damp the rising fire," cut short the indulgence of her poetic world, and lamentably force Wheatley to end her short-lived lyric: "Cease then, my song, cease the unequal lay." Her lyric must end because no poet can indefinitely sustain a mythic world.

In her use of the imagination to create "new worlds," Wheatley's departure from eighteenth century theories of this faculty is radical and once again points toward Coleridge. Although she does not distinguish between "primary" and "secondary" imagination as he does, Wheatley nevertheless constructs a theory which approaches his "secondary" imagination. According to Coleridge, the secondary imagination, which attends the creative faculty, intensifies the primary imagination common to all people. Coleridge describes how the secondary imagination operates in this well-known passage: "It dissolves, diffuses, dissipates, in order to recreate;/ or where this process is rendered impossible, yet still at all/ events it struggles to idealize and to unify." In spite of the fact that Wheatley's attempt to dissolve, diffuse, and dissipate is assuredly more modest than Coleridge's "swift half-intermitted burst" in "Kubla Khan," she does, nevertheless, like the apocalyptic Romantics, idealize, unify, and shape a mythopoeic world. Proceeding in a systematic fashion, she first constructs a theory of mental faculty that, when assisted by the associative fancy, builds, out of an act of the mind, a new world that does indeed stand in "beauteous order." This faculty, which she identifies as the imagination, she uses as a tool to achieve freedom, however momentary.

Wheatley was, then, an innovator who used the imagination as a means to transcend an unacceptable present and even to construct "new worlds [to] amaze the unbounded soul"; this practice, along with her celebration of death, her loyalty to the American struggle for political independence, and her consistent praise of nature, places her firmly in that flow of thought that culminated in nineteenth century Romanticism. Her diction may strike a modern audience as occasionally "got up" and stiff, and her reliance on the heroic couplet may appear outdated and worn, but the content of her poetry is innovative, refreshing, and even, for her times, revolutionary. She wrote during the pre-Revolutionary and Revolutionary War eras in America, when little poetry of great merit was produced. Wheatley, laboring under the disadvantages of being not only a black slave but also a woman, nevertheless did find the time to depict that political struggle for freedom and to trace her personal battle for release. If one looks beyond the limitations of her sincere if dogmatic piety and her frequent dependence on what Wordsworth called poetic diction, one is sure to discover in her works a fine mind engaged in creating some of the best early American poetry.

Other major works

MISCELLANEOUS: *Memoir and Poems of Phillis Wheatley: A Native African and a Slave*, 1833; *The Collected Works of Phillis Wheatley*, 1988 (John Shields, editor).

Bibliography

Cook, William W., and James Tatum. *African American Writers and Classical Tradition.* Chicago: University of Chicago Press, 2010. Examines the relationship of African American writers, beginning with Wheatley, to Greek and Roman classics.

Engberg, Kathrynn Seidler. *The Right to Write: The Literary Politics of Anne Bradstreet and Phillis Wheatley.* Lanham, Md.: University Press of America, 2010. Examines the first two published women poets of the United States and the problems and challenges they faced.

Gates, Henry Louis, Jr. *The Trials of Phillis Wheatley: America's First Black Poet and Her Encounters with the Founding Fathers.* 2003. Reprint. New York: Basic Civitas Books, 2010. A biography of Wheatley that examines her life and works, including Thomas Jefferson's harsh critique of her work and her lack of popularity among African Americans.

Hayden, Lucy K. "*Poems on Various Subjects, Religious and Moral.*" In *Masterplots II: African American Literature*, edited by Tyrone Williams. Rev. ed. Pasadena, Calif.: Salem Press, 2009. Examines this work in detail, looking at themes and meanings and the critical context.

Morton, Gerald W. *Phillis Wheatley: Slave and Poet.* Baltimore: PublishAmerica, 2008. A biography that looks at Wheatley's life and writings.

Robinson, William H. *Phillis Wheatley and Her Writings.* New York: Garland, 1984. A fine introduction to Wheatley, by an eminent Wheatley scholar. Presents a brief biography, the text of all the poems and surviving letters (several in facsimile) with an analysis, nine appendixes providing background information, bibliography, and index.

Shields, John C. *Phillis Wheatley and the Romantics.* Knoxville: University of Tennessee Press, 2010. Looks at the poetry of Wheatley and how it influenced the Romantics who followed her.

_____. *Phillis Wheatley's Poetics of Liberation: Backgrounds and Contexts.* Knoxville: University of Tennessee Press, 2008. Examines how evaluation of Wheatley's poetry has changed over the years.

John C. Shields

WALT WHITMAN

Born: West Hills, New York; May 31, 1819
Died: Camden, New Jersey; March 26, 1892

PRINCIPAL POETRY
"Song of Myself," 1855
Leaves of Grass, 1855, 1856, 1860, 1867, 1871, 1876, 1881-1882, 1889, 1891-1892
Drum-Taps, 1865
Sequel to Drum-Taps, 1865-1866
After All, Not to Create Only, 1871
Passage to India, 1871
As a Strong Bird on Pinions Free, 1872
Two Rivulets, 1876
November Boughs, 1888
Good-bye My Fancy, 1891
Complete Poetry and Selected Prose, 1959 (James E. Miller, editor)

OTHER LITERARY FORMS

Walt Whitman published several important essays and studies during his lifetime. *Democratic Vistas* (1871), *Memoranda During the War* (1875-1876), *Specimen Days and Collect* (1882-1883, autobiographical sketches), and the *Complete Prose Works* (1892) are the most significant. He also tried his hand at short fiction, collected in *The Half-Breed, and Other Stories* (1927), and a novel, *Franklin Evans* (1842). Many of his letters and journals have appeared either in early editions or as parts of the New York University Press edition of *The Collected Writings of Walt Whitman* (1961-1984; 22 volumes).

ACHIEVEMENTS

Walt Whitman's stature rests largely on two major contributions to the literature of the United States. First, although detractors are numerous and the poet's organizing principle is sometimes blurred, *Leaves of Grass* stands as the most fully realized American epic poem. Written in the midst of natural grandeur and burgeoning materialism, Whitman's book traces the geographical, social, and spiritual contours of an expanding nation. It embraces the science and commercialism of industrial America while trying to direct these practical energies toward the "higher mind" of literature, culture, and the soul. In his preface to the first edition of *Leaves of Grass*, Whitman referred to the United States itself as "essentially the greatest poem." He saw the self-esteem, sympa-

Walt Whitman
(Library of Congress)

thy, candor, and deathless attachment to freedom of the common people as "unrhymed poetry," which awaited the "gigantic and generous treatment worthy of it." *Leaves of Grass* was to be that treatment.

The poet's second achievement was in language and poetic technique. Readers take for granted the modern American poet's emphasis on free verse and ordinary diction, forgetting Whitman's revolutionary impact. His free-verse form departed from stanzaic patterns and regular lines, taking its power instead from individual, rolling, oratorical lines of cadenced speech. He subordinated traditional poetic techniques, such as alliteration, repetition, inversion, and conventional meter, to this expansive form. He also violated popular rules of poetic diction by extracting a rich vocabulary from foreign languages, science, opera, various trades, and the ordinary language of town and country. Finally, Whitman broke taboos with his extensive use of sexual imagery, incorporated not to titillate or shock, but to portray life in its wholeness. He determined to be the poet of procreation, to celebrate the elemental and primal life force that permeates humans and nature. Thus, "forbidden voices" are unveiled, clarified, and transfigured by the poet's vision of their place in an organic universe.

Whitman himself said he wrote but "one or two indicative words for the future." He expected the "main things" from poets, orators, singers, and musicians to come. They would prove and define a national culture, thus justifying his faith in American democracy. These apologetic words, along with the early tendency to read Whitman as "untranslatable," or barbaric and undisciplined, long delayed his acceptance as one of America's greatest poets. In fact, if judged by the poet's own test of greatness, he is a failure, for he said the "proof of a poet is that his country absorbs him as affectionately as he has absorbed it." Whitman has not been absorbed by the common people to whom he paid tribute in his poetry. However, with recognition from both the academic community and such poets as Hart Crane, William Carlos Williams, Karl Shapiro, and Randall Jarrell, his *Leaves of Grass* has taken its place among the great masterworks of American literature.

Biography

Walter Whitman, Jr., was born in West Hills, Long Island on May 31, 1819. His mother, Louisa Van Velsor, was descended from a long line of New York Dutch farmers, and his father, Walter Whitman, was a Long Island farmer and carpenter. In 1823, the father moved his family to Brooklyn in search of work. One of nine children in an undistinguished family, Whitman received only a meager formal education between 1825 and 1830, when he turned to the printing trade for the next five years. At the age of seventeen, he began teaching at various Long Island schools and continued to teach until he went to New York City to be a printer for the *New World* and a reporter for the *Democratic Review* in 1841. From then on, Whitman generally made a living at journalism. Besides reporting and freelance writing, he edited several Brooklyn newspapers, including the *Daily Eagle* (1846-1848), the *Freeman* (1848-1849), and the *Times* (1857-1859). Some of Whitman's experiences during this period influenced the poetry that seemed to burst into print in 1855. While in New York, Whitman frequented the opera and the public library, both of which furnished him with a sense of heritage and of connection with the bards and singers of the past. In 1848, Whitman met and was hired by a representative of the New Orleans *Crescent*. Although the job lasted only a few months, the journey by train, stagecoach, and steamboat through what Whitman always referred to as "inland America" certainly helped to stimulate his vision of the country's democratic future. Perhaps most obviously influential was Whitman's trade itself. His flair for action and vignette, as well as descriptive detail, surely was sharpened by his journalistic writing. The reporter's keen eye for the daily scene is everywhere evident in *Leaves of Grass*.

When the first edition of his poems appeared, Whitman received little money but some attention from reviewers. Included among the responses was a famous letter from

Ralph Waldo Emerson, who praised Whitman for his brave thought and greeted him at the beginning of a great career. Whitman continued to write and edit, but was unemployed during the winter of 1859-1860, when he began to frequent Pfaff's bohemian restaurant. There he may have established the "manly love" relationships that inspired the "Calamus" poems of the 1860 edition of *Leaves of Grass*. Again, this third edition created a stir with readers, but the outbreak of the Civil War soon turned everyone's attention to more pressing matters. Whitman himself was too old for military service, but he did experience the war by caring for wounded soldiers in Washington, D.C., hospitals. While in Washington as a government clerk, Whitman witnessed Abraham Lincoln's second inauguration, mourned over the president's assassination in April, printed *Drum-Taps* in May, and later added to these Civil War lyrics a sequel, which contained "When Lilacs Last in the Dooryard Bloom'd."

The postwar years saw Whitman's reputation steadily increasing in England, thanks to William Rossetti's *Selections* in 1868, Algernon Swinburne's praise, and a long, admiring review of his work by Anne Gilchrist in 1870. In fact, Gilchrist fell in love with the poet after reading *Leaves of Grass* and even moved to Philadelphia in 1876 to be near him, but her hopes of marrying Whitman died with her in 1885. Because of books by William D. O'Connor and John Burroughs, Whitman also became better known in the United States, but any satisfaction he may have derived from this recognition was tempered by two severe blows in 1873. He suffered a paralytic stroke in January, and his mother, to whom he was very devoted, died in May. Unable to work, Whitman returned to stay with his brother George at Camden, New Jersey, spending summers on a farm at Timber Creek.

Although Whitman recuperated sufficiently to take trips to New York or Boston, and even to Colorado and Canada in 1879-1880, he was never again to be the robust man he had so proudly described in early editions of *Leaves of Grass*. His declining years, however, gave him time to revise and establish the structure of his book. When the seventh edition of *Leaves of Grass* was published in Philadelphia in 1881-1882, Whitman had achieved a total vision of his work. With the money from a centennial edition (1876) and an occasional lecture on Lincoln, Whitman was able by 1884 to purchase a small house on Mickle Street in Camden. Although he was determined not to be "house-bound," a sunstroke in 1885 and a second paralytic stroke in 1888 made him increasingly dependent on friends. He found especially gratifying the friendship of his secretary and companion, Horace Traubel, who recorded the poet's life and opinions during these last years. Despite the care of Traubel and several doctors and nurses, Whitman died of complications from a stroke on March 26, 1892.

ANALYSIS

An approach to Walt Whitman's poetry profitably begins with the "Inscriptions" to *Leaves of Grass*, for these short, individual pieces introduce the main ideas and methods of Whitman's book. In general, they stake out the ground of what Miller has called the prototypical New World personality, a merging of the individual with the national and cosmic, or universal, selves. That democratic principles are at the root of Whitman's views becomes immediately clear in "One's-Self I Sing," the first poem in *Leaves of Grass*. Here, Whitman refers to the self as a "simple separate person," yet utters the "word Democratic, the word En-Masse." Citizens of America alternately assert their individuality—obey little, resist often—and yet see themselves as a brotherhood of the future, inextricably bound by the vision of a great new society of and for the masses. This encompassing vision requires a sense of "the Form complete," rejecting neither body nor soul, singing equally of the Female and Male, embracing both realistic, scientific, modern humanity and the infinite, eternal life of the spirit.

LEAVES OF GRASS

Whitman takes on various roles to lead his readers to a fuller understanding of this democratic universal. In "Me Imperturbe," he is at ease as an element of nature, able to confront the accidents and rebuffs of life with the implacability of trees and animals. As he suggests in *Democratic Vistas*, the true idea of nature in all its power and glory must become fully restored and must furnish the "pervading atmosphere" to poems of American democracy. Whitman must also empathize with rational things—with humanity at large and in particular—so he constructs what sometimes seem to be endless catalogs of Americans at work and play. This technique appears in "I Hear America Singing," which essentially lists the varied carols of carpenter, boatman, shoemaker, woodcutter, mother, and so on, all "singing what belongs to him or her and to none else" as they ply their trades. In longer poems, such as "Starting from Paumanok," Whitman extends his catalog to all the states of the Union. He intends to acknowledge contemporary lands, salute employments and cities large and small, and report heroism on land and sea from an American point of view. He marks down all of what constitutes unified life, including the body, sexual love, and comradeship, or "manly love." Finally, the poet must join the greatness of love and democracy to the greatness of religion. These programs expand to take up large parts of even longer poems, such as "Song of Myself" or to claim space of their own in sections of *Leaves of Grass*.

Whitman uses another technique to underscore the democratic principle of his art: He makes the reader a fellow poet, a "camerado" who joins hands with him to traverse the poetic landscape. In "To You," he sees the poet and reader as passing strangers who desire to speak to one another and urges that they do so. In "Song of the Open Road," Whitman travels the highways with his "delicious burdens" of men and women, calling them all to come forth and move forever forward, well armed to take their places in "the procession of souls along the grand roads of the universe." His view of the reader as fellow traveler and seer is especially clear in the closing lines of the poem:

> Camerado, I give you my hand!
> I give you my love more precious than money,
> I give you myself before preaching or law;
> Will you give me yourself? will you come travel with me?
> Shall we stick by each other as long as we live?

Finally, this comradeship means willingness to set out on one's own, for Whitman says in "Song of Myself" that the reader most honors his style "who learns under it to destroy the teacher." The questions one asks are one's own to puzzle out. The poet's role is to lead his reader up on a knoll, wash the gum from his eyes, and then let him become habituated to the "dazzle of light" that is the natural world. In other words, Whitman intends to help his reader become a "poet" of insight and perception and then release him to travel the public roads of a democratic nation.

This democratic unification of multiplicity, empathic identification, and comradeship exists in most of Whitman's poems. They do not depend on his growth as poet or thinker. However, in preparing to analyze representative poems from *Leaves of Grass*, it is helpful to establish a general plan for the various sections of the book. Whitman revised and reordered his poems until the 1881 edition, which established a form that was to remain essentially unchanged through succeeding editions. He merely annexed materials to the 1881 order until just before his death in 1892, then authorized the 1891-1892 version for all future printings. Works originally published apart from *Leaves of Grass*, such as *Drum-Taps* or *Passage to India*, were eventually incorporated in the parent volume. Thus, an analysis of the best poems in five important sections of this final *Leaves of Grass* will help delineate Whitman's movement toward integration of self and nation, within his prescribed portals of birth and death.

"Song of Myself"

"Song of Myself," Whitman's great lyric poem, exemplifies his democratic "programs" without diminishing the intense feeling that so startled his first readers. It successfully combines paeans to the individual, the nation, and life at large, including nature, sexuality, and death. Above all, "Song of Myself" is a poem of incessant motion, as though Whitman's energy is spontaneously bursting into lines. Even in the contemplative sections of the poem, when Whitman leans and loafs at his ease observing a spear of summer grass, his senses of hearing, taste, and sight are working at fever pitch. In the opening section, he calls himself "nature without check with original energy." Having once begun to speak, he hopes "to cease not till death." Whitman says that although others may talk of the beginning and the end, he finds his subject in the now—in the "urge and urge and urge" of the procreant world.

One method by which Whitman's energy escapes boundaries is the poet's ability to "become" other people and things. He will not be measured by time and space, nor by physical form. Rather, he effuses his flesh in eddies and drifts it in lacy jags, taking on new identities with every line. His opening lines show that he is speaking not of himself alone but of all selves. What he assumes, the reader shall assume; every atom of him, and therefore of the world, belongs to the reader as well. In section 24, he represents himself as a "Kosmos," which contains multitudes and reconciles apparent opposites. He speaks the password and sign of democracy and accepts nothing that all cannot share. To stress this egalitarian vision, Whitman employs the catalog with skill and variety. Many parts of "Song of Myself" list or name characters, places, occupations, or experiences, but section 33 most clearly shows the two major techniques that give these lists vitality. First, Whitman composes long single-sentence movements of action and description, which attempt to unify nature and civilization. The poet is alternately weeding his onion patch, hoeing, prospecting, hauling his boat down a shallow river, scaling mountains, walking paths, and speeding through space. He then follows each set of actions with a series of place lines, beginning with "where," "over," "at," or "upon," which unite farmhouses, hearth furnaces, hot-air balloons, or steamships with plants and animals of land and sea. Second, Whitman interrupts these long listings with more detailed vignettes, which show the "large hearts of heroes"—a sea captain, a hounded slave, a fireman trapped and broken under debris, an artillerist. Sections 34-36 then extend the narrative to tales of the Alamo and an old-time sea fight, vividly brought forth with sounds and dialogue. In each case, the poet becomes the hero and is actually in the scene to suffer or succeed.

This unchecked energy and empathy carry over into Whitman's ebullient imagery to help capture the physical power of human bodies in procreant motion. At one point Whitman calls himself "hankering, gross, mystical, nude." He finds no sweeter flesh than that which sticks to his own bones, or to the bones of others. Sexual imagery, including vividly suggestive descriptions of the male and female body, is central to the poem. Although the soul must take its equal place with the body, neither abasing itself before the other, Whitman's mystical union of soul and body is a sexual experience as well. He loves the hum of the soul's "valved voice" and remembers how, on a transparent summer morning, the soul settled its head athwart his hips and turned over on him. It parted the shirt from the poet's "bosom-bone," plunged its tongue to his "bare-stript heart," and reached until it felt his beard and held his feet. From this experience came peace and the knowledge that love is fundamental to a unified, continuous creation. Poetic metaphor, which identifies and binds hidden likenesses in nature, is therefore emblematic of the organic world. For example, in answering a child's question, "What is the grass?" the poet offers a series of metaphors that join human, natural, and spiritual impulses:

> I guess it must be the flag of my disposition, out of
>   hopeful green stuff woven.
> Or I guess it is the handkerchief of the Lord,
> A scented gift and remembrancer designedly dropt,
> Bearing the owner's name someway in the corners,
>   that we may see and remark, and say *Whose*?

The grass becomes hair from the breasts of young men, from the heads and beards of old people, or from offspring, and it "speaks" from under the faint red roofs of mouths. The sprout shows there is no death, for "nothing collapses," and to die is "luckier" than anyone had supposed. This excerpt from the well-known sixth section of "Song of Myself" illustrates how image making signifies for Whitman a kind of triumph over death itself.

Because of its position near the beginning of *Leaves of Grass* and its encompassing of Whitman's major themes, "Song of Myself" is a foundation for the volume. The "self" in this poem is a replica of the nation as self, and its delineation in the cosmos is akin to the growth of the United States in the world. Without putting undue stress on this nationalistic interpretation, however, the reader can find many reasons to admire "Song of Myself." Its dynamic form, beauty of language, and psychological insights are sufficient to make Whitman a first-rate poet, even if he had written nothing else.

CELEBRATION OF SELF AND SEXUALITY

The passionate celebration of the self and of sexuality is Whitman's great revolutionary theme. In "Children of Adam," he is the procreative father of multitudes, a champion of heterosexual love and the "body electric." In "From Pent-Up Aching Rivers," he sings of the need for superb children, brought forth by the "muscular urge" of "stalwart loins." In "I Sing the Body Electric," he celebrates the perfection of well-made male and female bodies. Sections 5 and 9 are explicit descriptions of sexual intercourse and physical "apparatus," respectively. Whitman does not shy away from the fierce attraction of the female form or the ebb and flow of "limitless limpid jets of love hot and enormous" that undulate into the willing and yielding "gates of the body." Because he sees the body as sacred, as imbued with divine power, he considers these enumerations to be poems of the soul as much as of the body.

Indeed, "A Woman Waits for Me" specifically states that sex contains all—bodies and souls. Thus, the poet seeks warm-blooded and sufficient women to receive the pent-up rivers of himself, to start new sons and daughters fit for the great nation that will be these United States. The procreative urge operates on more than one level in "Children of Adam"—it is physical sex and birthing, the union of body and soul, and the metaphorical insemination of the poet's words and spirit into national life. In several ways, then, words are to become flesh. Try as some early Whitman apologists might to explain them away, raw sexual impulses are the driving force of these poems.

"CALAMUS" POEMS

Whitman's contemporaries were shocked by the explicit sexual content of "Children of Adam," but modern readers and critics have been much more intrigued by the apparent homoeroticism of the poems in the "Calamus" section of the 1860 edition of *Leaves of Grass*. Although it is ultimately impossible to say whether these poems reflect Whitman's gay associations in New York, it is obvious that comradeship extends here to both spiritual and physical contact between men. "In Paths Untrodden" states the poet's intention to sing of "manly attachment" or types of "athletic love," to celebrate the need of comrades. "Whoever You Are Holding Me Now in Hand" deepens the physical nature of this love, including the stealthy meeting of male friends in a wood, behind some rock in the open air, or on the beach of some quiet island. There the poet would permit the comrade's long-dwelling kiss on the lips and a touch that would carry him eternally forth over land and sea. "These I Singing in Spring" refers to "him that tenderly loves me" and pledges the hardiest spears of grass, the calamus-root, to those who love as the poet himself is capable of loving.

Finally, two of Whitman's best lyrics concern this robust but clandestine relationship. "I Saw in Louisiana a Live-Oak Growing" is a poignant contrast between the live oak's ability to "utter joyous leaves" while it stands in solitude, without companions, and the poet's inability to live without a friend or lover near. There is no mistaking the equally personal tone of "When I Heard at the Close of the Day," probably Whitman's finest "Calamus" poem. The plaudits of others are meaningless and unsatisfying, says Whitman, until he thinks of how his dear friend and lover is on his way to see him. When his friend arrives one evening, the hissing rustle of rolling waves becomes congratulatory and joyful. Once the person he loves most lies sleeping by him under the same cover, face inclined toward him in the autumn moonbeams and arm lightly lying around his breast, he is happy.

Other short poems in "Calamus," such as "For You O Democracy," "The Prairie Grass Dividing," or "A Promise to California," are less obviously personal. Rather, they extend passionate friendship between men to the larger ideal of democratic brotherhood. Just as procreative love has its metaphorical implications for the nation, so too does Whitman promise to make the continent indissoluble and cities inseparable, arms about each other's necks, with companionship and the "manly love of comrades." Still other poems move this comradeship into wider spans of space and time. "The Moment Yearning and Thoughtful" joins the poet with men of Europe and Asia in happy brotherhood, thus transcending national and continental boundaries. "The Base of All Metaphysics" extends this principle through historical time, for the Greek, Germanic, and Christian systems all suggest that the attraction of friend to friend is the basis of civilization. The last poem in the "Calamus" section, "Full of Life Now," completes Whitman's panoramic view by carrying friendship into the future. His words communicate the compact, visible to readers of a century or any number of centuries hence. Each seeking the other past time's invisible boundaries, poet and reader are united physically through Whitman's poetry.

"Crossing Brooklyn Ferry"

"Crossing Brooklyn Ferry" is the natural product of Whitman's idea that love and companionship will bind the world's peoples to one another. In a sense it gives the poet immortality through creation of a living artifact: the poem itself. Whitman stands motionless on a moving ferry, immersed in the stream of life and yet suspended in time through the existence of his words on the page. Consequently, he can say that neither time nor place nor distance matters, because he is with each reader and each fellow traveler in the future. He points out that hundreds of years hence others will enter the gates of the ferry and cross from shore to shore, will see the sun half an hour high and watch the seagulls floating in circles with motionless wings. Others will also watch the endless scallop-edged waves cresting and falling, as though they are experiencing the same moment as the poet, with the same mixture of joy and sorrow. Thus, Whitman confidently calls upon the "dumb ministers" of nature to keep up their ceaseless motion—to flow, fly, and frolic on—because they furnish their parts toward eternity and toward the soul.

Techniques match perfectly with these themes in "Crossing Brooklyn Ferry." Whitman's frequent repetition of the main images—sunrise and sunset, ebb and flow of the sea and river, seagulls oscillating in the sky—reinforces the belief in timeless, recurring human experience. Descriptions of schooners and steamers at work along the shore are among his most powerful evocations of color and sound. Finally, Whitman's employment of pronouns to mark a shift in the sharing of experiences also shows the poem's careful design. Whitman begins the poem with an "I" who looks at the scenes or crowds of people and calls to "you" who are among the crowds and readers of present and future. In section 8, however, he reaches across generations to fuse himself and pour his meaning into the "you." At the end of this section, he and others have become "we," who understand and receive experience with free senses and love, united in the organic continuity of nature.

"Sea-Drift" poems

The short section of *Leaves of Grass* entitled "Sea-Drift" contains the first real signs of a more somber Whitman, who must come to terms with hardship, sorrow, and death. In one way, this resignation and accommodation follow the natural progression of the self from active, perhaps callow, youth to contemplative old age. They are also an outgrowth of Whitman's belief that life and death are a continuum, that life is a symphony of both sonatas and dirges, which the true poet of nature must capture fully on the page. Whereas in other poems the ocean often signifies birth and creation, with fish-shaped Paumanok (Manhattan) rising from the sea, in "Tears," it is the repository of sorrow. Its white shore lies in solitude, dark and desolate, holding a ghost or "shapeless lump" that cries streaming, sobbing tears. In "As I Ebb'd with the Ocean of Life," Whitman is distressed with himself for daring to "blab" so much without having the least idea who or what he really is. Nature darts on the poet and stings him, because he has not understood anything and because no man ever can. He calls himself but a "trail of drift and debris," who has left his poems like "little wrecks" on Paumanok's shores. However, he must continue to throw himself on the ocean of life, clinging to the breast of the land that is his father, and gathering from the moaning sea the "sobbing dirge of Nature." He believes the flow will return, but meanwhile he must wait and lie in drifts at his readers' feet.

"Out of the Cradle Endlessly Rocking"

"Out of the Cradle Endlessly Rocking" is a fuller, finally more optimistic, treatment of the poet's confrontation with loss. Commonly acknowledged as one of Whitman's finest works, this poem uses lyrical language and operatic structure to trace the origin of his poetic powers in the experience of death. Two "songs" unite with the whispering cry of the sea to communicate this experience to him. Central to the poem is Whitman's seaside reminiscence of a bird and his mate, who build and tend a nest of eggs. When the female fails to return one evening, never to appear again, the male becomes a solitary singer of his sorrows, whose notes are "translated" by the listening boy-poet. The bird's song is an aria of lonesome love, an outpouring carol of yearning, hope, and finally, death. As the boy absorbs the bird's song, his soul awakens in sympathy. From this moment forward, his destiny will be to perpetuate the bird's "cries of unsatisfied love." More important, though, Whitman must learn the truth that this phrase masks, must conquer "the word" that has caused the bird's cries:

>Whereto answering, the sea,
>Delaying not, hurrying not,
>Whisper'd me through the night, and very plainly
>   before daybreak,
>Lisp'd to me the low and delicious word death,
>And again death, death, death, death.

Whitman then fuses the bird's song and his own with death, which the sea, "like some old crone rocking the cradle," has whispered to him. This final image of the sea as an old crone soothing an infant underscores the central point of "Out of the Cradle Endlessly Rocking": Old age and death are part of a natural flux. Against the threat of darkness, one must live and sing.

Drum-Taps

Like the tone of the "Sea-Drift" section, darker hues permeate Whitman's Civil War lyrics. His experiences as a hospital worker in Washington, D.C., are clearly behind the sometimes wrenching imagery of *Drum-Taps*. As a wound dresser, he saw the destruction of healthy young bodies and minds at first hand. These spectacles were in part a test of Whitman's own courage and comradeship, but they were also a test of the nation's ability to survive and grow. As Whitman says in "Long, Too Long America," the country had long traveled roads "all even and peaceful," learning only from joys and prosperity, but now it must face "crises of anguish" without recoiling and show the world what its "children enmasse really are." Many of the *Drum-Taps* lyrics show Whitman facing this reality, but "The Wound Dresser" is representative. The poet's persona is an old man who is called on years after the Civil War to "paint the mightiest armies of earth," to tell what experience of the war stays with him latest and deepest. Although he mentions the long marches, rushing charges, and toils of battle, he does not dwell on soldiers' perils or soldiers' joys. Rather, he vividly describes the wounded and dying at battlegrounds, hospital tents, or roofed hospitals, as he goes with "hinged knees and steady hand to dress wounds." He does not recoil or give out at the sight of crushed heads, shattered throats, amputated stumps of hands and arms, the putrid gangrenous foot or shoulder. Nevertheless, within him rests a burning flame, the memory of youths suffering or dead.

Confronted with these horrors, Whitman had to find a way to surmount them, and that way was love. If there could be a positive quality in war, Whitman found it in the comradeship of common soldiers, who risked all for their fellows. In "As Toilsome I Wander'd Virginia's Woods," for example, Whitman discovers the grave of a soldier buried beneath a tree. Hastily dug on a retreat from battle, the grave is nevertheless marked by a sign: "Bold, cautious, true, and my loving comrade." That inscription remains with the poet through many changeful seasons and scenes to follow, as evidence of this brotherly love. Similarly, "Vigil Strange I Kept on the Field One Night" tells of a soldier who sees his comrade struck down in battle and returns to find him cold with death. He watches by him through "immortal and mystic hours" until, just as dawn is breaking, he folds the young man in a blanket and buries him in a rude-dug grave where he fell. This tale of tearless mourning perfectly evokes the loss caused by war.

Eventually, Whitman finds some ritual significance in these deaths, as though they are atonement for those yet living. In "A Sight in Camp in the Daybreak Gray and Dim," he marks three covered forms on stretchers near a hospital tent. One by one he uncovers their faces. The first is an elderly man, gaunt and grim, but a comrade nevertheless. The second is a sweet boy "with cheeks yet blooming." When he exposes the third face, however, he finds it calm, of yellow-white ivory, and of indeterminable age. He sees in it the face of Christ himself, "dead and divine and brother of all." "Over the Carnage Rose Prophetic a Voice" suggests that these Christian sacrifices will finally lead to a united Columbia. Even though a thousand may have to "sternly immolate themselves for one," those who love one another shall become invincible, and "affection shall solve the problems of freedom." As in other sections of *Leaves of Grass*, Whitman believes the United States will be held together not by lawyers, paper agreements, or force of arms, but by the cohesive power of love and fellowship.

"When Lilacs Last in the Dooryard Bloom'd"

"When Lilacs Last in the Dooryard Bloom'd," another of Whitman's acknowledged masterpieces, repeats the process underlying *Drum-Taps*. The poet must come to terms with the loss of one he loves—in this case, the slain President Lincoln. Death and mourning must eventually give way to consolation and hope for the future. Cast in the form of a traditional elegy, the poem traces the processional of Lincoln's coffin across country, past the poet himself, to the president's final resting place.

To objectify his emotional struggle between grief, on one hand, and spiritual reconciliation with death on the other, Whitman employs several vivid symbols. The lilac blooming perennially, with its heart-shaped leaves, represents the poet's perpetual mourning and love. The "powerful fallen star," which now lies in a "harsh surrounding could" of black night, is Lincoln, fallen and shrouded in his coffin. The solitary hermit thrush that warbles "death's outlet song of life" from a secluded swamp is the soul or spiritual world. Initially, Whitman is held powerless by the death of his departing comrade. Although he can hear the bashful notes of the thrush and will come to understand them, he thinks only of showering the coffin with sprigs of lilac to commemorate his love for Lincoln. He must also warble his own song before he can absorb the bird's message of consolation. Eventually, as he sits amidst the daily activities described in section 14, he is struck by the "sacred knowledge of death," and the bird's carol becomes intelligible to him. Death is lovely, soothing, and delicate. It is a "strong deliveress" who comes to nestle the grateful body in her flood of bliss. Rapt with the charm of the bird's song, Whitman sees myriad battle corpses in a vision—the debris of all the slain soldiers of the war—yet realizes that they are fully at rest and no longer suffering. The power of this realization gives him strength to let go of the hand of his comrade. An ever-blooming lilac now signifies renewal, just as death takes its rightful place as the harbinger of new life, the life of the eternal soul.

Matters of spirit

Whitman's deepening concern with matters of the spirit permeates the last sections of *Leaves of Grass*. Having passed the test of the Civil War and having done his part to reunite the United States, Whitman turned his attention to America's place in the world and his own place in God's design. As he points out in "A Clear Midnight," he gives his last poems to the soul and its "free flight into the wordless," to ponder the themes he loves best: "Night, sleep, death and the stars." Such poems as "Chanting the Square Deific" and "A Noiseless Patient Spider" invoke either the general soul, the "Santa Spirita" that pervades all created life, or the toils of individual souls, flinging out gossamer threads to connect themselves with this holy spirit.

"Passage to India"

Whitman was still able to produce fine lyrics in his old age. One of these successful poems, "Passage to India," announces Whitman's intention to join modern science to fables and dreams of old, to weld past and future, and to show that the United States is but a "bridge" in the "vast rondure" of the world. Just as the Suez Canal connected Europe and Asia, Whitman says, America's transcontinental railroad ties the eastern to the western sea, thus verifying Christopher Columbus's dream. Beyond these material thoughts of exploration, however, lies the poet's realm of love and spirit. The poet is a "true son of God," who will soothe the hearts of restlessly exploring, never-happy humanity. He will link all human affections, justify the "cold, impassive, voiceless earth," and absolutely fuse nature and humanity. This fusion takes place not in the material world but in the swelling of the soul toward God, who is a mighty "centre of the true, the good, the loving." Passage to these superior universes transcends time and space and death. It is a "passage to more than India," through the deep waters that no mariner has traveled, and for which the poet must "risk the ship, ourselves and all."

"Prayer of Columbus"

Whitman also uses a seagoing metaphor for spiritual passage in "Prayer of Columbus," which is almost a continuation of "Passage to India." In the latter, Whitman aggressively flings himself into the active voyage toward God, but in "Prayer of Columbus" he is a "batter'd, wreck'd old man," willing to yield his ships to God and wait for the unknown end of all. He recounts his heroic deeds of exploration and attributes their inspiration to a message from the heavens that sped him on. Like Columbus, Whitman is "old, poor, and paralyzed," yet capable of one more effort to speak of the steady interior light that God has granted him. Finally, the works of the past fall away from him, and some divine hand reveals a scene of countless ships sailing on distant seas, from which "anthems in new tongues" salute and comfort him. This implied divine sanction for his life's work was consolation to an old poet, who, at his death in 1892, remained largely unaccepted and unrecognized by contemporary critics and historians.

Legacy

The grand design of *Leaves of Grass* appears to trace self and nation neatly through sensuous youth, crises of maturity, and soul-searching old age. Although this philosophical or psychological reading of Whitman's work is certainly encouraged by the poet's tinkering with its structure, many fine lyrics do not fit into neat patterns, or even under topical headings. Whitman's reputation rests more on the startling freshness of his language, images, and democratic treatment of the common American citizen than on his success as epic bard. Common to all his poetry, however, are certain major themes: reconciliation of body and soul, purity and unity of physical nature, death as the "mother of beauty," and above all, comradeship or love, which binds and transcends all else. In fact, Whitman encouraged a complex comradeship with his readers to bind his work to future generations. He expected reading to be a gymnastic struggle and the reader to be a re-creator of the poem through imaginative interaction with the poet. Perhaps that is why he said in "So Long" that *Leaves of Grass* was no book, for whoever touches his poetry "touches a man."

OTHER MAJOR WORKS

LONG FICTION: *Franklin Evans*, 1842.

SHORT FICTION: *The Half-Breed, and Other Stories*, 1927.

NONFICTION: *Democratic Vistas*, 1871; *Memoranda During the War*, 1875-1876; *Specimen Days and Collect*, 1882-1883; *Complete Prose Works*, 1892; *Calamus*, 1897 (letters; Richard M. Bucke, editor); *The Wound Dresser*, 1898 (Bucke, editor); *Letters Written by Walt Whitman to His Mother, 1866-1872*, 1902 (Thomas B. Harned, editor); *An American Primer*, 1904; *Walt Whitman's Diary in Canada*, 1904 (William S. Kennedy, editor); *The Letters of Anne Gilchrist and Walt Whitman*, 1918 (Harned, editor).

MISCELLANEOUS: *The Collected Writings of Walt Whitman*, 1961-1984 (22 volumes).

BIBLIOGRAPHY

Canning, Richard. *Whitman*. London: Hesperus, 2010. Part of the Poetic Lives series, this is a basic biography that examines Whitman's life and poetry.

Folsom, Ed. *Re-scripting Walt Whitman: An Introduction to His Life and Work*. Malden, Mass.: Blackwell, 2005. A good starting point for readers of Whitman, delving into his life and literary works.

Genoways, Ted. *Walt Whitman and the Civil War: America's Poet During the Lost Years of 1860/1862*. Berkeley: University of California Press, 2009. Uses unpublished letters and manuscripts to explore Whitman's involvement in the war, debunking his supposed indifference.

Herrero-Brassas, Juan A., ed. *Walt Whitman's Mystical Ethics of Comradeship: Homosexuality and the Marginality of Friendship at the Crossroads of Modernity*. Albany: State University of New York Press, 2010. This collection of essays examines Whitman's mystical religious beliefs, his concept of comradeship, and his homosexuality.

Killlingsworth, M. Jimmie, ed. *The Cambridge Introduction to Walt Whitman*. New York: Cambridge University Press, 2007. A comprehensive work that covers Whitman's life and presents extensive analysis of his poetry, including his prewar poetry, *Leaves of Grass*, "Calamus," "Children of Adam," earth and body poems, and elegies. Also looks at critical reception of his works and the image that was created around him.

Kummings, Donald D., ed. *A Companion to Walt Whitman*. Malden, Mass.: Blackwell, 2006. These thirty-five essays by prominent scholars delve into the life and writing of Whitman. The essays are classified under four sections, concentrating on the author's life, the cultural and literary contexts of his writing, and the texts themselves.

Topics such as nature, the city, gender, civil war, and pop culture are discussed at length in relation to Whitman and his writing. Readers will also find this book valuable for the publication history it provides, as well as the thorough bibliography of criticism of Whitman's prose.

Reynolds, David S. *Walt Whitman*. New York: Knopf, 2005. Part of the Lives and Legacies series, this work examines the life and work of Whitman. Reynolds calls Whitman the founder of free verse and the first poet to treat sex candidly.

Robertson, Michael. *Worshipping Walt: The Whitman Disciples*. Princeton, N.J.: Princeton University Press, 2008. In his later years, Whitman developed "disciples," people who admired and supported him. This work examines his disciples, including Anne Gilchrist, John Burroughs, John Addington Symonds, and Horace Traubel.

Stacey, Jason. *Walt Whitman's Multitudes: Labor Reform and Persona in Whitman's Journalism and the First "Leaves of Grass," 1840-1855*. New York: Peter Lang, 2008. Focuses on the political views of Whitman as expressed in his journalism and in the first edition of *Leaves of Grass*. Whitman wrote on artisans who had lost their economic status, blaming them in part for becoming involved in consumerism and affectation.

Williams, C. K. *On Whitman*. Princeton, N.J.: Princeton University Press, 2010. Part of the Writers on Writers series, this work looks at Whitman from the standpoint of another poet and delves into Whitman's influence.

Perry D. Luckett

JOHN GREENLEAF WHITTIER

Born: Haverhill, Massachusetts; December 17, 1807
Died: Hampton Falls, New Hampshire; September 7, 1892

PRINCIPAL POETRY
Legends of New-England, 1831
Moll Pitcher, 1832
Mogg Megone, 1836
Poems Written During the Progress of the Abolition Question in the United States, 1837
Poems, 1838
Lays of My Home, and Other Poems, 1843
Hymns, 1846 (pb. in Samuel Longfellow and Samuel Johnson's *A Book of Hymns*)
Voices of Freedom, 1846
Poems, 1849
Songs of Labor, and Other Poems, 1850
The Chapel of the Hermits, and Other Poems, 1853
The Panorama, and Other Poems, 1856
The Sycamores, 1857
The Poetical Works of John Greenleaf Whittier, 1857, 1869, 1880, 1894
Home Ballads and Poems, 1860
In War Time, 1863
Snow-Bound: A Winter Idyl, 1866
The Tent on the Beach, and Other Poems, 1867
Among the Hills, and Other Poems, 1869
Ballads of New England, 1869
Maud Muller, 1869
Miriam, and Other Poems, 1871
The Pennsylvania Pilgrim, and Other Poems, 1872
Hazel-Blossoms, 1875
Mabel Martin, 1876
Favorite Poems, 1877
The Vision of Echard, and Other Poems, 1878
The King's Missive, and Other Poems, 1881
The Bay of Seven Islands, and Other Poems, 1883
Saint Gregory's Guest and Recent Poems, 1886
At Sundown, 1890

John Greenleaf Whittier
(Library of Congress)

Other literary forms

Besides his extensive poetry, John Greenleaf Whittier (WIH-tee-uhr) wrote numerous antislavery tracts, compiled editions of New England legends, edited various newspapers, and was active in abolitionist politics. Whittier's *Legends of New-England*, his earliest collection, was followed by the antislavery arguments in *Justice and Expediency: Or, Slavery Considered with a View to Its Rightful and Effectual Remedy, Abolition* (1833), and *The Supernaturalism of New England* (1847). Whittier's finest prose work is perhaps *Leaves from Margaret Smith's Journal* (1849), a Quaker novel in journal form. *Old Portraits and Modern Sketches* (1850) and *Literary Recreations and Miscellanies* (1854) followed, and the *Prose Works of John Greenleaf Whittier* were collected in two volumes in 1866.

Whittier also edited *Child Life* (1872) and *Child Life in Prose* (1874), as well as *Songs of Three Centuries* (1876). He wrote a masterful introduction to his edition of *The Journal of John Woolman* (1871), another notable American Quaker writer. A full collection of Whittier's prose can be found in *The Writings of John Greenleaf Whittier* (1888-1889).

ACHIEVEMENTS

John Greenleaf Whittier was a remarkably prolific writer and reformer. As poet, editor, abolitionist, and religious humanist, Whittier managed to produce more than forty volumes of poetry and prose during his lifetime, not counting his uncollected journalistic work. Through his antislavery poems, he spoke for the conscience of New England, and he later celebrated the virtues of village life for an age that looked back on them with nostalgia. Although honored and venerated as a poet during his later years, he was curiously guarded about his literary reputation, remarking to his first biographer, "I am a *man*, not a mere verse-maker." His belief that morality was the basis of all literature may have made him finally more of a moralist than a poet; his Quaker conscience would not permit him to produce art for art's sake.

Early in life, he patterned his verse after Robert Burns, writing dialect imitations of the Scottish poet to the extent of being called the American Burns. He further corrupted his muse by imitating the worst of the popular, sentimental, and genteel verse of his age and did not achieve a distinctive poetic voice until midcareer. Like many a self-educated poet, Whittier lacked a clear sense of critical taste and judgment, especially in regard to his own work. He wrote too much too quickly and could not distinguish between his best poems and his inferior work. Even his later work is often tainted by melodrama, moralizing, and sentimentality; yet when the worst has been said, the abiding strength of his work transcends its weaknesses.

His most obvious poetic strength is accessibility. Whittier wrote popular poetry that did not make great intellectual demands on his readers. Unlike the modernists, who wrote for a select, highly educated audience, Whittier tried to reach the ordinary reader. Instead of composing dense, ironic, highly allusive verse requiring careful explication, Whittier's narratives and ballads were written in a common idiom that could be readily understood. His poetical materials were regional legend and folklore, topical events, and the personal resources of his Quaker faith. Their moral perspective is clear and forthright, at times didactic or moralistic, and it lacks the ambiguity or tentativeness favored by the New Critics. George Arms argues persuasively that Whittier and the other schoolroom poets (also known as the Fireside poets) simply cannot be appreciated according to current standards of taste and, therefore, have been too often simply dismissed instead of being understood. Their strengths are seen as liabilities and they are faulted for lacking qualities foreign to their age.

The purview of Whittier's work was "common, natural things"—the realm of ordinary life. He rarely dealt with the extremes of human experience, except in some of his abolitionist poems. He shared the optimism and piety of his age and held to a romantic view of nature and a belief in the moral progress of humanity. His sense of moral order and probity may seem merely quaint or old-fashioned to the modern reader, but his poems reflect moral convictions sincerely held. He devoted thirty years to the struggle against slavery and committed the better part of his talents and energy to that issue. If he lost his sense of social justice later in life and failed to comprehend the problems of an industrial society, that might well be excused by his age. Few people are capable of devoting themselves to more than one cause in a lifetime.

The alleged deficiencies in Whittier's poetics should also be judged in terms of his commitment to a popular rather than an academic style. Whittier favored a light, relaxed approach to his verse. Perhaps he overused mechanical rhymes, ballad meter, apostrophe, and hyperbole, but in his "Proem," he is frank to confess his limitations. His muse was not given to exalted flights but spoke plainly for freedom and democracy. Whittier's readership steadily grew during his later years so that his reputation once seemed secure, but like those of the other Fireside poets, it has suffered a sharp decline since his death. He is now read, if at all, as the author of "Snow-Bound: A Winter Idyl" and other nostalgic portraits of New England village life rather than as one of the leading poets of his age. Though his reputation may now be eclipsed by those of Walt Whitman, Emily Dickinson, and Herman Melville, no American poet of the nineteenth century better deserves the title of "poet of the common man" than Whittier.

Biography

John Greenleaf Whittier was born in Haverhill, Massachusetts, on December 17, 1807, in an old family homestead built by a Quaker ancestor. He was the second of four children in the family of John Whittier and Abigail Whittier, of old Quaker stock. Besides John Greenleaf, the Whittier children included an older sister Mary, a younger brother Matthew Franklin, and a younger sister Elizabeth Hussey. Several other relatives lived with the family, including a paternal grandmother, a bachelor uncle, and a maiden aunt. The poet's father was an honest, industrious farmer who tilled his hard, rocky land in the Merrimack Valley with only marginal success. Whittier's mother was a model of quiet strength and deep refinement. She was noted in the community for her domestic industry and "exquisite Quaker neatness." The entire family attended Friends' services at Amesbury, nine miles away, even in poor weather.

Whittier's childhood was one of hard farmwork (that eventually weakened his health) and the occasional freedom of the outdoors—a life of frugality, harmony, and affection later idealized in "Snow-Bound" and "The Barefoot Boy." There were few books in the Whittier household besides the Bible and John Bunyan's *The Pilgrim's Progress* (1678, 1684), and the family depended for entertainment on the tales of his uncle Moses and the stories brought by itinerant Yankee peddlers and gypsies. Whittier's education was meager, consisting of sporadic attendance at the district school and several terms at Haverhill Academy. One of the local teachers, Joshua Coffin, introduced him to the poetry of Burns, and made such a lasting impression on young Whittier that he was later commemorated in "To My Old School Master." As a boy, Whittier showed a natural gift for rhymes and verse, and wrote simple ballads in imitation of Burns and Sir Walter Scott. His sister Mary sent one of these to the local newspaper, the Newburyport *Free Press*. The editor there,

William Lloyd Garrison, was so impressed that he paid a personal visit to the Whittiers to urge further education for their son. Whittier's father was said to have replied to Garrison, "Sir, poetry will not get him bread."

His father finally relented, and Whittier was allowed to enter Haverhill Academy at the age of nineteen. To pay his expenses, he learned the craft of shoemaking, a common winter vocation among New England country folk. Meanwhile, his poems continued to appear in the Haverhill *Gazette* and other publications. At Garrison's behest, Whittier entered the world of Boston journalism and at twenty-two became editor of the *American Manufacturer*, a Whig trade weekly. In the summer of 1829, he was called home by the illness and death of his father, which required him to manage the farm and provide for his family. Still unhappy with the drudgery of farm life, Whittier gladly accepted an invitation from Hartford, Connecticut, in July, 1830, to edit the *Weekly Review*. Unfortunately, his health failed, and Whittier was forced to resign from this attractive position within eighteen months and return to Haverhill in 1832. He was now twenty-five years old, ambitious, but without purpose or direction. A letter from Garrison in the spring of 1833 restored Whittier's spirits when he was invited to apply his talents to the abolitionist movement. From 1833 to the end of the Civil War, the abolition of slavery became the abiding goal of Whittier's life.

Immersion in abolitionist politics made him a master of satire and invective but at the expense of his literary gifts. Out of his new commitment came *Justice and Expediency*, and that same year he was elected to the National Anti-Slavery Convention in Philadelphia. Thus began a thirty-year career of antislavery advocacy and agitation. Several times he was exposed to the threat of mob violence and barely escaped personal injury. He later said that he was prouder of his abolitionist work than of all his authorship, but this comment must be taken in the perspective of his career.

As a young man, Whittier had struggled to reconcile his worldly literary ambitions with his Quaker reticence and piety. As a poor country boy, he had aspired to Boston gentility but lacked the education or means to move in Brahmin circles. One-third of his poetry was written before he was twenty-five, though much of it was sentimental and imitative. When he shrewdly realized that poetry would not bring him the fame he sought, he turned to politics and reformism instead. The abolitionist movement gave him a focus for his talents and energies. He became involved in Essex County politics and by 1835 was elected to the Massachusetts legislature. The following year he sold the Haverhill farm and moved to a small house in Amesbury, where he briefly edited the Amesbury *Village Transcript*. The next twenty years saw him editing various antislavery newspapers and writing numerous abolitionist poems and articles. Much of this was obviously hackwork, but occasionally he would write a notable poem in the heat of indignation, such as "Massachusetts to Virginia," "Barbara Frietchie," or "Laus Deo." His reform efforts interfered with his lyric gifts as a poet, however, and his best work came later in life, in his fifties and sixties, especially after the Civil War. The War Between the States presented a particular dilemma to Whittier in pitting his antislavery sentiments against his Quaker commitment to nonviolence. He saw the need for emancipation but did not approve of secession or the drift toward armed conflict. However, he remained a loyal unionist and wrote poems and broadsides in favor of the Union cause. Titles such as "Our Countrymen in Chains" and "The Sabbath Scene" are little more than propaganda, but Whittier was writing to appeal to the emotions and feelings of ordinary people, and these antislavery verses enjoyed great popular success. Next to Harriet Beecher Stowe, he was perhaps the most effective propagandist for the abolitionist cause.

In his personal life, Whittier remained a resolute bachelor, despite several romantic attractions to Quaker admirers. He lived with his mother, two sisters, and a brother in Amesbury and cherished the company of his family. Their successive deaths in the 1850's and 1860's, however, particularly the loss of his beloved sister Elizabeth in 1864, left him increasingly isolated. The idyllic poem "Snow-Bound" was written partially in memory of his tight-knit family, and with its publication in 1866, Whittier enjoyed his first large commercial success and thereafter was able to live comfortably on his literary earnings. Henceforth his volumes of poetry came out regularly and sold well, but he was plagued with persistently poor health and never felt fully comfortable with his new fame or with the many visitors to his Amesbury cottage. Occasionally he would venture into Boston to join Ralph Waldo Emerson, Henry Wadsworth Longfellow, and Oliver Wendell Holmes at the Saturday Club, but more often he preferred to enjoy the simple company of his niece and her family at their country estate in Danvers.

After the war, Whittier had gradually become institutionalized as one of the Fireside poets, and with this increased popularity came other honors. He served as a Harvard overseer from 1858 onward and as a trustee of Brown University from 1869 to 1892. Harvard also awarded him an honorary LL.D., in 1886, although Whittier was prevented by illness from attending the ceremony in person. On his seventieth birthday, his friends held a formal dinner in his honor, on which occasion Mark Twain embarrassed the guests when his humor misfired, his intended tribute being taken by some as parody.

In his later years, Whittier increasingly assumed the role of New England patriarch, invoking in his poems a sentimental and nostalgic view of village life. He felt out of touch with the changes in the postwar America of the Gilded Age, and increasingly withdrew to the quiet meditation of his Quaker faith. On September 3, 1892, he suffered a paralytic stroke, which led to his death four days later, on September 7, at the age of eighty-four. Holmes spoke at his funeral, after which Whittier was buried in the Friends' section of the Union Cemetery in Haverhill, next to his parents and sister.

Analysis

In the collected edition of his work, John Greenleaf Whittier decided to arrange his poems by topic, in ten categories, rather than present them in chronological order. He also suppressed many of the early verses that had proved embarrassing to him so that the supposedly complete 1894 edition of *The Poetical Works of John Greenleaf Whittier* is not really definitive, though it reflects the poet's final intentions. This arrangement obscures Whittier's development as a poet, but it does tell something about his major concerns and about the poetic forms in which he felt most comfortable. These include antislavery poems, songs of labor and reform, ballads, narratives and legends, nature poems, personal poems, historical poems, occasional verses, hymns and religious lyrics, and genre poems and country idylls.

From Whittier's collected verse, perhaps a dozen or so titles are distinctive. These include "Ichabod," "Massachusetts to Virginia," "Barbara Frietchie," "Telling the Bees," "Laus Deo," "The Trailing Arbutus," "Skipper Ireson's Ride," "First-Day Thoughts," and of course "Snow-Bound." A few other selections should be mentioned—"In School-Days," "The Barefoot Boy," and "Dear Lord and Father of Mankind"—simply because they are part of America's popular culture.

Abolitionist poems

Many of Whittier's abolitionist poems are little more than crude propaganda, but with "Ichabod," he produced a masterpiece of political satire and invective. Cast in terms of a prophetic rebuke, the poem is directed at Daniel Webster, whose "Seventh of March" speech in favor of the Fugitive Slave Law aroused the wrath and enmity of many Northern abolitionists, who accused him of selling out to slave interests. Whittier portrays Webster, in terms of bitter denunciation, as a leader who has betrayed his countrymen and extinguished the life of his soul. His audience would certainly have caught the disparaging reference to I Samuel 4:21, "And she named the child Ichabod, saying the glory is departed from Israel!" Webster, a contemporary "Ichabod" in his fall from glory, becomes the object of scorn and pity for his betrayal of the antislavery cause.

This same contentious tone is also evident in another antislavery poem, "Massachusetts to Virginia," which contrasts the free strength of the North with the moral decadence brought about by slavery in the South. The poem recalls that both Commonwealth States had stood united in the War for Independence, and appeals to that sense of common fellowship in freedom. Though some passages are marred by stock declamatory phrases and excessive use of formal diction and hyperbole, the poem ably makes its point and ends with a ringing slogan, "No fetters in the Bay State,—No slaves upon our Land!"

To a staunch abolitionist, the ratification of the Thirteenth Amendment on December 18, 1865, was reason enough for an occasional poem, but Whittier's "Laus Deo" (literally "praise God") expresses his personal jubilation at seeing a lifetime's work brought to completion. The poem describes the ringing of bells and firing of guns in Amesbury that accompanied the announcement that slavery had officially been abolished throughout the Union. The ten stanzas of trochaic tetrameter create a hymn of celebration and gratitude in which the Lord sanctions the righteousness of the Union cause.

On a more personal note, Whittier wrote many memorable verses in tribute to his Quaker faith, the finest of these perhaps being "First-Day Thoughts," in which he evoked the quiet grace and deep spirituality of the Friends' service. He captures the essence of Christian worship in the soul's contemplation of its creator through "the still small voice" of silent meditation. This same note of profound spiritual depth and reverence for the inner life appears in his famous hymn, "Dear Lord and Father of Mankind," which was adapted from the last six stanzas of "The Brewing of Soma." This inner faith grew with age and led Rufus M. Jones to comment later that Whittier "grasped more steadily, felt more profoundly, and interpreted more adequately the essential aspects of the Quaker life and faith" than any other of his age.

COUNTRY IDYLLS AND GENRE POEMS

Whittier's most lasting accomplishment, however, rests with his country idylls and genre poems, those set pieces and descriptive verses in which he evokes a memory of his childhood or presents an idealized view of the pleasures of rural life. In "The Trailing Arbutus," for example, a glimpse of this early spring flower on an otherwise cold and bitter day becomes the occasion for a moment of natural rapture. A better poem, "Telling the Bees," uses the New England custom of draping bee hives after a family death as a way of foreshadowing the narrator's sorrow at the loss of his beloved Mary. This particular poem, occasioned by the death of the poet's mother, contains some of his finest descriptive passages. Another genre poem, "In School-Days," treats of bashful love and childhood regrets nostalgically remembered, while "The Barefoot Boy" presents a stilted and somewhat generalized picture of rural childhood: Only in the middle stanzas does the poem rise above platitudes to a realistic glimpse of the poet's actual boyhood. With "Skipper Ireson's Ride," Whittier turned a New England legend into the material for a memorable folk ballad, although at the expense of historical veracity. The poem's mock-heroic tone does not mask the cruelty of the incident, in which Old Floyd Ireson was "tarred and feathered and carried in a cart" by the women of Marblehead for allegedly failing to rescue the survivors of another sinking fishing vessel. However factually inaccurate, Whittier's version of the legend captures the essential qualities of mob behavior in what one critic has called the most effective nineteenth century American ballad.

"SNOW-BOUND"

"Snow-Bound," subtitled "A Winter Idyl," is probably Whittier's most lasting achievement. The founding of *The Atlantic Monthly* in 1857 had given him a steady market for his verse, and when the editor, James Russell Lowell, wrote to him in 1865 requesting a "Yankee pastoral," Whittier responded with "Snow-Bound," which was published in the February, 1866, issue. The epigrams from Agrippa von Nettesheim's *Occult Philosophy* (1533) and Emerson's "The Snow Storm" establish the parameters of the poem in what John B. Pickard has called the protective circle of the family and hearth against the ominous power of the winter storm. Through an extended narrative in four-beat rhymed couplets, Whittier recalls the self-sufficiency of his family and recounts their close-knit circle of domestic affection as seen through a week of enforced winter isolation. This theme is enhanced through a series of contrasts between light and dark, warmth and cold, indoors and outdoors, fire and snow. After taking the reader through the round of barnyard chores, the poet shifts his perspective indoors to describe the sitting room of the Whittier homestead. Part 2 of the poem begins with Whittier's recollections of the tales and stories the family shared during their long evenings before the fire, with father, mother, uncle, aunt, schoolteacher, and another female guest each taking turns with the storytelling. The evening's entertainment finally ends as the fire burns low in the hearth and each family member retires from the pleasant circle of light and warmth. Part 3 of the poem gradually shifts from the past back to the present, as the poet's memories of "these Flemish pictures of old days" gradually fade; just as the fireplace logs had earlier faded to glowing embers covered with gray ash, so the poet will now gradually relinquish these recollections that have warmed "the hads of memory." His concluding lines express the hope that these memories will touch other readers and uplift their hearts, like the fresh odors of newly cut meadows, or pond lilies' fragrance on a summer breeze. The shift in season enforces the contrast between past and present, distancing Whittier from his family, most of whom had since died.

Legacy

While he was not a major poet, Whittier learned early from Burns the value of the commonplace, and his best poetry reflects an affectionate understanding of New England country life. If his muse flew no higher than popular and occasional verse, at least he wrote well of what he knew best—the customs and folkways of Yankee farming; the spiritual resources of his Quaker faith, which taught him to place spiritual concerns over material needs; and the history and legends of Essex County. His most accomplished poems look ahead to Edwin Arlington Robinson and Robert Frost, who would further probe the diminished world of the New England farm and village. Whittier stands directly in this tradition. His reputation has held better than those of the other Fireside poets, and he will continue to be read for his grasp of several essential truths: the value of family affections, the importance of firm moral character, and the simple attractions of country life.

Other major works

LONG FICTION: *Narrative of James Williams: An American Slave*, 1838; *Leaves from Margaret Smith's Journal*, 1849.

EDITED TEXTS: *The Journal of John Woolman*, 1871; *Child Life*, 1872; *Child Life in Prose*, 1874; *Songs of Three Centuries*, 1876.

NONFICTION: *Justice and Expediency: Or, Slavery Considered with a View to Its Rightful and Effectual Remedy, Abolition*, 1833; *The Supernaturalism of New England*, 1847; *Old Portraits and Modern Sketches*, 1850; *Literary Recreations and Miscellanies*, 1854; *Whittier on Writers and Writing: The Uncollected Critical Writings of John Greenleaf Whittier*, 1950 (Edwin H. Cady and Harry Hayden Clark, editors); *The Letters of John Greenleaf Whittier*, 1975 (John B. Pickard, editor).

MISCELLANEOUS: *Prose Works of John Greenleaf Whittier*, 1866; *The Writings of John Greenleaf Whittier*, 1888-1889.

BIBLIOGRAPHY

Fenner, Pamela, ed. and comp. *Celebrating Whittier: New England's Quaker Poet and Abolitionist—America's 1907 Centennial.* Foreword by John B. Pickard. Amesbury, Mass.: Michaelmas Press, 2010. Republication of documents relating to the one-hundredth anniversary of Whittier's birth.

Grant, David. "'The Unequal Sovereigns of a Slaveholding Land': The North as Subject in Whittier's 'The Panorama.'" *Criticism* 38, no. 4 (Fall, 1996): 521-549. Whittier's "The Panorama" discusses the interdependence of the two ideals exploited by the Republicans and Democrats: sovereignty and Union. The poem places the slave system at the root of the threats to the North.

Kribbs, Jayne K., comp. *Critical Essays on John Greenleaf Whittier.* Boston: G. K. Hall, 1980. Kribbs's extended introduction locates four periods of the poet's writing career and suggests in conclusion that the central question about Whittier is not how great, but how minor a figure he is in American literature. All the essays are written by respected scholars. Contains a bibliography and an index.

Leonard, Angela M. "The Topography of Violence in John Greenleaf Whittier's 'Antislavery Poems.'" In *Political Poetry as Discourse: Rereading John Greenleaf Whittier, Ebenezer Elliot, Hip-hop-ology.* Lanham, Md.: Lexington Books, 2010. Examines Whittier's antislavery poems and the violence contained within.

Pickard, Samuel Thomas. *Life and Letters of John Greenleaf Whittier.* Vol. 1. Honolulu, Hawaii: University Press of the Pacific, 2005. The first volume in a biography of Whittier that covers his life and works.

Rogal, Samuel J. *Congregational Hymns from the Poetry of John Greenleaf Whittier: A Comparative Study of the Sources and Final Works, with a Bibliographic Catalog of the Hymns.* Jefferson, N.C.: McFarland, 2010. Compares Whittier's original poems with the hymns, showing how they were adapted and, in the process, providing extensive explication of the poetry.

Wagenknecht, Edward. *John Greenleaf Whittier: A Portrait in Paradox.* New York: Oxford University Press, 1967. Wagenknecht arranges his facts and anecdotes topically rather than chronologically. The result is a vibrant and energetic portrait of Whittier that displays the richness of his inner and outer life. The thesis of this book is that many facets of Whittier's life seem paradoxical to one another. Includes bibliography.

Warren, Robert Penn. *John Greenleaf Whittier's Poetry: An Appraisal and a Selection.* 1971. Reprint. Minneapolis: University of Minnesota Press, 1992. Warren discusses "Snow-Bound," "Telling the Bees," "Ichabod," "To My Old Schoolmaster," and other poems addressing themes of childhood and nostalgia, as well as a controversial Freudian view of the poet's development. Includes thirty-six poems by Whittier.

Woodwell, R. H. *John Greenleaf Whittier: A Biography.* Haverhill, Mass.: Trustees of the John Greenleaf Whittier Homestead, 1985. This biography, based on years of research, is encyclopedic but has a very good index. Includes a useful review of Whittier's criticism.

Andrew J. Angyal

CHECKLIST FOR EXPLICATING A POEM

I. The Initial Readings

A. Before reading the poem, the reader should:
  1. Notice its form and length.
  2. Consider the title, determining, if possible, whether it might function as an allusion, symbol, or poetic image.
  3. Notice the date of composition or publication, and identify the general era of the poet.

B. The poem should be read intuitively and emotionally and be allowed to "happen" as much as possible.

C. In order to establish the rhythmic flow, the poem should be reread. A note should be made as to where the irregular spots (if any) are located.

II. Explicating the Poem

A. *Dramatic situation.* Studying the poem line by line helps the reader discover the dramatic situation. All elements of the dramatic situation are interrelated and should be viewed as reflecting and affecting one another. The dramatic situation serves a particular function in the poem, adding realism, surrealism, or absurdity; drawing attention to certain parts of the poem; and changing to reinforce other aspects of the poem. All points should be considered. The following questions are particularly helpful to ask in determining dramatic situation:
  1. What, if any, is the narrative action in the poem?
  2. How many personae appear in the poem? What part do they take in the action?
  3. What is the relationship between characters?
  4. What is the setting (time and location) of the poem?

B. *Point of view.* An understanding of the poem's point of view is a major step toward comprehending the poet's intended meaning. The reader should ask:
  1. Who is the speaker? Is he or she addressing someone else or the reader?
  2. Is the narrator able to understand or see everything happening to him or her, or does the reader know things that the narrator does not?
  3. Is the narrator reliable?
  4. Do point of view and dramatic situation seem consistent? If not, the inconsistencies may provide clues to the poem's meaning.

C. *Images and metaphors.* Images and metaphors are often the most intricately crafted vehicles of the poem for relaying the poet's message. Realizing that the images and metaphors work in harmony with the dramatic situation and point of view will help the reader to see the poem as a whole, rather than as disassociated elements.
  1. The reader should identify the concrete images (that is, those that are formed from objects that can be touched, smelled, seen, felt, or tasted). Is the image projected by the poet consistent with the physical object?
  2. If the image is abstract, or so different from natural imagery that it cannot be associated with a real object, then what are the properties of the image?
  3. To what extent is the reader asked to form his or her own images?
  4. Is any image repeated in the poem? If so, how has it been changed? Is there a controlling image?
  5. Are any images compared to each other? Do they reinforce one another?
  6. Is there any difference between the way the reader perceives the image and the way the narrator sees it?
  7. What seems to be the narrator's or persona's attitude toward the image?

D. *Words.* Every substantial word in a poem may have more than one intended meaning, as used by the author. Because of this, the reader should look up many of these words in the dictionary and:
  1. Note all definitions that have the slightest connection with the poem.
  2. Note any changes in syntactical patterns in the poem.
  3. In particular, note those words that could possibly function as symbols or allusions, and refer to any appropriate sources for further information.

E. *Meter, rhyme, structure, and tone.* In scanning the poem, all elements of prosody should be noted by the reader. These elements are often used by a poet to manipulate the reader's emotions, and therefore they should be examined closely to arrive at the poet's specific intention.
  1. Does the basic meter follow a traditional pattern such as those found in nursery rhymes or folk songs?
  2. Are there any variations in the base meter? Such changes or substitutions are important thematically and should be identified.
  3. Are the rhyme schemes traditional or innovative, and what might their form mean to the poem?
  4. What devices has the poet used to create sound patterns (such as assonance and alliteration)?
  5. Is the stanza form a traditional or innovative one?
  6. If the poem is composed of verse paragraphs rather than stanzas, how do they affect the progression of the poem?

7. After examining the above elements, is the resultant tone of the poem casual or formal, pleasant, harsh, emotional, authoritative?

F. *Historical context.* The reader should attempt to place the poem into historical context, checking on events at the time of composition. Archaic language, expressions, images, or symbols should also be looked up.

G. *Themes and motifs.* By seeing the poem as a composite of emotion, intellect, craftsmanship, and tradition, the reader should be able to determine the themes and motifs (smaller recurring ideas) presented in the work. He or she should ask the following questions to help pinpoint these main ideas:
1. Is the poet trying to advocate social, moral, or religious change?
2. Does the poet seem sure of his or her position?
3. Does the poem appeal primarily to the emotions, to the intellect, or to both?
4. Is the poem relying on any particular devices for effect (such as imagery, allusion, paradox, hyperbole, or irony)?

BIBLIOGRAPHY

General Reference Sources

Biographical sources

Colby, Vineta, ed. *World Authors, 1975-1980*. Wilson Authors Series. New York: H. W. Wilson, 1985.

_____. *World Authors, 1980-1985*. Wilson Authors Series. New York: H. W. Wilson, 1991.

_____. *World Authors, 1985-1990*. Wilson Authors Series. New York: H. W. Wilson, 1995.

Cyclopedia of World Authors. 4th rev. ed. 5 vols. Pasadena, Calif.: Salem Press, 2003.

Dictionary of Literary Biography. 254 vols. Detroit: Gale Research, 1978- .

International Who's Who in Poetry and Poets' Encyclopaedia. Cambridge, England: International Biographical Centre, 1993.

Seymour-Smith, Martin, and Andrew C. Kimmens, eds. *World Authors, 1900-1950*. Wilson Authors Series. 4 vols. New York: H. W. Wilson, 1996.

Thompson, Clifford, ed. *World Authors, 1990-1995*. Wilson Authors Series. New York: H. W. Wilson, 1999.

Wakeman, John, ed. *World Authors, 1950-1970*. New York: H. W. Wilson, 1975.

_____. *World Authors, 1970-1975*. Wilson Authors Series. New York: H. W. Wilson, 1991.

Willhardt, Mark, and Alan Michael Parker, eds. *Who's Who in Twentieth Century World Poetry*. New York: Routledge, 2000.

Criticism

Brooks, Cleanth, and Robert Penn Warren. *Understanding Poetry*. 4th ed. Reprint. Fort Worth, Tex.: Heinle & Heinle, 2003.

Classical and Medieval Literature Criticism. Detroit: Gale Research, 1988- .

Contemporary Literary Criticism. Detroit: Gale Research, 1973- .

Day, Gary. *Literary Criticism: A New History*. Edinburgh, Scotland: Edinburgh University Press, 2008.

Draper, James P., ed. *World Literature Criticism 1500 to the Present: A Selection of Major Authors from Gale's Literary Criticism Series*. 6 vols. Detroit: Gale Research, 1992.

Habib, M. A. R. *A History of Literary Criticism: From Plato to the Present*. Malden, Mass.: Wiley-Blackwell, 2005.

Jason, Philip K., ed. *Masterplots II: Poetry Series, Revised Edition*. 8 vols. Pasadena, Calif.: Salem Press, 2002.

Lodge, David, and Nigel Wood. *Modern Criticism and Theory*. 3d ed. New York: Longman, 2008.

Magill, Frank N., ed. *Magill's Bibliography of Literary Criticism*. 4 vols. Englewood Cliffs, N.J.: Salem Press, 1979.

MLA International Bibliography. New York: Modern Language Association of America, 1922-   .

Nineteenth-Century Literature Criticism. Detroit: Gale Research, 1981-   .

Twentieth-Century Literary Criticism. Detroit: Gale Research, 1978-   .

Vedder, Polly, ed. *World Literature Criticism Supplement: A Selection of Major Authors from Gale's Literary Criticism Series*. 2 vols. Detroit: Gale Research, 1997.

Young, Robyn V., ed. *Poetry Criticism: Excerpts from Criticism of the Works of the Most Significant and Widely Studied Poets of World Literature*. 29 vols. Detroit: Gale Research, 1991.

POETRY DICTIONARIES AND HANDBOOKS

Carey, Gary, and Mary Ellen Snodgrass. *A Multicultural Dictionary of Literary Terms*. Jefferson, N.C.: McFarland, 1999.

Deutsch, Babette. *Poetry Handbook: A Dictionary of Terms*. 4th ed. New York: Funk & Wagnalls, 1974.

Drury, John. *The Poetry Dictionary*. Cincinnati, Ohio: Story Press, 1995.

Kinzie, Mary. *A Poet's Guide to Poetry*. Chicago: University of Chicago Press, 1999.

Lennard, John. *The Poetry Handbook: A Guide to Reading Poetry for Pleasure and Practical Criticism*. New York: Oxford University Press, 1996.

Matterson, Stephen, and Darryl Jones. *Studying Poetry*. New York: Oxford University Press, 2000.

Packard, William. *The Poet's Dictionary: A Handbook of Prosody and Poetic Devices*. New York: Harper & Row, 1989.

Preminger, Alex, et al., eds. *The New Princeton Encyclopedia of Poetry and Poetics*. 3d rev. ed. Princeton, N.J.: Princeton University Press, 1993.

Shipley, Joseph Twadell, ed. *Dictionary of World Literary Terms, Forms, Technique, Criticism*. Rev. ed. Boston: George Allen and Unwin, 1979.

INDEXES OF PRIMARY WORKS

Frankovich, Nicholas, ed. *The Columbia Granger's Index to Poetry in Anthologies*. 11th ed. New York: Columbia University Press, 1997.

_____. *The Columbia Granger's Index to Poetry in Collected and Selected Works*. New York: Columbia University Press, 1997.

Guy, Patricia. *A Women's Poetry Index*. Phoenix, Ariz.: Oryx Press, 1985.

Hazen, Edith P., ed. *Columbia Granger's Index to Poetry*. 10th ed. New York: Columbia University Press, 1994.

Hoffman, Herbert H., and Rita Ludwig Hoffman, comps. *International Index to Recorded Poetry.* New York: H. W. Wilson, 1983.

Kline, Victoria. *Last Lines: An Index to the Last Lines of Poetry.* 2 vols. Vol. 1, *Last Line Index, Title Index*; Vol. 2, *Author Index, Keyword Index.* New York: Facts On File, 1991.

Marcan, Peter. *Poetry Themes: A Bibliographical Index to Subject Anthologies and Related Criticisms in the English Language, 1875-1975.* Hamden, Conn.: Linnet Books, 1977.

Poem Finder. Great Neck, N.Y.: Roth, 2000.

POETICS, POETIC FORMS, AND GENRES

Attridge, Derek. *Poetic Rhythm: An Introduction.* New York: Cambridge University Press, 1995.

Brogan, T. V. F. *Verseform: A Comparative Bibliography.* Baltimore: Johns Hopkins University Press, 1989.

Fussell, Paul. *Poetic Meter and Poetic Form.* Rev. ed. New York: McGraw-Hill, 1979.

Hollander, John. *Rhyme's Reason.* 3d ed. New Haven, Conn.: Yale University Press, 2001.

Jackson, Guida M. *Traditional Epics: A Literary Companion.* New York: Oxford University Press, 1995.

Padgett, Ron, ed. *The Teachers and Writers Handbook of Poetic Forms.* 2d ed. New York: Teachers & Writers Collaborative, 2000.

Pinsky, Robert. *The Sounds of Poetry: A Brief Guide.* New York: Farrar, Straus and Giroux, 1998.

Preminger, Alex, and T. V. F. Brogan, eds. *New Princeton Encyclopedia of Poetry and Poetics.* 3d ed. Princeton, N.J.: Princeton University Press, 1993.

Spiller, Michael R. G. *The Sonnet Sequence: A Study of Its Strategies.* Studies in Literary Themes and Genres 13. New York: Twayne, 1997.

Turco, Lewis. *The New Book of Forms: A Handbook of Poetics.* Hanover, N.H.: University Press of New England, 1986.

Williams, Miller. *Patterns of Poetry: An Encyclopedia of Forms.* Baton Rouge: Louisiana State University Press, 1986.

Maura Ives
Updated by Tracy Irons-Georges

GUIDE TO ONLINE RESOURCES

Web Sites

The following sites were visited by the editors of Salem Press in 2010. Because URLs frequently change, the accuracy of these addresses cannot be guaranteed; however, long-standing sites, such as those of colleges and universities, national organizations, and government agencies, generally maintain links when their sites are moved.

Academy of American Poets
http://www.poets.org
    The mission of the Academy of American Poets is to "support American poets at all stages of their careers and to foster the appreciation of contemporary poetry." The academy's comprehensive Web site features information on poetic schools and movements; a Poetic Forms Database; an Online Poetry Classroom, with educator and teaching resources; an index of poets and poems; essays and interviews; general Web resources; links for further study; and more.

Contemporary British Writers
http://www.contemporarywriters.com/authors
    Created by the British Council, this site offers profiles of living writers of the United Kingdom, the Republic of Ireland, and the Commonwealth. Information includes biographies, bibliographies, critical reviews, and news about literary prizes. Photographs are also featured. Users can search the site by author, genre, nationality, gender, publisher, book title, date of publication, and prize name and date.

LiteraryHistory.com
http://www.literaryhistory.com
    This site is an excellent source of academic, scholarly, and critical literature about eighteenth, nineteenth, and twentieth century American and English writers. It provides individual pages for twentieth century literature and alphabetical lists of authors that link to articles, reviews, overviews, excerpts of works, teaching guides, podcasts, and other materials.

Literary Resources on the Net
http://andromeda.rutgers.edu/~jlynch/Lit
    Jack Lynch of Rutgers University maintains this extensive collection of links to Web sites that are useful to researchers, including numerous sites about American and English literature. This collection is a good place to begin online research about poetry, as it

links to other sites with broad ranges of literary topics. The site is organized chronologically, with separate pages about twentieth century British and Irish literature. It also has separate pages providing links to Web sites about American literature and to women's literature and feminism.

LitWeb
http://litweb.net

LitWeb provides biographies of hundreds of world authors throughout history that can be accessed through an alphabetical listing. The pages about each writer contain a list of his or her works, suggestions for further reading, and illustrations. The site also offers information about past and present winners of major literary prizes.

The Modern Word: Authors of the Libyrinth
http://www.themodernword.com/authors.html

The Modern Word site, although somewhat haphazard in its organization, provides a great deal of critical information about writers. The "Authors of the Libyrinth" page is very useful, linking author names to essays about them and other resources. The section of the page headed "The Scriptorium" presents "an index of pages featuring writers who have pushed the edges of their medium, combining literary talent with a sense of experimentation to produce some remarkable works of modern literature."

Outline of American Literature
http://www.america.gov/publications/books/outline-of-american-literature.html

This page of the America.gov site provides access to an electronic version of the ten-chapter volume *Outline of American Literature*, a historical overview of poetry and prose from colonial times to the present published by the Bureau of International Information Programs of the U.S. Department of State.

Poetry Foundation
http://www.poetryfoundation.org

The Poetry Foundation, publisher of *Poetry* magazine, is an independent literary organization. Its Web site offers links to essays; news; events; online poetry resources, such as blogs, organizations, publications, and references and research; a glossary of literary terms; and a Learning Lab that includes poem guides and essays on poetics.

Poet's Corner
http://theotherpages.org/poems

The Poet's Corner, one of the oldest text resources on the Web, provides access to about seven thousand works of poetry by several hundred different poets from around the world. Indexes are arranged and searchable by title, name of poet, or subject. The site also offers its own resources, including "Faces of the Poets"—a gallery of portraits—and "Lives of the Poets"—a growing collection of biographies.

Representative Poetry Online
http://rpo.library.utoronto.ca
   This award-winning resource site, maintained by Ian Lancashire of the Department of English at the University of Toronto in Canada, has several thousand English-language poems by hundreds of poets. The collection is searchable by poet's name, title of work, first line of a poem, and keyword. The site also includes a time line, a glossary, essays, an extensive bibliography, and countless links organized by country and by subject.

Voice of the Shuttle
http://vos.ucsb.edu
   One of the most complete and authoritative places for online information about literature, Voice of the Shuttle is maintained by professors and students in the English Department at the University of California, Santa Barbara. The site provides countless links to electronic books, academic journals, literary association Web sites, sites created by university professors, and many other resources.

Voices from the Gaps
http://voices.cla.umn.edu/
   Voices from the Gaps is a site of the English Department at the University of Minnesota, dedicated to providing resources on the study of women artists of color, including writers. The site features a comprehensive index searchable by name, and it provides biographical information on each writer or artist and other resources for further study.

ELECTRONIC DATABASES

Electronic databases usually do not have their own URLs. Instead, public, college, and university libraries subscribe to these databases, provide links to them on their Web sites, and make them available to library card holders or other specified patrons. Readers can visit library Web sites or ask reference librarians to check on availability.

Canadian Literary Centre
   Produced by EBSCO, the Canadian Literary Centre database contains full-text content from ECW Press, a Toronto-based publisher, including the titles in the publisher's Canadian fiction studies, Canadian biography, and Canadian writers and their works series; *ECW's Biographical Guide to Canadian Novelists*; and *George Woodcock's Intro-*

duction to *Canadian Fiction*. Author biographies, essays and literary criticism, and book reviews are among the database's offerings.

Literary Reference Center

EBSCO's Literary Reference Center (LRC) is a comprehensive full-text database designed primarily to help high school and undergraduate students in English and the humanities with homework and research assignments about literature. The database contains massive amounts of information from reference works, books, literary journals, and other materials, including more than 31,000 plot summaries, synopses, and overviews of literary works; almost 100,000 essays and articles of literary criticism; about 140,000 author biographies; more than 605,000 book reviews; and more than 5,200 author interviews. It contains the entire contents of Salem Press's MagillOnLiterature Plus. Users can retrieve information by browsing a list of authors' names or titles of literary works; they can also use an advanced search engine to access information by numerous categories, including author name, gender, cultural identity, national identity, and the years in which he or she lived, or by literary title, character, locale, genre, and publication date. The Literary Reference Center also features a literary-historical time line, an encyclopedia of literature, and a glossary of literary terms.

MagillOnLiterature Plus

MagillOnLiterature Plus is a comprehensive, integrated literature database produced by Salem Press and available on the EBSCOhost platform. The database contains the full text of essays in Salem's many literature-related reference works, including *Masterplots*, *Cyclopedia of World Authors*, *Cyclopedia of Literary Characters*, *Cyclopedia of Literary Places*, *Critical Survey of Poetry*, *Critical Survey of Long Fiction*, *Critical Survey of Short Fiction*, *World Philosophers and Their Works*, *Magill's Literary Annual*, and *Magill's Book Reviews*. Among its contents are articles on more than 35,000 literary works and more than 8,500 poets, writers, dramatists, essayists, and philosophers; more than 1,000 images; and a glossary of more than 1,300 literary terms. The biographical essays include lists of authors' works and secondary bibliographies, and hundreds of overview essays examine and discuss literary genres, time periods, and national literatures.

Rebecca Kuzins
Updated by Desiree Dreeuws

GEOGRAPHICAL INDEX

CHINA
    Du Fu, 54
    Wang Wei, 205

ENGLAND
    Cowper, William, 44
    Hardy, Thomas, 87
    Hopkins, Gerard Manley, 101
    Thomas, Edward, 159

INDIA
    Tagore, Rabindranath, 147

JAPAN
    Matsuo Bashō, 117

SPAIN
    Castro, Rosalía de, 34

UNITED STATES
    Ammons, A. R., 5
    Bryant, William Cullen, 15
    Carver, Raymond, 23
    Emerson, Ralph Waldo, 61
    Frost, Robert, 75
    Merwin, W. S., 125
    Swenson, May, 138
    Thoreau, Henry David, 166
    Very, Jones, 177
    Wagoner, David, 183
    Walker, Alice, 196
    Wheatley, Phillis, 215
    Whitman, Walt, 228
    Whittier, John Greenleaf, 244

CATEGORY INDEX

AESTHETIC POETS
   Emerson, Ralph Waldo, 61
AFRICAN AMERICAN CULTURE
   Walker, Alice, 196
   Wheatley, Phillis, 215
AMERICAN COLONIAL POETS
   Wheatley, Phillis, 215
AMERICAN EARLY NATIONAL POETS
   Bryant, William Cullen, 15
   Emerson, Ralph Waldo, 61
   Thoreau, Henry David, 166
   Very, Jones, 177
   Whitman, Walt, 228
   Whittier, John Greenleaf, 244
AUGUSTAN AGE, ENGLISH
   Cowper, William, 44

BALLADS
   Hardy, Thomas, 87
   Whittier, John Greenleaf, 244
BLACK ARTS MOVEMENT
   Walker, Alice, 196

CHILDREN'S/YOUNG ADULT POETRY
   Swenson, May, 138
CLASSICAL PERIOD, CHINA
   Du Fu, 54
   Wang Wei, 205

DIALECT POETRY
   Frost, Robert, 75

ECOPOETRY
   Ammons, A. R., 5
   Emerson, Ralph Waldo, 61
   Merwin, W. S., 125
   Wagoner, David, 183
   Whitman, Walt, 228

EDWARDIAN AGE
   Hardy, Thomas, 87
ELEGIES
   Wheatley, Phillis, 215
EPICS
   Whitman, Walt, 228
EPIGRAMS
   Ammons, A. R., 5
   Thoreau, Henry David, 166

FEMINIST POETS
   Walker, Alice, 196
FIRESIDE POETS
   Bryant, William Cullen, 15
   Whittier, John Greenleaf, 244

GAY AND LESBIAN CULTURE
   Walker, Alice, 196
   Whitman, Walt, 228
GRAVEYARD SCHOOL
   Cowper, William, 44

HAIKU
   Matsuo Bashō, 117
HYMNS
   Bryant, William Cullen, 15
   Cowper, William, 44
   Very, Jones, 177
   Wheatley, Phillis, 215
   Whittier, John Greenleaf, 244

JOHNSON, AGE OF
   Cowper, William, 44

LOVE POETRY
   Swenson, May, 138
LYRIC POETRY
   Du Fu, 54

Frost, Robert, 75
Hardy, Thomas, 87
Very, Jones, 177

MODERNISM
Frost, Robert, 75
Hopkins, Gerard Manley, 101
MODERNISMO
Castro, Rosalía de, 34

NARRATIVE POETRY
Emerson, Ralph Waldo, 61
Frost, Robert, 75
Whittier, John Greenleaf, 244
NEOCLASSICAL POETS
Cowper, William, 44
Wheatley, Phillis, 215
NEOPLATONISM
Thoreau, Henry David, 166
NEO-ROMANTICISM
Hopkins, Gerard Manley, 101

OCCASIONAL VERSE
Du Fu, 54
Emerson, Ralph Waldo, 61
Wheatley, Phillis, 215
Whittier, John Greeleaf, 244
ODES
Thoreau, Henry David, 166
OXFORD MOVEMENT
Hopkins, Gerard Manley, 101

PATTERN POETS
Swenson, May, 138
POLITICAL POETS
Du Fu, 54
Merwin, W. S., 125
Walker, Alice, 196
Wheatley, Phillis, 215
Whittier, John Greenleaf, 244

POSTMODERNISM
Carver, Raymond, 23
Merwin, W. S., 125
PROSE POETRY
Tagore, Rabindranath, 147

REALISM
Frost, Robert, 75
RELIGIOUS POETRY
Castro, Rosalía de, 34
Cowper, William, 44
Hopkins, Gerard Manley, 101
Tagore, Rabindranath, 147
Very, Jones, 177
Wang Wei, 205
Wheatley, Phillis, 215
Whittier, John Greenleaf, 244
RENAISSANCE, AMERICAN
Emerson, Ralph Waldo, 61
Thoreau, Henry David, 166
Whitman, Walt, 228
ROMANTICISM, AMERICAN
Bryant, William Cullen, 15
Emerson, Ralph Waldo, 61
Whitman, Walt, 228
Whittier, John Greenleaf, 244

SONGS
Tagore, Rabindranath, 147
SONNETS
Frost, Robert, 75
Hardy, Thomas, 87
Hopkins, Gerard Manley, 101
Very, Jones, 177
SYMBOLIST POETS
Emerson, Ralph Waldo, 61

TOPOGRAPHICAL POETRY
Bryant, William Cullen, 15
Whitman, Walt, 228

TRANSCENDENTALISM
    Ammons, A. R., 5
    Emerson, Ralph Waldo, 61
    Thoreau, Henry David, 166
    Very, Jones, 177

VERSE DRAMATISTS
    Hardy, Thomas, 87
VICTORIAN ERA
    Hardy, Thomas, 87
    Hopkins, Gerard Manley, 101

VISIONARY POETRY
    Merwin, W. S., 125

WAR POETS
    Thomas, Edward, 159
WOMEN POETS
    Castro, Rosalía de, 34
    Swenson, May, 138
    Walker, Alice, 196
    Wheatley, Phillis, 215

SUBJECT INDEX

Absolute Trust in the Goodness of the Earth (Walker), 201
"Adlestrop" (Thomas), 162
"After Apple-Picking" (Frost), 79
"Airiños, airiños, aires" (Castro), 39
Ammons, A. R., 5-14
    A Coast of Trees, 11
    Collected Poems, 1951-1971, 9
    Corsons Inlet, 8
    "Easter Morning," 11
    Expressions of Sea Level, 7
    Garbage, 12
    Glare, 12
    Lake Effect Country, 11
    The Really Short Poems of A. R. Ammons, 12
    The Snow Poems, 10
    Sphere, 9
    Sumerian Vistas, 11
    Tape for the Turn of the Year, 8
Another Animal (Swenson), 140
"As the Team's Head-Brass" (Thomas), 161
"August 19, Pad 19" (Swenson), 142

Beside the River Sar (Castro), 41
"Brahma" (Emerson), 69
Bryant, William Cullen, 15-22
    "A Forest Hymn," 20
    "The Prairies," 20
    "Thanatopsis," 18

Cantares gallegos (Castro), 39
"Car, The" (Carver), 27
Carrier of Ladders, The (Merwin), 130
"Carrion Comfort" (Hopkins), 114
Carver, Raymond, 23-33
    "The Car," 27

Fires, 26
"Near Klamath," 26
A New Path to the Waterfall, 29
"NyQuil," 28
Ultramarine, 27
"Winter Insomnia," 26
"Castaway, The" (Cowper), 49
Castro, Rosalía de, 34-43
    "Airiños, airiños, aires," 39
    Beside the River Sar, 41
    Cantares gallegos, 39
    Follas novas, 40
    "I Used to Have a Nail," 38
    "Saint Scholastica," 41
    "They Say That Plants Do Not Speak," 41
Coast of Trees, A (Ammons), 11
Collected Poems, 1951-1971 (Ammons), 9
"Concord Hymn" (Emerson), 72
Corsons Inlet (Ammons), 8
Cowper, William, 44-53
    "The Castaway," 49
    "The Diverting History of John Gilpin," 50
    "On the Receipt of My Mother's Picture Out of Norfolk," 47
    "The Poplar Field," 50
    The Task, 51
"Crossing Brooklyn Ferry" (Whitman), 237

Dancing Bears, The (Merwin), 128
"Days" (Emerson), 68
"Deer Park" (Wang Wei), 209
"Dicen que no hablan las plantas." *See* "They Say That Plants Do Not Speak"
"Diverting History of John Gilpin, The" (Cowper), 50
Drum-Taps (Whitman), 238
Drunk in the Furnace, The (Merwin), 129

Dry Sun, Dry Wind (Wagoner), 187
Du Fu, 54-60
    "Moonlit Night," 58
    "The River by Our Village," 59
    "The Winding River," 59
"Duns Scotus's Oxford" (Hopkins), 112
Dynasts, The (Hardy), 98

"Each and All" (Emerson), 70
"Easter Morning" (Ammons), 11
Emerson, Ralph Waldo, 61-74
    "Brahma," 69
    "Concord Hymn," 72
    "Days," 68
    "Each and All," 70
    "Give All to Love," 70
    "Hamatraya," 68
    "The Humble Bee," 71
    "Ode," 72
    "The Problem," 68
    "The Rhodora," 71
    "The Snow-Storm," 68
    and Henry David Thoreau, 169
    "Threnody," 70
    "Uriel," 69
    and Jones Very, 178
    "Woodnotes," 71
Expressions of Sea Level (Ammons), 7

"Fire and Ice" (Frost), 85
Fires (Carver), 26
Flight of Swans, A (Tagore), 154
Folding Cliffs, The (Merwin), 133
Follas novas (Castro), 40
"Forest Hymn, A" (Bryant), 20
"Friendship" (Thoreau), 172
Frost, Robert, 75-86
    "After Apple-Picking," 79
    "Fire and Ice," 85
    "Mending Wall," 84

Gallagher, Tess, 25
Garbage (Ammons), 12
Gitanjali Song Offerings (Tagore), 153
"Give All to Love" (Emerson), 70
Glare (Ammons), 12
Good Morning and Good Night (Wagoner), 193
Good Night, Willie Lee, I'll See You in the Morning (Walker), 200

"Hamatraya" (Emerson), 68
Hardy, Thomas, 87-100
    The Dynasts, 98
    Moments of Vision and Miscellaneous Verses, 97
    Poems of the Past and Present, 95
    Satires of Circumstance, 96
    Time's Laughingstocks, and Other Verses, 96
    Wessex Poems, and Other Verses, 94
Her Blue Body Everything We Know (Walker), 201
Hopkins, Gerard Manley, 101-116
    "Carrion Comfort," 114
    "Duns Scotus's Oxford," 112
    "Pied Beauty," 111
    "The Windhover," 108
    "The Wreck of the *Deutschland*", 105
"Horses in Central Park" (Swenson), 140
Horses Make a Landscape Look More Beautiful (Walker), 200
House of Song, The (Wagoner), 192
"Humble Bee, The" (Emerson), 71

"I Used to Have a Nail" (Castro), 38
"Ichabod" (Whittier), 250
Iconographs (Swenson), 141
In Broken Country (Wagoner), 190
In Other Words (Swenson), 144
"In the City" (Matsuo Bashō), 122

"Lady Xi" (Wang Wei), 208
Lake Effect Country (Ammons), 11
Landfall (Wagoner), 190
"Lately, Alas, I Knew a Gentle Boy" (Thoreau), 173
Leaves of Grass (Whitman), 232
Lice, The (Merwin), 129

Map of the Night, A (Wagoner), 194
Mask for Janus, A (Merwin), 128
Matsuo Bashō, 117-124
   "In the City," 122
   The Narrow Road to the Deep North, 123
"Mending Wall" (Frost), 84
Merwin, W. S., 125-137
   The Carrier of Ladders, 130
   The Dancing Bears, 128
   The Drunk in the Furnace, 129
   The Folding Cliffs, 133
   The Lice, 129
   A Mask for Janus, 128
   Migration, 134
   Opening the Hand, 131
   Present Company, 133
   The Pupil, 133
   The Rain in the Trees, 132
   The River Sound, 133
   The Shadow of Sirius, 134
   Travels, 132
   The Vixen, 132
Migration (Merwin), 134
Moments of Vision and Miscellaneous Verses (Hardy), 97
"Moonlit Night" (Du Fu), 58

Narrow Road to the Deep North, The (Matsuo Bashō), 123
"Near Klamath" (Carver), 26
New and Selected Things Taking Place (Swenson), 143

"New Birth, The" (Very), 180
New Path to the Waterfall, A (Carver), 29
"No One So Much as You" (Thomas), 163
"NyQuil" (Carver), 28

"October" (Swenson), 143
"Ode" (Emerson), 72
"On the Receipt of My Mother's Picture Out of Norfolk" (Cowper), 47
Once (Walker), 199
Opening the Hand (Merwin), 131
"Out of the Cradle Endlessly Rocking" (Whitman), 238

"Passage to India" (Whitman), 240
Patraput (Tagore), 155
"Pied Beauty" (Hopkins), 111
Poem Traveled Down My Arm, A (Walker), 202
Poems of the Past and Present (Hardy), 95
"Poplar Field, The" (Cowper), 50
"Prairies, The" (Bryant), 20
"Prayer of Columbus" (Whitman), 241
Present Company (Merwin), 133
"Problem, The" (Emerson), 68
Pupil, The (Merwin), 133

Rain in the Trees, The (Merwin), 132
Really Short Poems of A. R. Ammons, The (Ammons), 12
Revolutionary Petunias, and Other Poems (Walker), 199
"Rhodora, The" (Emerson), 71
"River by Our Village, The" (Du Fu), 59
River Sound, The (Merwin), 133
Roethke, Theodore, 184

"Saint Scholastica" (Castro), 41
Satires of Circumstance (Hardy), 96
"Seven Songs for an Old Voice" (Wagoner), 188

Shadow of Sirius, The (Merwin), 134
"Snow-Bound" (Whittier), 251
Snow Poems, The (Ammons), 10
"Snow-Storm, The" (Emerson), 68
"Song of Myself" (Whitman), 233
Sphere (Ammons), 9
Sumerian Vistas (Ammons), 11
Swenson, May, 138-146
   Another Animal, 140
   "August 19, Pad 19," 142
   "Horses in Central Park," 140
   Iconographs, 141
   In Other Words, 144
   New and Selected Things Taking Place, 143
   "October," 143
   "A Thank-You Letter," 144

Tagore, Rabindranath, 147-158
   A Flight of Swans, 154
   Gitanjali Song Offerings, 153
   Patraput, 155
Tape for the Turn of the Year (Ammons), 8
Task, The (Cowper), 51
"Thanatopsis" (Bryant), 18
"Thank-You Letter, A" (Swenson), 144
"They Say That Plants Do Not Speak" (Castro), 41
Thomas, Edward, 159-165
   "Adlestrop," 162
   "As the Team's Head-Brass," 161
   "No One So Much as You," 163
Thoreau, Henry David, 166-176
   "Friendship," 172
   "Lately, Alas, I Knew a Gentle Boy," 173
"Threnody" (Emerson), 70
Time's Laughingstocks, and Other Verses (Hardy), 96
Traveling Light (Wagoner), 192
Travels (Merwin), 132
Tu Fu. *See* Du Fu

Ultramarine (Carver), 27
"Uriel" (Emerson), 69

Very, Jones, 177-182
   "The New Birth," 180
   "The Wind-Flower," 181
   "Visiting the Temple of Gathered Fragrance" (Wang Wei), 210
Vixen, The (Merwin), 132

Wagoner, David, 183-195
   Dry Sun, Dry Wind, 187
   Good Morning and Good Night, 193
   The House of Song, 192
   In Broken Country, 190
   Landfall, 190
   A Map of the Night, 194
   "Seven Songs for an Old Voice," 188
   Traveling Light, 192
   Walt Whitman Bathing, 191
   Who Shall Be the Sun?, 189
Walker, Alice, 196-204
   Absolute Trust in the Goodness of the Earth, 201
   Good Night, Willie Lee, I'll See You in the Morning, 200
   Her Blue Body Everything We Know, 201
   Horses Make a Landscape Look More Beautiful, 200
   Once, 199
   A Poem Traveled Down My Arm, 202
   Revolutionary Petunias, and Other Poems, 199
Walt Whitman Bathing (Wagoner), 191
Wang Wei, 205-214
   "Deer Park," 209
   "Lady Xi," 208
   "Visiting the Temple of Gathered Fragrance," 210

Wessex Poems, and Other Verses (Hardy), 94
Wheatley, Phillis, 215-227
"When Lilacs Last in the Dooryard Bloom'd" (Whitman), 240
Whitman, Walt, 228-243
    "Crossing Brooklyn Ferry," 237
    Drum-Taps, 238
    Leaves of Grass, 232
    "Out of the Cradle Endlessly Rocking," 238
    "Passage to India," 240
    "Prayer of Columbus," 241
    "Song of Myself," 233
    and Henry David Thoreau, 170

"When Lilacs Last in the Dooryard Bloom'd," 240
Whittier, John Greenleaf, 244-254
    "Ichabod," 250
    "Snow-Bound," 251
Who Shall Be the Sun? (Wagoner), 189
"Wind-Flower, The" (Very), 181
"Windhover, The" (Hopkins), 108
"Winding River, The" (Du Fu), 59
"Winter Insomnia" (Carver), 26
"Woodnotes" (Emerson), 71
Wordsworth, William
    Henry David Thoreau, 171
"Wreck of the *Deutschland*, The" (Hopkins), 105